1 MONTH OF
FREE
READING

at

www.ForgottenBooks.com

By purchasing this book you are eligible for one month membership to ForgottenBooks.com, giving you unlimited access to our entire collection of over 1,000,000 titles via our web site and mobile apps.

To claim your free month visit:

www.forgottenbooks.com/free54071

HARRISON AND SONS,
PRINTERS IN ORDINARY TO HER MAJEST
ST. MARTIN'S LANE, LONDON.

COUNCIL, 1897.

CONTENTS.

———o———

CONTENTS.

No. cXliv. March

No. cXlv. April.

No. cXlvi. May.

PROCEEDINGS

OF

THE SOCIETY

OF

BIBLICAL ARCHÆOLOGY.

————❦❦————

VOL. XIX. TWENTY-SEVENTH SESSION.

First Meeting, January 12th, 1897.

————❦❦————

CONTENTS.

————❦❦————

PUBLISHED AT

THE OFFICES OF THE SOCIETY,

37, GREAT RUSSELL STREET, BLOOMSBURY, W.C.

——

1897.

[No. CXLII.]

SOCIETY OF BIBLICAL ARCHÆOLOGY,

37, GREAT RUSSELL STREET, BLOOMSBURY, W.C.

TRANSACTIONS.

			To Members.		To Non-Members.						To Members.		To Non-Members.	
					s.	*d.*							*s.*	*d.*
Vol.	I, Part	1 ...	10	6	... 12	6	Vol. VI, Part	1 ...	10	6	...	12	6
,,	I, ,,	2 ...	10	6	... 12	6	,, VI, ,,	2 ...	10	6	...	12	6
,,	II, ,,	1 ...	8	0	... 10	6	,, VII, ,,	1 ...	7	6	...	10	6
,,	II, ,,	2 ...	8	0	... 10	6	,, VII, ,,	2 ...	10	6	...	12	6
,,	III, ,,	1 ...	8	0	... 10	6	,, VII, ,,	3 ...	10	6	...	12	6
,,	III, ,,	2 ...	8	0	... 10	6	,, VIII, ,,	1 ...	10	6	...	12	6
,,	IV, ,,	1 ...	10	6	... 12	6	,, VIII, ,,	2 ...	10	6	...	12	6
,,	IV, ,,	2 ...	10	6	... 12	6	,, VIII, ,,	3 ...	10	6	...	12	6
,,	V, ,,	1 ...	12	6	... 15	0	,, IX, ,,	1 ...	10	6	...	12	6
,,	V, ,,	2 ...	10	6	... 12	6	,, IX, ,,	2 ...	10	6	...	12	6

PROCEEDINGS.

Vol.					To Members.				To Non-Members.	
Vol.	I,	Session	1878–79	...	2	0	...	...	2	6
,,	II,	,,	1879–80	...	2	0	...	...	2	6
,,	III,	,,	1880–81	...	4	0	...	...	5	0
,,	IV,	,,	1881–82	...	4	0	...	...	5	0
,,	V,	,,	1882–83	...	4	0	...	..	5	0
,,	VI,	,,	1883–84	...	5	0	...	..	6	0
,,	VII,	,,	1884–85	...	5	0	...	...	6	0
,,	VIII,	,,	1885–86	...	5	0	...	...	6	0
,,	IX,	,,	1886–87	...	2	0 per Part	...	2	6
,,	IX,	Part 7,	1886–87	...	8	0 ,, ,,	...	10	6
,,	X,	Parts 1 to 7,	1887–88	...	2	0 ,, ,,	...	2	6
,,	X,	Part 8,	1887–88	...	7	6 ,, ,,	...	10	6
,,	XI,	Parts 1 to 7,	1888–89	...	2	0 ,, ,,	...	2	6
,,	XI,	Part 8,	1888–89	...	7	6 ,, ,,	...	10	6
,,	XII,	Parts 1 to 7,	1889–90	...	2	0 ,, ,,	...	2	6
,,	XII,	Part 8,	1889–90	...	5	0 ,, ,,	...	6	0
,,	XIII,	Parts 1 to 7,	1890–91	...	2	0 ,, ,,	...	2	6
,,	XIII,	Part 8,	1890–91	...	5	0 ,, ,,	...	6	0
,,	XIV,	Parts 1 to 7,	1891–92	...	2	0 ,, ,,	...	2	6
,,	XIV,	Part 8,	1891–92	...	5	0 ,, ,,	...	6	0
,,	XV,	Parts 1 to 7,	1892–93	...	2	0 ,, ,,	...	2	6
,,	XV,	Part 8,	1892–93	...	5	0 ,, ,,	...	6	0
,,	XVI,	Parts 1 to 10,	1893–94	...	2	0 ,, ,,	...	2	6
,,	XVII,	Parts 1 to 8	1895	...	2	0 ,, ,,	...	2	6
,,	XVIII,	Parts 1 to 8	1896	...	2	0 ,, ,,	...	2	6
,,	XIX,	In progress	1897							

A few complete sets of the Transactions still remain for sale, which may be obtained on application to the Secretary, W. H. RYLANDS, F.S.A., 37, Great Russell Street, Bloomsbury, W.C.

PROCEEDINGS

OF

THE SOCIETY

OF

BIBLICAL ARCHÆOLOGY.

TWENTY-SEVENTH SESSION, 1897.

First Meeting, 12*th January*, 1897.
[ANNIVERSARY.]

JOSEPH POLLARD, ESQ. (MEMBER OF COUNCIL),

IN THE CHAIR.

————✻————

The following Presents were announced, and thanks ordered to be returned to the Donors :—

From the Author, Prof. G. Maspero :—Histoire Ancienne des Peuples de l'Orient classique. II, Les premières mêlées des Peuples. 8vo. Paris. 1897.

From the Publishers, The Theosophical Publishing Society :— Pistis Sophia, a Gnostic Gospel (with extracts from the books of the Saviour appended), originally translated from Greek into Coptic, and now for the first time into English from Schwartze's Latin version of the only known Coptic MS., and checked by Amélineau's French version, with an introduction by G. R. S. Mead, B.A., M.R.A.S. 8vo. London. 1896.

[No. CXLII.] 1

From the Author, Dr. John P. Peters :—The Seat of the Earliest
Civilization in Babylonia, and the date of its beginnings.
(*American Oriental Society.*) 8vo. 1896.

From the Author, Dr. John P. Peters :—Christ's Treatment of
the Old Testament. (*American Journal of Biblical Literature.*)
8vo.

From the Author, Dr. John P. Peters :—Notes on the Old
Testament. (*American Journal of Biblical Literature.*) 8vo.

From the Author, G. Margoliouth, M.A. :—The Liturgy of the
Nile (*Journ. Roy. Asiatic Soc.*) 8vo. London. 1896.

From Rev. R. Gwynne (*Sec. For. Corr.*):—Address to the
Assyrian Section of the Ninth Congress of Orientalists by
Prof. A. H. Sayce. 8vo. London. 1892.

From Rev. R. Gwynne (*Sec. For. Cor.*):—Die Lehre von der
übernatürlichen Geburt Christi. P. Lobstein. 8vo. Freiburg,
i. B. 1896.

From Rev. R. Gwynne (*Sec. For. Corr.*) :—Western Asia according to the most recent Discoveries, by C. P. Tiele. 8vo.
London. 1896.

From Innes Whitehouse :—Monumental Egypt, by W. Osborn.
Vol. I. 8vo.

The following Candidates were nominated for election at
the next Meeting to be held on the 2nd February, 1897 :—

Rev. James Hastings, M.A., The Manse, Kinneff, Bervie.
W. Jacks, Crosslets, Dumbartonshire.
Miss Martha Izod, The Hawthorns, Church Road, Edgbaston,
Birmingham.
John N. Duncan, Johannesburg.

The following Candidates were elected Members of the
Society, having been nominated at the last Meeting, held
on the 1st December, 1896.

Mahomad Barakat Ullah-Moulvie, Oriental Academy, 5, Bloomsbury Square.
Miss Vera F. Mameroff, P.O. Box 93, New York City, U.S.A.

SECRETARY'S REPORT

FOR THE YEAR 1896.

During the year just passed it has been my sad duty to notice from time to time the heavy loss the Society has suffered by the death of some of its distinguished Members.

The number on the Roll of Members has, however, been fairly maintained. I have to thank many who recognize the duty they owe to the Society by making an effort to secure at least *one new Member*, and it is sincerely to be hoped that others during the coming year will realize the same duty, and make an effort to give their help in this direction. It is in every way desirable that the number of Members should be increased, as if this were done the Council would be able to print more original material, and illustrate the various communications more fully.

The Society is certainly to be congratulated on the number of Papers which have been printed; and their interest is quite equal to those of former years. Still, with so much valuable material only waiting for publication, it is to be regretted that sufficient funds are not placed at the disposal of the Council, so as to enable them to at least double the size of the Parts of the *Proceedings*. This could easily be done if each Member now on the Roll would make a determined effort to obtain such a desirable result.

The Twenty-sixth Session of the Society commenced in November, 1895, but the present Volume, according to the more convenient arrangement, includes only the *Proceedings* from January to December, 1895, those Parts for November and December, 1895, having been issued with the previous Volume.

Again, classing the papers according to subjects, it will be well to take, in the first place, those which bear more directly on matters connected with the Bible. I am pleased to be able to state that communications on similar subjects will be submitted to the Society during the present and future Sessions.

REV. DR. M. FRIEDLANDER, On Some Fragments of the Hebrew Bible with peculiar Abbreviations and peculiar Signs for Vowels and Accents (read in March). REV. C. J. BALL, M.A., the Blessing of Moses (Deuteronomy xxxiii) (April). REV. G. MARGOLIOUTH, More Fragments of the Palestinian Syriac Version of the Holy Scriptures (November and December). PROFESSOR FLINDERS PETRIE, the Period ot the Judges (December). DR. M. GASTER, Two Unknown Hebrew Versions of the Tobit Legend (November and December).

Other papers have been read, which will appear in future parts of the *Proceedings.* For example, DR. GASTER, Some unique Hebrew Manuscripts of the Bible of the 9th or 10th century. REV. C. J. BALL, M.A., the first chapter of Genesis and its Babylonian cosmogonies. REV. DR. LÖWY, the Song of Deborah. JOSEPH OFFORD, the Tell-Amarna Tablets relating to Jerusalem and Central Palestine.

Of papers dealing with the antiquities and mythology of Egypt, the following may be mentioned. Still continuing his complete translation of the Book of the Dead, THE PRESIDENT has added to those already printed Chapters CXXV, Part IV (January), Notes to Chapter CXXV (February, March, April), Chapters CXXVI, CXXVII (May), Chapter CXXVIII (June). F. LL. GRIFFITH, Chaereu to Hermopolis on a Bilingual Milestone (February). JOSEPH OFFORD, the Name Chaereu (March). PROFESSOR FLINDERS PETRIE, the Arrangement of the XXIst Dynasty (February). R. D. FOTHERINGHAM, Some Considerations regarding Professor Petrie's Egyptian Chronology (March). PROFESSOR PETRIE, Note on Chronology (April). E. TOWRY WHYTE, Some Remarks on the Sepulchral Figures usually called Ushabti, with ten plates of examples (April and May). F. LL. GRIFFITH, Note on Demotic Philology (March). DR. W. MAX MÜLLER, on a Hieroglyphic Sign (June). F. LL. GRIFFITH, Stela of Mentuhetep, Son of Hepy (November). W. E. CRUM, a Stele of the XIIIth Dynasty.

Babylonian and Assyrian antiquities have also as in former years found a place in our publications. PROFESSOR DR. FRITZ HOMMEL, Assyriological Notes (January). ROBERT BROWN, junr., Euphratean Stellar Researches (*continued*) (January). THE HON. MISS PLUNKET, *Gu*, the Eleventh Constellation of the Zodiac (February). REV. A. J. DELATTRE, *A-mur-ri* ou *A-ḫar-ri?* (February). ALFRED BOISSIER, Lettre de Labâ au roi d'Égypte. PROFESSOR SAYCE, Roman Inscriptions at Assuân (March). JOSEPH OFFORD, the Nude Goddess in Assyrio-Babylonian Art (May). ALFRED BOISSIER, Bas-Reliefs de Tiglat-Pileser III (May). PROFESSOR SAYCE, Assyriological Notes, No. 1 (June). REV. C. H. W. JOHNS, a New Eponym List (November). ALFRED BOISSIER, Notes Assyriologiques (November). THEOPHILUS G. PINCHES, Assyriological Gleanings (December).

The best thanks of the Society are due to the many writers who have so willingly given their assistance by submitting so varied and interesting a series of Papers to the Society.

Of the Large Paper Edition of SIR P. LE PAGE RENOUF'S Translation with Commentary and Notes of the Book of the Dead, Parts I to V have been issued to Subscribers.

The Society has undertaken the publication, as has already been notified to the Members, of a limited number of copies, in large paper, of some recently discovered portions of the Palestinian Syriac Version of the Holy Scriptures, edited by the REV. G. MARGOLIOUTH, M.A. The work will contain a photographic facsimile of the whole of the text, a printed transcription, translation, and notes.

The number of books in the Library still, I am happy to say, continues to increase, as well as the number of readers. Notwithstanding the kindness of many members who, by valuable donations, not only of the whole of their own writings as issued, but by the works of others, have added so much to the interest and value of our collection, there are very many books required, the possession of which by the Society would be of great advantage to students. The Society exchanges publications with a large number of kindred Institutions; a list of many works especially wanted for the use of the Members has been printed at the end of each number of the *Proceedings*. This list is necessarily altered from time to time, owing to the kind responses made in the form of works asked for. I cannot too often point out that, as the books may be borrowed by Members, to have a good representative Library is one of the most important portions of the Society's functions. As the funds allow, the Council purchases whatever it is in their power to supply of the immediate requirements. The amount at their disposal, however, is quite inadequate to meet the demands on it. It is therefore to the kind generosity of those possessing spare copies of the books required, or of others connected with the objects of the Society, that the Members must look for assistance in this very desirable object.

The audited Statement of Receipts and Expenditure annexed shows that the funds available for the year 1896 have been £713 14s. 6d., including the donations already mentioned for which the Society has been indebted to ADMIRAL OMMANEY and MR. ROBERT BROWN, junr., F.S.A. The expenditure has been £647 15s. 4d. The balance carried forward to the current year is therefore £65 19s. 2d.

W. HARRY RYLANDS,
Secretary.

New Year's Day, 1897.

The thanks of the Society were voted to the President, the Secretary, and Officers for their efforts in behalf of the Society.

The following Officers and Council for the current year were elected :—

COUNCIL, 1897.

President.
SIR P. LE PAGE RENOUF.

Vice-Presidents.
THE MOST REV. HIS GRACE THE LORD ARCHBISHOP OF YORK.
THE MOST NOBLE THE MARQUESS OF BUTE, K.T., &c., &c.
THE RIGHT HON. LORD AMHERST OF HACKNEY.
THE RIGHT HON. LORD HALSBURY.
THE RIGHT HON. W. F. GLADSTONE, D.C.L., &c.
ARTHUR CATES.
F. D. MOCATTA, F.S.A., &c.
WALTER MORRISON, M.P.
SIR CHARLES NICHOLSON, BART., D.C.L., M.D., &c.
ALEXANDER PECKOVER, LL.D., F.S.A.
REV. GEORGE RAWLINSON, D.D., Canon of Canterbury.

Council.

REV. CHARLES JAMES BALL, M.A.
REV. PROF. T. K. CHEYNE, D.D.
THOMAS CHRISTY, F.L.S.
DR. J. HALL GLADSTONE, F.R.S.
CHARLES HARRISON, F.S.A.
GRAY HILL.
PROF. T. HAYTER LEWIS, F.S.A.
REV. ALBERT LOWY, LL.D., &c.

REV. JAMES MARSHALL, M.A.
CLAUDE G. MONTEFIORE.
WALTER L. NASH, F.S.A.
PROF. E. NAVILLE.
J. POLLARD.
EDWARD B. TYLOR, LL.D., F.R.S., &c.
E. TOWRY WHYTE, M.A., F.S.A.

Honorary Treasurer.
BERNARD T. BOSANQUET.

Secretary.
W. HARRY RYLANDS, F.S.A.

Hon. Secretary for Foreign Correspondence.
REV. R. GWYNNE, B.A.

Honorary Librarian.
WILLIAM SIMPSON, F.R.G.S.

PRE-MOSAIC PALESTINE.

By Joseph Offord.

It is now nearly a century since Young and Champollion first wrested from the mysterious hieroglyphs of Egypt the key to their secrets ; and almost half a century has elapsed since the educated world was astonished and enriched by the epoch-making discoveries of Layard and Botta in the Mesopotamian mounds. During all these years, first the temples, tombs and papyri of Egypt, and then also the Babylonian bricks, Chaldean cylinders, and Assyrian slabs have gradually been unfolding to us the history, culture, religion and mythology of these great peoples of antiquity.

Incidentally both from Egyptian monuments and papyri, and from Assyrian and Babylonian records, matters connected with the history of Palestine and her Syrian neighbours, as depicted in the Bible, have been illustrated in many ways, but it is only quite recently that a series of documents has been discovered that are almost exclusively concerned with events either in Palestine itself or the immediately contiguous countries of Western Asia.

Early in the year 1888, some Egyptian peasants, searching for relics among the ruins at Tel el-Amarna, a site some hundred miles up the Nile from Cairo, found several hundreds of baked clay tablets of diverse dimensions, all having carefully inscribed upon both sides texts in the cuneiform or arrow-headed characters, so well known from Babylonian, Assyrian and Persian inscriptions.

The majority of these relics were acquired by the Berlin and British Museums, a portion by the Egyptian Museum of Gizeh, some by a Russian savant, M. Golenischef, and Rostovich Bey of Cairo ; one may be seen in the Louvre, a few are in private hands, and altogether the whereabouts of more than 300 are known.

The deep impression produced among scholars by such a

discovery may be imagined, and their elucidation and publication may be said to have been anxiously awaited by the whole civilised world.

Such a task, however, for various reasons, which will appear as we study the subject, takes time, and it is only just lately that summaries of all their contents have been published, and it will be very many years indeed before their elucidation is finally accomplished ; and many more before all the information they afford as to history and philology is utilised.

The period has however now arrived when the results accomplished may be summarised and popularised with advantage. Translations have been attempted or made by the most erudite scholars in such matters, and although nine years have not elapsed since their discovery, the number of more or less learned works relating to them is already in excess of that of the tablets themselves.

The first question that anyone having an acquaintance with ancient history will naturally ask is, how can it be that in Egypt and far up her Nile valley away from Syria, buried deep in the ruins of an almost unknown Egyptian city, a collection of documents written in the script of nations beside the Tigris and Euphrates should be preserved, to thus so fortunately enrich our museums and our knowledge.

The answer to this question will explain that in these clay tablets and their strange characters we have come upon what has been justly termed a " priceless treasure," for they contain nothing less than the diplomatic archives of two well known Egyptian Pharaohs, Amenophis III and IV.

To set forth who these monarch were, and why their foreign correspondence thus pigeon-holed at El Amarna should give us so much information concerning pre-Mosaic Palestine, it will be necessary in a few words to touch upon a short period of Egyptian history.

Anyone who has read even an elementary history of Egypt, knows that after the long ages of the early dynasties, during which many of the most marvellous monuments, such as the pyramids, were constructed, and almost all Egyptian literature was written, Egypt was invaded and partly conquered, and for centuries governed by an alien race known as the Hykshos or Shepherd Kings, and it is almost certain that it was to one of these monarchs that Joseph was " Grand Vizier." At length, however, the native Egyptian royal race, which had never been extinguished, roused up the lovers of their fatherland, and descending the Nile, drove out the hated foreigners from Lower Egypt and the Delta, and freed their country from what they considered their oppressors. The native monarch who thus regained the throne of a united Egypt and his immediate descendants constituted the celebrated XVIIIth dynasty, which together with the subsequent XIXth dynasty reigned, roughly speaking, for 400 years, from about 1600 to 1200 B.C.

During this period Egypt was frequently brought into close connexion with Palestine and Syria, and even with countries farther to the east and north, for no sooner did the early XVIIIth dynasty kings find themselves securely masters of all Egypt, than they commenced those Asiatic campaigns which occupy such a glorious place in the national annals, and which were to the outer world the sign of that zenith level of power and prosperity which Egypt at the period attained. Actuated doubtless partly by revenge for centuries of subjection, as well as by the lust of conquest engendered by renewed strength at home, Amasis, who expelled the Shepherds, entered Palestine and took Sharhan to the south of Gaza, mentioned in Joshua xix, 6; and a great Pharaoh named Thothmes I marched through Palestine and Syria and on to Mesopotamia, added to Egyptian sway also the countries of Canaan and Phœnicia, and even ruled as suzerain as distant a land as that on the further bank of the Euphrates. Whether Assyria itself became an appanage of Egypt we cannot say, but her rulers certainly paid tribute; and under a later Pharaoh, Thothmes III, who among other cities captured Aradus, Tyre, Tunip,* Kadesh, and Carchemish, Egypt undoubtedly possessed the districts called by her Naharina and Mitanni, which were in north Mesopotamia, and shortly afterwards Babylonia itself became her tributary.

The most distant of her conquests did not however remain permanently beneath Egyptian sway, the long line of communications between the Nile and Euphrates after leaving the Jordan valley, was open to constant flank attack from the rising power of the Hittites; gradually the Mesopotamian plains and north Syrian valleys and hills ceased to be subject, and became semi-independent, though still on friendly terms with their temporary rulers.

The coasts of Phœnicia and the inland region of Palestine, however, still owned Egypt as their lord; their proximity enabled

* Tunip was south of Aleppo near Damascus.

her to hold them with firmer hand. She appears to have retained them in subjection by means of governors subservient to herself, selected from their own chiefs, assisted by resident Egyptian advisers, and maintained by small Egyptian garrisons, and to have received tribute from all just as Assyria had done at other times. Rebellion if it arose was crushed by the mercenaries stationed in the various cities, or if they were insufficient, by them further assisted by fresh troops from the Delta.

Such evidently were the political conditions of Palestine under kings Amenophis II and Thothmes IV, the immediate successors of Thothmes III. Under the monarch who next ascended the Egyptian throne, Amenophis III, however, Egypt's prestige waned, and her grasp of the territories still remaining to her weakened.

His campaigns were few,* and do not appear to have terminated victoriously, for his return in quasi triumph home seems to have ever been the signal for fresh revolt, if not in Palestine, certainly in far off satrapies bordering on Assyria and Babylonia. The tribute, at all events from Naharina, which lay thereabouts, we know ceased to be paid. By the time he was gathered to his fathers and Amenophis IV reigned in his stead, matters were going from bad to worse. Even the adulation of the official scribes who compiled his temple inscriptions could only once venture to record the tribute from the comparatively contiguous territories of the Ruten, that is Syria, Palestine, and the Syrian shore.

To provide some idea of the chronology of the events so hastily narrated, it is well to mention that Thothmes III assumed the double crown of Egypt about 1500 B.C.. and Amenophis III about 1430 B.C., so that from the date of the extreme extension of Egyptian power in Asia to the commencement of its declension was a space of about 70 years.

Besides the gradual diminution of the will, or prowess, necessary to maintain her conquests, that befell Egypt in the reigns of Thothmes IV and Amenophis III, in the time of Amenophis IV there appears, so rapidly was the decline accelerated, to have been some special reason at home for her impotence abroad ; and the cause is not far to seek, for we know that under that strange monarch a most remarkable revolution, nothing less than a nearly

---

* His lion hunts in the earlier part of his reign, in north and eastern Syria, we know were many, for in the first ten years we have records of 102 slain by his hand alone.—(BEZOLD, XVIII.)

total reversal of the most cherished dogmas of his country's religion, was attempted, and temporarily carried out, and although he reigned more than 3000 years ago, we have a very considerable knowledge of the crisis.

Like many great historical events, it probably owed its origin to a woman. Amenophis III, among other wives, married a certain lady named Thi or Tii, daughter of parents called on the monuments Iuaa and Tuaa. Who she was is not known, but from her name being familiarly mentioned on two of the Tel el Amarna Tablets which were received from Asia, it is probable she had been an Asiatic, and her portrait, showing fair hair, blue eyes, and the colour assigned by Egyptian painters to the Syrians, confirm this.* Her husband also took at least four other spouses from the beautiful Asiatic princesses ; one of whom, Kilkipa, is spoken of in a scarab graven in honour of the occasion, which tells us she arrived in Egypt acccompanied by 317 ladies of honour.

It seems almost certain that if Amenophis IV did not inherit his heterodox religious views through the instructions of queen Thi, she sympathised with her son-in-law's notions, for she is depicted upon monuments as uniting in the peculiar worship favoured by him.

He was, when a young prince, made a priest of the great temple of the sun god at Heliopolis, and became a member of its sacred college, and it may be that there, apart from any bias imparted to him in youth, he conceived a hatred of the powerful Theban hierarchy whose supreme god was Amen Ra.

His portraits, of which we have many (more or less mutilated by inconoclasts who disapproved of his tenets, and some apparently caricatures), show most peculiar features, evidently an admixture of utterly diverse races ; features perhaps accounting for his fanaticism, and at any rate his head betrays a very low type of cranial development.

No sooner had he ascended the throne than he endeavoured to banish the worship of Amen Ra and establish that of Aten, or the form of god as revealed to man in the symbol of the solar disk, and so determined was he that none should mistake his wishes that he changed his sacred royal name of Amenophis to that of Khuenaten, or "splendour of the sun." Wherever he could. he had the name of Amen erased from the ancient monuments in whose inscriptions it occurred, and persecuted his worshippers.

* Professor Maspero still thinks Thi was an Egyptian lady.

This abolition of a long received form of the Deity, however, was impossible to be carried out to the full, in a conservative country like Egypt and with a city like Thebes for a capital, where the prestige of the cult was so great; so he determined to build a new capital and royal residence where Aten alone should be reverenced, where the temple,* which in Egypt was ever the nucleus of the town, should be consecrated to him alone. So to gratify the royal will, about 180 miles above Memphis a city rose as if by magic, and was named almost precisely as himself, a splendour of Aten. There he erected a palace, and like a good Egyptian, near by a tomb, and there by, while it lasted, his great officials constructed sepulchres for themselves. Whether Khuenaten's change in the form under which the Deity was to be adored involved any return to, or commencement of, a purer form of religion we cannot positively tell, but by the transiency of the result we are tempted to think otherwise. Instead of being a prophet of a purer faith, he appears, it has been said, to have merely endeavoured by his auto-cratic power to enforce on his people a new form of worship, for upon his death it soon fell into disuse. After a short period of ineffectual rule by his sons-in-law, the dethroned Amen Ra was restored to theological honours, and the sacred city of Khuenaten's folly abandoned for ever; and is now known only by the title of its mound heap of ruins and rubbish, as Tel Amarna.

It will have been noticed that these two kings Amenophis III and IV, or Khuenaten, are the identical monarchs of whose reigns the oriental correspondence was said to have been embodied in the tablets whose wonderful discovery we are considering; and it will by this time be clear why it is that the archives containing the dispatches between their Asiatic possessions and themselves should, if found, be concealed, as was pointed out, in such a strange place as Tel Amarna far up the Nile.

But we are not left to conjecture, or even to historical proba-bility, for one of the tablets bearing a letter addressed to Khuen-aten's father, and therefore a document which would have been placed among the records before the court and with it the foreign office, was transferred to Tel Amarna; has a docket in Egyptian

---

* The temple's title was Pa-Aten. A magnificent tomb, much mutilated, has been discovered recently near Tel Amarna, being that of Khuenaten's second daughter Maquet-Aten; three of her sisters are mentioned in the inscriptions, Ankhsnpaaten, Merit-Aten, and Nefer-nefru-Aten-ta-Serat.

telling us it had been brought away from the "Record Chamber" of Thebes when Khuenaten removed to his model sacred metropolis.

Why a collection of dispatches to and from the Egyptian Government should be embodied in the cuneiform script, and in the Babylonian language, interspersed however in the Syrian and Palestinian letters, by a number of semi Hebrew or Aramaic words, has still to be explained, and this can best be done by a preliminary survey of the contents of the tablets and of some documents found with them.

First as to the contents : they easily sever themselves into two parts ; a series of letters to the Pharaohs, or their ministers for foreign affairs, from rulers of the north and western provinces of Assyria and Babylonia, in *Naharina, Mitanni, Assapi, and Alashiya ; the three last of doubtful situation : together with one or two drafts of replies from a Pharaoh to a king of part of Babylonia. Secondly, a larger series of despatches from officials or chiefs subservient to Egypt at various places along the coast of Palestine, in the interior, and in the region immediately to the north of that country. There are a few tablets, or fragments of tablets, bearing mythological texts and dictionaries, the former marked in red (an Egyptian practice). These evidently served as text books to Egyptians learning to read the writing and language of the letters. However, her scholars had at least one, if not two, interpreters to assist them in properly appreciating and in writing the dispatches, with the absolute accuracy we know to be so essential even now in reading diplomatic documents, for his seal has been disinterred by Dr. Petrie, and tells us his name was Tetunu, and he was servant (*or* slave) of one Samas-aki-iddin. But even with his help their task must have been tremendous, for the cuneiform script was intended for an idiom different to those it now embodied, its prolixity a scholar tells us was quite unsuited for diplomatic correspondence, and if ever such writings were said to have been used to conceal the thoughts of their authors, that may truly be stated of some of these curious dispatches.

Coming now to the question of the letters and language, it would seem that cuneiform writing must at this time have been used for all, and the Babylonian language for nearly all, official purposes in Western Asia, although at this period Babylon was in more senses than one in low water, for her power was restricted to the low lands

* This is the Aram Naharaim, or Syria of the two rivers of the Bible.

of the rivers Tigris and Euphrates, and she was ruled by a conquering race of kings known as Kassites. How was it that Egypt was unable to impress her letters and language, at all events on her subject peoples, and that they and foreign nations with whom she had alliance, all in addressing her used Babylonian letters, and nearly all that rival's language? for some few tablets are written in unknown and untranslatable tongues emanating from the lands of Arsapi and Mitanni.

The reasons seem certainly to have been that at some time in its chequered history Syria and her neighbours had been for a long period subject to Babylonia, and this adds another to the many proofs that the Chaldean scribes were not vaingloriously falsifying history when they state that far back in the time of their great king Sargon, who reigned 3800 years B.C., their armies had conquered, not only Syria and Phœnicia, but even crossed over to Cyprus under his victorious leadership.

With their warriors the Babylonians would introduce their writing, and so long must their supremacy have endured, and so deep the impression which their civilisation made on the inhabitants have been, that it fixed irrevocably the form of their writing until the merchants of Phœnicia invented a simpler script. It must be remembered this effect would be much assisted by the similarity of language among the peoples we find using the cuneiform letters and the Babylonians who introduced them to them; and as an illustration of this it must not be forgotten that the alien and unsubdued Hittites always used a graphic system of their own.

With regard to the inability of the Egyptians to impress their language upon the tribes they conquered, it must be borne in mind that theirs was a wholly alien tongue—Canaanites, Amorites and Syrians were as brothers to the great Semitic people of Mesopotamia, whilst with Egypt they had no such affinity.

Then the richest part of Egypt had been for centuries under the domination of a race of Asiatic origin, no doubt using a branch of the very language of the tablets, during all which time their relatives in Palestine and Syria had been pursuing their own way. Then came the Egyptian campaigns immediately preceding the time in which the Tel Amarna dispatches were written, in which Egypt was victorious, it is true, but these expeditions seem to have been more of the nature of gigantic forays, and ended by leaving the people she had plundered pretty much to manage their own affairs, provided they acknowledged the supremacy of the Pharaohs and paid them tribute.

It has been said that these tablets divide into two series, one of dispatches from the regions to the east and north-east of Palestine and Syria, reaching as far as Babylonia, and the other of records referring to affairs in Palestine or the sea coast and the districts immediately to the north. The first of these portions we shall not have time to discuss on this occasion. They are, however, supremely interesting. The peculiar matrimonial negotiations, the almost childish clamour for presents, and the subtle way in which wishes or fears of the writers are frequently conveyed, borders sometimes upon the grotesque.

The list of articles of tribute or gifts present a complete epitome of the civilisation of the age, including gold, silver, bronze, lapis-lazuli, precious stones, horses, chariots, elephants' tusks, and " men who could run as swift as eagles' flight."

Turning now to the second series of dispatches, those relating to Palestine and Syria : the keenest interest will naturally be aroused in connection with the five or six letters from Abed-heba (or Ebed Tob), governor of Jerusalem and the surrounding districts. He appears to have had control of a large portion of Palestine, including Hebron, Gezer, Askalon, Lachish and Ajalon. That he was Canaanite is proved by his name, and the manner in which he some-times employs Canaanitish words, but his nationality would have been, on the Egyptian system, no objection in the way of utilising him as a governor ; indeed, he appears to have been more than an ordinary governor or " ḥazânu," as he terms it, for he often tells us he is not that, but a " u-e-u " which in Egyptian signifies an official of the Pharaoh, and must have been higher than a " ḥazânu," for he seems to have been superior to several such, or ordinary governors, who were included in his viceroyalty.

These " ḥazânus " appear, except in cases where their names show them to have been native Egyptian officials, to have been descendants of chiefs formerly governing the cities or districts they now superintended for the Egyptians.

Abed-heba says he too was descended from a family that had been lords over the lands of Jerusalem, but now (as stated) he was an " u-e-u " officer of the king. This superiority of status of the governorship of Jerusalem seems to indicate that at this primitive period it was a city of greater importance than the others.

These five or perhaps six letters present a most valuable index of the state of affairs in Syria and Palestine as generally described by the Tel Amarna tablets, but before proceeding to describe them it will be well to devote a few words to the question of the name by which Jerusalem was known.

Her title in the tablets is always " Urusalem," though in the lapse of time the Babylonians dropped the second u, for in the cuneiform inscriptions containing Sennacherib's account of the war against Hezekiah it had become " Ursalem." This discovery of the extreme antiquity of the title of Jerusalem disproves conclusively the theory that the gloss in Judges xix, 10, " Jerusalem which is Jebus," means that Jebus was an older name for Jerusalem, for here some centuries before we find Urusalem is its name, and indeed 1 Chronicles xi, 4, "and David and all Israel went to Jerusalem which is Jebus," shows that Jebus and Jerusalem were not names distinct from being anterior one to the other, but used interchangeably.*

However, the manner in which Urusalem is spoken of in the tablets shows it included not only the city, but a district round. The tablets are explicit, speaking of "the country," or district of Urusalem; twice omitting the sign for city and once saying "districts of the city of Urusalem." Now we know this, it gives a clearer meaning to the gloss in Judges and Chronicles, showing that those texts indicate to us that Jerusalem included Jebus, so that the Jebusites were embraced in the district of Jerusalem.†

That this really is the view set forth in the Bible seems clear from the statement in 1 Chronicles xxviii and xxxii, where a list of more than 60 Benjamite clans are said to have lived in Jerusalem, where it must obviously refer to a district and not to the space confined within the city walls.

The etymology of the word Uru-salem is uncertain. Most scholars consider it to be derived from Uru, a city, and Salem the name of some deity. The use of Salem alone in the 76th Psalm, and by the writer of the Epistle to the Hebrews, who appears to have had knowledge of some extremely ancient tradition, shows it was considered by the Jews to be a compound word, and if, as is probable, the Salem of Geneses xiv, 18 (and Melchizedek king of

---

* See Morris Jastrow, in *Journal of Biblical Literature*, 1892, p. 103.
† See Morris Jastrow, *l.c.*, p. 104, 105.

Salem brought forth bread and wine), is Jerusalem, this is an additional confirmation of the word Salem being used singly, a translator of the chief reference to Urusalem, as we shall presently see, considers the tablet to tell us that Jerusalem was sacred to the god Ninip, and his worship consisted frequently in libations of wine, which, as M. Pinches points out, may be connected with the offering of bread and wine to the guests by Melchizedek.

But it is just possible that Melchizedek's Salem was " Shalem, a city of Shechem," to which Jacob came as stated in Genesis xxxii, 18, which is probably the Shalim of 1 Samuel ix, 4, and the Salim in Ænon, where John the Baptist was, as recorded in John's Gospel, iii, 23.

Coming back to the title Uru-salem, it may be that the word Uru is the name of a god and not connected directly with Uru city.* Mr. Pinches' decipherment of the most distinct reference to Jerusalem, quotes the tablet as saying, "The city of the mountain of Jerusalem, the city of the temple of Ninip is its name. Now the deity Ninip was entitled Uru when spoken of as the god of planting, and the prefix Uru may therefore be his name. It is true that the usual sign or determinative placed by Babylonian scribes before any word being the name of a god, is omitted, but one of the peculiarities of the El Amarna tablets is, that such signs for deity are frequently left out.

Leaving aside this somewhat philological discussion, and concentrating our attention upon the letters of Abed-heba himself, which have been fully discussed and illustrated by Professor Morris Jastrow, to whose erudition I am much indebted, and whose translations have been appropriated, we find from them the following interesting particulars. They are all more or less occupied with petitions for assistance, and explanations of the serious position in which their writer was placed, owing to attacks upon his district of a foe he entitles the "Habiri," or Confederates, who were under a chief named Ili Milku, or Elimelech (often called Milkil, or Melech), and consisted of several tribes, or clans, the most prominent of whom seem to have been led by chiefs named Laba and Šuadatum.

In addition to such dangers of environment, threatened by such energetic enemies, Abed-heba seems to have felt still more keenly

---

* See "The Most High God of Salem," in *Proc. Soc. Bibl. Arch.*, Vol. XVI, p. 225.

that owing to his loyalty having been questioned in some "evil
reports" to the Pharaoh, that monarch failed to forward him the
necessary troops to maintain his position and the power of his
Egyptian superiors. The following letter, probably the first in point
of date of those we have, and one of supreme interest, because it
contains the important passage relating to Jerusalem, gives a good
idea of Abed-hebas epistles to his sovereign:—

"To the king my lord, speaks as follows Abed-heba thy servant:—
To the feet of the king my lord, seven times and seven times I prostrate myself. See the deed which Milkil * and Šuardatum have done
against the king my lord. They have hired the soldiery of Gezer and
Gath and the troops of Kilti (? Keilah). They have taken the district
of Rubute. The province of the king has gone over to the Habiri
people. And now also a city of the province of Jerusalem known as
Bit Ninip, a city of the king, has revolted, just as the people of Kilti
have done. Let the king, therefore, listen to Abed-heba thy servant
and send troops, so that the province of the king may be restored to
the king, but if no troops are forthcoming the province of the king
goes over to the Habiri. This is the deed that Šuardatum and
Milkil have done . . . ."

Here unfortunately the tablet breaks off, excepting that on the
edge of it may be deciphered the words, "Let the king have a care
for his province."

There is a difference of opinion among specialists as to whether
the "city known as Bit Ninip, which had become disaffected," is
not another name for Jerusalem, and it appears most probable that
this is the case, and we should, with Mr. Pinches, read the sentence
thus: "and now the city of the mountain of Jerusalem, the city of
the temple of Ninip is its name, the city of the king, has become
disaffected."

Looking at a map it will easily be seen that Abed-beba's foes
were coming upon him from the south and west, for there lay
Gezer, Gath, and Keilah.

The Pharaoh does not, however, appear to have been favourably
impressed by Abed-heba's appeals and statements; perhaps with
good reason, for the three chiefs he so denounces all appear by
letters from themselves to have also been protesting their allegiance
to Egypt and Elimelech even applies for Egyptian troops to be sent

* Or (Eli) Melech.

him ; whilst Laba actually writes a letter repudiating Abed-heba's charges against him and Elimelech.

"See," he declares, " I am the faithful servant of the king ; I have not committed sin, neither have I transgressed ; I have not withheld my tribute."

Further, he says, the reports against him are calumnies, and he only entered Gezer in good faith and to succour Elimelech, and having done so handed over his soldiers to Yapti Addi, an Egyptian emissary. Finally, he winds up his protestation of loyalty thus :—

"If the king were to send to me " (the order) "plunge thy bronze sword into thy heart I could die without fail," a somewhat Japanese challenge to fidelity, but an offer which may charitably be taken as proving his loyalty.*

Šuardatum deliberately denounces Abed-heba as a traitor, saying : " *He* sent to Keilah instigating it to revolt, saying, 'Take money and follow me.'" Elimelech,† however, confirms Abed-heba's statement that he was an ally of Šuardatum, by the way he mentions him, though that incidental corroboration does not in any way prove that Abed-heba was the true, and the other three chiefs false friends to Egypt.

Abed-heba evidently became aware of the denunciations of his loyalty, either through a friend at the Egyptian court, or perhaps from his own consciousness of guilt, for in a letter, probably the last that we have of his, he says :—

"What have I done against the king my lord that they should slander me in the presence of the king (declaring) Abed-heba has revolted against the king his lord. See, as for me, neither my father nor my mother put me in this place ; the arm of the mighty king brought me to the house of my father. Why then should I commit a wrong against the king my lord as long as he lives ? I speak to the king's envoy, 'Why showest thou favour to the Habiri and oppose the prefects, whereas it is they (the Habiri) who plot against the king, my lord ?' And, furthermore, I say the lands of the king are lost because they plot against the king my lord. And may the king know that when he sent garrisons, Yanhamu took them."

The tablet is mutilated here, but it contains complaint of

---

* See " Lettre de Labâ au roi d'Égypte," *Proc. Soc. Bibl. Arch.*, February, 1896.

† There are at least three letters of Elimelech.

Yanhamu having deprived him of his reinforcements.   He goes on
to say :—

    " The cities of the king have revolted, for Elimelech has ruined
the whole of the king's province.   Therefore let the king have a
care for his province and direct his countenance to his province
. . . . . . as long as the king, my lord, lives; whenever his envoys
come I declare that lost are the provinces of the king, and though
thou dost not hearken unto me, yet lost are all the governors.   Not
a single *ḥazânu* is left to the king.   May he direct his countenance
therefore to the troops, and may the king send the troops.   There
are no longer any provinces to the king, for the Habiri have
destroyed all the king's provinces.   If the troops are forthcoming
during the year, then the provinces of the king my lord will remain,
but if troops are not forthcoming this year, then are surely lost the
provinces of the king."   Then he adds a summary of affairs in the
subscription : " To the king's scribe, Abed-heba, thy servant, bring
the plain message to the king my lord, lost are all the provinces of
the king."

    The mention of one Yanhamu in this letter is of interest, because
it shows another of the letters, known as number 105, must have
predated it by some time, for in it, after again denouncing Elimelech
and the son of Laba and others who had deserted from Abed-heba's
authority, he asks the king to send Yanhamu to investigate his
truthfulness, boldly saying, " Send men as a garrison for the
protection of the country, inasmuch as the entire province is in
revolt, and send Yanhamu that he may find out the condition of
the entire province of the king."

    This Yanhamu appears to have been the greatest official from
Egypt employed in Syria and Palestine.   We find him referred to in
numerous tablets relating to many parts of the country.   Some of the
chiefs praise him for his assistance, others suggest him as a referee
as to their good faith, and tell the Egyptian government they have
aided him with their troops.   Others again denounce him, and
sometimes he appears to have been first the friend and finally
the foe of the correspondents ; so that altogether his office can have
been no sinecure.

    One document distinctly accuses him of treachery, saying he
was favourable to the Habiri.   This or some similar slander caused
Amenophis to send one Shipti-Adda to ascertain the truth, and we
have his confidential report and result of his inquiry, wherein he

tells the Pharaoh, "Yanhamu *is* a faithful servant of the king and the dust of the king's feet." This proof of the fidelity of Yanhumu throws a suspicious light upon the true nature of Abed-heba's obedience and loyalty. *

Yanhamu apparently generally had his headquarters at Jarmuda, (the Jarmuth of Joshua x, 3), but his name occurs as the special Egyptian commissioner in connection with affairs in the extreme north, in the Amorite country, being mentioned by Rib-addi, governor of Gebal, or Byblos, also by Abed-ashera and his son Aziru (the Biblical Ezer), who were rulers of the Amorite districts, and had Tunip as chief city. In this case the rival rulers were, as at Jerusalem, mutually reporting against each other. There were other similar Egyptian officials to Yanhamu, all of which bore Egyptian names, which, as far as we can judge, Yanhamu's was not.

Among these were Amanappa = Amenapt, Rianapa = Egyptian Renapa, and Pahura or Paur; a colonel of the Egyptian guard at Jerusalem is called Khapi, the Egyptian Hapi, and we are told his father was Miyariya = Meri-ra. This Hapi was the father of Amenhotep, who built the colossus of Memnon, and he is spoken of in the Amarna tablets as Khatbi.

As we saw by the second letter of Abed-heba's, Yanhamu had been sent as he requested, but the consequence was not as he had hoped, the rehabilitation of his loyalty: for Yanhamu, if accompanied by the reinforcements, or if they arrived subsequent to his coming, kept the garrisons in his own hands the Pharaoh had sent, which probably means that his investigations on the spot failed to satisfy him as to Abed-beba's good faith.

The third Abed-heba tablet, which we summarised in reference to the request for Yanhamu's presence, alluded to other rebels or enemies than Melech and Šuadatum of the Habiri confederates; these new foes are the "son of Laba,"† the "sons of Arza," and a certain

---

* A letter, No. 62 in B.M. series, from one Melech, probably the same who Abed-heba so denounces, accuses Yanhamu of gross tyranny in carrying off his goods, wives, and children, and appeals to Egypt for restitution.

† There is a letter from Laba to the king of Egypt in the B.M. collection, No. 61, in which he promises to hold out for the Pharaoh to the last extremity. Another letter, No. 72, speaks of an officer named Zurata having captured Laba at Megiddo. Zurata promised to forward Laba prisoner to Egypt by sea, and the writer of the letter paid Zurata a ransom or bribe to do so. However, Zurata subsequently took Laba home and let him get away. See "The Tel el-Amarna Tablets in the British Museum," p. 83.

Puru. Further light upon the performances of some of these chiefs in
the continued revolts and razzias, which were going in Palestine at this
epoch is shown by the (Berlin) letter No. 103, probably in chronological order the third of Abed-beba's series. After repeating, as
in a later letter of his we have described, his protest against the
Pharaoh believing the evil reports of his conduct, he says :—

" See, the provinces round about are hostile to me, let the king
therefore have a care for the land. See, the district of the city of
Gezer, of Ascalon, and of Lachish have given them (the Habiri)
assistance, inasmuch as they furnished food, oil, and various things.
Therefore let the king have a care and send troops against the
men who have committed sin against the king my lord. If the
troops come this year, the provinces and governors will remain
to the king my lord, but if not, there will be neither lands nor
governors left to the king. See, this district of the city of Jerusalem,
neither my father or mother gave it to me, but the mighty king's
arm gave it me. See the deed Melech and the sons of Laba have
done, giving the land to the Habiri. See, O king, and be just
towards me with regard to the Kasi. Let the king find out through
emissaries that they have done violence and grave offences."

He then continues his troubles, saying Adda and some garrisons
had revolted, and begging that troops might be concentrated at or
near Ajalon, and adds that the Kasi, whoever they were, are in his
power, and the king can do what he likes with them. Abed-heba
pleads for clemency towards them in a half-hearted way, seeking
first security for himself.

There is only one other letter (No. 104, Berlin) of Abed-heba's
correspondence to be now considered ; it probably follows the last
described. After the customary laudation of the king, and stating
" his name is fixed from the rising of the sun to the setting of the
sun," he goes on to assert his faithful sending of tribute, and reports
the safe arrival and departure of two envoys who had had handed
over to them from him valuable captives as hostages and ladies
for Pharaoh's concubines. He then gives a dismal account of his
position ; all the country is lost to Egypt ; the enemy have occupied
Seeri (probably Mount Seir) and Gimticarmel.[*] He then rather
taunts the king, no doubt in hope of thus obtaining his assistance,

---

* A Phœnician inscription from Larnaka in Cyprus, published in the *Révue
d'Assyriologie*, Vol. III, mentions a Quormel, or Carmel, in Cyprus, a counterpart
of that upon the Syrian coast.

by reminding him that Egypt still holds the distant Naharina, upon the Euphrates, and says, "How then shall the Habiri be permitted to hold the king's cities?" meaning the cities of his district, so much nearer to Egypt. He then goes on to say, "Not a single Ḥazânu (Egyptian governor) is left to the king; all have perished: Turbazu has been killed at the great gate of Zilu. Zimrida of Lachish has been put to death by his subjects, and Yapti Addi has been killed at Zilu, and if the troops do not come this year, then irrevocably lost are all the lands of the king. If troops are not forthcoming this year, then let the king send an envoy to fetch me with other officials that we may die near the king."

The subscription adds:—

"To the scribe of my lord the king, Abed-heba, thy servant, I prostrate myself. Being these plain words to the king: a faithful servant am I."

To shortly summarise the information contained in these letters of Abed-heba, supplementing it by what may be derived from other of the Tel Amarna dispatches from persons mentioned by Abed-heba, it may be seen that the district of Jerusalem was threatened by an adversary who at the final attack was advancing from the western coast districts.

By comparison of a number of letters, it appears the foe descended the coast from north to south, finally capturing Gezer and Askalon; then marching inland they took Lachish, and turning northward, Gath and Zorah. Then turning south, Keilah and Gimti Carmel were captured, and in the end apparently Jerusalem itself. Some of the cities, such as Askelon and Lachish, according to Abed-heba, went over to the enemy through the treachery of Elimelech and Laba. Abed-heba begs for troops and envoys; both were sent, but the Commissioners appear to have found his loyalty doubtful, and retain the troops in their own hands, and do not employ them in defending the neighbouring cities of the Jerusalem satrapy from Abed-heba's foes. Many of his local governors now desert; others, such Zimrida at Lachish and Yapti Addi at Zilu (or Zelah),* were slain. The position becomes critical, and Abed-heba makes a last appeal for the help he had so often craved, with what result we know not.

The way in which Gezer, Askelon, Lachish, and Ajalon are

---

* Joshua xviii, 28; 1 Sam. xxv, 2–5.

mentioned in one of the letters, seems to show that they formed part of probably the boundary cities of the priest-king of Jerusalem.

We have two letters from the Ajalon governor, and they are interesting, because she was a lady. When she writes the rebellion had burst forth, and the Habiri were close by; Zarkhu or Zorah has fallen, doubtless the Zorah of Joshua xv, 23, and Zorah of Judges xiii, 25. She also speaks of a city of Zabuba or Zebub, and M. Halévy, the celebrated Jewish scholar, suggests from this that the deity Baal Zebub of 2 Kings i, 2 is not lord of flies, but the Baal of Zebub, the city.*

The writer from Gezer is named Yapakhi, and he of Askelon Pidya (or Widya). Yapakhi,† is perhaps known from other tablets sent to Egypt, stating his fleet attacked the ships of Byblos.‡ The "ḥazânu" of Lachish, Zimrida, however, is to us by far the most important of all. He, too, is known from his letters, one of which is dated from Sidon, when he was the Egyptian official there, and one from Lachish. It is of him from the latter city that we have received the most wonderful contemporaneous evidence of the genuineness of these Tel Amarna dispatches.

In 1892 the Palestine Exploration Fund were excavating at Lachish, the Amorite city whence Zimrida wrote his dispatch, and where he must have dictated and received many others. Among various small relics their explorer, Dr. Bliss, found an Egyptian ornament bearing the name of Queen Tii, wife of Amenophis II, father of the king to whom Zimrida's dispatch, now at Berlin, was sent, and far more fortunate than this, a clay tablet turned up similar to these from Tel Amarna, having the same peculiar idioms as did those of that collection emanating from Southern Palestine, and the same forms of cuneiform letters, and bearing twice upon it the name of Zimrida himself. In the words of Professor Sayce, "Nothing more extraordinary has ever happened in the annals of archæology. The discovery had hardly been made that a governor of Lachish wrote letters in the Babylonian language and syllabary to his suzerain, the Pharaoh of Egypt, when on the site of Lachish, only just then identified, is found a letter similar to those of Zimrida, in which his name occurs. For more than 4,000 years the broken halves of a correspondence carried on before the

The characters may be read Zabuma, so Halévy's reading is not certain.
† See "The Tel-el-Amarna Tablets in the British Museum," pp. 75 and 76.
‡ *Ibid.*, p. 47.

Exodus had been lying under the soil, one half on the bank of the Nile, the other half in Canaan, and the recovery of the one from its long continued oblivion was followed almost immediately by the recovery of the other."

Space will not permit of further description of any among the series of tablets or even of any single tablet, but enough information about them has probably been given to encourage an intense desire to know more of them.   As an instance of some of the interesting results to be apprehended from a study of them, it may be mentioned that a perusal of the various translations of them presents the following allusions to Biblical sites in addition to those which have transpired in the reading of Abed-heba's letters :—

Akko,* the city of Judges i, 3 ; Akzabu, see Joshua xix, 29, and Micah i, 14; (Achzib) Arka, Genesis x, 7 ; Arvad, Genesis x, 18 ; Ashtarti or Ashteroth of Genesis xiv, 5 ; Burza or Bene-berek of Joshua xix, 45 ; Gebal of Psalms lxxxiii, 7 ; Hosah, see Joshua xix, 29 ; Hobah, see Genesis xiv, 5 ; Hazor (or Khazor), see Joshua xi, 1 ; Kadesh, see Joshua xv, 33 ; Magdalim of Genesis xxxvi, 43 (?) and Migdol, Exodus xiv, 2, and Numbers xxxiii, 7 ; Megiddo, Judges i, 27; Rabbah, perhaps the city of Joshua xv, 60 ; Sunama, the Shunem of Joshua xix, 18, and Samhuna, the Shimron or Sumoon of Joshua xix, 15.   The writer from this place was son of a person named Balimi or Balaam.   Zelah, Joshua xviii, 28, and 2 Samuel xxi, 14, and Zemer or Simyra, see Genesis x, 18 ; and Urma, the Ummah of Joshua xix, 30.

Two other matters are worthy of mention as having been apparently satisfactorily decided by these tablets: one is the evident existence in pre-Mosaic Palestine of a deity named Melech.   We have in Scripture Akhimelech, "my brother is Melech," and Abimelek, "my father is Melech," and it has been suggested the Melek there is merely a title of Jehovah, but in the tablets we have A-bi-mil-ki (or Abimelech) and Mil-ki-ilu or Melek is god ; perhaps the similarity of Melech to Moloch, Dr. Barton has suggested, caused it to be dropped by the Jews, as they dispensed with compounds of Baal in later names.

The second deity upon which light is thrown is Ashera, the

---

* The governor of Akko had a Babylonian's feet amputated : he was a Canaanite, and cruel like Adoni-Bezek, who cut off the thumbs and great toes of 70 kings, Judges i, 5 (see Prof. C. P. Tiele, "Western Asia according to the most recent Discoveries," p. 29).

goddess of 1 Kings xv, 13, and perhaps of Judges iii, 7. In the Berlin series of tablets a name of one Arad-a-si-irta, or Ebedashera is often mentioned. That the name is theophorous we know because twice the D. P. ilu is found, and not long ago a Phœnician inscription of Cyprus was found dedicated "to my lady the mother Ashera." This interesting point has been cleared up by Dr. Barton, to whose essays reference should be made.*

It in very remarkable also that the word " ilani " is used in plural for the singular god as the Israelites used Elohim, so that the use of the plural by the latter cannot now be used as an argument, for their having formerly had many deities, and Dr. Tiele has pointed out how the Syrian governors in speaking of Amen to Amenophis III do not acknowledge him as a deity except in an indirect manner, always qualifying him as the "god creator of my brother's life" ("ilu šabŭ aḫia ").

NOTE.

In the Berlin tablets recently published by Dr. Winckler the name U-ru-sa-lim occurs seven times, and once Winckler has supplied it conjecturally.

In B[103], line 25, the phrase is *māt maḫāz Urusalim*, "the land (or district) of the town (or stronghold) of Jerusalem;" in line 46 it is *māt al Urusalim*, "the land of the city of Jerusalem;" in line 61 simply *māt Urusalim*, "the district of Jerusalem;" and in line 63 it is *mālāti al Urusalim*, "the lands (or territories) of the city of Jerusalem." This seems to be the only place where the scribe has written the plural (𒌝 𒌈 or 𒌈 𒈨𒌍) instead of the usual 𒌈 sing.

In B[106] we have, according to Winckler, in line 14 sqq., *alu māt Urusalim šu-mu-ša* (?) (*alu*) *Bit-Nin-ib al šarri*, "a city of the district of Jerusalem, whose name is Bit-Ninib, "a city of the kings." Here *Bit-Ninib* appears to be some place within the territory of Jerusalem.

In B[199] we have *al* or *alu* (𒌷) Urusalim, the town of Jerusalem, twice; viz., in line 1 and line 16, with *ki*, "place," appended on the latter occasion.

* See article " On Native Israelitish Deities," in *Papers of the Oriental Club of Philadelphia*, and " Ashtoreth and her influence in the Old Testament," in *Journal of Biblical Literature*," 1891.

TWO UNKNOWN HEBREW VERSIONS OF THE TOBIT LEGEND.

[*Concluded.*]

By Dr. M. Gaster.

26 (11) And it came to pass in the middle of the night, about the cockcrowing, that Reuel cried to his servants : " Arise and dig quickly a grave for Tobiyah, (12) for I know that mischief has befallen him as it happened to the other seven men who made marriage with us." **27** (13) And when they had finished digging the grave, Reuel returned to the house, and said to his wife : (14) Send the maid and let her see and ascertain whether the young man be dead or alive.* **28** (15) And the maid went, and behold, both were alive, lying in their bed and sleeping. (16) And she returned and brought the good tidings, and their heart rejoiced. **29** (17) And they blessed the Lord, and said : Blessed art thou, O Lord God of Israel, for thou hast done well unto us, and thou hast wrought wonders (18), and thou hast rebuked the Satan, so that he should not be able to harm us nor our children for ever, (19) and all the nations shall know that thy name is called upon us.† (20) And Reuel commanded them to fill up the pit from one end to another. **30** (21, 22) And he commanded, and they prepared a feast (slaughtered animals), and he called all his neighbours, and they ate and drank and made a

---

* J. adds, that I may bury him before it be day.

† J. (18 and 19) reads : For thou hast shown thy mercy to us, and hast shut out from us the enemy that persecuted us. (19) And thou hast taken pity upon two only children. Make them, O Lord, bless thee more fully : and to offer up to thee a sacrifice of thy praise, and of their health, that all nations may know that thou alone art God in all the earth.

great banquet.* **31** (23) And Reuel begged of Tobiyah to abide with him two weeks. **32** (24) And he gave him one half of his riches and substance, and treasures and his sheep, and his cattle and his oxen, and his household, and of whatever he possessed he would give (one half of) it to him in his lifetime, and after his death he would take it all.

IX. **1** (1, 2) And Tobiyah said to the angel : I beseech thee, my lord, let not thine anger burn against me, I have taken upon me to speak but this once, and do thou show more kindness in the latter end than at the beginning. **2** (3) And go for me to Gabael into the town (city) of . . . . and take these tokens into thy hands, and receive the silver from him, and invite him to come to the joy and to rejoice with us, (5 ?) as I cannot depart from here before the end of the two weeks, the days of the feast.† **3** (4) And thou knowest that my father will not rest nor be still until I return in peace. **4** (6) So the angel listened to him, and he took four of Reuel's servants and two camels with him, and came to Rage, and he gave the token to Gabael and took the silver from him. **5** (7) And he told what had happened to Tobiyah, the son of Tobi, and that he had asked him to come and rejoice with the invited on the day of his marriage, the day of the rejoicing of his heart. **6** [And Gabael arose and saddled his camel and went with him.] **7** (8) And when he had come into Reuel's house, he found him and Tobiyah with him, sitting at the table, and he fell upon his neck and kissed him and he wept. **8** (9) And he blessed him and said : The Lord bless thee and keep thee, for thou art the son of a good man, Godfearing and avoiding evil. **9** (10, 11) May thy house be as the house of Perez, who begat Hezron.‡ (12) And all the people answered : Amen ! and they ate and drank and made merry.

X. **1** (1-3) But Tobi was heavy and wretched, and it grieved him at his heart, and he said : my son, my son, why dost thou tarry, why

---

* J. (21 and 22) reads : And he spoke to his wife to make ready a feast and prepare all kinds of provisions that are necessary for such as go on a journey. (22) He caused also two fat kine and four wethers to be killed, and a banquet to be prepared for all his neighbours and all his fiends.

† J. reads (5) : And indeed thou seest how Raguel had adjured me, whose adjuring I cannot despise.

‡ J. reads : (10) And may a blessing come upon thy wife and upon your parents ; (11) and may you see your children and your children's children unto the third and fourth generation, and may your seed be blessed by the God of Israel who reigneth for ever.

are thy steps so long in coming?* Such was his custom all the days. 2 (4) And Hanna wept and did not eat, for her sighs were many and her heart was faint. 3 And she said to her husband : thou are verily guilty of this great tribulation which thou hast brought upon us, 4† for thou hast sent away our son, the joy of our heart, the nourisher of our old age, under whose shadow we would live among the nations. 5 (6) And Tobi answered her : fear not, my sister, for [I trust in the lovingkindness of my God, that he will bring him back] in peace, as the man who went with him is very trusty [and he is an angel from the Lord of hosts]. 6 (7)‡ Go outside, my sister, and see, perhaps it might be the will of God, through his mercy, that thou bring me tidings and rejoice my fainting heart. Such was his custom all the time his son was abroad.§ 7 (9) Tobiyah was thinking in his own heart, and he said to Reuel, his father-in-law : why dost thou make me tarry, and God has made my way prosperous, whilst the sleep has fled from my father and my mother, they do not rest nor are they still [until I return home in peace?]‖ 8 [But Reuel said to his son-in-law : be content, I pray thee, and tarry with me ; fulfil these two weeks, and I will send thee away with mirth and with song. 9 But Tobi answered : no, my lord, listen to me, and send me away, so that I go to my country, and my wife with me.] 10 (10) When Reuel saw that he could not prevail upon him, he sent him away, and his wife with him, with silver and gold, and precious things, and cattle, and great household, and with great mirth. 11 (11)¶ And

---

* X. J. (1–3) reads : But as Tobias made longer stay upon occasion of the marriage, Tobias his father was solicitous, saying, Why thinkest thou doth my son tarry, or why is he detained there ? (2) Is Gabelus dead, thinkest thou, and no man will pay him the money ? (3) And he began to be exceeding sad both he and Anna his wife with him : and they began both to weep together, because their son did not return to them on the day appointed.

† J. (5) (here missing) : We having all things together in thee alone, ought not to have let thee go from us.

‡ J. (7) reads : But she could by no means be comforted, but daily running out looking round about, and went into all the ways by which there seemed any hope he might return, that she might if possible see him coming afar off.

§ J. (8) (here missing) reads : But Raguel said to his son-in-law, stay here, and I will send a messenger to Tobias thy father, that thou art in health.

‖ J. (9) : And Tobias said to him, I know that my father and mother now count the days, and their spirit is grievously afflicted within them."

¶ J. (11) : "saying, the holy angel of the Lord be with you in your journey, and bring you through safe, and that you may find all things well about your parents, and my eyes may see your children before I die."

Reuel blessed his daughter, and said: may the Lord God of Israel give unto thee seed of men, and prosper thy way!*

XI. **1** And they sent him away, and his wife [and all his relations and friends and acquaintances went with him one day's journey, and they gave him gifts, everyone a ring of gold, a Qesitah and a piece of silver; (1) and they went on their way to the city of Nineveh.] **2** (2) And when they came near the city, the angel of the Lord said to Tobiyah: thou knowest that it is a long time since we have separated ourselves from your father. **3** (3) Set thy steps on thy walk and go quickly to thy father, and I will lead on softly according to the pace of the flock. **4** (4) And Tobiyah said: the word is good which thou hast spoken. And he hastened and saddled his ass, and he arose and went.† **5** (7) And the angel charged Tobiyah: as soon as thou shalt come into the house, forthwith give thanks to God and bless him, and go to thy father and kiss him. **6** (8) And the gall of the fish which thou hast put up to keep, take with thee and anoint the eyes of thy father, and he will see, and his heart will rejoice. **7** Then Tobiyah went away from him and came into the town; (5)‡ when he came near his mother perceived him (6)§ and she ran and told it to her husband.‖ **8** (10) And Tobi rejciced exceedingly, and he arose from his bed and wanted to run to meet his son, and he dashed his foot against a stone [and he fell down, for his eyes were blind]. **9** And Tobiyah hastened (11) [and descended from the ass and lifted his father up from the ground] and kissed him, and they wept (12) and worshipped God; they praised him and blessed him with a loud voice. **10** (13) And Tobiyah took the gall of the fish and annointed the eyes of his father with it (14, 15) and his eyes were opened; and the white substance which

---

* J. adds (12-13): And the parents taking their daughter kissed her and let her go. (13) Admonishing her to honour her father and mother-in-law, to love her husband, to take care of the family, to govern the house, and to behave herself irreprehensibly.

† J. reads (4): And as their going pleased him, Raphael said to Tobias, Take with thee of the gall of the fish, for it will be necessary. So Tobias took some of that gall and departed.

‡ J. (5): But Anna sat beside the way daily, on the top of a hill, from whence she might see afar off.

§ J. (6) And while she watched his coming from that place, she saw him afar off, and presently perceived it was her son coming.

‖ J. (9) omitted: Then the dog which had been with them in the way, ran before, and coming as if he had brought the news, showed his joy by his fawning and wagging his tail.

covered the eyes fell off, and he rejoiced exceedingly.* **11** (16) When Hannah saw that her husband was seeing, she worshipped God. **12** (17) And she said : blessed be the Lord God of Israel, who has comforted us and has magnified his mercy.† **13** (18) And it came to pass after the completion of seven days that Sarah arrived with all the cattle and the young and the camels and beasts which her father Reuel had given her. **14** (19) And Tobiyah told his father all that had happened to him, and what the angel had done for him, and how God had prospered him.‡

XII. **1** (1) And Tobi said to his son : in what manner shall we honour this man ? (2, 3) for all that thou hast, has come to thee through him. He has moreover killed the demon, and has done many wondrous things for thee ? **2** (4) And now, my son, call him, that he may take one half of the riches which thou hast brought. **3** (5) And he listened to his father, and called the angel. And he besought him and said : I pray thee, my Lord, man of God, behold the Lord has blessed me for thy sake : choose thee from all that I possess, and take one half thereof. (6) And he answered : I will not take anything ; **4** but do ye serve God with fear, and worship him and praise his holy name, for he renders to every man according to his work. **5** And blessed be now the Lord who has rendered thee thy reward, for thou hast acted towards the dead in piety and in truth. **6** And the strength of Israel will not lie or utter falsehood, for he is truthful. **7** (9) And righteousness (alms) delivers from death.§ .**8** (13) And God has tried thee and has brought upon thee tribulations,

---

* J. (14 and 15) : (14) And he stayed about half an hour ; and a white skin began to come out of his eyes, like the skin of an egg (15) and Tobias took hold of it and drew it from his eyes, and immediately he recovered his sight.

† J. (17) : And Tobias said, I bless thee, O Lord God of Israel, because thou hast chastised me, and thou hast saved me : and behold I see Tobias my son.

‡ J. (20 and 21) omitted in our text. (20) And Achior and Nabath the kinsmen of Tobias came rejoicing for Tobias, and congratulating with him for all the good things that God had done for him. (21) And for seven days they feasted and rejoiced all with great joy.

§ J. (6–13) corresponding to end of **3** and **4-7** differs greatly ; J. (7–8) and (10–12) are missing here. (7) For it is good to hide the secret of a king : but honourable to reveal and confess the works of God. (8) Prayer is good with fasting and alms, more than to lay up treasures of gold. (10) But they that commit sin and iniquity, are enemies to their own soul. (11) I discover then the truth unto you and I will not hide the secret from you. (12) When thou didst pray with tears, and didst bury the dead, and didst leave thy dinner, and hide the dead by day in thy house, and bury them by night, I offered thy prayer to the Lord.

and has purified thee as silver and has heard thy prayer. **9** (15) And he has sent me, the angel Raphael, one of the seven princes who minister first in the presence of the King, the Lord of hosts. **10** (14) And he commanded me to heal thee and to save thee and to conduct thy son and to bring him back; for God had listened to thy prayer and to thy reproach, and to the prayer and reproach of Sarah. **11** (16) And when they had heard his words, they were amazed one at another, and they fell down upon their faces. **12** (17) And he said to them, fear not,* (18) for I came by the word of God, and by his command have I done all these things [and not by any will of mine], (19) and behold, at the sight of your eyes I appeared to eat and drink,† and yet did I neither eat bread nor drink water.‡ **13** (21, 22) So they arose and blessed God, and the angel had disappeared, and they did not know it (see it), for they feared that they would die, as their eyes had seen an angel of the Lord of hosts.

XIII. **1** (1) And they arose and blessed God the Lord their God. And Tobi said: blessed art thou, O Lord, and great are thy works, and thou shalt reign for ever and ever. **2** (2) For [thine is the kingdom], thou leadest down to Sheol and bringest up again, he wounds and he heals, and there is none who could deliver out of his hand. **3** (3)§ O give thanks unto the Lord, for he is good : for his mercy endureth for ever. **4** Who can utter the mighty acts of the Lord, or show forth all his praise? unto thee praise shall be given. **5** Bless the Lord, O my soul, O Lord my God, thou art very great ; thou art clothed with honour and majesty. **6** Blessed be the Lord God of Israel from everlasting even to everlasting. And all the people say : Amen ! **7** And it came to pass that before they had finished their repast Tobiyah was told : lo, thy wife has come with the cattle and the flock. And they arose and went to meet them with timbrels and dances, and they brought them into the house with mirth and songs. **8** And they fulfilled the days of the feast, and they blessed God with a loud voice : Oh that men would praise the Lord for his loving kindness, and for all the good deeds and the wondrous things which God has wrought for us. **9** And

* J. adds, Peace be to you.

† J. reads : but I use an invisible meat and drink, which cannot be seen by men.

‡ J. (20) omitted here : It is time therefore that I return to him that sent me : but bless ye God, and publish all his wonderful works.

§ (3) till end of chapter totally different from J.

Tobi said : blessed art thou, oh Lord God of Israel, because thou hast not denied us thy love and thy truth, thou who art the keeper of the covenant, and of the love for those who love thee and keep thy covenant.   10 And Tobi said to his son and to his wife Sarah, O give thanks unto the Lord, call upon his name ; make known his doing among the peoples, because he has dealt wondrously with us, and has changed our mourning into mirth, and our sorrow into dance and a day of feasting.   And all the people answered : Amen ! and Tobi said to his son Tobiyah : blessed be our Lord, of whose gifts we have eaten, and through whose goodness we live.   And all the people answered : blessed be our Lord, of whose gifts we have eaten, and through whose goodness we live.   12 And all the people arose and blessed Tobi and his wife, and Tobiyah his son, and his daughter-in-law, and they said to Tobiyah : may thy house be like unto the house of Perez.   And they answered : Amen !   And they went, everyone of them, to their tents, joyful and glad of heart.

XIV. 1 (1) And Tobi lived after he had recovered his sight forty-nine years, and the days of his life were one hundred and seventy years.   2 (2) And he died and was gathered unto his people in a good old age in the city of Nineveh.*   3 (4) And the rest of his works were in the love of God, in gladness of heart and abundance in everything, and in the fear of God and clinging to him.   4 (5) And it was before his death, and he spake to his son, saying : come near to me, my son, and do not stand aside, for I will counsel thee before God, ere I (die). . . . .

BE STRONG.

TOBIT LEGEND II (H.G).

(FOR THE SECOND DAY OF SHEBUOTH).

Thou shalt surely tithe all the increase of thy seed, that which cometh forth of the field year by year.   And thou shalt eat before the Lord thy God, in the place which he shall choose to cause his name to dwell there, the tithe of thy corn, of thy wine, and of

---

* J. (3) omitted here : For he was six and fifty years old when he lost the sight of his eyes, and sixty when he recovered it again.

thine oil, and the firstlings of thy herd and of thy flock; that thou mayest learn to fear the Lord thy God always. Our sages say: "Thou shalt surely tithe" (Asser te 'asser), which means: tithe in order that thou become rich, and tithe surely, in order that thou have no wants. This is an indication to those that travel on the high seas to give the tenth to those that are engaged in the study of the law. If thou tithest then it is thy corn, but if not, it is my corn, as it is said (Hosea ii, 11), "therefore will I take back my corn in its due time." If thou art worthy, it is thy wine, but if not, it is mine. Rabbi Levi said: (Prov. xxviii, 22) "He that hath an evil eye hasteth after riches, and knoweth not that want shall come upon him," this verse applies to the man who does not bring out his tithes in a proper manner. For R. Levi said: It happened once (a history is told) of a man who brought out his tithes in a proper manner (etc.), therefore Moses warned the Israelites to tithe surely.

1. The history is told of a man whose name was Tobi, of the tribe of Napthali, who all his days walked in the right path, and performed many good deeds for his brethren who were with him in the captivity in Nineveh: and he was left an orphan by his father, and he was brought up by Deborah his father's mother, and she led him in the right path. And when he became a man he took a wife of his own kindred and family, whose name was Hannah, and she bare him a son, and he called his name Tobiyah. And when he was in the captivity, in the city of Nineveh, all his brethren and kindred polluted themselves, and did eat the bread of the sons of the Gentiles. But he did not eat, for he feared God with all his heart. And therefore God gave him grace and favour in the eyes of Shalmanesser, the king, and he appointed him master over all that he had, to the day of his death. And at that time he committed to the hand of Gabael his kinsman ten talents of gold. And after the death of the king Shalmanesser, his son Sennacherib reigned in his stead. And in the days of Sennacherib Tobi did many charitable deeds for the poor, and he fed the hungry and the orphans; and when he saw one of the Jews slain, cast out in the street, he buried him. Now when Sennacherib returned in haste from Judah, he went to Nineveh in fierce wrath against the ten tribes, and killed many of them, and their corpses were cast out in the streets, and none buried them. When Tobi saw that, his wrath was kindled, and he arose in the night and buried them; and thus he did many times. Once Sennacherib asked for the bodies of the slain,

but found them not. And the men of Nineveh said to the king: Tobi buries them. And the king commanded that he be put to death. When Tobi heard it, he fled. And the king commanded that they should pillage his house, and he hid himself from him five and forty days, until Adramelech and Sharezer his sons killed Sennacherib with the sword, and Esarhaddon his son reigned in his stead. And the king appointed Aqiqar over all his affairs. And Aqiqar spake good words for Tobi, and he brought him back to Nineveh.

II. When the feast of Weeks came, his wife prepared a plentiful meal, and as he sat at the table, he said to his son Tobiyah: go, and bring to me some of our poor brethren, such as fear God, to eat with us. Then Tobiyah went and found a man slain, cast out in the street, and he told his father. What did his father do? he rose from the table and he went with him, and he took him from the street of the city, and brought him into a house until the going down of the sun, that he might be able to bury him. And he turned to his house and ate his bread in mourning And he said : Woe that on us is fulfilled, "and I will turn your feasts and your songs into mourning." And he wept very sore. And when the sun went down he went and buried him. And he returned to his house, and he lay upon his bed, and his face was uncovered, and dust fell from the wall into his eyes. And in the morning he went to the physician to cure his eyes, but it did not avail him, until he became blind of both eyes, which lasted for four years. And Aqiqar his friend nourished him. After many days his wife did work for women, and they gave her a kid for her wages. And Tobi heard the kid bleating in the house, and he asked her : from whence hast thou this kid? hast thou stolen it perhaps? And his wife Hannah said: they have given it to me as the wages of the work of mine hands ; I have not stolen it ! But Tobi did not believe her, and they quarrelled concerning the kid. Hannah said to Tobi : Where are thy goodnesses and thy merits? hence thy worthlessness is manifest to all !

III. When Tobi heard this he was much grieved, and he wept and prayed to the Holy One, blessed be he, in the anguish of his soul, and he said : Lord of the universe ! take my soul from me, for it is better for me to die than to live, so that I shall no more hear shame. And the same day, Sarah, the daughter of Reuel, who lived in Agbatanis, in the land of Media, heard a great reproach because she had been given to seven men as wife, and not one of them came in unto her according to the way of all the earth. And

thou hast done. And he told him. And he said : Blessed be the Lord who hath sent his angel with my son, and hath prospered his way, and hath cured two poor people like ourselves. In after days God blessed Tobiyah also, because he fulfilled the command of his father, and gave tithes of everything that he possessed.

Hence we learn how great is the power of alms and tithes, and how, because Tobi gave alms and separated his tithes as is meet, the Holy One, blessed be he, rewarded him ! And because the Patriarchs of the world knew the power of alms and tithes they were careful in observing them. Therefore did Moses warn the Israelites, saying to them : Thou shalt surely tithe all the increase of thy seed.

MORE FRAGMENTS OF THE PALESTINIAN SYRIAC· VERSION OF THE HOLY SCRIPTURES.

[Concluded.]

BY THE REV. G. MARGOLIOUTH.

2 *Kings* ii, 19–22.

V. 19. And the men of the city said to Elisha, Behold the habitation of the city is good, as our Lord seeth, but the water is bad, and the land is barren.

V. 20. And Elisha said, Bring me one new pot, and throw salt into it, and they brought [it] to him.

V. 21. And Elisha went out unto the springs of the water, and he threw salt therein and said, Thus saith the Lord, I have healed the waters, and there shall no more be thence that which is dead or is bereft.*

V. 22. And these waters were healed unto this day, according to the word of Elisha which he spake.

Amos ix, 5–14a.

V. 5. Thus saith the Lord God, the all apprehending One; he who toucheth the whole earth, and shaketh it,† and all those that inhabit it shall mourn; and it shall rise up like the river of Egypt which‡ buildeth its rising in heaven.

V. 6. And establisheth its§ promises on the earth; he who calleth the waters of the sea, and poureth them out upon the face of the earth, the Lord God, the all apprehending One, is his name.

* Or, barren.
† Or, " and it shaketh." See the note on p. 47.
‡ Or, " He who buildeth . . ." See the note on p. 48.
§ Or, " his."

V. 7. Are ye not like children of the Ethiopians, O ye children of Israel? saith the Lord. Israel have I brought up from the land of Egypt, and the Philistines from Cappadocia,* and the Syrians from the depth.

V. 8. Behold, the eyes of the Lord God are against the kingdom of the sinners, and I will remove it from the face of the earth; only so as not to destroy completely will I remove† the house of Jacob, saith the Lord.

V. 9. For behold, I command, and I shall winnow among all nations the house of Israel, as one winnoweth straw with a winnowing fork;‡ there shall not [anything] fall upon the earth in the pounding§ thereof.

V. 10. By the sword, then, shall die the sinners [of my people], who say,‖ These evils will not approach us, nor come upon us.

V. 11. And on that day will I raise up the tabernacle of David which had fallen down, and I will build up its ruin, and raise up its destruction, and I will build it up as in the days of old.

V. 12. In order that the rest of men and all the nations upon whom my name is called may seek [it]¶ saith the Lord who doeth these things.

V. 13. Behold, the days come, saith the Lord, and the threshing shall overtake the vintage, and the vintage the seed [-time], and the grapes shall mix with the seed, and the mountains shall drop sweetness, and all the hills shall be planted.

V. 14a. And I will bring again the captivity of my congregation Israel.

Translation.

Acts xvi, 16–34.

V. 16. In those same days, as the Apostles were going to the House of prayer, there met them a certain young woman who had

---

* It may also be rendered "from the Cappadocians;" but "from Cappadocia" is required by the Hebrew, LXX, and Peshitta. See note on p. 48.

† See note on p. 49.   ‡ See note on p. 57.

§ See note on p. 49.   ‖ Or, "those who say."

¶ I.e., the tabernacle spoken of in v. 11, or [him], i.e., "the Lord," with the Alexandrine text of the LXX.

a spirit of divination,* and she was bringing her masters much gain by the divination which she was divining.

V. 17. And she was following Paul and us, and she was thus crying and saying, These men are the servants of the Most High God, and they announce to you the way of life.

V. 18. And thus was she doing many days, and Paul became angry, and said to that spirit, I command thee in the name of Jesus Christ that thou go out of her ; and in that same hour did the spirit depart.

V. 19. And when her masters saw that the hope of their gain had gone out from her, they seized Paul and Silas, and they dragged them and brought them to the market place.

V. 20. And they brought them to the magistrates and to the chief men of the city, and they said, that these men trouble our city, because they are Jews.

V. 21. And they teach customs which are not lawful for us to receive, or to observe, because we are Romans.

V. 22. And a great assembly was assembled against them ; then did the magistrates tear their clothes, and commanded that they should scourge them.

V. 23. And when they had scourged them much, they cast them into prison, and commanded the prison-keeper that he should keep them carefully.

V. 24. He, therefore, having received such a command, brought [them in and] bound them in the inner prison house,† and made their feet fast in the stocks.

V. 25. And in the middle of the night, Paul and Silas were praying and praising God, and the prisoners heard them.

V. 26. And suddenly there was a great earthquake, and the foundations of the prison were shaken, and all the doors were suddenly opened, and the bands of all of them were loosed.

V. 27. And when the prison-keeper awoke, and saw that the doors of the prison were open, he took a sword, and wanted to kill himself, because he thought that the prisoners had fled.

V. 28. And Paul called unto him with a loud voice, and said unto him. Do thyself no harm, because we are all here.

V. 29. And he lighted himself a lamp, and sprang and came in trembling, and fell at the feet of Paul and Silas.

* Literally : of a diviner.
† Literally : in the inner house of the prison house.

παραδεισῳ), as this would in any case be the natural Syriac rendering which is also adopted in Pesh.

ﺍ‏ﻣﻜﻮ‏‏ evidently represents τοῦ εἰδέναι γνωστόν of the LXX. In v. 17, however, where Pal. Syr. has the same rendering, the LXX. have only τοῦ γινώσκειν.

V. 10. In ﺍ‏ﺣﻤﻮ‏ ﻭ‏‏ the "*waw* conjunctionis" was unnecessary, as ﻭ‏‏ follows. This pleonasmus appears to show that the force of the Greek particle δέ was not understood by the translator (or the copyist ?).

The definite tense ﺍ‏ﻣﻜﻮ‏‏ is here used instead of the infinitive form of M., LXX., and Pesh.

ﻭ‏ﺍﻣﻮ‏‏ after ﻣﻜﻮ‏‏ agrees with M., Pesh., and the "alia exempl." mentioned in *Field's Originis Hexapla*.

V. 11. ﻭ‏ﺍﻟﻮ‏‏ = LXX. Εὐειλάτ (Εὐιλάτ), which is the Greek transcription of חוילה; the so-called Targum Jonathan b. Uzziel has ארע הינדיקי.

V. 12. ﻭ‏ﻣﻮﺣﻮ‏‏ (so also Pesh.) is in closer agreement with Lucian's καὶ τὸ χρυσίον . . . than with τὸ ἐκ χρυσίον . . .

ﻭ‏ﻣﻜﻮ‏‏ = LXX. ἄνθραξ. ﻭ‏ﺣﻤﻮ‏‏ ﻣﻜﻮ‏‏ = LXX. ὁ λίθος ὁ πράσινος.

Mr. Ball suggests that the Greek translator connected שֹׁהַם with שׁוּם, leek, and, therefore, rendered ὁ λίθος ὁ πράσινος, "green like the leek." *ﻭ‏ﺣﻤﻮ‏‏ ﻣﻜﻮ‏‏ is, indeed, literally אבן השום, the stone of leek.

V. 14. ﻣﻜﻮﻣﻮ‏‏ agrees with LXX. κατέναντι, Pesh. ﻣﻜﻮﻣﻮ‏‏. Onkelos and Jonathan have למדינחא and למידנח respectively.

ﻣﻜﻮ‏‏, the Syrians, represents the LXX. Ἀσσυρίων.

V. 15. ﻭ‏ﻣﻜﻮ‏‏ = LXX. ὃν ἔπλασεν; it is found neither in M. nor in Pesh. ﻭ‏ﻣﻜﻮ‏‏ = M. בגן עדן, Pesh. ﻭ‏ﻣﻜﻮ‏‏. LXX. only ἐν τῷ παραδείσῳ. L. adds τῆς τρυφῆς, a reading adopted in Field's, Or. H. as the accepted reading of the LXX.

Note the paraphrastic rendering ﻣﻜﻮ‏‏ . . . ﻣﻜﻮ‏‏, both M. and LXX. using the infinitive. Pesh. ﻣﻜﻮ‏‏.

V. 16. Here only ﻣﻜﻮ‏‏ without ﻣﻜﻮ‏‏.

ﻣﻜﻮ‏‏ ﻣﻜﻮ‏‏ = Pesh. ﻣﻜﻮ‏‏ ﻣﻜﻮ‏‏; comp. LXX. βρώσει φαγῇ.

* ﻣﻜﻮ‏‏ = Arab. كَرَاث, Jew. Ar. כרייא.

V. 17. For ܕܡܢ ܐܝܠܢܬܐ see the note on v. 9.

ܕܐܢܬ ܬܐܟܘܠ (singular) agrees with E. which has φαγη (so also M. and Pesh.), against A. which has φαγησθε (L. φαγητε), and so also is the preceding clause.

ܠܐ ܬܐܟܘܠ (sing.) against LXX. φαγεσθε.

Note also the emphasized pronoun ܕܐܢܬ ܬܐܟܘܠ, where Pesh. only has ܕܬܐܟܘܠ.

V. 18. ܕܗܐ (that behold), is a free addition, M., LXX, and Pesh. having no introductory particle.

ܐܠܐ (but) is also a free addition. ܢܥܒܕ = LXX. ποιησωμεν; Pesh. has the sing. (ܐܥܒܕ), like M.

ܟܐܬܘܬܗ, Pesh. ܐܟܘܬܗ = LXX. κατ' αὐτον.

V. 19. ܡܪܝܐ ܐܠܗܐ agrees with M. and Pesh., LXX. only ὁ θεος.

For ܥܘܕ (= LXX. ἐτι) see note on v. 9.

ܠܘܬ ܐܕܡ (without ܒܪܢܫܐ), the LXX. also rendering here προς τον 'Αδαμ; so also ܐܕܡ, LXX. 'Αδὰμ lower down in the verse.

ܠܗܘܢ (Pesh. ܐܢܘܢ) agrees with LXX. αὐτα, the Hebrew text having no object after ויבא.

ܠܗܘܢ, in both cases for the Hebrew sing. לוֹ, agrees with Pesh., the LXX. using the plural αὐτα for the first, and the singular αὐτο for the second.

---

2 *Kings* ii, 19–22.*

V. 19. The Hebrew נא remains unrepresented, as is also the case with the LXX. (in Lucian's recension, however, 'Ιδου δη) and Pesh.

ܠܡܘܬܒܘܬܐ answers more closely to the LXX. κατοικησις than Pesh. ܡܘܬܒܐ (. . . ܕ ܡܘܬܒܗ).

Lucian's ταυτης after πολεως is not represented in this version.

ܕܡܪܢ = Pesh. ܕܡܪܝ. M. has אדֹנִי. LXX. ὁ κυριος (without a possessive pronoun), L. συ κυριε ὁρᾳς, but Syr. Hex. also ܕܡܪܝ.

* These verses are marked in the margin of Brit. Mus. MS. Add. 14,620 as [קר]ינא דבית [דנ]חא בלליא. After v. 22 ש (שלם); see Lagarde's Vet. Test. Fragmenta, (Gottingæ, 1880).

ܬܥܩܪܐ must no doubt be taken in an intransitive sense, "barren," and the same meaning or that of "bereft" will have to be assigned to ܬܥܩܪܢ at the end of v. 21. It would, of course, be possible to translate והארץ מְשַׁכָּלֶת by "and the land causeth barrenness or bereavement [among men]." But the LXX. ἀτεκνουμενη is, probably, the word which the Palestinian translator is rendering. Pesh. ܡܬܟܠܐ may be either active or passive, but ܘܡܬܟܠܢܐ in v. 21 can only be active (passive ܡܬܟ̈ܠܢ). L., on the contrary, has ἀτεκνουντα in this verse, and ἀτεκνουμενη in v. 21. Syr. Hex. ܡܬܟܠܢܝܬܐ = ἀτεκνουντα in this place, and ܡܬܟܠܢܘܬܐ (= sterilitas, or orbitas) in v. 21. For the suggestion that ܡܬܬܟܠܢܝܬܐ (= ἀτεκνουμενη) should be read instead of ܡܬܟܠܢܝܬܐ, see P. Sm. Thes., col. 696.

V. 20. The name Elisha at the beginning of this verse and of v. 21 (omitted by L. in the latter instance) evidently comes from the LXX. Pesh, follows M. in omitting it, but Syr. Hex. also ܐܠܝܫܥ in both places.

The word ܡ̈ܝܐ after ܩܠܬܐ appears to come from Pesh.

ܘܪܡܘ (Pesh. ܘܐܪܡܘ = ἐμβαλετε) agrees with L. Syr. Hex. ܘܣܝܡܘ (=θετε).

ܘܐܝܬܝܘ (Pesh. ܘܐܝܬܝܘ)=και ἠνεγκαν, whereas ܘܢܣܒܘ of Syr. Hex. = και ἐλαβον; *see Field's Or. H., in loco.*

V. 21. Note the ܐܢܐ after ܐܣܝܬ; Pesh. merely ܐܣܝܬ, agreeing exactly with M. and LXX.; Syr. H. ܐܢܐ ܡܐܣܐ.

The "waw" conjunctive in ܘܠܐ ܗܘܐ agrees with L. and Pesh. (ܘܬܗܘܐ ܠܐ).

Note ܕܡܝܬ, "that which is dead;" but perhaps ܕܡܝܬ = Pesh. ܕܡܐܬ, "that which dieth." LXX. θανατος = M. מָוֶת. L. has ἀποθνησκων.

On ܘܡܬܥܩܪܢ = LXX. ἀτεκνουμενη; *see* note on v. 19.

At the end of the verse L. adds δι' αὐτα.

V. 22. ܗܠܝܢ after ܡ̈ܝܐ is taken from Pesh. Syr. Hex. similarly ܡ̈ܝܐ ܗܢܘܢ, LXX. τα ὑδατα agrees with M. המים.

ܕܐܡܪ at the end agrees with M., most recensions of the LXX., and Pesh. L. has ὁ ἐλαλησεν 'Ελισαιε.

Amos ix, 5–14a.

V. 5. ܗܘܝܘ ܡܪܐ is apparently an addition made for Lectionary purposes (comp. Acts xvi, 16). Pesh. begins with ܡܪܐ, but LXX., like M., opens the sentence with καί.

ܡܪܐ ܚܝܠܘܬܐ is evidently, like ܐܠܗܐ ܚܝܠܐ of Syr. Hex., a literal rendering of LXX. παντοκρατωρ; but instead of the double κυριος of the LXX. Pal. Syr. only has ܡܪܐ. Syr. Hex. also ܘܡܪܝܐ only.

ܗܘ ܕܓܫܦ represents the LXX. ὁ ἐφαπτόμενος; similar instances of rendering the definite article ὁ when followed by a participle are found in vv. 6, 10, 11, and 12 (also once more in this verse: ܗܘ ܕܡܣܩܠ); see Nöldeke, op. cit., p. 510. Similarly Syr. Hex. ܗܘ ܕܢܩܦ.

ܠܟܘܠܗ before ܐܪܥܐ is not represented either in M., LXX., or Pesh.

ܠܗ after ܘܡܙܝܥ represents LXX. αὐτην. One should expect ܘܡܙܝܥ, the active form, but we probably have a conflated rendering, ܘܡܙܝܥ representing the sense of ותמוג as translated in Pesh. (ܘܪܝܕ), and the following accusative pronoun ܠܗ being taken over from the LXX.; Syr. Hex. consistently ܘܡܙܝܥ ܠܗ.

ܘܢܬܐܒܠܘܢ (Imperf.) represents the LXX. πενθησουσιν, as it can hardly be supposed that the Palestinian translator deliberately used the imperf. to represent the Hebrew perfect with the *waw* consecutive. Syr. Hex. also ܘܢܬܐܒܠܘܢ.

ܠܗ after ܗܝܟܢܡܣ also appears to represent the accusative (αὐτην) of the LXX., the Hebrew having בה. Syr. Hex. ܒܗ·

ܘܣܩܘܗ ܣܡܪ ܢܗܪܐ ܘܢܚܬ ܐܝܟ ܢܗܪܐ represent the following M. and LXX. on both sides of the [ ] :—

וְעָלְתָה [כִיאֹר כֻּלָּה וְשָׁקְעָה] כִיאֹר מִצְרַיִם ׃

καὶ ἀναβήσεται [ὡς ποταμος συντελεια

αὐτης, καὶ καταβήσεται] ὡς ποταμος Αἰγυπτου.

In this important reading Pal. Syr. agrees with Syr. Hex. as given in Middledorff's " Codex Syriaco-Hexaplaris," but in Ceriani's facsimile (*Monumenta Sacra et Profana*, Vol. VIII) : ܘܣܩܘ ܐܝܟ ܢܗܪܐ ܟܠܗ : ܘܣܩܘ ܐܝܟ ܢܗܪܐ ܕܡܨܪܝܢ, in agreement with the usual recension of the LXX.

It is possible that the adoption of this reading is due to the character of the Service. It was the rising of the Nile, and not the falling, which was the subject of the celebration.

No break is indicated in the MS. after ܕܡܨܪܝܢ, and the clause that follows is, therefore, probably to be attached to v. 5. In this case, the Nile, instead of God, would be here said to build a rising [or aqueduct?] in heaven. It is, however, possible that ܗܕܝܢ ܪܒܐ takes up the same subject (ܡܨܐ ܠܥܠ) as ܗܕܝܢ ܪܡܝܢ nearer the beginning of the verse. If so, v. 5 would end (as in the Hebrew text, LXX., etc.) with the word "Egypt." In Syr. Hex. ܗܘ ܪܡܝܐ begins v. 6.

ܡܣܩܘܬܐ (comp. Syr. Hex. ܠܡܣܩܘܬܐ) is probably to be read as a singular, the LXX. having ἀνάβασιν, though Pesh. (in agreement with M.) ܡܣܩܘܬܗ.

ܘܡܘܠܟܢܗ = LXX. καὶ τὴν ἐπαγγελίαν αὐτοῦ, and Pesh. and Syr. Hex. ܘܡܘܠܟܢܗ.

The accusative pronoun contained in יְסָדָהּ is not represented, although such a pronoun might easily have been placed after ܣܡܗ. This is probably due to the fact that the translation was made from the LXX., and not from the Hebrew. Pesh. and Syr. Hex. also omit the acc. pronoun.

In place of ܡܨܐ ܕܡܪܝ ܠܥܠ ܗܘ at the end of the verse, LXX. have only Κύριος Παντοκράτωρ (Pesh. ܡܪܝܐ ܚܝܠܬܢܐ), and M. יהוה alone. Syr. Hex. ܡܪܝܐ ܐܝܣܪ ܟܠ, in agreement with the usual reading of the LXX.

V. 7. Notice that the Hebrew לִי (AQ. ἐμοί, B. ἐμοῦ; Pesh. ܠܝ) remains here untranslated. Syr. Hex. has ܠܝ.

The second הֲלוֹא (LXX. οὐ τὸν Ἰσραηλ) is not translated either. Pesh. opens the clause with ܗܐ. Syr. Hex. ܠܐ ܠܐܝܣܪܝܠ.

ܘܠܦܠܫܬܝܐ is in agreement with M. and Pesh.; Syr. Hex. ܘܠܦܠܫܬܝܐ ܘܠܥܡܡܐ = LXX. καὶ τοὺς ἀλλοφύλους.

ܡܢ ܩܦܘܕܩܝܐ agrees (apart from the different spelling) with Pesh. and Syr. Hex., representing LXX. ἐκ Καππαδοκίας.

ܡܢ ܓܘܒܐ (Syr. Hex. ܡܢ ܢܘܩܪܐ) = LXX. ἐκ βόθρου (the root meaning of קוּר being "to hollow out"). Pesh., like M., ܡܢ ܩܝܪ. It is noticeable that in Josh. xii, 23. מֶלֶךְ־גּוֹיִם is translated

48

ܡܠܟܐ ܡܢ ܕܩܘܡܘܪܐ in Pesh., the LXX. rendering being there *βασιλεα Γεει*. See P. Sm. Thes., col. 2917.

V. 8. ܕܣܟܠܐ (Syr. Hex. ܕܚܛܝܐ)=LXX. *των ἁμαρτωλων*, Pesh. ܚܛܝܬܐ=M. החטאה.

. . . ܒܪܡ ܕܝܢ ܕ represents LXX. *πλην ὁτι*=M. אפס כי.

ܠܐ ܠܫܘܠܡܘܢ ܐܢܐ ܡܚܪܒ=LXX. *οὐκ εἰς τελος ἐξαρω*. If the Palestinian translator had made his version from the Hebrew, he would probably not have used two different verbs to represent השמד אשמיד. In the Syr. Hexaplar the LXX. clause is rendered by ܕܠܐ ܠܡܫܠܡܘܬ ܡܚܪܒ* ܐܢܐ.

"The house of Jacob" with B. against "Israel" of A. So also Pesh., Syr. Hex., and M.

V. 9. ܠܡܛܠ ܕܗܐ ܐܢܐ=*διοτι ἰδου ἐγω* of AQ, as opposed to B, which leaves out *ἰδου*. Syr. Hex., also ܕܗܐ

. . . ܠܟܢܐ ܕ appears to be a free addition. See the note on p. 57.

ܠܐ ܢܦܘܠ, where M., LXX., Syr. Hex., and Pesh. (but in Ceriani's facsimile ܕܠܐ) have "and" at the beginning of the clause.

For ܒܫܘܦܝ one should probably read ܒܫܘܦܗܘܢ, or only ܫܘܦܗܘܢ; Pesh. ܕܨܘܗܘܢ. LXX *συντριμμα* (Syr. Hex. ܬܒܪܐ) without a possessive pronoun following.

V. 10. There is here no particle in the LXX corresponding with ܕܝܢ after ܒܚܪܒܐ. Syr. Hex. ܒܚܪܒܐ ܢܡܘܬܘܢ.

There is in this version no word to represent the Hebrew כל, LXX. *παντες*, Pesh. ܟܠ, Syr. Hex. ܟܠܗܘܢ.

It appears best to add ܕܥܡܝ after ܣܟܠܘܗܝ, so as to bring the clause into accord with M., LXX., and Pesh. Otherwise we should have to translate, "By the sword, then, shall die *his* sinners," which is not likely. The omission of ܕܥܡܝ is probably due to an oversight on the part of the scribe. Syr. Hex. ܕܥܡܐ ܕܝܠܝ.

The plural forms of the participles ܡܩܪܒܝܢ and ܐܬܝܢ (see note on p. 57) make it necessary to read ܒܝܫܬܐ pl.; LXX. also *τα κακα*, though M. and Pesh. use the singular. Syr. Hex. ܒܝܫܬܐ.

* Middledorff emends the ܡܚܪܒܐ which he had before him into ܐܚܪܒ, but ܡܚܪܒ stands in Ceriani's facsimile edition, and this word is also nearer ܡܚܪܒܐ.

ܗܠܟܝܢ before ܟܡܝܬܐ is free.

V. 11. The conjunction "and" at the beginning of the verse is neither in M., nor in LXX., Syr. Hex., and Pesh.

Note the rendering of the definite tenses used in the Hebrew, LXX., Syr. Hex., and Pesh. by the participles ܐܢܐ ܡܬܡܣܟ (*bis*) and ܡܟܒܝܢ ܐܢܐ. On the other hand, ܗܘܝܐ ܕܢܦܠܐ represents the participial forms הנפלת, *την πεπτωκυιαν*, and one should vocalize ܕܢܦܠܐ (but Pesh. ܕܢܦܠܐ (?).) See note on v. 5, Syr. Hex. ܠܗܘ ܕܢܦܝܠ.

ܡܦܠܬܗ, "its (or his?) ruin," does not agree completely either with פרציהן (pl. subst. with pl. suffix), or with LXX. *τα πεπτωκοτα αὐτης* pl. subst., or with Pesh. ܠܘܪ̈ܥܠܬܗܘܢ (like M. pl. subst. with pl. suffix). If, however, ܡܦ̈ܠܬܗ (pl.) is read, agreement is established with LXX.; Syr. Hex. ܠܕܢܦܠܝܢ ܡܢܗܘܢ.

ܘܡܦܣܩܬܗ, "and its (or his?) destruction" also differs from והריסתיו and *τα κατεσκαμμενα αὐτης*; but ܘܡܦܣܩ̈ܬܗ would agree with both. Pesh. *ܘܡܦܣܩܬ̈ܝܗܘܢ (pl. subst. with pl. suffix); Syr. Hex. in agreement with M. and LXX., ܠܡܦܣܩܬܐ ܕܝܠܗ.

V. 12. This verse agrees with LXX. (following B against A in points of difference between them; see Swete's edition *in loco*). Pesh. follows M. Syr. Hex. adds ܠܡܪܝܐ as the object of the verb "to seek," thus agreeing with A against B. The reading ידרשו for יירשו of M. must here be supposed.

ܕܥܒܕ is best taken as a participle (M. עֹשֶׂה, Pesh. ܕܥܒܶܕ); Syr. Hex. also ܕܥܒܕ.

V. 13. ܕܪܟܐ "threshing," agrees with AQ[a] (*ἀλοητος*) against A (*ἀμητος*); Pesh. ܐܕܪܐ. Notice that this version, like Pesh., uses the substantives "threshing" and "vintage" in conformity with LXX., M. having the participial forms חוֹרֵשׁ and קוֹצֵר. Syr. Hex. also ܕܪܟܐ ܠܩܛܦܐ; Pesh. ܐܕܪܐ ܠܩܛܦܐ.

ܘܩܛܦܐ ܠܙܪܥܐ "and the vintage the seed [-time]" is evidently a free rendering of the clause as it stands in M. Pesh. ܘܡܥܨܪܐ ܕܥܢܒܐ is nearer ודרך ענבים than ܘܩܛܦܐ, though again using a substantive for the participle דֹּרֵךְ. Syr. Hex. has no equivalent to

* Ceriani: ܘܡܦܣܩܬܗܘܢ.

ܟܪܡܐ ܘܡܥܨܪܐ, and as LXX. has here καὶ περκασει κ.τ.λ. (*vide infra*). there appears to be a strong indication in this place of the Hebrew original having been used by the translator.

The next clause: ܘܡܬܚܠܛܝܢ ܒܙܪܥܐ is evidently an attempt to render the LXX. καὶ περκασει ἡ σταφυλὴ ἐν τῷ σπόρῳ, though ܘܡܬܚܠܛܝܢ "and shall mix" is by no means a literal rendering of περκασει. On the Syr. Hex. ܘܢܬܒܫܠ ܥܢܒܐ ܒܙܪܥܐ see Field "*in loco*" and also P. Sm. Thes. col. 561. ܘܡܬܚܠܛܝܢ of Pal. Syr. appears to support the reading ܘܢܬܒܫܠ (so also in Ceriani's facsimile edition) against ܘܢܬܒܥ.

It is to be noted that Pal. Syr. has a duplicate rendering of the original clause, attempting to translate both the reading of M. and of LXX.

ܢܬܒܫܠ is an attempt to translate LXX. σύμφυτοι. Syr. Hex. ܟܚܕܐ ܢܨܝ̈ܒܘ ܕܩܘܦܐ.

V. 14*a*. Note the rendering ܕܥܡܝ̈ܠܘ, which is the usual Pal. Syr. equivalent for עַמִּי (LXX. λαου μου; Pesh. ܕܥܡܝ Syr. Hex, ܕܥܡܗ ܕܝܠܝ).

Acts xvi, 16–34.

The Palestinian-Syriac translation of these verses is, as can be seen at a glance from the comparison of passages given in the Introduction, an adaptation from the Peshitta. For the sake of fuller demonstration, however, the more salient points of likeness between these two versions on the one hand, and their differences from the Harklensian translation on the other, will be specially marked in the course of the following notes :—

V. 16. The opening clause, "in those same days," is an addition, made in order to provide a suitable beginning for a Lectionary lesson; comp. Amos ix, 5. The introduction of the word ܟܚܝܡܐ as the grammatical subject in the third person, and the subsequent use of the personal pronoun (ܠܗܘܢ) in the same person instead of the second (ἡμιν, Pesh. and Hark. ܢܟ) is no doubt due to the same cause.

ܠܒܝܬ ܨܠܘܬܐ (= εἰς την προσευχην) is in agreement with Pesh. Hark. has ܠܨܠܘܬܐ.

ﬥﻛﻮﻣﻖﻤﻯ ﻟﻤﻮﻯ (genitive construction) agrees, like Pesh. and Ḥark., with πνευμα Πυθωνος, against the more usual Πυθωνα.

Note that the Palestinian transcriber* employs the "nomen agentis" ﬥﻛﻮﻣﻖﻤ, where Pesh. and Ḥark. have the abstract noun ﬥﻛﻮﻮﻖ.

The reading of Pesh. ﻟﻮﻋﻯ ﬥﻛﻮﻮﻯﻣﻯ ﬥﻛﻮﻮﻣﻯ is here altered into ﬥﻛﻮﻣﻖﻤ ﻟﻮﻋﻯﻣﻯ ﬥﻛﻮﻣﻖﻤﻤ. Compare the rendering ﬥﻛﻮﻮﻤﻯ ﻟﻮﻋﻯ of Ḥark., representing exactly the Greek μαντευομενη.

In connection with this phrase the rendering by Ḥark. of the Greek participle by ﻖ with the following verbal form may be noted. Pesh. and Pal.-Syr. are here found to agree in another rendering; so also e.g. ﻟﻤﻤﻯ ﻖ in v. 17 is the Ḥark. translation of κατακολουθουσα, whilst Pesh. and Pal.-Syr. have ﻯﻟﻤ (Pal. ﻟﻮﻟﻮﻋﻯ) ﻟﻮﻋﻯ ﻟﻤﻟﻮ).

V. 17. ﻖﻮﻤ after ﻟﻤﻤﻮﻮﻤ is evidently a free addition. ﻖﻮﻋﻤ is in agreement with Pesh., Ḥark.; and the more usual Greek reading ὑμιν (against ἡμιν) is also to be noted. The rest of the verse is clearly modelled after Pesh. Compare the close following of the Greek text in Ḥark.

V. 18. ﻟﻤﻮﻯ is peculiar to Pal., but the rest closely follows Pesh. Note particularly that Pal. agrees with Pesh. in leaving out ﻖﻤﻮﻟﻮ (και ἐπιστρεψας).

V. 19. The likeness to Pesh. is very striking in this verse. Note especially: (1), ﻮﻤﻮﻖﻤ after ﻮﻤﻟ ﻤﻮﻋﻯﻣﻯ; (2), ﻮﻖﻮﻤﻟ = ﻮﻤﻟﻮﻟﻤ in Pesh.; (3), the closing of the verse with ﻟﻮﻮﻖﻮﻟ, "to the market place," and introducing ﻟﻟﻤﻤﻮﻮﻤﻯ ﻟﻤﻤﻮﻮﻟﻮ into the next verse.

On the other hand, mark the close agreement of Ḥark. with the Greek, the possessive pronouns being, e.g., translated by separate words (ﻮﻤﻟﻤﻮﻯ ﻟﻤﻮﻮﻖ = οἱ κυριοι αὐτης; ﻖﻮﻮﻤﻟﻤﻮﻯ ﻟﻤﻤﻮﻟﻮﻮﻯ = της ἐργασιας αὐτων).

Vv. 20–21. The likeness to Pesh. is also much apparent. Besides ﻟﻟﻤﻤﻮﻮﻤﻯ ﻟﻤﻤﻮﻮﻟﻮ in v. 20, note the phrases ﻖﻮﻋﻯ ﻤﻮﻮﻮﻯﻮﻮﻤﻟ ﻟﻟﻤﻮﻮﻤﻟﻤ, ﻤﻮﻟﻤ ﻟﻤ.. ﻖﻮﻮﻮﻮﻮﻤﻤﻯ ﻟﻟﻤﻮﻮﻤﻟﻤ; answering closely to ﻖﻮﻟﻤ ﻟﻤﻮﻯﻮﻮﻮﻤﻟﻤ ﻟﻟﻤﻮﻮﻟﻤﻮ, ﻤﻮﻟﻤ ﻟﻤﻤﻮﻮﻮﻤﻮﻤﻯﻮﻮ ﻟﻟﻤﻮﻮﻟﻤﻮ, in Pesh.

---

* I use this term advisedly, as the Pal.-Syr. version of the lesson is in reality only a modified transcription of Pesh.

[ܡܩܕܡܝܢ] in v. 21 is common to Pal. and Pesh. against [ܡܩܕܡܝܢ] in Ḥark.; [ܩܕܡ] agrees, however, with Ḥark., Pesh. having [ܡܩܕܡ].

Vv. 22–24. The differences between Pal.. and Pesh. in these verses consist merely in the special usage of words and forms, presumably owing to preferences of dialect; thus Pesh. [ܣܘܡ], Pal. [ܣܡܟ]; Pesh. [ܢܘܗܝ], Pal. [ܡܟܢܘܢ]; Pesh. [ܐܙܕܝܢ]. Pal. [ܢܟܘ].

V. 25. Clearly a recension of Pesh., only note [ܕܘ] after [ܥܠܘܗܝ].

V. 26. Only a few alterations from Pesh., owing to peculiarities of dialect.

V. 27. Also like Pesh. Mark especially [ܢܣܒ] [ܣܝܦܐ] against [ܣܠܩ] (σπασαμενος) of Ḥark.

V. 28. Pesh. and Pal. agree in the order of words, Ḥark. following a different order.

The use of [ܪܒ] by both Pal. and Ḥark. against [ܪܒܐ] of Pesh. may be accidental.

V. 29. Clearly modified from Pesh.

V. 30. Also like Pesh., but notice the paraphrastic form [ܗܘܐ ܟܕ] instead of [ܟܕܡܟ], as in Pesh.

V. 31. Differs from both Pesh. and Ḥark. by the addition of [ܘܩܒܠܗ] before [ܣܡܟ]. The same reading is found in E. 13, and the Armenian version of Misrob, made in the 4th century. See Tregelles *in loco*.

V. 32. Quite like Pesh.

[ܢܗܘܘܬܗ] may be a plural, but the analogy of Pesh. [ܢܗܘܘܢ] suggests the singular.

V. 33. Note the omission of [ܗܘ] after [ܡܛܠܟ], where both Pesh. and Ḥark. have that pronoun after the corresponding word [ܗܘ] (Gr. ἐβαπτισθη αὐτος).

V. 34. [ܕܘ] after [ܠܗܘܢ] is an addition apparently due to some special usage of this particle in the Palestinian dialect.

Note the omission of [ܩܠܗܘܢ] after [ܘܡܢܝܬܗ]. The reading of Pal. Syr. is nearer συν τῳ οἰκῳ αὐτου of D. and Lucif. than to πανοικι, which appears to be followed by Pesh. and Ḥark (the latter having [ܠܟܠ ܟܝܬܘܗܝ ܥܡ]).

NOTES ON PALESTINIAN WORDS AND PHRASES.

Gen. ii, 4–19.

V. 5. ܛܘܪܐ in the sense of ἀγρός is not uncommon in the Palestinian dialect. Nöldeke (Beiträge zur Kenntniss der aramäischen Dialecte II, Z.D.M.G., Band 22, p. 518) thinks that this use of the word may be taken to show that the translator (or translators?), lived in a district where only the uplands were fit for cultivation.

V. 7. For ܥܦܪܝ, dust, see Miniscalchi Erizzo, Evangeliarium Hierosolymitanum (Lexicon sub loco), and Nöldeke, *op. cit.*, p 515; also Schwally *Id. in loco.*

ܢܫܘܡܝ appears to be a feminine noun with the termination *ī*, or perhaps *ai*; compare ܡܠܘܫܝ, ܬܢܘܝ, etc., in Syriac.

Note the use of ܘܐܬܥܒܕ, literally: "and he was made," to represent the Hebrew וַיְהִי = Greek καὶ ἐγένετο. *See* P. Sm., Thes. Syr., col. 2778. The Peshitta has ܘܗܘܐ.

ܚܝܐ at the end of the verse can only be taken as an adjective qualifying ܢܦܫܐ, and the *seyāmē* must, therefore, be due to a mistake.

V. 8. The letter ܝ which is written over the vacant space between the last two letters of the word, for the purpose of correcting it into ܘܐܫܪܝܗ, may be an afterthought; *see* however, v. 15, where the full form ܘܐܫܪܝܗ is used.

V. 9. In view of the scarcity of infinitives in this dialect (Nöldeke, *op. cit.* p. 505), one should notice the infinitival forms ܠܡܚܙܝܐ, and ܠܡܝܟܘܠ, besides ܐܟܪܘܬܐ, on which see the following note. So also in v. 16 ܡܝܟܘܠ, and in v. 17 ܡܘܬ, infinitive absolute before ܬܡܘܬ.

ܐܟܪܘܬܐ, used here and in v. 17, is a verbal noun of the Af'el conjugation from the root ܢܟܪ; comp. הכרת פניהם, Is. III, 9. *See* the notes on this root as used in the Palest. Syr. and cognate dialects in Z.D.M.G. op. cit. p. 515, and Payne Smith, col. 2378; also Schwally *in loco.*

V. 10. The form ܡܦܪܫܢ as a participle of the Pa'el conjugation in Palest. Syr. is mentioned by Payne Smith (col. 3310), and a form ܡܦܪܫ as a participle Pa'el act. is given by Nöldeke, *op. cit.*, p. 504, but the more usual form is no doubt ܡܦܪܫܐ. Or is ܡܦܪܫܢ an Af'el participle?

V. 11. ܐܩܦܬܗ should perhaps also be noted from a lexical point of view, although it is merely the Palestinian transcription of the Greek word which represents חוילה. See note on p. 44.

V. 12. ܟܐܘܣܪܐ as representing "carbuncle," and ܣܡܩ ܘܟܐܪ for "emerald," should be noted for the vocabulary.

V. 13. Note the difference in the construction between ܗܪ ܘܗܘ ܘܗܝܢܝܠ (where, however, the ܘ was added after ܗܝܢܝܠ had been written) and ܗܪ ܘܗܘ ܣܝܢܝܠ in v. 11, which agrees with ܗܪ ܘܗܘ ܐܝܠ in v. 14.

V. 14. ܐܝܢܝܠ is the Palestinian Syriac for ܘܩܠܐ (Pesh.). Comp. the Assyrian 'Idiḳlat.

ܣܡܪܣܘ = ܣܡܪܣܝ. See Nöldeke, *op. cit.*, p. 477.

V. 15. Note the separation of ܢܝܗ and ܝܐܪܣ by the subject (ܣܪܝ ܝܠܗܘܐ).

V. 19. On the use of ܟܘܪܐ in the sense of ἀγρός see note on v. 5.

Note the spelling ܘܐܝܢܘ for ܘܐܝܢܘ; see the note on Acts xvi, 19.

---

2 *Kings* ii, 19–22.

V. 19. Note the form ܙܘܒܠ, barren, in this verse, and also ܝܢܙܘܠ in v. 21, the latter appearing to be the absolute form of ܙܘܒܠ, just as ܘܡܠܟܘ in v. 20 is the absolute form of ܗܡܠܟܘ in v. 21.

V. 20. For ܝܢܝܣܘ, see P. Sm., Thes., col. 3520.

V. 21. ܝܗܘܣܘܟܝܠ is at first sight curious, but it is probably = ܝܗܘܣܘܟܝܠ, the ܟ being here pronounced like ܟ, and therefore written so. It answers in sense to the Hebrew מוצא. Comp. ܝܗܘܣܘܟܝ in St. Luke ix, 31. Another possible explanation is that the ܟ represents the ע of ܟܘܣܘܥ, just as ארקא in Jer. x, 11, is the same as ארעא. See Gesen. Thesaurus, *in loco*; also P. Sm., Thes., cols. 397 and 400. Pesh. has ܟܘܣܘܡܠ.

Amos ix, 5–14a.

V. 5. ܘܗܘ ܝܝ here and at the end of v. 6, as representing παντοκρατωρ should be noted for the vocabulary; comp. اسم ܘܢ in the same sense.

With ܫܡܝܐ, cœlum, compare the Samaritan "shumejja," as vocalised by Petermann (Brevis Linguæ Samaritanæ Grammatica .. ... cum glossario).

With ܫܡܝܘܬܐ, compare ܫܡܝܐ (P. Sm. Thes., col. 2650).

V. 6. ܣܘܪܝܐ is to be noted as a variation of ܣܘܪܝܐ (see P. Sm., Thes., col. 3702).

In ܐܫܡܥ, the root ܐܫܡ appears in a verbal form, though such use is rather rare in Semitic languages in general. For instances see Levy's Neuhebräisches und Chaldäisches Wörterbuch under

אשׁשׁ (comp. اسّ in Arabic), and Castel's Lexicon Heptaglotton under the same root.

ܟܡܝܣܘ can only be taken as a form of the active participle analogous to the Samaritan form "Katol" (see Petermann's Grammar, p. 21). As the verb is transitive, it cannot be looked upon as an instance of the form Katūl for the perfect (see Dalman's "Grammatik des Jüdisch-Palästinischen Aramaisch," pp. 199, 206). ܟܡܝܣ could, of course, as far as the form goes, be the imperative, but the context is against this view. For the participial form speak also LXX. ($\dot{\epsilon}\kappa\chi\epsilon\omega\nu$), and Pesh. (ܐܡܪ).

V. 7. ܗܘ ܠܐ ܟܡܐ represents the LXX. $o\dot{v}\chi$ $\dot{\omega}s$ (Hebrew הלוא כ ··); Pesh. only ܗܐ ܐܣܘ.

Note the form ܟܒ before ܣܘܡܐܝܢ for the construct plural, as noted by Nöldeke (op. cit., p. 479).

The form ܟܣܘܪܝܬܐ is mentioned in P. Sm., Thes., col. 3688, as one of the forms used in place of ܟܣܘܪܝܐ.

V. 8. On the use of ܚܛܝܐ in the sense of "sinner," see Nöldeke, op. cit., pp. 518, 519; Schwally, Id., in loco.

On the form ܐܘܡܐ = ܐܘܡܐ (1st pers. sing. imperfect) see Nöldeke, op. cit., p. 499. So also, e.g., ܘܐܡܪ in v. 9, and ܘܐܡܪ in v. 11.

For the substantive form ܣܘܝܘ see Nöldeke, op. cit., p. 517

For the use of the Af'el of ܢܘܕ as exemplified in ܟܡܘܕܥ see Nöldeke, op. cit., pp. 516, 517. Comp. the note on p. 49.

V. 9. On ܟܝܢܝܐ see Nöldeke, op. cit., p. 515. Compare the uses of מין, מינא as given in Levy (op. cit. pp. 104, 105).

One should expect ܐܢܐ after ܘܐܡܪ to supply a subject.

ܠܬܒܢܐ ܕܡܕܪܝܐ is literally rendered "the straw of a winnowing fork." ܡܕܪܝܐ is probably the same as מזרה, which is shown by H. Vogelstein (Die Landwirthschaft in Palästina zur Zeit der Mišnâh, p. 69) to be the seven-pronged winnowing fork.

V. 10. The fem. of the part. plur. ܐܙܠܝ agrees with ܟܢܘܫܬܐ, and we should also expect ܩܝܡܢ instead of ܩܝܡܝܢ.

On the form ܥܠܝܗܝܢ = ܥܠܝܗܘܢ see Nöldeke, *op. cit.*, pp. 469, 482.

V. 11. ܟܘܒܪܝܗ in the sense of "ruin" or "destruction" should be noted for the vocabulary.

V. 12. For ܠܥܠܟ see P. Sm., Thes., col. 2130. The full form is . . ܕ ܠܥܠܟ (Nöldeke, *op. cit.*, p. 489).

For ܩܪܝܒ see Noldeke, *op. cit.*, p. 519.

V. 13. The fem. ܐܙܠܝ construed with ܗܘܢܠܟܘ is irregular.

V. 14a. ܕܥܡܠܟ exhibits the use of ܥܡܐ in Palest. Syriac as the regular representative of the Hebrew עם, Greek λαος.

Acts xvi, 16-34.

V. 16. The ܣ instead of ܙ in ܩܘܣܡܐ reminds one of the Hebrew spelling (קוסם). In Land's "Anecdota Syriaca," vol. iv, pp. 200, 203, ܠܩܘܣܡܝܗܘܢ, is found.

V. 17. ܟܪܝ, also found in the form ܟܪ = Jewish Aram. כדין, Samaritan כדן.

V. 18. ܝܣܘܣ (elsewhere ܝܣܘ) occurs again in the same form in v. 31.

V. 19. ܕܝ after ܡܒܪܗ is altogether meaningless. It might have been possible (?) to take it as equal in sense to the relative prefix ܕ (compare Jewish Aram. דו, and see Adler's "Novi Testamenti Versiones Syriacæ" (Hafniæ, 1789, p. 142), if that prefix itself did not follow.

ܐܬܝܗ (= ܐܬܝܗ = ܐܬܝܗ) points to the state of considerable decay which the dialect had reached when the MS. was written. Comp. ܘܐܬܝ in Gen. ii, 19, and ܘܐܬܝܗ in 2 Kings, ii, 20.

V. 20. For ܘܡܟܪܙܝܢ see P. Sm., Thes , col. 2985.

V. 21. ܕܝ at the end of the verse is very strange.

V. 22. For the vocabulary note ܟܘܝܐ (= Pesh. ܟܘܝܐ); also ܟܟܢ (= Jewish Aram. בכין), corresponding here in meaning to ܗܝܟܢ.

V. 24. Note the forms ܩܡܝܠܠ, ܐܟܝܠܠ, ܢܣܟܡ, and ܗܣܪ. Comp. Nóldeke, *op. cit.*, p. 492.

ܕܝ after ܠܗܘܢ, is strange.

V. 26. Note the use of ܐܬܟܠ, where Pesh. and Hark. have ܗܘܐ (ἐγένετο). Comp. Gen. ii, 7.

V. 28. For ܩܣܠܣܣ, and the various other forms of the same word, see P. Sm., Thes., col. 1738; also Schwally, *Id. in loco*.

V. 29. Note the spelling ܩܥܪܝܟܡ instead of the usual ܩܥܪܝܟ.

V. 30. There are in this verse two instances of the first person singular imperfect having the peculiarly Palestinian prefix ܢ instead of ܐ, namely, ܝܗܘܐ and ܝܚܝܢ.

Note that ܢܘܠܠܟ ܡܟ was selected in the Palestinian adaptation instead of ܟܠ ܘܠܐ ܡܟܠ of Pesh.

V. 32. Note the writing ܣܟܡܝܠܗ in one word; so also ܣܟܡܝܠܗ in v. 33. In v. 34 the two words are written separately, but ܡܟܝ is at the end of the line in the latter case.

V. 33. For ܝܘܕܗܘܢ, see P. Sm., Thes., col. 2281.

Note ܐܘܟܣ=ܐܟܘܟܐ,. The form with ܣ is more common in Pal. Syr. than in the Edessene dialect.

VOCABULARY OF UNUSUAL WORDS
AND FORMS.*

ܐܘܝܠܐ (=Εὐειλατ, חוילה), Gen. ii, 11.

ܐܪܝܠ, Gen. ii, 14.

ܐܬܝ (=ܐܬܝ), Gen. ii, 19.

ܐܬܝܘ (=ܐܬܝܘ=ܐܬܝܘ), Acts xvi, 19

ܐܬܝܘ, 2 Kings ii, 20.

ܐܡܪ (and similar forms of the perfect tense), Acts xvi, 24.

ܐܘܐ (in ܟܐܘܐ), Amos ix, 6.

ܒܬܒ (=in meaning to Ed. Syr. ܗܘܡܪ), Acts xvi, 22.

ܟܒ (as a construct plural), Amos ix, 7.

ܝܘܩܢܐ, carbuncle, Gen, ii, 12.

ܘܪ (=δέ), very extensively used.

ܚܩܠܐ, ἀγρός, Gen. ii, 5, 19.

ܪܣܝܣܐ, raindrops, Ps. lxv, 11.

ܢܘܪܕܝܐ, Gen. ii, 5.

ܣܟܘܠܬܢ, Acts xvi, 28.

ܟܐܦܐ ܪܝܩܐ, emerald, Gen. ii, 12.

ܟܬܝܒ, Acts xvi, 22.

ܡܐ ܠܐ ܗܘ (=ουχ ὡς), Amos ix, 7.

ܡܕܝܢܬܐ, nations, Amos ix, 9.

ܡܐܐ (in ܟܐܘܐ, without following ?), Amos ix, 12.

ܢܣܒ (for ܢܣܒ) in ܡܣܒܘܗܝ, 2 Kings ii, 21.

ܢܘܪܕܝܗܘܢ, Acts xvi, 33.

ܢܒ (in ܪܟܝܢܘܪ), Gen. ii, 9, 17.

ܢܣܘܡܝ, Gen. ii, 7.

ܣܡܡ (for ܘܣܒ) in ܐܣܡܟܗ, Acts xvi, 33.

ܣܟܠܐ, sinner, Amos ix, 8.

ܣܠܟ (in the form ܐܣܘܩܬܐ), Amos ix, 5 (6).

ܥܒܕ (in ܐܬܥܒܪ=ἐγένετο), Gen. ii, 7; Acts xvi, 26.

ܥܠܝ, Gen. ii, 9, 19.

ܥܠܝܗܘ (=ܥܠܝܗܘ), Amos ix, 10.

ܥܒܪܟܘ (in ܡܟܪܟܘ), Acts xvi, 20.

ܩܪܝ (in the form ܐܩܪܘܢܝܐ), Amos ix, 11.

---

* A vocabulary containing the more important words and forms occurring in the entire "Liturgy of the Nile" will be found at the end of the publication bearing that title. In this vocabulary the more or less unusual forms contained in the Biblical passages treated on are collected on a somewhat fuller scale.

NOTICES.

SUBSCRIPTIONS to the Society become due on the 1st of January each year.   Those Members in arrear for the current year are requested to send the amount, £1 1s., at once to Messrs. Lloyds' Bank, Limited, 16, St. James's Street, S.W.

PAPERS proposed to be read at the Monthly Meetings must be sent to the Secretary on or before the 10th of the preceding month.

Members having NEW MEMBERS to propose, are requested to send in the names of the Candidates on or before the 10th of the month preceding the meeting at which the names are to be submitted to the Council.

A few complete sets of the publications of the Society can be obtained by application to the Secretary, W. HARRY RYLANDS, 37, Great Russell Street, Bloomsbury, W.C.

The LIBRARY of the Society, at 37, GREAT RUSSELL STREET, BLOOMSBURY, W.C., is open to Members on Monday, Wednesday, and Friday, between the hours of 11 and 4, when the Secretary is in attendance to transact the general business of the Society.

As the new list of members will shortly be printed, Members are requested to send any corrections or additions they may wish to have made in the list which was published in Vol. IX of the *Transactions*.

THE FOLLOWING BOOKS ARE REQUIRED FOR THE LIBRARY OF THE SOCIETY.

Members having duplicate copies, will confer a favour by presenting them to the Society.

ALKER, E., Die Chronologie der Bucher der Könige und Paralipomenōn im Einklang mit der Chronologie der Aegypter, Assyrer, Babylonier und Meder.

AMÉLINEAU, Histoire du Patriarche Copte Isaac.

————————— Contes de l'Égypte Chrétienne.

————————— La Morale Egyptienne quinze siècles avant notre ère.

AMIAUD, La Légende Syriaque de Saint Alexis, l'homme de Dieu.

————————— A., AND L. MECHINEAU, Tableau Comparé des Écritures Babyloniennes et Assyriennes.

————————— Mittheilungen aus der Sammlung der Papyrus Erzherzog Rainer. 2 parts.

BAETHGEN, Beitrage zur Semitischen Religiongeshichte. Der Gott Israels und die Götter der Heiden.

BLASS, A. F., Eudoxi ars Astronomica qualis in Charta Aegyptiaca superest.

BOTTA, Monuments de Ninive. 5 vols., folio. 1847–1850.

BRUGSCH-BEY, Geographische Inschriften Altaegyptische Denkmaeler. Vol. I—III (Brugsch).

————————— Recueil de Monuments Égyptiens, copiés sur lieux et publiés pas H. Brugsch et J. Dümichen. (4 vols., and the text by Dümichen of vols. 3 and 4.)

BUDINGER, M., De Colonarium quarundam Phoeniciarum primordiis cum Hebraeorum exodo conjunctis.

BURCKHARDT, Eastern Travels.

CASSEL, PAULUS, Zophnet Paneach Aegyptische Deutungen.

CHABAS, Mélanges Égyptologiques. Séries I, III. 1862–1873.

DÜMICHEN, Historische Inschriften, &c., 1st series, 1867.

————————————————— 2nd series, 1869.

—————— Altaegyptische Kalender-Inschriften, 1886.

————————————— Tempel-Inschriften, 1862. 2 vols., folio.

EBERS, G., Papyrus Ebers.

ERMAN, Papyrus Westcar.

Études Égyptologiques. 13 vols., complete to 1880.

GAYET, E., Stèles de la XII dynastie au Musée du Louvre.

GOLÉNISCHEFF, Die Metternichstele. Folio, 1877.

————————— Vingt-quatre Tablettes Cappadociennes de la Collection de.

GRANT-BEY, Dr., The Ancient Egyptian Religion and the Influence it exerted on the Religions that came in contact with it.

HAUPT, Die Sumerischen Familiengesetze.

HOMMEL, Dr., Geschichte Babyloniens und Assyriens. 1892.

JASTROW, M., A Fragment of the Babylonian "Dibbarra" Epic.

JENSEN, Die Kosmologie der Babylonier.

JEREMIAS, Tyrus bis zur Zeit Nubukadnezar's Geschichtliche Skizze mit besonderer Berucksichtigung der Keilschriftlichen Quellen.

JOACHIM, H., Papyros Ebers, das Älteste Buch über Heilkunde.

JOHNS HOPKINS UNIVERSITY. Contributions to Assyriology and Comparative Semitic Philology.

KREBS, F., De Chnemothis nomarchi inscriptione Aegyptiaca commentatio.

LEDERER, Die Biblische Zeitrechnung vom Auszuge aus Aegypten bis zum Beginne der Babylonische Gefangenschaft mit Berichsichtignung der Resultate der Assyriologie und der Aegyptologie.

LEDRAIN, Les Monuments Égyptiens de la Bibliothèque Nationale.

LEFÈBURE, Le Mythe Osirien. 2me partie. "Osiris."

LEGRAIN, G., Le Livre des Transformations. Papyrus démotique du Louvre.

LEHMANN, Samassumukin König von Babylonien 668 vehr, p. xiv, 173; 47 plates.

LEPSIUS, Nubian Grammar, &c., 1880.

MARUCHI, Monumenta Papyracea Aegyptia.

MULLER, D. H., Epigraphische Denkmaler aus Arabien.

NOORDTZIG, Israël's verblijf in Egypte bezien int licht der Egyptische outdekkingen.

POGNON, Les Inscriptions Babyloniennes du Wadi Brissa.

RAWLINSON, CANON, 6th Ancient Monarchy.

ROBIOU, Croyances de l'Égypte à l'époque des Pyramides.

———— Recherches sur le Calendrier en Égypte et sur le chronologie des Lagides.

SAINTE MARIE, Mission à Carthage.

SARZEC, Découvertes en Chaldée.

SCHAEFFER, Commentationes de papyro medicinali Lipsiensi.

SCHOUW, Charta papyracea graece scripta Musei Borgiani Velitris.

SCHROEDER, Die Phönizische Sprache.

STRAUSS and TORNEY, Der Altägyptishe Götterglaube.

VIREY, P., Quelques Observations sur l'Épisode d'Aristée, à propos d'un Monument Égyptien.

VISSER, I., Hebreeuwsche Archaeologie. Utrecht, 1891.

WALTHER, J., Les Découvertes de Ninive et de Babylone au point de vue biblique. Lausanne, 1890.

WILCKEN, M., Actenstücke aus der Königl. Bank zu Theben.

WILTZKE, De Biblische Simson der Agyptische Horus-Ra.

WINCKLER, HUGO, Der Thontafelfund von El Amarna. Vols. I and II.

———— Textbuch-Keilinschriftliches zum Alten Testament.

WEISSLEACH, F. II., Die Achaemeniden Inschriften Zweiter Art.

WESSELEY, C., Die Pariser Papyri des Fundes von El Fajum.

Zeitsch. der Deutschen Morgenl. Gesellsch., Vol. I, 1847 ; Vols. IV to XII, 1850 to 1858, inclusive ; Vol. XX to Vol. XXXII. 1866 to 1878.

ZIMMERN, H., Die Assyriologie als Hulfswissenschaft für das Studium des Alten Testaments.

SOCIETY OF BIBLICAL ARCHÆOLOGY PUBLICATIONS.

Society of Biblical Archæology.

COUNCIL, 1897.

President.

Sir P. le Page Renouf, Knt.

Vice-Presidents.

The Most Rev. His Grace The Lord Archbishop of York.
The Most Noble the Marquess of Bute, K.T., &c., &c.
The Right Hon. Lord Amherst of Hackney.
The Right Hon. Lord Halsbury.
The Right Hon. W. E. Gladstone, M.P., D.C.L., &c.
Arthur Cates.
F. D. Mocatta, F.S.A., &c.
Walter Morrison, M.P.
Sir Charles Nicholson, Bart., D.C.L., M.D., &c.
Alexander Peckover, LL.D., F.S.A.
Rev. George Rawlinson, D.D., Canon of Canterbury.

Council.

Rev. Charles James Ball, M.A.	Rev. James Marshall, M.A.
Rev. Prof. T. K. Cheyne, D.D.	Claude G. Montefiore.
Thomas Christy, F.L.S.	Walter L. Nash, F.S.A.
Dr. J. Hall Gladstone, F.R.S.	Prof. E. Naville.
Charles Harrison, F.S.A.	J. Pollard.
Gray Hill.	Edward B. Tylor, LL.D., F.R.S.,
Prof. T. Hayter Lewis, F.S.A.	&c.
Rev. Albert Löwy, LL.D., &c.	E. Towry Whyte, M.A., F.S.A.

Honorary Treasurer—Bernard T. Bosanquet.

Secretary—W. Harry Rylands, F.S.A.

Honorary Secretary for Foreign Correspondence—Rev. R. Gwynne, B.A.

Honorary Librarian—William Simpson, F.R.G.S.

Harrison and Sons, Printers in Ordinary to Her Majesty, St. Martin's Lane.

PROCEEDINGS

OF

THE SOCIETY

OF

BIBLICAL ARCHÆOLOGY.

—————❦❀————

VOL. XIX. TWENTY–SEVENTH SESSION.

Second Meeting, February 2nd, 1897.

————————❦❀————————

CONTENTS.

————————❦❀————————

PUBLISHED AT

THE OFFICES OF THE SOCIETY,

37, GREAT RUSSELL STREET, BLOOMSBURY, W.C.

————

1897.

SOCIETY OF BIBLICAL ARCHÆOLOGY,

37, Great Russell Street, Bloomsbury, W.C.

TRANSACTIONS.

			To Members.		To Non-Members.					To Members.		To Non-Members.
					s. *d.*							*s.* *d.*
Vol.	I,	Part 1	... 10	6	... 12	6	Vol.	VI,	Part 1	... 10	6	... 12 6
,,	I,	,, 2	... 10	6	... 12	6	,,	VI,	,, 2	... 10	6	... 12 6
,,	II,	,, 1	... 8	0	... 10	6	,,	VII,	,, 1	... 7	6	... 10 6
,,	II,	,, 2	... 8	0	... 10	6	,,	VII,	,, 2	... 10	6	... 12 6
,,	III,	,, 1	... 8	0	... 10	6	,,	VII,	,, 3	... 10	6	... 12 6
,,	III,	,, 2	... 8	0	... 10	6	,,	VIII,	,, 1	... 10	6	... 12 6
,,	IV,	,, 1	... 10	6	... 12	6	,,	VIII,	,, 2	... 10	6	... 12 6
,,	IV,	,, 2	... 10	6	... 12	6	,,	VIII,	,, 3	... 10	6	... 12 6
,,	V,	,, 1	... 12	6	... 15	0	,,	IX,	,, 1	... 10	6	... 12 6
,,	V,	,, 2	... 10	6	... 12	6	,,	IX,	,, 2	... 10	6	... 12 6

PROCEEDINGS.

				To Members.			To Non-Members.
Vol.	I,	Session	1878–79	... 2	0	...	... 2 6
,,	II,	,,	1879–80	... 2	0	...	... 2 6
,,	III,	,,	1880–81	... 4	0	...	... 5 0
,,	IV,	,,	1881–82	... 4	0	...	... 5 0
,,	V,	,,	1882–83	... 4	0	...	... 5 0
,,	VI,	,,	1883–84	... 5	0	...	... 6 0
,,	VII,	,,	1884–85	... 5	0	...	... 6 0
,,	VIII,	,,	1885–86	... 5	0	...	... 6 0
,,	IX,	,,	1886–87	... 2	0 per Part	...	... 2 6
,,	IX,	Part 7,	1886–87	... 8	0 ,, ,,	...	... 10 6
,,	X,	Parts 1 to 7,	1887–88	... 2	0 ,, ,,	...	... 2 6
,,	X,	Part 8,	1887–88	... 7	6 ,, ,,	...	... 10 6
,,	XI,	Parts 1 to 7,	1888–89	... 2	0 ,, ,,	...	... 2 6
,,	XI,	Part 8,	1888–89	... 7	6 ,, ,,	...	... 10 6
,,	XII,	Parts 1 to 7,	1889–90	... 2	0 ,, ,,	...	... 2 6
,,	XII,	Part 8,	1889–90	... 5	0 ,, ,,	...	... 6 0
,,	XIII,	Parts 1 to 7,	1890–91	... 2	0 ,, ,,	...	... 2 6
,,	XIII,	Part 8,	1890–91	... 5	0 ,, ,,	...	... 6 0
,,	XIV,	Parts 1 to 7,	1891–92	... 2	0 ,, ,,	...	... 2 6
,,	XIV,	Part 8,	1891–92	... 5	0 ,, ,,	...	... 6 0
,,	XV,	Parts 1 to 7,	1892–93	... 2	0 ,, ,,	...	... 2 6
,,	XV,	Part 8,	1892–93	... 5	0 ,, ,,	...	... 6 0
,,	XVI,	Parts 1 to 10,	1893–94	... 2	0 ,, ,,	...	... 2 6
,,	XVII,	Parts 1 to 8	1895	... 2	0 ,, ,,	...	... 2 6
,,	XVIII,	Parts 1 to 8	1896	... 2	0 ,, ,,	...	... 2 6
,,	XIX,	In progress	1897				

A few complete sets of the Transactions still remain for sale, which may be obtained on application to the Secretary, W. H. Rylands, F.S.A., 37, Great Russell Street, Bloomsbury, W.C.

PROCEEDINGS

OF

THE SOCIETY

OF

BIBLICAL ARCHÆOLOGY.

TWENTY-SEVENTH SESSION, 1897.

Second Meeting, 2nd February, 1897.

ALEX. PECKOVER, LL.D., VICE-PRESIDENT.

IN THE CHAIR.

————❦❦————

The following. Presents were announced, and thanks ordered to be returned to the Donors :—

From the Author, G. H. Gwilliam,. B.D. :—The Palestinian Version of the Holy Scriptures. Five more fragments recently acquired by the Bodleian Library. Anecdota Oxoniensia. Semitic Series. Vol. I, Part V. 4to. Oxford. 1893.

From the Author, Prof. Paul Haupt :—The Origin of the Pentateuch. 8vo. New York. 1895.

From the Author, Prof. Paul Haupt :—The Beginning of the Judaic Account of the Creation. (*American Oriental Soc. Proc.*, April, 1896.)

From Prof. Paul Haupt:—The Oriental Seminary at the Johns Hopkins University, by the Rev. Joseph Brunneau, S.S. Translated from *La Revue Biblique*, July, 1895. 8vo. Baltimore. 1895.

From E. Towry Whyte (*Member of Council*):—Regni Davidici et Salomonœi, Descriptio Geographica et Historica, una cum delineatione Syriæ et Ægypti ***** juncta est huic operi consideratio Urbium Maximarum ***** auctore Johanne Matthia Hasio. Norembergæ. Folio. 1739.

The following Candidates were elected Members of the Society, having been nominated at the last Meeting, held on the 12th January, 1897:—

John N. Duncan, Johannesburg.
Rev. James Hastings, M.A., The Manse, Kinneff, Bervie.
Miss Martha Izod, The Hawthorns, Church Road, Edgbaston, Birmingham.
W. Jacks, Crosslet, Dumbarton.

A Paper was read by the Rev. C. J. Ball, M.A.: "Th Prophecy of the Servant" (Isa. lii, liii).

Remarks were added by the Rev. Dr. Löwy.

Mr. Jos. Offord read a Note on:

Thanks were returned for these communications.

BOOK OF THE DEAD.

By Sir P. le Page Renouf.

CHAPTER CXXIX
is a repetition of Chapter C.

CHAPTER CXXX.

A Book whereby the Soul is made to live for ever, on the day of entering into the Bark of Rā, and to pass the Sheniu of the Tuat. Made on the Birthday of Osiris. (1)

Opened be the gates of Heaven; opened be the gates of Earth; opened be the gates of the East; opened be the gates of the West; opened be the gates of the Southern and of the Northern sanctuaries.

Opened be the gates and thrown wide the portals as Rā riseth up from the Mount of Glory; opened to him be the doors of the Sektit boat, thrown open to him be the portals of the Māātit, as he scenteth Shu and setteth in motion Tefnut, and those follow who are in the train of the Osiris *N*, who followeth Rā and taketh possession of his arms of steel. (2)

I am coffined in an ark like Horus, to whom his cradle (3) is brought: and secret is the place, hard by his own shrine, which the god openeth to whom he willeth.

And so it cometh that I lift up Right to the Lord of Right, and that I make fast the cord which windeth about the shrine.

The Osiris *N* avoideth the raging storm: the Osiris *N* is not to be kept away from Rā, not to be repulsed is he.

Let not the Osiris *N* advance into the Valley of Darkness: let not the Osiris *N* enter into the dungeon of the captives: let him not leap into the grip of Fate, let him not fall among those who imprison souls or come forth among those who would drag him behind the slaughtering block of the Armed god. (4)

Salutations to you, ye sejant gods. (5)

The divine Sword (6) is concealed in the hands of Seb, at daybreak, for he delighteth in drawing to himself both old and young at his own season.

And now behold Thoth in the secret of his mysteries. He maketh purifications and endless reckonings; piercing the steel firmament and dissipating the storms around him.

And so it cometh that the Osiris N hath reached every station of his.

He hath fashioned his staff, and received the oblations of Rā, the swift of speed and beautiful in his rising and almighty through what he hath done.

He putteth an end to his pain and suffering, and the Osiris N putteth an end to his own pain; yea, he gladdeneth the countenance of Thoth by the worship of Rā and Osiris.

The Osiris N entereth the Mount of Glory of Rā, who hath made his Bark and saileth prosperously, lightening up the face of Thoth, that he may listen to Rā and beat down the obstacles in his way, and put an end to his adversaries.

Let not the Osiris N be shipwrecked on the great voyage by him whose face is in his own lap: (7) for the name of Rā is upon the Osiris, and his token of honour is on his mouth, which speaketh to him who listeneth to the words of the Osiris N.

Glory to thee, O Rā, Lord of the Mount of Glory. Hail to thee, who purifiest the generations yet unborn and to whom this great quarter of heaven offereth homage.

The steering keepeth clear from misadventure.

Lo, here is Osiris who proclaimeth Right, because of the marvel in the West, for he hath put an end to the rage of Apepi, for he is himself the god in Lion form among the associate gods and protecteth Rā against Apepi daily, that he may not approach him, and he keepeth watch upon him. Osiris seizeth the scrolls and receiveth the offerings.

And Thoth supplieth the Osiris N with that which he shall perform for him. It is granted that the Osiris shall carry Maāt at the head of the great Bark, and hold up Maāt among the associate gods, and that Osiris gain endless triumphs.

The Sheniu marshal the Osiris *N*, and they procure for the Osiris a voyage amid acclamations.

The Satellites of Rā make their round, in the train of the exaltation of Maāt, who followeth her Lord.   And glory is given to the Inviolate one.

The Osiris receiveth the Amsu-staff (8) wherewith he goeth round Heaven.

The unborn generations of men give him glory, as to one who standeth without ever resting.   Rā exalteth him by this, that he alloweth the Osiris to disperse the cloud and behold his glories.   He maketh firm his rudders that the Bark may go round in Heaven and that he may make his appearance in Antu.   Thoth is in the centre of his eye, sejant in the great Bark of Chepera.   The Osiris becometh one whose words come to pass.   He it is who passeth over Heaven unto the West, and the Chabasu gods of Light rise up to him with acclamation.   They receive the cable of Rā from his rowers, and Rā goeth on his round and seeth the Osiris who issueth his decrees ; (9) the Osiris *N*, the Victorious ; in peace ! in peace !

Not to be repelled is he ; not to be caught by the fire of thy fate. Let not the tempest of thy mouth come forth against him.

Let not the Osiris *N* advance upon the paths of misfortune : let him avoid disasters, let them not attain him.

The Osiris *N* enters into the Bark of Rā, he succeedeth to thy throne ; he receiveth thine insignia.

The Osiris *N* inaugurateth the paths of Rā and prayeth that he may drive off the Lock which cometh out of the flame against thy Bark out of the great Stream.

But the Osiris *N* knoweth it, and it attaineth not thy Bark.   For the Osiris *N* is within it ; the Osiris *N* who maketh the divine offerings.

Said over a Bark of Rā, coloured in pure green. (10)   *And thou shalt place a picture of the deceased at the prow thereof.   And make a Sektit boat on the right side of it and an Atit boat on the left side of it.* (11)

ASSYRIOLOGICAL NOTES. No. 2.

By Professor A. H. Sayce.

In the summer of 1889 I copied in the Hermitage at St. Petersburg a very interesting inscription on a seal-cylinder, which I afterwards sent to the *Zeitscrift für Assyriologie*. There, however, it was so badly printed that it is necessary to publish it again, more especially as Prof. Jensen has recently misread it. Accordingly I here give a correct copy of the text.

Seal in the Hermitage, St. Petersburg.

(A. vi, 3. No. 7).

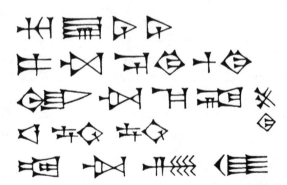

This must be transcribed :—

    (1) Khu-un-ni-ni

    (2) pa-te-śi Ki-mas-KI

    (3) GIR-NITAKH (sakkanakku) Ma-ad (?)-qat-KI

    (4) UD-GU-GU

    (5) ? NITAKH ZI MI.

(I.) "Khunnini (or Khun-ili), (2) the high-priest of Kimas, (3) the viceroy of Madqat (?)." The last word, however, may also be read *Mat Qit*, "the land of Qit," the third character in it being No. 156 in the list of Amiaud and Méchineau. The second character, moreover, may be *la*. Of the last two lines I do not know the signification; indeed I do not even know to what language they belong. *Ud-gugu* can hardly be a dialectic variant of the Sumerian *adgigi*, "counsellor." Nor do I know what is the value of the first character of l. 5, as it is differently formed from that which corresponds with the Assyrian ⟨cuneiform⟩.

Kimas is frequently mentioned in the early Babylonian contract-tablets of the age of the Third dynasty of Ur and of the First dynasty of Babylon which followed it. Thus one of them is dated MU KI-MAS-KI SI-SU-KHU KI-TI-KI BA-KHUL, "the year when Kimas, Sisukhu (?) and Kiti were overrun," and in another we read I BI DU LUGAL US KI-MAS-KI ME . . . . KI-MAS-KI SA-DU-NI (?), "one (*qa*) of common beer of the king for the males* from Kimas." According to Dr. Scheil the name is sometimes preceded by the ideograph NIM, from which he infers that the country was situated in Elam. This, however, does not necessarily follow, as NIM merely signifies "Highlands," and it is possible that Prof. Hommel and myself may be right in making Ki-mas "the land of Mas," or northern Arabia. Moreover, the texts published by M. Dangin in the *Revue d'Assyriologie*, iii, 4, show that he is correct in considering that the character in question is not really NIM, but an ideograph which he believes to signify "servant," since it is prefixed not only to the gentilic names Ansan, Simas, Kimas, and Markhasi (*i.e.*, Mer'ash, in northern Syria), but also to the proper name Khunimas. It really is, however, "male" or "eunuch" (see note). At all events the Arabian desert to the west of Ur is called Ki-sarra "the land of the (Bedawin) hordes" in early Babylonian texts (see W.A.I., III, 60, 2, 83), and Ki-mas would be a parallel formation to this. Mas was the name given to the great desert of northern Arabia, the Mash, Massa, or Mesha of the Old Testament.

---

* The character is written ⟨cuneiform⟩ and has been confounded with NIM by Dr. Scheil (see above). It is really the Assyrian ⟨cuneiform⟩, "male" or "eunuch." In the same text we read: "5 *qa* of common beer of the king for the goddess Nin-sug-ga of *Khu-un*-KI SA-DU . . ," where "the land of Khun" may contain the same element as *Khunnini*.

The supposition that ⊀⊀ ⊁ *Mat Mas* should be read *Madbar*, and identified with the Hebrew מדבר, "desert," is devoid of probability.

Kimas seems to have given a name to "copper" among the Sumerians, from which we may gather that copper was brought from it, as is expressly affirmed by Gudea. The name is usually written ⊀ ⊁ ⊁, D.P. *Ka-mas*, from which the Semites borrowed their *Kêmassu* (W.A.I., II, 18, 54, IV, 4, 42). *Kêmassu* is certainly not a compound of *qu*, "the bright," and *masâsu*, "to rub," as has been suggested by Prof. Delitzsch.

If Kimas is northern Arabia, we might see in Madqat the land of Madga, near the river Urruda, from which Gudea derived a substance, conjectured by Amiaud to be "bitumen." Amiaud further believed that it was brought from the neighbourhood of Sodom and Gomorrah, and he told me that he saw in the Urruda the river Jordan. That the name of the river, the first syllable of which is written with the ideograph of "man," can really be read Ur-ruda is plain from an inscription published by Dr. Scheil (*Recueil de Travaux*, XVIII, 1, 2, p. 71), where the ideograph in question interchanges with the sign for *ur*.

It must not be forgotten, however, that in most of the early texts the sign *la* has the same form as the *at* in our inscription, and that consequently we might read the name Malaqat, and compare the Dur-Malgi of Khammurabi's tablets.

(II.) In the Museum of Warwick there is a small broken half-column of black stone, the rounded portion of which is covered by a cuneiform inscription, while on the flat side is the figure of a king in relief, holding a bow in the left hand and two arrows in the right. The inscription consisted of two columns, of the first of which only a few characters remain. It is written in Babylonian characters of the 12th century B.C., which I here transcribe into ordinary Assyrian :

Column II.

1.	𒀭𒌷𒂊 𒊹 𒌋 𒐕 𒂍𒐐 𒉺 𒀸 𒌷𒁉 𒂍 𒃻
2.	𒁹 𒂍 𒉺 𒀭𒂗𒉪 𒁉 𒐕
3.	𒂍𒌋 𒁹 𒉺 𒌍 𒃻 𒉪 𒁹 𒌋 𒉿 𒂍 𒁉 𒌋
	𒉺𒌋 𒂍 𒃻
4.	𒉺 𒌷𒁉 𒂍 𒃻 𒌍 𒃻 𒂍
5.	𒉺𒌋 𒐕 𒃻 𒂍 𒐖 𒉺 𒉪 𒉺𒌋 𒂍 𒃻
6.	𒁹 𒂍 𒉺 𒀭𒂗𒉪 𒃻 𒃻 𒌋
7. . . . . . 𒐊	𒂍𒌋 𒂍 𒐖 𒌋 𒐖 𒐊 𒂍 𒐖 𒐊 𒋼
8. . . . . 𒉺	
9. . . . . . 𒂍	𒂍 𒌋 𒉺 𒀭𒂗 𒂍𒌋 𒉪 𒃻
10. . . . 𒂍 𒉿	𒁹 𒂍 𒂍 𒉺 𒂍 𒃻 𒁹 𒃻 𒉿
11. . . . . . 𒂍𒌋	𒁹 𒂍 𒁉 𒉺 𒐖 𒐊 𒂍𒌋 𒃻 𒁹 𒉺 𒌍
12. . . . . . 𒂍	𒁹 𒂍 𒌋 𒃻 𒃻 𒁹 𒂍 𒃻
13. . . . 𒐊𒉺	𒁹 𒂍 𒂍 𒃻 𒁹 𒂍 𒉺 𒂍
14. . . . . . 𒁉	𒁹𒉺𒐊𒉺𒉪𒉺 𒉺𒃻 𒉪 𒃻𒁹𒉺𒁹𒐊
15.	𒁹 𒂍(?) 𒐖 𒁉 𒁉 𒉺𒌍 𒁉 𒃻 𒃻 𒉺
16.	𒁹 𒉺 𒁉 𒂍 𒂍𒃻 𒃻 𒃻 𒁹 𒉺
17.	𒀭𒌷 𒂍 𒂍 𒂍 𒉺𒐖 𒉪 𒂍 𒐖 𒂍
18.	𒂍𒌋 𒀭𒐖 𒉺𒐊 𒊹 𒊹 𒂍𒃻 𒃻 𒀸𒐖 𒐊
19.	𒉺 𒌷𒁉 𒂍 𒃻 𒂍𒃻 𒂍𒌋 𒁉
20.	𒃻 𒂍𒌋 𒃻 𒂍𒌋 𒁹 𒉺𒌍 𒂍𒌋 𒐊 𒃻

1. iklu   xx   SE-KUL   sa   AN-Marduk-nadin-akhê
   A field of 20 gur *of corn* (*land*)   *which*   *Merodach-nadin-akhê*
   [sarru]
   [*the king*]

2. ana Iddin-AN-Nin-ip   abil
   to Iddin-Ninip   *the son*

3. sa   D.P.   AN-Sin-TUR-US-ba-sa   NIS ir-śi ri-ya . . .
   of   *Sin-pal-basa,*   *the* . . . .

71

4. AN-Marduk-nadin-akhê   sarru
    of Merodach-nadin-akhê   the king

5. ik-nu-uk-ma   a-na   khu-tal-la   [sa]
    has sealed and   for   the heritage (?)   [of]

6. D.P. Iddin-AN-Nin-ip   NIS   ir-śi-[ri]
    Iddin-Ninip   the . . .

7. arad-śu   a-na   yu-um   tsa - a - [ri iddinu]*
    his servant   for   future days   [has granted]

---

9. i-na   ka-nak   dup-pi   [an-ni]
    At   the sealing   of [this] tablet (were)

10. D.P. Er-ba-ilu-rabu   abil   D.P   Nazir-kal-sa . . .
    Erba-ilu-rabu   the son   of Nazir-kal-sa (?)

11. D.P. Ba-bi-la-â-u   abil   D.P.   AN-Sin-[lisir]
    Babilâu   the son   of Sin-[lisir]

12. D.P. Ê-[Ul-mas]-surqi-iddin   abil   D.P.   Ba-zi-[i]†
    Ê-Ulmas-surqi-iddin   the son   of Bazi

13. D.P. . . . . . su   abil   D.P.   Ê-Saggil- . .
    . . . su   the son   of Ê-Saggil- . .

14. D.P. AN-Bilu-LIL-GI-NA-TUR-US   abil   D.P.   AN-Bilu- . . .
    Bel-yukin-pal   the son   of Bel- . . .

15. [D.P. E]-a-ku-dur-ri-ib-ni   abil   D.P.   Arad-[Ea]
    [Ea]-kudurri-ibni   the son   of Arad-[Ea]

16. D.P. Nabu-nadin-akhê   abil   D.P.   Nam-[ri]
    Nebo-nadin-akhê   the son   of Nam[ri]

17. lib-ba   bit   u-na-a-tı   iz-za-az
    In   the house   of stores   it is placed

---

* Or possibly *yuzakku*, "has made free."

† E-Ulmas-surqi-iddin is also mentioned in a deed dated in Merodach-nadin-akhê's 10th year, and if, as it seems necessary to suppose, he is the E-Ulmas-surqi-iddin who founded the dynasty of Bit-Bazi, Merodach-nadin-akhê must be the 10th king of the dynasty of Isin who died, after a reign of 13 years, 52 years before the death of E-Ulmas-surqi-iddin. As the same officials appear in documents of Merodach-nadin-akhê and Bel-nadin-pal, the last 5 kings of the dynasty of Isin will have been : (7) Nebuchadrezzar I., (8) Bel-nadin-pal, (9) Merodach-nadin- . . , (10) Merodach-nadin-akhê, (11) Nebo-nadin- . . . .

18. al   Kar-AN-Bil-matâti   arkhi Âri sanat   XIII KAM
    (*in*)   *the city of Kar-Bel-matâti,   the month Iyyar,   the 13th year*

19. D.P.   Marduk-nadin-akbê   sarri   E-[ki]
              of Merodach-nadin-akhê   king   of Babylon.

20. TAK-DUB   sarri   sa   me-ri-e-ri-[su]
    The seal of   of the king,   whose (is) the figure.

Mereti, "a bas-relief," (l. 20) is from *erû*, "to carve." But Dr.
Peiser's reading *sip rêti* is also possible. The character *kar* is written
{⊠⌐ (l. 18). The *Bit unâti* (l. 17) seems to have been the record-
office ; but public stores of all kinds were placed in it : we hear, for
instance, of the *satam bit unâti* or "superintendent of the public
granary." *Babilâu* (l. 11) is an interesting form. I can throw no
light on the name of the official in ll. 3, 6.

The importance of the text lies in its mention of the 13th year
of Merodach-nadin-akbê, the contemporary of Tiglath-pileser I of
Assyria, and shows that he must have reigned at least that number
of years. The latest date of his reign hitherto met with is his 10th
year (W.A.I., III, 43, I, 28).

(III.) The Museum of Warwick contains another Babylonian
antiquity, the cylinder-seal of green stone, $1\frac{1}{2}$ inch in diameter, on
which is the dedicatory inscription of Kilulla the throne-bearer, the
son of Ur-babi, for the life of his liege lord Dungi of Ur. A copy of
the text given to me by Dr. Haigh formed the subject of my article
on "An Akkadian Seal" in the *Journal of Philology*, 1870. The
cylinder was unfortunately broken in 1895. A god is represented
upon it standing with a trident in the left hand, while the worshipper
and the priest stand before him. In Winckler's copy of the inscription (*Keilschriftiche Bibliothek*, III, 1, p. 82) the character *ka* has
been omitted in line 6 after *Ur*-KI-*ma*, the reading being *Ur*-KI-*ma-
ka-ku.*

(IV.) Certain early Babylonian contract-tablets of the age of the
"Second" (more correctly Third) Dynasty of Ur, which I have lately
been copying, are dated in the reign of "*Ri-im*-(AN) *A-nu-um* the
king." Rim-Anu must therefore be added to the rulers of Ur. It
is probable that the name influenced the Semitic subjects of Eri-Aku
in transforming his name into Rim-Sin. It is noticeable that one
of the dates I have copied is that of "the 3rd day of S'van in the
year of Rim-Anum (and) the land of Emutbalum " (*ma-da E-mu-ut-
ba-lum*).

73

(V.) In the Hermitage at St. Petersburg is a gem of Syrian workmanship on which is the figure of a god and the characters ▶◀ ▶◀ ◀, *i.e.*, the god Salim-mu, the god of Peace.   M. Clermont-Ganneau has recently pointed out (*Études d'Archéologie orientale*, in the *Bibliothèque de l'École des Hautes Études*, CXIII, Vol. II, pp. 36, 48) that the name of the same god under the form of Shalman is found on a stele discovered at Sidon, and under the form of Selamanês in the inscriptions of Shêkh Barakât, north-west of Aleppo.

(VI.) On another seal in the Hermitage (A VI, 3, 15) a god is represented standing, with a priest before him, and at the back of the priest are two smaller men placed one above the other.   The following two lines of inscription are attached :—

▶◀ 𒂍 𒐊 ◀ 𒁹	1. AN Ra-ta (?)-nu-um.
▶◀ ▶ 𒂍 ▶◀	2. AN As-ra-tum.

Asratum is the Canaanitish goddess Ashêrah, whose existence was demonstrated in the Tel el-Amarna tablets.   Ratanum ought to be the Baal who was conjoined with her, but I cannot explain the name, unless it is to be connected with Rutennu, the Egyptian name of Syria.   In this case, just as the Palestinian god who was identified with Rimmon was called Amurru, "the Amorite," by the Babylonians (Reisner, *Mittheilungen aus den orientalischen Sammlungen*, X, p. 139, l. 142), so the consort of Ashêrah might have been known to them as Ratanum, "the Rutennian."   In the Berlin tablet published by Reisner, Amurru, which is given as the Assyrian equivalent of the Accadian Martue, "the lord of the mountain," is coupled with Asratum, which is given as the equivalent of the Sumerian Gubarra, "the mistress of the plain."   For Gubarra, see my Hibbert Lectures on the *Religion of the Ancient Babylonians*, p. 211.

(VII.) The land of Zabsali or Subsalla, in the mountains of the "Amorites," of which I have spoken in my last Paper (No. I), may perhaps be identified with the Zuzim and Zamzummim of Scripture (Gen. xiv, 5 ; Deut. ii, 20), who were located in the land of Ham or Ammon.   I have pointed out elsewhere that the double form of the two names implies a cuneiform original, as a Babylonian *Zam* or *Zav* might be transcribed in Hebrew either זם or זו, while *Am* could be written either הם or עם.   A comparison of Zabsali with Samsalla, moreover, shows that the second consonant was v (w), and Sumerian l could pass into a semi-vowel.*

(VIII.) *Tuktú*, which I have left untranslated in my last Paper (No. VII), means "remains," "remnant," not "bones" as Prof. Jensen suggests. Thus in Smith's *Assur-bani-pal* we have (p. 172, l. 17) *terra tuktê abi bani-ka*, "bring back the remains of the father who begat thee," and the passage in the astronomical work must be rendered: "It is prophesied that after 30 years a remnant shall return, and the great gods shall be restored with them." The word accordingly corresponds with the Hebrew שאר, and the Assyrian expression is in close parallelism with such verses of the Old Testament as Is. x, 21 and Jer. xxv, 11, 12.

(IX.) I withdraw my explanation of the form *Amraphel* in place of *Khammurabi*, in favour of one which has just been proposed by Dr. Lindl. He considers it to stand for *Ammirabi ilu*, "Khammurabi the god." We know that many of the early Semitic kings of Babylonia, including Khammurabi himself, were deified like the Pharaohs of Egypt, and though in the cuneiform texts the title is prefixed to the name, there is no reason why it should not have followed it in the usage of the subjects of the Babylonian sovereigns in the distant West.

(X.) It is generally assumed that northern Babylonia received the name of Kar Duniyas, "the Wall of the god Duniyas," after the Kassite conquest of the country, since the name of the god (or deified king) seems to have a Kassite termination. It has even been asked whether it is not a Kassite form of the Sumerian Dungi, who was deified during his lifetime. In one of the tablets, however, relating to Kudur-Laghamar and Eri-Âku, which have been discovered by Mr. Pinches, Babylon (E-KI) is called "the city of Kar-Dunyas" (*al Kar-*AN*-Dun-ya-as*, Sp. II, 987, *Obv.*, 8), and if these texts are copied from contemporaneous documents, the name would go back to an older period than that of the Kassite domination. However this may be, the name must have been derived from a line of fortification which protected Babylonia from its enemies, and I would accordingly identify it with "the Median Wall" (τὸ Μηδίας καλούμενον τεῖχος) mentioned by Xenophon (*Anab.*, II, 4, 12), which he says "is not far from Babylon." It may be "the wall (διατείχισμα)

---

* As in *sae*, "thou," for *zale*, *mae* for *male*, "I:" see Hommel, *Zeitschrift für Keilschriftforschung*, I, 2, p. 172.

Proc. Soc. Bibl. Arch, Feb, 1897.

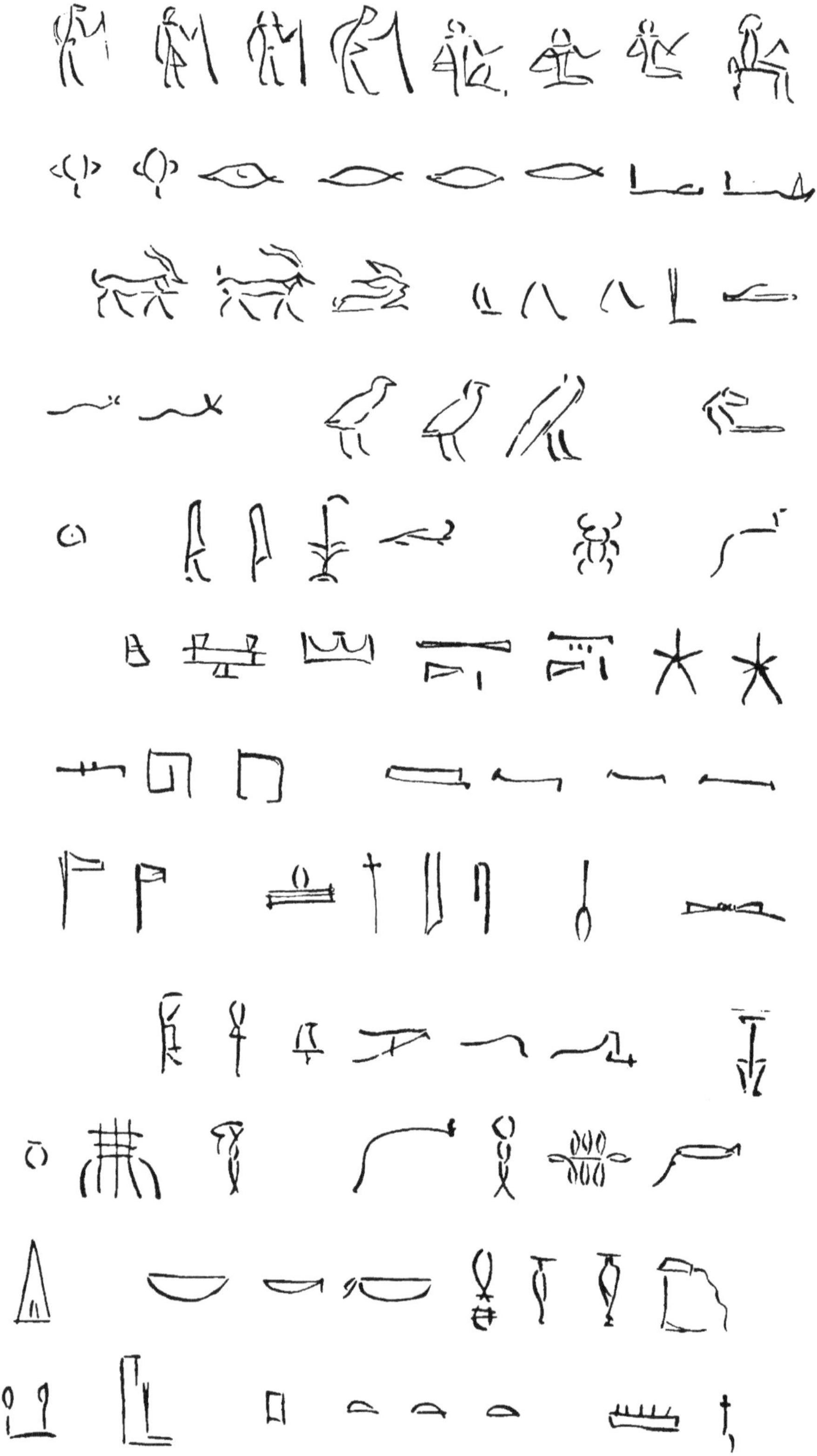

THE STELA OF DUÂ-ER-NEHEH.

Miss M. Murray.

This very interesting stela was found at Thebes by Professor Flinders Petrie, in the temple of Amenhotep II. It appears to have been thrown aside in an unfinished condition, owing to the stone being unsuitable; and it is this unfinished condition which gives the stela its peculiar interest, as we have here an example of the method of preparing a tablet for the sculptor. The inscription was rapidly sketched in by the scribe in red ink; and afterwards carefully re-drawn in black over the red, and accurately spaced. The main part of the inscription has not been re-drawn in black, but remains still in the original red ink, and it is to these hieroglyphs that I wish to draw attention. They present a fine example of the hieroglyphic, as apart from the hieratic, writing; and as the stela dates from the early part of the XVIIIth dynasty—a time when the hieroglyphs were more brilliantly and artistically rendered than, perhaps, at any other period—it seems worth while to study, from so good an example, the method which the Egyptians themselves used for forming the hieroglyphic characters, and so to learn the correct way of writing the signs rapidly and accurately. I have therefore copied all the written signs (omitting those that have been re-drawn in black), carefully imitating the characteristic brushwork. I have not repeated any sign except where there is some difference in the two examples, as in the seated man and the ḥs vase.

The Duâ-er-neheh of the stela held the titles of erpa-ha and royal chancellor, and in Champollion's "Notices" (I, 515–16 and 844) we find mention of a Duâ-i-heh ($\star$ ⌇ ⌇) who held the same titles and may possibly be the same man. That the two belonged to the same family is fairly certain from the similarity of the name, and from the fact that both had a brother, "the Uab Nebmes." As the two names are uncommon, it is evident that they would only occur together in one family, though perhaps in different generations. It is also possible that the tomb of Duâ-i-heh, described by Champollion, may be the tomb for which this stela was originally intended before the workmen discovered the faulty condition of the stone.

A description of the stela itself will appear in Professor Petrie's forthcoming book on his recent excavations at Thebes.

ASSYRIOLOGICAL NOTES.

By Professor Dr. Fritz Hommel.

§ 21. In his admirable "Handwörterbuch," Prof. DELITZSCH thinks *lubâru*, "dress," originated from *lubâšu* by rhotacism. The same form فَعَال gives us another instance for this kind of transmutation, viz., *nupâru*, "mind," which is evidently a derivate of the well-known *napištu*, "soul"; *nupâšu* became by the same manner *nupâru*, as *lubâšu* became *lubâru*. The root of *nupâru* is therefore not נבר, but נפש.

§ 22. Prof. DELITZSCH gives *nabâsu, napâsu*, very rare *nab̄ašu*, "rothgefarbte Wolle" (red wool), p. 445 of his "Handwörterbuch," and p. 426, *napâšu*, "to pick wool" (Wolle zerzupfen).

Both of these words belong originally to the same root, نفش, נבש (Aram. נְבַס, "to pick wool"), comp. the Arabic نفش, "to pick wool," نفش, "wool." The true form of the Babylonian substantive for "wool" is therefore not *nabâsu*, but *napâšu*.

For the other synonym, *ṣirpu*, "dyed wool" (*ṣarâpu*, "to dye, to colour"), may be compared the Arabic صرف *ṣirf*, "red dye," and probably too *ṣirf*, "unmixed wine" (because it has a red colour). Perhaps also أصفر *aṣfaru*, "yellow," is transposed from *aṣrafu*.

§ 23. Not seldom we have in Hebrew, Aramaic, and Arabic, *b*, where we find in Babylonian *p*, e.g., *dišpu*, "honey," דְּבַשׁ, دبس, ديس: *gapâru*, "to be strong," Hebr. גָּבַר· A new instance for this I see in the Babylonian word *piṣû*, "white" (opp., *ṣalmu*, "black"), lit. "egg-coloured," from *bîṣu*, بَيْض (*baiḍ*), בֵּיצָה, "egg"; in the same manner, as the Babylonians made *piṣû* (فِيضِي) from *pîṣu*, or *bîṣu*, بَيْض (comp. also Arab. فِضَّة, "silver"?) the Arabs formed their adjective أَبْيَض (*abyaḍ*), "white," from بَيْض, "eggs."

§ 24. The Sumerian word *ĝilib*, "god."

In W.A.I., II, 48, 28a, we read twice the ideogram 𒂍 ⟶𒀭 (i.e., *e-zil*, or perhaps *e-dun*, comp. 𒂊𒌌 *e-lum* for *e-dum*, "Bel"?) with the gloss *ĝi-li-bu*, and the translation *ilu*, "god." In the list of gods, partially published in these *Proceedings*, June, 1887 (Vol. IX, p. 377), we read:—

kadmu (ψ 68, 34)	*ilu*, "god"
digirû	*ilu, ḫilibû*
e-ne, the same (in the dialect of Su)	*nab*, the same (in the language of Elam)
malaḫum (מלך)	the same (in the language of Mar, *i.e.*, Phenicia).

Now, it is clear that *digirû* comes in the same manner from the Sumerian *dingir* (Turkish *tengri*), "god" as *ḫilibû* from another Sumerian word *ĝilib*, "god." We have here beyond doubt the old Turkish جلب *čeleb*, "lord, god" (comp. *čelebî*, "god-ful, elegant," in modern Arabic of Syria *šelebî*, "beautiful"), which expression was originally in use with the Turks of Asia Minor and Armenia, as *tengri* with the Turks of Central Asia. So the word is probably of Alarodian origin; indeed, we find in the Georgian languages the expressions *ghmerth*, *ghmerthi*, *ghormoth*,[*] and *gherbeth* (ERCKERT, "die Sprachen des kaukasischen Stammes," p. 74) for "god"— *gherbeth* being only a derivation from an old word *gherb* (comp., too, Baskian *cerub*, *ceru*, "heaven,") which, of course, is the same as Sumerian *ĝilib* and Old Turki *čeleb*. If we were allowed to read the

---

[*] Compare the element ἑρμα in Lycian names ('Ερμα-δάπιμις, etc), SACHAU, Z.A., VII. 95, and 'Αρμα-δάπιμις, and perhaps Οὐβρα-μύνασις by the side of Ὄρβις, 'Ορβα-λασήτας, and *Urballaï* (in Tabal).

above cited 𒂷 ►𒑏 *e-rib* (comp. ►𒑏 *sub* in 𒂼 ►𒑏 *mun-sub*),
we would have in Sumerian, too, an older *erib* (out of *ǧerib*) instead
of the later *ǧilib*.

In this connection it is of the greatest interest to find this old
Alarodian word *ghirib*, *ghilib*, "god,"* in some proper names of the
same region, viz., Armenia and its neighbourhood.   I think on the
well-known names—

>   *Ḳarpa-runda*, *Garpa-ruda* (גברד, *Z.A.*, VI, 432), a king
>   of Gurgum.
>
>   *Girpa-ruda*, a servant of the Khattinians in North-Western
>   Syria.
>
>   *Aḥlib-šir* (*Aḥ-li-ib-* 𒂊𒇻, servant of the god Rammân or
>   Tišup." Seal cylinder of the Berlin Museum, V.A.,
>   518), Winckler, "Geschichte Israels," p. 135, note 2,
>   and last but not least the Hethite names—
>
>   *Kherpa-sir* or *Khelpa-sir*, of the time of Ramesses II.
>
>   *Gerba-tusa*† (same time), comp. W. Max Müller, "Asien
>   und Europa," p. 332, note 2.

Finally, we see from the Aramaic transcription גברד (for
Garpa-ruda), that also *Ghipa* in the Mitannian names *Tadu-ghipa*,
Gilu-ghipa (1400 B.C.), and *Pû-ḥipa* ("queen of the Cheta,"
W. Max Müller, p. 335) was originally *Ghirpa* (like גב for
garpa), these names containing the same element *ghirpa*, "god."
Was 'Abd-ghipa of Jerusalem (1400 B.C.) generally read 'Abd-tôb,
too, a king of Alarodian (Hethitic) origin? comp. the writing
'Abd- 𒂼 -ba besides 'Abd- 𒀸 -ba, and Gen. 23, Ezech. xvi, 45.

§ 25. We see in the preceeding paragraph that the first element of
Hethitic names like *Herpa-sir*, *Aḥlib-sar* is the name of a god. So
the meaning of such names is probably " Herpa (or god) is great, or
mighty." The necessary conclusion from this is that too the other
Hethitic names ending in *-sar* or *-sir* must contain the name of a
god in their first element. We have in the time of Rameses II,
Maura-sir, father of *Kheta-sir*, both kings of the Hethites, and we
meet in the inscription of Tiglatpileser I (*c.* 1100, B.C.), 2, 44, a

---

* Quite another word is the Sumerian *ghi-li* (perhaps to pronounciate
shar-gub), joy, pride, splendour.

† Or *Gerbatu-sa*? comp. *gherbeth* above.

certain *Shadi-Teshup*, son of *Ḥattu-* ◭, i.e., *Ḥattu-shar*, king of
Uarṭinaš in the mountains of Panari (between Kilikia and Armenia);
compare in the same inscription, 2, 25, *Kili-Teshup*, son of *Kali-
Teshup*,* king of the Kurdi (*or* Kurkhi) on the Upper Tigris.

So, as the result of this investigation, we have two names of
Alarodian, respecting Hethitic gods, viz., *Maura* and *Ḥattu*. For
Maura compare NONNUS, "Dion.," 34, 188 (cited in "Zeitschrift
der Deutschen Morgenl. Gesellschaft," Vol. XXXI, p. 738), who
speaks of a Cilician god *Morrheus*, and adds that Morrheus was
only another name for Sandan. Since the Hethitic god *Tarku* is
also found in the Etruscan name Tarquinius, we may find our
Morrheus, or Maura, in the Roman (original Etruscan) *Mavor-s*,
Mars. The final *t* in Mavors (gen. Mavortis) would be the same
suffix as in Georgian *ghmer-th*, or *gherbeth*.

The other god, *Ḥattu*, is most probably the well-known god עתי
in the Lydian names Σαεϋ-αττης (comp. above *Sadi-Teshup*), Μυ-
άττης (comp. Μοα-γέτης and Μοα-φέρνης, 'Οπρα-μοας, Ηαναμύης, etc.)
and Αλυ-αττης (on the coins *Valviattes*, but originally Galvi-gate,
comp. above *Kali-Teshup*). The name of this god originally began
with a weak guttural sound; so we find him in עתרעתי (for
עשתר־עתי, i.e., Ishtar, wife of 'Ate), in Greek transcription
'Αταρ-γάτη and Δερ-κετώ (for עתר־עתי). The centre of the worship
of the god עתי was (at least in later times) in Northern Syria
(Hierapolis); moreover we find him in Cyprus (comp. the proper
noun גדעת, i.e., gad-'Ate), Damascus, Palmyra and Askalon, to
which places his adoration was brought by the Aramaeans of
Northern Syria. The Egyptians of the so-called New Kingdom
(XVIIIth dynasty) knew in Syria the gods Resheph, Ba'al, Astarte
(lady of Kadesh), and ענת (Ghannat, the goddess *Ghanna* of the
Babylonians), but not yet עתי or Khate, except in the Hethitic
nomen proprium Kheta-sir. Now it is clear that the oldest centre
of the worship of this god was not Syria, but the east of Asia Minor;
from there it came to Western Asia Minor (the Lydian god Attes, or
Attis, the Tammuz-Adonis of the mythology of Asia Minor) and to
Northern Syria (Hierapolis-Bambyke, in the neighbourhood of
Karchemis). The origin of the name is, of course, not Semitic
but Hethitic. Of great interest is also the form of the name in the
Armenian literature (comp. PAUL DE LAGARDE, "Mittheilungen,"

---

* For the god Teshup see these "Notes," § 19 (*Proceedings*, January, 1896).

Vol. I, p. 78) *Hat, Hatay, Atay* (viz., in Thara-hat, Thar-hat, Thar-hatay = Atar-gatis). At the same time, the history of this principal god of the Hethites is too the history of the spreading out of the Hethitic civilization, marked by the spots where Hethitic inscriptions have been found (Lydia, Kappadocia, Northern Cilicia, Northern Syria).

Whether the name of the land Khattu (חַת) is originally identical with the name of the god Khattu (עתי) or not, is still an open question (comp. perhaps Assur, but the land Assur is originally *A-usar*, the god Assur originally *An-šur* ►►❙ ◁, "heavenly hosts," a surname of the god Anu). I think it most probable that *Khattu* (land) originated from *Khantu;* we would so have *Khattu* besides *Khani,* like *Martu* (orig. Amartu) besides *Amurri, Subartu* besides *Subari, Elamtu* besides *Elamu. Khani, Amurri, Subari, Elamu,* are so-called nisba-forms from *Khana* (see next paragraph), *Amur, Subar, Elam* (עילם), whilst *Khattu, Subartu,* etc., are the feminine forms of the same.

§ 26. W.A.I. I, 28, 17 and following lines we read that Tiglath-pilesar I. hunted in several mountains of Assyria, of *Khana* (written: *mât Kha-a-na*), of the districts (*šid-di*) of the land of the *Lulumi,* and in the mountains of the *Naïri*-lands.

In a geographical list, W.A.I. II, 50, 69 (and add.), we read *mât Khi-a-na(-ki)*, with the explanation mat *Kha-ni-i* (comp. some lines before, mat *Mar-tu-ki*, explained by mat *A-mur-ri-i*), i.e. land Khyana, or land of the Khanites. In the following line we read *mât Lu-lu-bi*[*-ki = mat Lu-lu-bi-i*].

In the inscription of the Kassite king Agu-kak-rimi (about 1600 B.C.), W.A.I. V, 33, the statue of Bel is brought back from the "far land of the Khanites" (*a-na mâti ruk-ti a-na mât Kha-ni-i lu-u aš-pur* i.e. to . . . . I sent my ambassadors).

Moreover, in an inscription found in Abu Habba (Sippar) which belongs most probably to the time of Assur-naṣir-pal, a king of Khana itself (written *mât Kha-na*), *Tukulti-Mir,* son of *Ilu-ḳa'ish,* boasts to have given to the sun-god of Sippar some present.*

Now, this land *Khâna* or *Khyâna* is the same district as *Akhânu* in the inscription of Assurnazirpal (3, 71). He went out from Karchemis to Khazâz (the modern 'Azâz, N.W. of Haleb), marching

---

* Comp. Th. G. PINCHES, in *T.S.B.A.,* VIII, p. 352.

between the mountains *Munzigani* and *Khamurga*, and leaving the land *Akhânu** at his left side. Therefore Akhânu, or at least the western part of it, must have been situated in the northern neigh-bourhood of Haleb, where the well-known town Arpad (to-day Tell Erfâd) was placed in olden times, see the following sketch :—

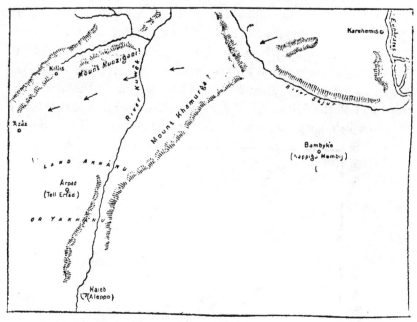

SKETCH OF THE MARCH OF ASSUR-NAZIR-PAL FROM KARCHEMIS
TO KHAZÂZ.

Concerning this Akhânu and his town Arpad, I will draw the attention to a most remarkable fact, namely, that (as HUGO WINCKLER in his " Altorientalische Forschungen," p. 8, has proved) the residence of the king *Mati-el* of *Yakhan* (dynasty of Bit-Agûsi), in the time of Tigl. III, has been the same Arpad. I conclude, therefore, that *Akhânu* is not only the fuller form of *Khâna* (comp. *Amadai* and *Madai*, *Agûsi* and *Gûsi*, *Azalla* and *Zalla*, *Atun* and *Tun*), but that also the names *Akhânu* and *Yakhan* are identical.†

In close connection with this land *Yakhânu*, *Akhânu* or *Khana* (*Khyana*) seems to stand the land *Khani-galbat* or *Khani-rabbat*.

---

* *Mât A-kha-a-nu ;* Lay. 44, 28 : *mât A-kha-nu.*

† Even in my " Geschichte Babylonicas und Assyriens," p. 581, I added to *Yakkan* in brackets : " or Yakhânu ? comp. Khana ? " For *bît Agûsi = mat Ya-kha-na-i*, see SCHRADER, " Keilinschr. u. Geschichts f., p. 207, note."

In the Tell Amarna letters we find the forms *Kha-ni-*𒂍*-bat*, *Kha-ni-*𒂍*-ba-tu-ú*, *Kha-ni-*𒈗*-bat-i*, but also the forms *Kha-na-*𒂍*-bat* and *Kha-na-*𒈗*-bat*. In the Assyrian inscriptions (Tigl. I, Assurn., Asarh.) it is always written *Kha-ni-*𒂍*-bat*. Now it is clear that this name consists of two elements, *Khani* or *Khana* (comp. above *Kha-ni-í* and *Kha-a-na*) and 𒂍*-bat*, Var. 𒈗*-bat*. 𒂍*-bat* is *gal-bat* and 𒈗*-bat kal-bat;* but 𒈗*-bat* is also *rab-bat* (comp. 𒈗 *rab* besides *rib*, W.A.I. V, 45, Col. V, line 55, *tu-kar-ràb*), and since 𒂍 is the ideogram for *rabû*, "great," as well as for *rabbu*, "great," the reading *mât khani rab-bat*, "the great land of the Khani," is the most probable one. *Rab-bat* is an adj. fem., belonging to *mâtu*, "land," whilst *galbat* would be a quite

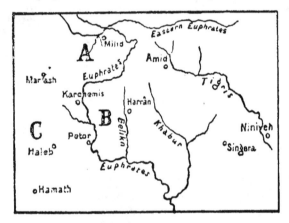

A *Kheta-'o* ("the great Kheta") of the Egypt inscriptions = *Khani-rabbat* ("the great Khani") of the Assyrian and Mitanni inscriptions.

B The land Mitanni of the Tell Amarna period (also called sometimes *Khani-rabbat*).

C The land Yakhânu (Akhânu, Khâna) of the Babylonian and Assyrian inscriptions.

unknown word. The best proof for the correctness of the reading *Khani-rabbat*, is the fact that in the same region in which we must seek *Khani-*𒂍*-bat*, or at least a part of it, namely in the neighbourhood of Malatiye (*see* below), the Egyptians knew a land *Kheta-'o*, i.e., "the great (land) of the Kheta;" comp. my "Geschichte Babyloniens und Assyriens," p. 348 and 418 (printed, 1887), W. Max Muller, "Asien und Europa" (1893), p. 320. This is at the same time a new argument for the identification of *Kheta*, *Khattu* (in the Bible בָּתִים and חִתִּים) and *Khana*.

Now let us look, what geographical position has this term Khani-rabbat in the inscriptions? In the Tell el-Amarna letters, it is a mere synonym of Mitanni; the official name of the kingdom of Dushratta was, it is true, Mitanni, but a more general signification of his land must have been Khani-rabbat. Compare the letter, B. 22, 17, "Khani-rabbat and Miṣru (Egypt) are in peace," where we necessarily expect Mitanni and Egypt. In a similar manner stands Khani-rabbat for Mitanni in the letter B. 9, 22, and in the letter B. 24, 49. We learn from this that Mitanni at least must have been a part of Khani-rabbat.

In the inscription of Shalmaneser I (c. 1300 B.C.), W.A.I. III, pl. 4, No. 1, a town Shu-un-⁂-ra (Shundura, Shungura?) of the land Kha-nt-𒂍-[....] is mentioned as situated in the neighbourhood of Kashiari (Masius) and Kirkhu; it is clear that only Khani-rabbat is meant.

Tiglatpileser I (c. 1100 B.C.) speaks of Milidia (Malatiya of to-day) as a town of the land Khani-rabbat ("Tigl.," 5, 33 ff.), whilst Assurnaçirpal receives the tribute of the "kings of Khani-rabbat" ("Assurn.," 2, 21) during his sojourn in the towns of the land Kirkhi (north-east of Amid or Diarbekr). In the Vannic inscriptions of king Argistis and his son Sarduri, the king Khilaruada * of Milidia is set in close connection with Khâti, or Khatina; † comp. above, Milidia and Khani-rabbat.

The last mention of Khani-rabbat is found in the cylinder C of Esarhaddon; when his father Sennacherib was murdered, Esarhaddon stood with his army in Khani-rabbat, where he defeated the army of his hostile brothers. Berosos names an otherwise unknown town Bizana in Western Armenia as the locality of the battle (comp. E. SCHRADER, Keilschr. u. Geschichtsforschung, p. 531); the Bible (2 Kings, xix, 37) gives Ararat (Assyr. Urartu) as the land into which the brothers fled.

Finally I should like to remark that (though Khattu and Khani-rabbat seem originally to be mere synonyms) in the Tell Amarna letters, as well as in the Assyrian inscriptions, Khattu is a geographical term different from Khani-rabbat. In the historical texts

* Or Khite-ruada (comp. Girpa-ruda?). Another king of Milidia, mentioned in the Vannic inscriptions, is Suli'a-uali = Sulumal of Milid (JENSEN, Recueil, XVIII, 114).

† Compare Khattin (𒄷 -ti-in) of the Assyrian inscriptions.

of the Assyrian kings, Khattu is the kingdom of Karchemis, some
time in a wider sense the whole Northern Syria, whilst Khani-
rabbat seems to be only the most northern part of the latter, including, especially, Milidia.   In the Tell el-Amarna letters, Khani-
rabbat is the same as Mitanni (between Euphrates and Belikhos),
whilst Khattu, at least politically, is different from it.   So Dushratta
relates (l. 9, 30 ff.) that the king of the land Khattu (*mât Kha-at-ti*)
had invaded his (Dushratta's) territory, and that the god of Mitan
delivered him into his hand, so that the Hethite king was slain by
Dushratta.*   In l. 5, 49 the king of Alashia (probably Cyprus)
warns the Pharaoh not to make any friendship with the king of
Khattu and with the king of *Shankhar* (Singara in Eastern Mesopotamia).   According to a letter of *Rabi-Mur* (otherwise called
Rib- ⊳⊷⟅ ◁⟊⧧⟅) of Gebal, the king of *Khattu* and the king of
Narima (אַרַם נַהְרִים) are the helpers of a certain Itakama of
Kinza, and Ḳidsha (Kadesh) in his attack against the cities of *Amki*
(*mât Am-ki* = عَمق or *Khattin* on the banks of the Orontes?)   In
another letter of the same prince of Gebal (B. 79), "the king of
Khatu, and the king of *Mittan,* and the king of *Naḥrima,*" are said
to have captured all the lands of *Kutiti* (=*Ḳode,* W. MAX MÜLLER,
"Asien u. Europa," p. 242, f.?).   Besides Amki, we see (according
to many of these letters) especially Nukhassi and Amurru (in
Cœlesyria), threatened by the invasions of the "king of the land
Khattu."   It is strange that no mention is made in the whole
Tell el-Amarna correspondence of *Karchemis;* perhaps Karchemis
belonged to Mitanni, or it was the residence of the king of Naharim,
whilst the land of the king of Khatti can only be sought for more
northwards (Mar'ash and Eastern Cappadocia, and perhaps including
too a part of Cilicia).

     To sum up the foregoing results (which are for the most part in
direct contradiction to Prof. JENSEN's assertions in *Zeitschr. d.
Morgenl. Gesellsch.,* Vol. XLVIII), we have found—

     a. Khattu (Kheta, עַתִּי, Attes), the name of a principal god of
Asia Minor from Lydia to the borders of Armenia and even to
Northern Syria (Karchemis) ;

     b. The element *Khani, Khana* in Khani-rabbat, is the same as
Khyana, Khana, Khani, which we find south-westwards from

---

     * Perhaps this victory gave the occasion for calling henceforth Mitan
Khani-rabbat ?

Karchemis—Khani-rabbat and Khana both being countries which were reckoned by the Assyrian inscriptions to the great land Khattu and both countries in which were found hieroglyphic (non-Semitic) inscriptions of the so-called Hethitic style ;

c. Khani-rabbat ("great land of Khani"), in its geographical position almost the same as *Kheta-'ō* ("great land of the Kheta") of the Egyptian inscriptions, so that Khana and Khattu are at least identical terms, if not the same words (*Khattu* from *Khantu*), though the latter identification can only be suggestive at present. Perhaps the existence of the great Hethitic god Ghati gave occasion to the Semites of Western Asia to transform *Khana*, the oldest name of the Hethitic people, to *Khanti*, resp. *Khatti ;* this must have happened even before 2000 B.C., to which time belongs the first mention of the Hethites, viz., in the astronomical work of the Babylonians (W.A.I. III, 60, 37 and 38, where we find both expressions, *shar mât Kha-a-ti* and *shar mât Kha-at-ti*).

§ 27. *Tuktû*, "blood, vengeance"= ﭏﭏﭏ (*tektô*) "blood (of the woman)" :

In the astronomical work of the Babylonians, W.A.I. III, 61, 21, we read : *Ummân-Manda itbâ-ma mâta ibîl, parakki ilâni rabûti innasiḫû, Bel ana mât Elamti alâka iḳbî, ina XXX šanâti tuk-tu-ú ut-tar-ru, ilâni rabûti itti-šunu iturrû*, i.e., " The Ummân-Manda shall come and possess the land, the sanctuaries of the great gods will be destroyed, the god Bel gives order to go to Elam (= his statue will be brought by the enemies to Elam), after thirty years they (the Babylonians) shall take vengeance, the great gods will return with them (back to Babylonia)." HUGO WINCKLER, in his "Altoriental. Forschungen," III (Leipsic, 1895), cites this passage, p. 239, note, translating the words *tuktû uttarrû*, by "wird man die *tuktu* zurückbringen"; but, p. 252, reviewing JENSEN's translation of Assurb. Cyl. B, 7, 18, *tirra tuk-ti-i abi banî-ka*, "bring back the bones of the father, thy begetter," he proposes a much better translation, viz., "Spolia oder Rache (vengeance)." That *turru tuktî* can only be translated "take vengeance" (syn. *turru gimilli*), will be clear by the following, but the original meaning of *tuktû* is, as the Ethiopic *tektô* proved, "blood" (comp. בְּקֵשׁ דָּם, "to take vengeance," lit., require the blood).

In the new discovered stele of Nabonid, published by Pater

SCHEIL, Recueil, XVIII, we read, Col. 2, 11 ff., *utir gimillu Tin-tir-(ki), i-ri-ba tuk-ti-i shar Umman-manda*. Pater SCHEIL translates: "il vengea Babylone, Iriba-tukte, roi des Umman-manda"; but the only right translation is that of M. L. MESSERSCHMIDT, "Die Inschrift der Stele Nabu-na'id's," Berlin, 1896, p. 25, "er rächte Babylon, mehrte die Vergeltung, der König der Umman-manda," etc. Even before the book of MESSERSCHMIDT was published, I wrote to several friends (*e.g.* to Dr. LEHMANN, in Berlin), as my own translation, "er rachte Babylon und nahm Vergeltung" (*iriba*, being so-called imperf. of continuation ending in *a*, and to be derived from a root רִיב, comp. 1 Sam. 25, 39) "der König der Umman-manda," thinking that Nabonid proposed to make an allusion (by a kind of pun) to Arbakes, whom Ktesias says to be the conqueror of Nineveh; at the same time I quoted the passage of a hymn published by Mr. STRONG in the "Journal Asiatic," 1893, May—June, line 17: *ana shakan gimilli u turri tukti* (written *tur-ri tuk-ti-i*), "um zu rächen und Vergeltung zu nehmen." But perhaps Mr. MESSER-SCHMIDT is more right with his translation of *iriba*, "he increased (vengeance)," than I with my etymology (*iriba*, from רִיב), for he cites, p. 43, a parallel name, given to him by Dr. PEISER, viz., *Nabu-tukti-irba* (Nerigl., 55, 3, 4, EVETTS, p. 68); because this name has the same verb as the well-known name *Sin-akhi-irba*, and similar names ending in -irba, also *iriba tukti* in the Nabonid-stele must come from *iribu* (יִרְב) "to increase," and not from רִיב to quarrel.

I am now in a position to give another proper name, in which *turru tukti* means clearly, "to take vengeance," viz. *Nabû-tuk-ti-i-tir-ri*, STRASSMAIER, Cyrus, No. 292, line 16 (reprinted and transl. in SCHRADER's "Keilinschr. Bibl.," IV, pp. 280 and 281), comp. the name of the eponym *Assur-gi-mil-tir-ri* (K. 382, in K. 364 written ideographically Aššur 𒂗 𒁷, BEZOLD, "Catalogue," Vol. I, p. 92).

§ 28. In a contract of the time of Sennacherib, W.A.I. III, 48, No. 3, a woman is called *Amat-𒂗 Su-'u-la* (*i.e.* handmaid of the god or goddess *Su'la*). Now this otherwise unknown deity Su'la can be nothing other than the Arabic demon سِعْلاة, or سِعْلاة, or سِعْلي (*si'lâ*) of the old Arabic poetry, comp., e.g., *Hamâsa*, 25, 3

(p. ٦٨), plur. السَّعالِى (as-sa'âlî), or *Labîd*, 41, 12, 20 (women like evil ghosts), or *Imrulḳais*, 53, 2, or *Mufaḍḍaliyât*, 23, 38.

§ 29. In the *Collection de Clercq*, Vol. II, Pl. X, No. 6, the following inscription is published (in archaic characters, about 4000 B.C.), which I translate as follows :—

[cuneiform]	"To the god En-ki-gal
[cuneiform]	Ur-Num-ma
[cuneiform]	king of Te
[cuneiform]	son of En-à-ab-she-rak (?)
[cuneiform]	king of Te
[cuneiform]	has built this temple."

The characters are quite clear ; the two (or three ?) last characters in line 4 are [cuneiform], which is perhaps [cuneiform] instead of [cuneiform]; [cuneiform] seems to be a compound of [cuneiform] *she*, and of [cuneiform] *rak*, or *shal*. For the country or town [cuneiform] (without *ki*, written only [cuneiform]), compare *irṣit Te-ki sha ki-rib Din-tir-ki** in a contract tablet, published by Pater STRASSMAIER (Liverpool Collection, No. 136 and 149), and perhaps [cuneiform] (W.A.I. II, 53, 5*a*), a name, as it seems, of Erech ([cuneiform]). Of great interest are the names of the gods *En-ki-gal* (of course Nergal as consort of Nin-ki-gal) and [cuneiform], in which I see an older form of Anum (comp. Nun, Num, fuller forms Anun, Anum).

M. MENANT gives the following transliteration and translation (*Collection de Clercq*, II, p. 92) :—

An En-ki-gal	Au grand dieu de la terre
Ur-An-Ḥum-ma (?)	Avil-Ea (?)
Lugal Te	Roi de Te (?)
Tur En-it- . . . . . *in*	fils de Bel-it- . . . . . in
Lugal Te	Roi de Te
E-mu-na-ni	a construit cc Temple.

and cites for Te the passage of the contract tablet.

---

* Comp. *Tema* in the annals of Nabonid (written *te-ma-a*) ?

89

§ 30. In Sc. 289 we read *i-mi*, ◁╫, *a-ḫu* and *ṭi-ṭu* (written di-du).   *Ṭiṭu* is "loam, clay, vessel of clay (syn. *ḳadûtu*, comp. طينة), tablet of clay."   Now it seems to me very probable, that *aḫu* is here not "border, coast" (so DELITZSCH, "Handwörterbuch," p. 40), or "brother," but Heb. אָח (Jer. xxxvi, 22), "brasier," specially for incense.   May we too compare Egypt. *ḫau-t*, *ḫaui*, *ḫ-t* (Copt. ϢΗΟⲦⲈ, ϢΗΟⲦⲒ), βωμός, "altar," and South Arab. (Minaean) خبى, خوهت, "censer" (Eth. ሰዉ, "fire")?

THE ROLLIN PAPYRI AND THEIR BAKING CALCULATIONS.

By Prof. Dr. August Eisenlohr.

(*Sent in* 1 *November*, 1895.)

A long while ago (1868) Mr. W. Pleyte at Leiden published the Rollin Papyri of the then Imperial, now National Library at Paris, and gave a kind of commentary and translation of them. Soon afterwards the skilful explanator of hieratic papyri, Mr. F. Chabas, made in the *Aegyptische Zeitschrift* (1869, p. 85 ff., "Sur quelques données des Papyrus Rollin") some very useful and ingenious remarks on Pleyte's work. My inclination for all kinds of ancient reckoning induced me also to study the same work. But forthwith I recognized that many faults must have glided in Pleyte's edition of the papyri. So, stopping on my way home from London a few days at Paris in 1872, I went to the library, and through the kindness of Dr. Derenbourg I was able to make a close comparison of Pleyte's edition with the original text. I found in the former so many differences that I consider it more as a free copy than a facsimile of the original.

For a long time it was my intention to publish and comment on in connection with the Rhind mathematical papyrus other documents of numerical character, the Edfu field donations, the Papyrus Louvre 3226 and the Rollin papyri. But every time I was preparing something of that kind I was forestalled by another. So in the Edfu field donations (on which I read a paper at the Leyden Oriental Congress) by Professor H. Brugsch in his *Thesaurus*, III, p. 531 ff., and by the same author with regard to the Louvre papyrus in *Thesaurus*, V, 1079. Still the explanation of the last document is in such a manner insufficient that I shall give a better

one at another occasion. To prevent a work of considerable time
being again over-run by another,[1] I give now what I have to correct
in Pleyte's edition of the Rollin Papyri, and what I brought out in
the explanation of their texts.

Of the twenty plates of Pleyte's edition I neglect wholly Pl. XV
(No. 1887) and Pl. XVI (No. 1888), because they contain quite
different subjects; Pl. XV is a praise to the honour of Amenophis II,
and Pl. XVI belongs to the judiciary document of Turin, which was
published and commented upon by Devéria in the *Journal Asiatique*,
1867, treating of a conspiracy in the hareem of Ramses (ḥek an) III.
Devéria gives Pl. V of his work a mended text of Rollin XVI and a
translation of it (p. 130).

As the numbers of the Rollin Papyri have been, since Pleyte's
publication, several times changed in the National Library at Paris,
I give the references of the corresponding numbers.

No. 1882 (Pleyte, I–IV) was afterwards 210–213.

No. 1883 (not in Pleyte's tables) was afterwards 209.

No. 1884 (Pleyte, V–IX) was afterwards 208 (V–VI) and 207
(VII–IX).

No. 1885 (Pleyte, X–XIV) was afterwards 204 (X–XII) and 206
(XIII, XIV).

No. 1886 (not in Pleyte's tables) was afterwards 203.

No. 1887 (Pleyte, XV) was afterwards 202.

No. 1888 (Pleyte, XVI) probably 201.

No. 1889 (Pleyte, XVII–XX) was afterwards 205.

To our investigation are now remaining from Pleyte's work:
1. Pl. V–IX (1884, V, VI = 208; VII–IX = 207). 2. Pl.

---

[1] At the time this article was put in type, appeared Dr. Spiegelberg's
Rechnungen aus der Zeit Seti I (K. Trubner. Strassburg, 1896). Bd. I,
Text und Commentar; Bd. II, 43 Tafeln, 70 Mark. This work treats of not
only the baking calculations of the Rollin Papyri, but also the other reckonings
of timber, etc. As I differ from the author's views in some essential points,
I let my text stand as it was, and only briefly point out the different views of
Dr. Spiegelberg. For the correction of the text, the five heliotype plates by
Mr. Chassinat, in the work alluded to, are of importance. Unfortunately, they
contain only Pleyte's Pll. X—XIV, and XVII—XX, but not Pll. V—IX. All
the other plates are only copies after the original, like Pleyte's and my own
revised ones. As Dr. Spiegelberg's edition is much more reliable than Pleyte's,
I refer to it instead of giving my own corrections, there being difficulties in
printing them.

X–XIV (1885, X, XI, XII = 204; XIII, XIV = 206). 3. Pl. XVII–XX (1889 = 205).

To these are to be added the fragmentary two plates, of which Pleyte has not given the facsimile, 1883 = 209, and 1886 = 203.

These different plates form, corresponding to their contents, different sections. Pl. V–IX and X–XIV form the first part, to which belong also 1883 (209). Pl. XVII–XIX, which are pasted on

the same card-board in the following order $\frac{19 \mid 18}{20 \mid 17}$, form a second

part, and 1886 = 203, very defective, does not treat of baking but of the providing the poultry-yard[1] 🐦 of Seti I with geese, and is dated in the third year of the same monarch.

The two sections of the first part, Pleyte, Pl. V–IX and Pl. X–XIV, treat of the baking of different kinds of loaves, but by the same bakers ; the first section the baking of only small loaves, called *kelešta*, weighing $3\frac{1}{2}$–4 ten (= 316–362 grammes); the second the baking of larger loaves (*ākuu*) weighing about $13\frac{1}{2}$ ten (= $1\frac{1}{4}$ kilg.). Pl. XII, and the reception of both kind of loaves in the magazine

of the royal court 🦅🦅🦅🦅,

pa ut'a en chennu, Pl. XIII, 10. To this is added on Pl. XI a reckoning of sacks of corn into loaves. Belonging to this date, the first section (Pl. V–IX) is dated only in the month of Thoth (5–23) of probably the second year, while Pl. XII, XIII and X, beginning with the second Thoth, runs through this and the following months to the fourth month (Choiak) of the first season. Pl. XIV in the same section is dated year 2, *Mesori* 23 of the King Seti I. Papyrus 1883 is also dated of the second year, and contained the names of the same bakers as the above. The king's household was not staying at the same place, but moving about, so we find it (XII, 1, XIV, 3) in Memphis, Pap. 209, as also Pleyte, *Rollin*, Pl. I, 1, in Heliopolis, Pl. XIII, 1,

🦅[2], travelling on the

---

[1] Dr. Spiegelberg's Text, p. 34, corrected this after Gr. Harris 28, 2 ; 48, 1, in 🦅.

[2] Spiegelberg reads 🦅 rut, "district." Though the first signs look more like 🦅, I adopt Spiegelberg's reading (*vide ib.* Text, p. 44).

western road; Pl. XVII, 3, , travelling in the northern district.

After these general remarks we now enter on the translation and explanation of the text.

TRANSLATION AND COMMENTARY OF PLATES V—IX.

PLATE V.

1. *Thoth 5.*[1] *Account of the receipt of the bakers in flour*
2. *for making kelešta bread, each of four ten to three ten*[2] *and a half.*

The missing year is doubtless the second year of Seti I, which we see commemorated XII, 1; XVII, 1. The word *ḥannu*  is met in the same phrase, XII, 2. It signifies different labours, especially in the field, but in connection with the following it must signify "receipt." The determinative of *ḥannu* is to be corrected according to XII, 2. The word 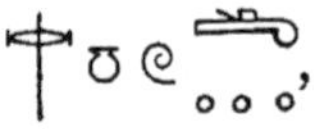, "flour," has been known for a long time. XII follows *er kefennu* for baking.

On *kelešta*, compare Herodot., II, 77, κυλλήστις (*cf.* Chabas, *Zeitschr.*, 1869, p. 67) made of ὄλυρα, spelt or *durra* (*sorghum vulgare*), which gives a tasteful bread (Kremer, *Aegypten*, I, p. 202; *cf.* Wiedemann, in Herodot., XXXVI, p. 158).[3] The word 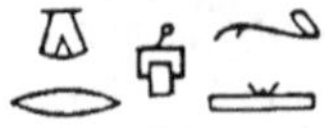 seems to be mended in 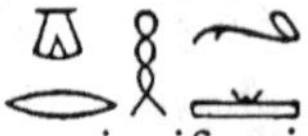. If it has not here (also Pl. XII 1) the unknown signification of *two* (in German *bis*), we must think on the verb ḳerḥ, "finish"

..... is written in red ink in the original. Pll. V and VI = Spiegelberg, Tafel VIII.

[2] Spiegelberg reads always  *deben*, but without sufficient reason. The word *ten*, written in the same manner, is met so often in the Great Harris Papyrus, and in the acts of silver robbery (Pap. Harris, No. 1, 498-9; Pap. Vasalli, and others of the British Museum).

[3] Indian corn, *Zea mais*, is now much planted in Egypt (Kremer, I, 190–194), but probably later introduced from Persia or even America.

(Br., *W.*, p. 1518), so that the unbaked bread weighs 4, the baked only 3½ ten, *i.e.*, 316 grammes. Before the number we must restore ⌒ ▭. The word (here) is met with in the didactical piece on the misery of different trades in comparison to that of the scribe or learned man. From the two copies in which this piece is found (1 Sallier, VII, 7; 2 Anastasi, VIII, 3) we borrow the following phrase, which demonstrates dramatically the work and the calamity of a baker:

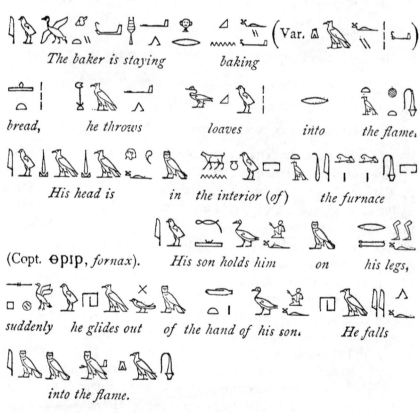

The baker is staying   *baking* (Var.)

bread,   *he throws*   *loaves*   *into*   *the flame.*

His head is   *in the interior (of)*   *the furnace*

(Copt. ⲑⲣⲓⲡ, *fornax*).   *His son holds him*   *on*   *his legs,*

suddenly   *he glides out*   *of the hand of his son.*   *He falls*

into the flame.

cf. Maspero, "Du Genre Epistolaire," p. 36.

V, 3. *That day.*

4. *Baker.*

5. *The baker T'at'a receives on flour tep sacks* 3,[1] *gives keleśta* 602, *rest* 28, *rest of* han 78½¼.

---

[1] Spiegelberg, 3½.

6. *The baker Chara receives flour* 2½, *gives keleŝta* 290,[1] *rest* 25,
    rest of 🐦 77.

7. *The baker.*   8. *Sum.*

There are mentioned in this and the following plates only four bakers, whose names are:— 𓅃 𓅃 ⊚ 🐦 *T'af'a*, verbally Head, 𓅃 ⊂ | 🐦 [2] *Chara*, the Syrian, ⌐ ʊ ℮ ⊙ 𓂀 | 𓎼 🐦 *Nennuamon* (who regards Amon), and 𓉔 ○ ◎ 𝕭 🐦 *Anchtu.*

The signs ⌐ [3] are known as the hieratic form of ⬛ *ŝop*, besides ⌒, the Egyptian palm; here they seem to represent the word 𓈖 *ŝop* to receive. ⌇ is often found in the Mathematical Papyrus as a corn measure; but here is ⌇ without doubt ϾΙΚε, molere, hierogl. 𓏤 ⌇ geschrieben. Br., Wort., 1325, Cont. 1140.

We can approximately determine the weight and the volume of the *tep saik* measure from the accounts given here and on Pl. XII. Line 15 of Pl. V we may take as an average production of keleŝta bread. Here 2½ tep sacks give 430 keleŝta and a rest of 20 + 59 = 79. Adding these last to 430, we have 509 keleŝta from 2½ tep sacks. Now the keleŝta are, as is told V, 2 from 3½ to 4 ten, and as we have here from the same amount of flour a higher number of breads than Pl. VI, we must presume that these breads had the lower weight, *i.e.*, 3½ ten. Now $509 \times 3½ = 1781$, 5 ten, divided by 2, 5 gives 712[4] ten for each tep sack. Pl. XII, 3 are made from 3½ tep sacks 168 great loaves (âkeku), which have a weight of 13½ ten with a loss of 1½ ten for baking, *i.e.*, $15 \times 168 = 2520$, divided by 3½ gives 720 ten for each tep sack. The *ten* reckoned to 90·46 grammes (Eisenlohr, *Math. Papyrus*, p. 206) gives for the tep sack the weight of 65 kilogr. and a litre flour weighing about 442 grammes (*cf.* Göriz, *Betriebslehre*), the volume of a tep sack is a little more than 147 litres or 4 English bushels.

[1] Spiegelberg omits this number, p. 16.
[2] Spiegelberg transcribes these names in the faulty Berlin fashion, Dod and Hor.
[3] Omitted by Spiegelberg, Tafel VIII.
[4] Considering the loss of weight in baking, 1/15 (see Pl. XII), the weight of the tep sack would rise to 790 ten.

In Pl. V and VI we find after each amount of *kelešta* noted two rests, of which the second is called ⏉ 〰 ⏉ *ut'a en han* (this alone Pl. VII and VIII).   If this ⏉ is an abbreviation of the ⏉ (above l. 1), and means the bread still in work or to be baked, or anything other, I ignore.   As they are added together V, 13, 18 (after my correction of line 18, end, we read there ⏥ loaves), we must add both, as we did above, to the number of kelešta, for determining the weight of a tep sack of flour.   Probably the first rest are loaves already baked, the other (〰 ⏉) still unbaked bread, dough.

9. *Thoth, day 6.*

10. *The baker T'at'a, flour tep sacks* $2\frac{1}{2}$*, gives kelešta* 440, *rest* 10, *rest of dough* $53\frac{1}{4}$.[1]

11. *The baker Chara,*   „   *sacks* $2\frac{1}{2}$*, gives kelešta* 450, *rest* 10, *rest of han* 67.

12. *The baker Nennuamon,*   „   *sacks* $2\frac{1}{2}$*, gives kelešta* 430, *rest* 20, *rest of han* $37\frac{1}{2}\frac{1}{4}$.

13. *Sum. Flour . . . . tep sacks* $7\frac{1}{2}$*, gives kelešta* 1310, *rest* 40, *rest of han* 158, *together* 198.

The real sum of the kelešta is not 1310, but 1320,[2] as Pleyte changed the number of the original 10.

14. *Thoth, day 7.*

15. *The baker T'at'a, flour tep sacks* $2\frac{1}{2}$*, gives kelešta* 430, *rest* 20, *rest of han* 59.

16. *The baker Chara* „ *tep sacks* $2\frac{1}{2}$*, gives kelešta* 430, *rest* 20 *rest of han* $57\frac{1}{2}\frac{1}{4}$.

17. *The baker Nennuamon,* „ *tep sacks* $2\frac{1}{2}$*, gives kelešta* 432, *rest* 20, *rest of han* $55\frac{1}{2}\frac{1}{4}$.

18. *Sum. Flour . . . . tep sacks* $7\frac{1}{2}$*, gives kelešta* 1290, *rest* 60, *rest of han* $172\frac{1}{2}$.

The account is in perfect accord.   *together rest loaves* $232\frac{1}{2}$.

[1] Spiegelberg, Tafel VIII, omits this line.
[2] Spiegelberg reads 1310.

PLATE VI.

1. *Thoth, day 9.*
2. *The baker T'at'a ground flour tep sacks* $2\frac{1}{2}$*, gives kelešta 365, rest* $17\frac{1}{2}$*, rest of ḥan* $52\frac{1}{4}\frac{1}{8}$*.*
3. *The baker Chara ground flour tep sacks* $2\frac{1}{2}$*, gives kelešta 365, rest* $17\frac{1}{2}$*, rest of ḥan 28.*
4. *The baker Nennuamon ground flour tep sacks* $2\frac{1}{2}$*, gives kelešta 360,[1] rest* $17\frac{1}{2}$*, rest of ḥan* $36\frac{1}{2}$*.*
5. *The baker Anchtu ground flour tep sacks* $2\frac{1}{2}$*, gives kelešta 365,[2] rest* $17\frac{1}{2}$*, rest of ḥan* $22\frac{1}{2}\frac{1}{4}$*.*
6. *Sum ground flour tep sacks* $8\frac{1}{2}$*, gives kelešta 1360, rest 70, rest of ḥan 139, together* $209\frac{1}{2}\frac{1}{4}\frac{1}{8}$*.*

4. In the original only 360, which Pleyte corrected to 365, so he brings out a o in the sums of breads. But this sum is 1360[3] in the original instead of 1460, which was corrected by Pleyte. We find here line 5 for the first time, the fourth baker called Anchtu. Pleyte gives him only 1 sack, while the original has $2\frac{1}{2}$, the sum $8\frac{1}{2}$ confirms Pleyte's correction. The fractions $\frac{1}{2}$, $\frac{1}{4}$, $\frac{1}{8}$, are only in the total sum. As above I join ⃒ ⚹ ÇIKE, *molere*, to flour, not to the tep sacks.

7. *Thoth, day 10.*
8–11. *Deest.*
12. *Brought by these kelešta . . . , 100, rest 1·8 rest of ḥan, 785[4] together rest.*
13. *Different loss[5] by the hands of the bakers and confectioners 100.*

---

[1] Spiegelberg reads 365.

[2] Spiegelberg, Pl. VIII, Col. 2.

[3] Spiegelberg has 1460.

[4] Spiegelberg, 788.

[5] Instead of Pleyte's ✕ ⌷ △ 🦉 ⌇ Spiegelberg has Tafel VIIIb, ✕ ⃒⌒℮ 𝄞 ⌇ ..... ⚹ 〰 , which he translates : "Einzelangabe der Restbetiage der Bäcker nach ihrem Namen." For the meaning of ✕ ⃒⌒ he gives good proofs, p. 52, of his own commentary.

L. 12, the numbers in this line are very uncertain, so I could not see Pleyte's 20 in 128.

The 5 in 785 is indistinct, and all the rest of the line obscure. The last word in l. 13 is probably ⟨glyphs⟩ corresponding to ⟨glyphs⟩ cf. Louvre Pap. 3226, Brugsch, *Wörtb. Contin.*, S. 277. It appears as an apposition to *chennu*, bakers; line 13 closes with 100.

> 14. *The baker T'at'a ground flour tep sacks* $12\frac{1}{2}$,[1] *mill sacks* $1\frac{3}{4}$, *gives keleśta* 2177, *rest* $85\frac{1}{2}$, *rest of han* 264[2] $\frac{1}{2}$ $1\frac{3}{8}$, *together in breads (hotep')* 33. $\frac{1}{8}$.

Pleyte made $65\frac{1}{2}$ instead of the $85\frac{1}{2}$ of the original, because only so he got the sum of 330 with the 264 $\frac{1}{2}$ $\frac{1}{4}$. The last number of 33. and the fractions before $\frac{1}{8}$ are not to be seen more.

> 15. *The baker Chara ground flour tep sacks* $10\frac{3}{4}$, *mill sacks* $1\frac{1}{4}$, *gives keleśta* 2075,[3] *rest* $137\frac{1}{2}$, *rest of han* $251\frac{3}{4}$, *together breads* 389 $\frac{1}{4}$.
>
> 16. *The baker Nennuamon ground flour tep sacks* $10\frac{3}{4}$, *mill sacks* $1\frac{3}{4}$, *gives keleśta* 2135, *rest* $82\frac{1}{2}$, *rest of han* 228, *together breads* $310\frac{1}{2}$.

To choose between ⟨glyph⟩ and ⟨glyph⟩ we miss here the heliotype. But as the following list contains not only the rest, but also a summary of all that has been delivered ⟨glyph⟩, and what remained in the foregoing days ⟨glyphs⟩ would be more adequate than ⟨glyphs⟩. How far it is founded to make a difference between ⟨glyphs⟩ and ⟨glyphs⟩ (Spiegelberg, Com. p. 39 "feingemahlenes and grobgemahlenes Noitkorn"), that would well explain the special record of these last, I cannot decide. But I think that Spiegelberg's translation of nut' with "Noitkorn," instead of the well-known meaning "flour," is surely erroneous, as his replacing the sack ⟨glyph⟩ by ⟨glyph⟩, which is found in the Pap. Louvre 3226, and in the Med. Abu Kalendar. There the ⟨glyph⟩ is a measure of 4 bescha (Pap. Louvre) and of 16 bescha = 18 and 72 liter, only the $\frac{1}{10}$ part of our flour measure.

[1] Spiegelberg reads $10\frac{1}{2}$ $\frac{1}{4}$.
[2] Spiegelberg omits the 4 and adds "im Ganzen," rest (not bread), 350 $\frac{1}{4}$ $\frac{1}{8}$.
[3] Spiegelberg reads 3075, in no accordance with the number of sacks.

13. *Thoth* 15.

14. *Thoth* 16.

15. *The baker T'at'a ground flour tep sacks* $1\frac{3}{4}$, *gives kelešta* 360, *rest loaves* (?).[1]

16. *The baker Chara ground flour tep sacks* $1\frac{3}{4}$, *gives kelešta* [3]255 *rest* 30 (?).

17. *The baker Nennuamon ground flour tep sacks* $1\frac{3}{4}$, *gives kelešta* 280.

18. *The baker Anchtu ground flour tep sacks* $1\frac{3}{4}$, *gives kelešta* 280.

19. *Sum ground flour tep sacks* 7, *gives kelešta* 1275,[2] *each of* 4 *ten coming out of the oven.*[3]

The end of l. 15 seems to be *hotepu*, but the number is not clear. The sum l. 19: 1275 asks a hundred more in the numbers, perhaps 355, l. 16, instead of 255. is coming forth from the oven. The rest is to be completed from Pl. VIII 2, where *t'a* may signify "received."[4]

PLATE VIII.

1. *Thoth day* 17.

2. *The baker T'at'a ground flour sacks* $2\frac{1}{2}$,[5] *gives kelešta* 120, *each of* 4 *ten in coming from the oven, received kelešta* 312[6] *each of* $3\frac{1}{2}$ *ten in coming from the oven.*

3. *The baker Chara ground flour sacks* $1\frac{3}{4}$, *gives kelešta* 130, *each of_____ received_____* 205 *_____together.*[7]

4. *The baker Nennuamon ground flour sacks* $1\frac{3}{4}$, *gives kelešta* 200 each of 50_____rest 50.

[1] Spiegelberg, Tafel VIII, has, after 360, , each of 4 ten, when baked.

[2] Spiegelberg, 1175.

[3] Spiegelberg repeats here : rest 30 the number crossed here and l. 16.

[4] Spiegelberg transcribes his indistinct sign nem, "ferner."

[5] Spiegelberg, $2\frac{1}{4}$.

[6] Spiegelberg, 313.

[7] This whole line is in Spiegelberg given to Nennuamon, but $2\frac{1}{2}$ for $1\frac{3}{4}$, 210 instead of 205, and Chara omitted ; in the following lines no numbers.

5. *The baker Anchtu ground flour sacks* 1¾, *gives* . . .
6. *Sum*   *sacks.*
7. *Thoth.*
8. *The baker T'at'a ground flour sacks* 2, *gives keleŝta* 350, *rest of ḥan* 30½.[1]
9. *The baker Chara ground flour sacks* 1½,[2] *gives keleŝta* 300.
10. *The baker Nennuamon ground flour sacks* 1⅓,[3] *gives keleŝta* 350, *rest of ḥan* 30.[4]
11. *The baker Anchtu ground flour sacks* 1½, *gives keleŝta* 300.
12. *Sum ground flour sacks* 6½, *gives keleŝta* 1300, *rest of ḥan* 60½.

The sum agrees well with the single numbers.

13. *Thoth day* 21.
14. *The baker T'at'a ground flour mill sacks* 2, *gives keleŝta* 400.
15. *The baker Chara* „ *sacks* 1¾.[5] *gives keleŝta* 250.
16. *The baker Nennuamon* „ *sacks* 1¾, *gives keleŝta* 250.[6]
17. *The baker Anchtu* „ *sacks* 1,[7] *gives keleŝta* 300
18. *Sum ground flour sacks* , *gives keleŝta* 1200.

In l. 18 the lost sum of sacks ought to be 6½.[8]

PLATE IX.[9]

1. *Thoth day* 22.
2. *The baker T'at'a ground flour mill sacks* 2, *gives keleŝta*
3. *The baker Chara* „ *sacks* 1¾, *gives keleŝta*
4. *The baker Nennuamon* „ *sacks* 1¾, *gives keleŝta*
5. *The baker Anchtu* *sacks* 1¾, *gives keleŝta*[10]
6. *Sum.*

---

[1] The whole line not preserved, Spiegelberg, Tafel VIII, Col. 2.
[2] The number not in Spiegelberg. [3] Spiegelberg, 1⅔.
[4] Spiegelberg, 20. [5] Spiegelberg, 1¼.
[6] Spiegelberg, 350. [7] Spiegelberg, 1½.
[8] Spiegelberg exhibits 6½ sacks, and 1300 not 1200 keleŝta.
[9] Spiegelberg, Tafel VIII, Col. 3.
[10] This line is wanting in Spiegelberg.

7. *Thoth day 23.*[1]

8. *The baker T'at'a ground flour mill sacks* 2, *gives keleŝta*

9. *The baker Chara* .. *sacks* 1$\frac{3}{4}$,[2] *gives keleŝta*

10. *The baker Nennuamon* ,, *sacks* 1$\frac{3}{4}$,[3] *gives keleŝta*

11. *The baker Anchtu* ,, *sacks* 1$\frac{3}{4}$, *gives keleŝta*[4]

12. *Sum ground flour sacks* ,, *gives keleŝta*

13. *Thoth day 2.*[5]

14. *The baker T'at'a* ,, *sacks* 2,[6] *gives keleŝta*

15. *The baker Chara* ,, *sacks* 2, *gives keleŝta*

16. *The baker Nennuamon* ,, *sacks* 2, *gives keleŝta*

17. *The baker Anchtu* ,, *sacks* 2, *gives keleŝta*

18. *Sum ground flour sacks*   *keleŝta*

Pl. IX is only partly preserved. The end of each line with the number of keleŝtas is wanting, and also the rest of ḥan, if this was given.

[1] Spiegelberg, day 25.
[2] Spiegelberg, 1$\frac{1}{4}$.
[3] Spiegelberg, 1$\frac{1}{2}$.
[4] This line not in Spiegelberg.
[5] No day in Spiegelberg.
[6] Spiegelberg has no number of sa

(To be continued.)

The next Meeting of the Society will be held at 37, Great Russell Street, Bloomsbury, W.C., on Tuesday, 2nd March, 1897, at 8 p.m., when the following Paper will be read :—

The late DR. GRANT-BEY : "The Climate of Egypt in Geological, Prehistoric, and Ancient Historic Times."

THE FOLLOWING BOOKS ARE REQUIRED FOR THE LIBRARY OF THE SOCIETY.

Members having duplicate copies, will confer a favour by presenting them to the Society.

ALKER, E., Die Chronologie der Bücher der Könige und Paralipomenōn im Einklang mit der Chronologie der Aegypter, Assyrer, Babylonier und Meder.

AMÉLINEAU, Histoire du Patriarche Copte Isaac.

——————— Contes de l'Égypte Chrétienne.

——————— La Morale Egyptienne quinze siècles avant notre ère.

AMIAUD, La Légende Syriaque de Saint Alexis, l'homme de Dieu.

—————— A., AND L. MECHINEAU, Tableau Comparé des Écritures Babyloniennes et Assyriennes.

—————— Mittheilungen aus der Sammlung der Papyrus Erzherzog Rainer. 2 parts.

BAETHGEN, Beitrage zur Semitischen Religiongeshichte. Der Gott Israels und die Götter der Heïden.

BLASS, A. F., Eudoxi ars Astronomica qualis in Charta Aegyptiaca superest.

BOTTA, Monuments de Ninive. 5 vols., folio. 1847–1850.

BRUGSCH-BEY, Geographische Inschriften Altaegyptische Denkmaeler. Vols. I—III (Brugsch).

——————— Recueil de Monuments Égyptiens, copiés sur lieux et publiés par H. Brugsch et J. Dümichen. (4 vols., and the text by Dümichen of vols. 3 and 4.)

BUDINGER, M., De Colonarium quarundam Phoeniciarum primordiis cum Hebraeorum exodo conjunctis.

BURCKHARDT, Eastern Travels.

CASSEL, PAULUS, Zophnet Paneach Aegyptische Deutungen.

CHABAS, Mélanges Égyptologiques. Séries I, III. 1862–1873.

DÜMICHEN, Historische Inschriften, &c., 1st series, 1867.

————————————— 2nd series, 1869.

—————— Altaegyptische Kalender-Inschriften, 1886.

———————————— Tempel-Inschriften, 1862. 2 vols., folio.

EBERS, G., Papyrus Ebers.

ERMAN, Papyrus Westcar.

Études Égyptologiques. 13 vols., complete to 1880.

GAYET, E., Stèles de la XII dynastie au Musée du Louvre.

GOLÉNISCHEFF, Die Metternichstele. Folio, 1877.

—————— Vingt-quatre Tablettes Cappadociennes de la Collection de.

GRANT-BEY, Dr., The Ancient Egyptian Religion and the Influence it exerted on the Religions that came in contact with it.

HAUPT, Die Sumerischen Familiengesetze.

HOMMEL, Dr., Geschichte Babyloniens und Assyriens. 1892.

JASTROW, M., A Fragment of the Babylonian "Dibbarra" Epic.

JENSEN, Die Kosmologie der Babylonier.

JEREMIAS, Tyrus bis zur Zeit Nubukadnezar's, Geschichtliche Skizze mit beson derer Berücksichtigung der Keilschriftlichen Quellen.

JOACHIM, H., Papyros Ebers, das Älteste Buch über Heilkunde.

JOHNS HOPKINS UNIVERSITY. Contributions to Assyriology and Comparative Semitic Philology.

KREBS, F., De Chnemothis nomarchi inscriptione Aegyptiaca commentatio.

LEDERER, Die Biblische Zeitrechnung vom Auszuge aus Aegypten bis zum Beginne der Babylonische Gefangenschaft mit Berichsichtigung der Resultate der Assyriologie und der Aegyptologie.

LEDRAIN, Les Monuments Égyptiens de la Bibliothèque Nationale.

LEFÈBURE, Le Mythe Osirien. 2me partie. "Osiris."

LEGRAIN, G., Le Livre des Transformations. Papyrus démotique du Louvre.

LEHMANN, Samassumukin König von Babylonien 668 vehr, p. xiv, 173. 47 plates.

LEPSIUS, Nubian Grammar, &c., 1880.

MARUCHI, Monumenta Papyracea Aegyptia.

MÜLLER, D. H., Epigraphische Denkmäler aus Arabien.

NOORDTZIG, Israël's verblijf in Egypte bezien int licht der Egyptische out dekkingen.

POGNON, Les Inscriptions Babyloniennes du Wadi Brissa.

RAWLINSON, CANON, 6th Ancient Monarchy.

ROBIOU, Croyances de l'Égypte à l'époque des Pyramides.

————— Recherches sur le Calendrier en Égypte et sur la chronologie des Lagides.

SAINTE MARIE, Mission à Carthage.

SARZEC, Découvertes en Chaldée.

SCHAEFFER, Commentationes de papyro medicinali Lipsiensi.

SCHOUW, Charta papyracea graece scripta Musei Borgiani Velitris.

SCHROEDER, Die Phönizische Sprache.

STRAUSS and TORNEY, Der Altägyptishe Götterglaube.

VIREY, P., Quelques Observations sur l'Épisode d'Aristée, à propos d'un Monument Égyptien.

VISSER, I., Hebreeuwsche Archaelogie. Utrecht, 1891.

WALTHER, J., Les Découvertes de Ninive et de Babylone au point de vue biblique. Lausanne, 1890.

WILCKEN, M., Actenstücke aus der Königl. Bank zu Theben.

WILTZKE, Der Biblische Simson der Agyptische Horus-Ra.

WINCKLER, HUGO, Der Thontafelfund von El Amarna. Vols. I and II.

————— Textbuch-Keilinschriftliches zum Alten Testament.

WEISSLEACH, F. H., Die Achaemeniden Inschriften Zweiter Art.

WESSELEY, C., Die Pariser Papyri des Fundes von El Fajum.

Zeitsch. der Deutschen Morgenl. Gesellsch., Vol. I, 1847; Vols. IV to XII, 1850 to 1858, inclusive; Vol. XX to Vol. XXXII, 1866 to 1878

ZIMMERN, H., Die Assyriologie als Hülfswissenschaft für das Studium des Alten Testaments.

OCIETY OF BIBLICAL ARCHÆOLOGY PUBLICATIONS.

I 8 Parts. Price 5s. each. The Fourth Part having been issued, the Price is now Raised to £5 for the 8 Parts. Parts cannot be sold separately.

THE EGYPTIAN BOOK OF THE DEAD.

Complete Translation, Commentary, and Notes.

By SIR P. LE PAGE RENOUF, KNT. (*President*);

CONTAINING ALSO

A Series of Plates of the Vignettes of the different Chapters.

The Bronze Ornaments of the Palace Gates from Balawat.

[SHALMANESER II, B.C. 859–825.]

Parts I, II, III, and IV have now been issued to Subscribers.

In accordance with the terms of the original prospectus the price for each part is now raised to £1 10s.; to Members of the Society (the original price) £1 1s.

Price 7s. 6d. Only a Limited Number of Copies will be Printed.

THE PALESTINIAN SYRIAC VERSION OF THE HOLY SCRIPTURES.

Four Recently Discovered Portions (together with verses from the Psalms and the Gospel of St. Luke). Edited, in Photographic Facsimile from a Unique MS. in the British Museum, with a Transcription, Translation, Introduction, Vocabulary, and Notes, by

REV. G. MARGOLIOUTH, M.A.,

Assistant in the Department of Oriental Printed Books and MSS. in the British Museum ; formerly Tyrwhitt Hebrew Scholar.

Subscribers' names to be Addressed to the Secretary.

SOCIETY OF BIBLICAL ARCHÆOLOGY.

COUNCIL, 1897.

President.

SIR P. LE PAGE RENOUF, KNT.

Vice-Presidents.

THE MOST REV. HIS GRACE THE LORD ARCHBISHOP OF YORK.
THE MOST NOBLE THE MARQUESS OF BUTE, K.T., &c., &c.
THE RIGHT HON. LORD AMHERST OF HACKNEY.
THE RIGHT HON. LORD HALSBURY.
THE RIGHT HON. W. E. GLADSTONE, M.P., D.C.L., &c.
ARTHUR CATES.
F. D. MOCATTA, F.S.A., &c.
WALTER MORRISON, M.P.
SIR CHARLES NICHOLSON, BART., D.C.L., M.D., &c.
ALEXANDER PECKOVER, LL.D., F.S.A.
REV. GEORGE RAWLINSON, D.D., Canon of Canterbury.

Council.

REV. CHARLES JAMES BALL, M.A.
REV. PROF. T. K. CHEYNE, D.D.
THOMAS CHRISTY, F.L.S.
DR. J. HALL GLADSTONE, F.R.S.
CHARLES HARRISON, F.S.A.
GRAY HILL.
PROF. T. HAYTER LEWIS, F.S.A.
REV. ALBERT LOWY, LL.D., &c.

REV. JAMES MARSHALL, M.A.
CLAUDE G. MONTEFIORE.
WALTER L. NASH, F.S.A.
PROF. E. NAVILLE.
J. POLLARD.
EDWARD B. TYLOR, LL.D., F.R.S., &c.
E. TOWRY WHYTE, M.A., F.S.A.

Honorary Treasurer—BERNARD T. BOSANQUET.

Secretary—W. HARRY RYLANDS, F.S.A.

Honorary Secretary for Foreign Correspondence—REV. R. GWYNNE, B.A.

Honorary Librarian—WILLIAM SIMPSON, F.R.G.S.

HARRISON AND SONS, PRINTERS IN ORDINARY TO HER MAJESTY, ST. MARTIN'S LANE.

PROCEEDINGS

OF

THE SOCIETY

OF

BIBLICAL ARCHÆOLOGY.

————— ✤ —————

VOL. XIX. TWENTY-SEVENTH SESSION.

Third Meeting, March 2nd, 1897.

————— ✥ —————

CONTENTS.

————— ✳ ✳ —————

PUBLISHED AT

THE OFFICES OF THE SOCIETY,

37, Great Russell Street, Bloomsbury, W.C.

——

1897.

[No. CXLIV.]

SOCIETY OF BIBLICAL ARCHÆOLOGY,

37, GREAT RUSSELL STREET, BLOOMSBURY, W.C.

TRANSACTIONS.

			To Members.		To Non-Members.					To Members.		To Non-Members.
					s.	*d.*						*s.*	*d.*
Vol.	I,	Part	1 ... 10	6	... 12	6	Vol.	VI,	Part	1 ... 10	6	... 12	6
,,	I,	,,	2 ... 10	6	... 12	6	,,	VI,	,,	2 ... 10	6	... 12	6
,,	II,	,,	1 ... 8	0	... 10	6	,,	VII,	,,	1 ... 7	6	... 10	6
,,	II,	,,	2 ... 8	0	... 10	6	,,	VII,	,,	2 ... 10	6	... 12	6
,,	III,	,,	1 ... 8	0	... 10	6	,,	VII,	,,	3 ... 10	6	... 12	6
,,	III,	,,	2 ... 8	0	... 10	6	,,	VIII,	,,	1 ... 10	6	... 12	6
,,	IV,	,,	1 ... 10	6	... 12	6	,,	VIII,	,,	2 ... 10	6	... 12	6
,,	IV,	,,	2 ... 10	6	... 12	6	,,	VIII,	,,	3 ... 10	6	... 12	6
,,	V,	,,	1 ... 12	6	... 15	0	,,	IX,	,,	1 ... 10	6	... 12	6
,,	V,	,,	2 ... 10	6	... 12	6	,,	IX,	,,	2 ... 10	6	... 12	6

PROCEEDINGS.

					To Members.				To Non-Members.	
Vol.	I,	Session		1878–79	... 2	0	...	...	2	6
,,	II,	,,		1879–80	... 2	0	...	...	2	6
,,	III,	,,		1880–81	... 4	0	...	...	5	0
,,	IV,	,,		1881–82	... 4	0	...	..	5	0
,,	V,	,,		1882–83	... 4	0	...	..	5	0
,,	VI,	,,		1883–84	... 5	0	...	..	6	0
,,	VII,	,,		1884–85	... 5	0	...	...	6	0
,,	VIII,	,,		1885–86	... 5	0	...	...	6	0
,,	IX,	,,		1886–87	... 2	0 per Part	...	2	6
,,	IX,	Part 7,		1886–87	... 8	0 ,, ,,	...	10	
,,	X,	Parts 1 to 7,		1887–88	... 2	0 ,, ,,	...	2	6
,,	X,	Part 8,		1887–88	... 7	6 ,, ,,	...	10	6
,,	XI,	Parts 1 to 7,		1888–89	... 2	0 ,, ,,	...	2	6
,,	XI,	Part 8,		1888–89	... 7	6 ,, ,,	...	10	6
,,	XII,	Parts 1 to 7,		1889–90	... 2	0 ,, ,,	...	2	6
,,	XII,	Part 8,		1889–90	... 5	0 ,, ,,	...	6	0
,,	XIII,	Parts 1 to 7,		1890–91	... 2	0 ,, ,,	...	2	6
,,	XIII,	Part 8,		1890–91	... 5	0 ,, ,,	...	6	0
,,	XIV,	Parts 1 to 7,		1891–92	... 2	0 ,, ,,	..	2	6
,,	XIV,	Part 8,		1891–92	... 5	0 ,, ,,	...	6	0
,,	XV,	Parts 1 to 7,		1892–93	... 2	0 ,, ,,	...	2	6
,,	XV,	Part 8,		1892–93	... 5	0 ,, ,,	...	6	0
,,	XVI,	Parts 1 to 10,		1893–94	... 2	0 ,, ,,	...	2	6
,,	XVII,	Parts 1 to 8		1895	... 2	0 ,, ,,	...	2	6
,,	XVIII,	Parts 1 to 8		1896	... 2	0 ,, ,,	...	2	6
,,	XIX,	In progress		1897						

A few complete sets of the Transactions still remain for sale, which may be obtained on application to the Secretary, W. H. RYLANDS, F.S.A., 37, Great Russell Street, Bloomsbury, W.C.

PROCEEDINGS

OF

THE SOCIETY

OF

BIBLICAL ARCHÆOLOGY.

TWENTY-SEVENTH SESSION, 1897.

Third Meeting, 2nd March, 1897.

REV. JAMES MARSHALL, M.A., MEMBER OF COUNCIL,

IN THE CHAIR.

————◆◆◆————

'The following Presents were announced, and thanks
dered to be returned to the Donors —:

From David J. Waugh:—Koptos, by W. M. Flinders Petrie,
D.C.L., LL.D., with a chapter by D. G. Hogarth, M.A. 4to.
London. 1896.

From David J. Waugh:—Two Hieroglyphic Papyri from Tanis.
4to. London. 1889.

Extra Memoir of the Egypt Exploration Fund.

From the Author, Prof. E. Lefébure:—La mention des Hebreux par les Égyptiens, s'accorde-t-elle avec la date de l'Exode? 4to.

Extrait des *Mélanges Charles de Harlez.*

The following Candidates were nominated for election at the next Meeting, to be held on the 6th April, 1897 :—

Miss Jane Alice Weightman, Fern Lea, Seaforth, Liverpool, and Mrs. Peirson, The Haven, Saltwood, Hythe, Kent.

———

A Paper by the late Dr. Grant-Bey was read : The Climate of Egypt in Geological, Prehistoric, and Ancient Historic Times.

Remarks were added by Rev. Dr. Löwy, Mr. E. Towry Whyte, M.A., F.S.A., Rev. James Marshall, and Mr. J. Pollard.

BOOK OF THE DEAD.

By Sir P. le Page Renouf.

CHAPTER CXXX.

Notes.

1. This title is given to the Chapter in the later recensions, and nearly resembles that given in the Berlin papyrus of Nechtu-amen of the XIXth dynasty). That given in another papyrus of the older period is quite different,—" *Chapter whereby the Chu is fortified.*" Instead of the *Sheniu of the Tuat, Ba* (the papyrus of Nechtuamen) has the *Sheniu of Fire* 𓂝𓏤𓅆𓇳, a reading suggested by the 𓂝𓏤𓇳 *the circuit of fire*, which occurs in the title of another chapter. The *Sheniu* of this chapter are living personages who attend upon the Osiris and greet him with their acclamations. The word is often translated 'princes,' 'officers,' but it signifies *those who are in the circle* of a king or god, hence 'ministrants,' 'courtiers,' as in the rubric of Chapter CXXV.

The words *made on the Birth-day of Osiris* are only found in the later texts, but the old papyrus *Lc*, which has another title, has the words 𓊹𓏤𓅆𓆓. The important word 𓉐𓅆𓇳 which is here carelessly omitted is supplied by the rubric. For the Birth-day of Osiris, was the first of the five supplementary days, added to the year of 360 days. On this day the chapter was to be recited and the usual oblations offered (see Note 11). So we must understand 𓂋𓏥, 'which is to be made or done.'

2. *Arms of steel,* 𓂝𓅃𓂋𓏤.

107

3. *Cradle* or *Nest*, [hieroglyphs]; the 'Nest of Reeds' [hieroglyphs] so often represented in pictures of the later periods.

4. *The Armed god,* [hieroglyphs] *Septu,* called [hieroglyphs] (*Unas* 282) and [hieroglyphs] *septu ābu,* 'armed with horns,' that is, rays of light. In pictures he is represented as a hawk armed with bow and arrows, and there is one picture in which he is in the form of Bes, destroyer of the *Menti.*

5. *Sejant gods* [hieroglyphs]. I am compelled for want of a better word to use the heraldic term which most nearly expresses the posture of gods sitting on the ground with their knees raised up against their breasts. The posture is a very common one in Egyptian pictures. The second Sallier Papyrus represents an unfortunate artisan as sitting, [hieroglyphs] [hieroglyphs] "with his two knees at the pit of his stomach." The [hieroglyphs] is the limb between the knee and the pelvis.

6. *This divine Sword* [hieroglyphs]. Unseen fate brings down the old and the young alike to the Grave ever ready to receive them. Seb, the φυσίζοος αἶα, is here, as elsewhere, spoken of in reference to his κατοχή of the dead in the Tuat, as in *Unas* 210.

7. *Whose face is in his own lap,* [hieroglyphs]. *Cf.* Notes 5.

8. *The Amsu staff.* The name of it is phonetically written [hieroglyphs] in the later texts. It is the emblem both of Osiris and of Horus, and is constantly represented along with bows, arrows, and other weapons, in the oldest coffins, as belonging to the celestial armoury of the deceased person.

9. *Who issueth his decrees.* See Maspero, *Bibl. Egyptol.* II., p 3 (note) and 39.

10. *Green.* The Egyptian [hieroglyphs] is probably nearer in meaning to the Greek χλωρός, 'pale green, yellowish-green.'

11. The Rubric ends here in *Pb. Lc.* adds, *They shall offer bread, beer, and all good things* on the Birth-day of Osiris. *And i,*

*hese rites are performed for him, his soul will rise up and live for
ver ; he will not ever die a second time in the divine Nether world."

The later texts add the information that the text was discovered
n the great hall of the palace in the time of king Septa, and that it
vas found in a pit or chamber in the rock, ⌂ ⌒ 〰 . It was
made by Horus for his father Osiris Unneferu. Septa is the fifth
oyal name on the great tablet of Abydos.

CHAPTER CXXXI.

Chapter whereby one proceedeth into Heaven by the side of Rā. (1)

Oh Rā (2) who art shining this night : if there be any one among
hy followers, let him present himself living as a follower of Thoth,
vho causeth Horus to come forth this night.

The heart of the Osiris is glad, because he is one at the head of
hem.

His adversaries are brought to a stop by the warriors (3) of the
Osiris *N*, who is a follower of Rā, and hath taken his arms of steel.

He cometh to thee, his father Rā, he followeth Shu and calleth
or the Crown. He putteth on Hu (4) and is arrayed with the
Lock which is on the path of Rā and is his glory.

And he arriveth at the Aged one, at the confines of the Mount
of Glory, and the crown awaiteth him.

The Osiris *N* raiseth it up.

Thy Soul is with thee, and strong is thy Soul through the terror
und the might which belong to thee, Oh Osiris *N*, who utterest the
decrees which Rā hath spoken in Heaven.

Hail to thee, great god in the East of Heaven, who enterest into
he Bark of Rā in the form of the Divine Hawk and executest the
decrees which have been uttered ; thou who strikest with thy sceptre
rom thy Bark.

The Osiris *N* entereth into thy Bark and saileth peacefully to the
Fair West ; and Tmu saith to him : Art thou coming in ?

Mehenit is millions upon millions in length from Amur to
Ta-ur (5) an endless river wherein the gods move.

(6) . . . . whose path is in the fire ; and they travel in
he fire who come behind him.

NOTES.

1. None of the oldest papyri yet known contain this chapter. This of itself is not an argument against its antiquity, and there is really no reason for supposing it to be less ancient than the chapter which precedes it. The latter portion of the text is, however, very corrupt and we have unfortunately no means as yet of correcting it.

2. *O Rā.* The name of the god is sometimes omitted in MSS. The context, however, requires its presence. It may nevertheless be asked : how can the Sun-god be said to be shining in the night?

The question might as pertinently be asked : how can Horus (in the very same line) be said to come forth in the night? The answer to both these questions is that the Sun, whether as Rā or as Horus or Osiris, shines in the night through the agency of Thoth, the Moon. For further information see Notes to next chapter.

3. *Warriors* ⟨glyph⟩. I take this group as = ⟨glyph⟩ or ⟨glyph⟩. But a papyrus gives the variant ⟨glyph⟩.

4. *He putteth on Hu.* This is certainly obscure ; but it is not the less in conformity with the doctrine of the Pyramid texts. The deceased (*Pepi* I. 432, *Merira* 618) is borne to a region where he is fed from night till daybreak, and then seizes upon the god Hu, ⟨glyphs⟩. And according to other texts (*Unas*, 446, *Teta*, 250) the deceased seizes (⟨glyph⟩) upon Hu, and after Sau has been fastened to his feet enters the bark and seizes upon (⟨glyph⟩) the Mount of Glory.

5. *Mehenit* ⟨glyphs⟩, or in the masculine form ⟨glyphs⟩, is the name of the mythological serpent which personifies the subterranean path from West to East of the Sun's nightly course. In the *Book of Hades* (*e.g.* on the Sarcophagus of Seti, *passim*) it is represented as extending over the back, top and front of the shrine in which the Sun-god is borne in his Bark. The many folds of the serpent are symbolical of the turnings and windings of the river or canal (⟨glyph⟩) over which the god is conveyed. This river is here described as infinite in *length*. This is one of the instances from which it is clear ⟨glyphs⟩, like the corresponding Coptic ⲟⲩⲉⲓ, has the meaning of *length*. See *P.S.B.A.*, XVII, 190.

The length 'from West to East' is described as 'from *Amur* to

Taur' 🦁✝🦁 [hieroglyphs] ⊗. *Amur* is known from many texts to signify the West (see *supra*, Chapter 64, note 13). The East is known as *Ta-ur* or *Ta-urit*. The royal Ritual at Abydos (Mariette, I. 37) says [hieroglyphs] [hieroglyphs]. And as one of the values of the sign [hieroglyph] is *ta* as in [hieroglyphs] (Louvre, B. 14), I feel sure that we should read *Ta-ur* (or in the feminine *Ta-urit*) rather than *Nif-ur* or *Nif-urit*, even in such passages as those quoted *supra* in Chapter 128, notes 1 and 2, which have no necessary references to earthly geography.

6. There is a corrupt passage here, which I have at present no means of correcting by manuscript authority. M. Pierret thus renders it: "Le dieu qui partage les paroles y fait son chemin de millions d'années, seigneur sans égal, dont le chemin est dans le feu."

CHAPTER CXXXII.

Chapter whereby a person is enabled to go round, to visit his dwelling in the Netherworld.

I am the Lion-god who issueth from the Bow, (1) and therefore nave I shot forth. (2)

I am the Eye of Horus; and the Eye of Horus is opened at the instant that I reach the strand, coming with happy issue.

I advance and, lo! there is no defect found in me, and the Balance is relieved of my case. (3)

NOTES.

1. *The Bow,* [hieroglyph], often written with the determinative Λ, of *stretching*, which is the conception implied in this name of the instrument. This mythological *Bow*, as I explained, *Proc. Soc. Bibl. Arch.*, VI, 131, is the moon's *crescent*, which during its course through the sky is always turned towards the sun; so that a line at right angles to the chord of the arc passes through the sun's centre. From this "very delicate observation," as Arago calls it, the Alexandrian astronomer Geminus infers that the moon derives

its light from the sun.   The observation evidently had been made in Egypt some thousands of years before Geminus, and explains why in several chapters the sun is spoken of as shining in or from the moon.

See also *Proc. Soc. Bibl. Arch.*, XVII, 37, on another form of the myth.

2. I follow the Turin text in omitting a word about which the earlier texts are not agreed, but which seems to have originated in an alternate reading for .

3. See end of Chapter 1 and note.   These words are omitted in Turin text.

KHIANA OR KHÂNA.

WESTON-SUPER-MARE,
February 2, 1897.

MY DEAR MR. RYLANDS,

I have read to-day, with lively interest, Prof. Hommel's "Assyriological Notes" in the *Proceedings* of February 2, and wish to make a few remarks on "the land of Khâna or Khyâna," in hope of possibly working a little more on the matter when I may have more leisure.

At once this name suggested to me my old association of the Pharaoh S-user-n-Râ *Khyan* with two princes of similar name in the region of northern Syria now in question. Let me quote from a paper of mine on the Hyksôs (*Journal of Anthropological Institute*, 1889, p. 185). I compared Khyan with the Hyksôs name IANNAΣ with rough breathing, and proceeded : "See the letters of Mr. Griffith and Mr. Petrie in the *Academy* of August 25th, and my letter in the *Academy* of September 1st of this year, in which I have shown reason for identifying the name Khian with Khaian, a name borne by a king of Khindani on the west side of Euphrates, south of the junction of the Khabûr, in the time of Assurnazirpal, and by another prince, the son of Gabbari, who dwelt at the foot of Khamanu, that is, the Amanus range, north-west of Syria. There is a Tell Khaïa, south of Kharran, at the head of a tributary of the Belîkh River, which may be connected with this name." In the *Records of the Past*, New Series, vol. ii, p. 144, Assurnatsirpal speaks of the former Khayanu, and in vol. iv, p. 59, the second Khayanu is also called Khânu (as Prof. Hommel says the name of the district is contracted) of the country of the Sam'alians.

Now we know how Lenormant believed that a Hyksôs dynasty was of Hittite race. At all events this trace of the fatherland of Khyan, and of the correctness of my suggestion as to the two princes Khayanu, is worth recording. I am not sure whether these rulers were Hittite or Amorite. That is a further question. But surely we have an additional reason for believing the statement that Zoan was built (or rebuilt) seven years after Hebron (Num. xiii, 22).

Allow me to take this opportunity of stating that I fancy I have found the name of *Pethor* alive at this day.

In the *Times* of August 19, 1880, is an account of the exploration of Jerablûs (Karkemish), and it is mentioned that the 'Ain-el-Bedder joins the Euphrates at the northern angle of the *enceinte*. This notice sent me to Rey's and Sachau's maps, where I find that this brook (not marked by name) must rise in its *'Ain* in the neighbourhood of Tash-atan, where Pethor appears to be found, called by the *Hittites* Pitru, and by the Egyptians *Pederi*. It is easy to believe that the spring should be called 'Ain-el-*B*edder on the spot, for a place called after the name of the river, el-*B*urât (not *P*urat), is found near the same part of the Eu-*ph*rates.

Hoping that the members of our Society will put up with these hasty notes,

Believe me,

Ever yours very truly,

Henry George Tomkins.

THE ROLLIN PAPYRI AND THEIR BAKING

CALCULATIONS.

[*Continued.*]

By Frof. Dr. August Eisenlohr.

(*Sent in* 1 *November,* 1895.)

Section II. Plates X—XIV.

The real order of these five plates, according to their date, is Pl. XII, XIII, X, XI, XIV. These plates are in time not subsequent to Pl. V–IX, but contemporary; but while the first section comprises only the month of Thoth, this section extends to the end of the fourth month of the first season, the Choiak, and Pl. XIV has even dates of the last month of this second year of Seti I. Also the subject of this section is different from that of the first section: while we saw there the dispensing of flour to different bakers, with their product in small loaves (*keleśta*), we have here the account of reception from the same bakers, first (Pl. XII) of big loaves (*ākuu*), then of big (XIII, 3) and small loaves (XIII, 4–23; X) to the magazine of the royal court, the 𓅱 𓏏 𓅆 𓎡 𓈖 𓄞 𓅱𓏏' *a en chennu*, XIII, 2, also 𓄞 𓎡 alone (XII, 3–13).

115

PLATE XII. TRANSLATION AND COMMENTARY.

1. *Year 2, Thoth 2, one was in Memphis in Pa Ranefer-cheperka, the deceased.*

⟨hieroglyphs⟩ *àutu* is the impersonal form, third pers. sing. of the auxiliary verb *àu; cf.* De Rougé, *Chrest.*, III, p. 32. Vainly I searched for it in Erman's grammars. It signifies the royal court, or the king himself.

Though the lists contain several ⟨cartouche⟩ Raneferka and Racheperka, also Ra-nefer-cheper (Wiedem. *Geschichte*, pp. 296, 282), we have only once in the Grant collection (Wiedem., S. 280, i), probably the same name, Nefer-cheper-ka. Without doubt he built a part of Memphis, which was called after him ⟨hieroglyphs⟩ Pa Ranefercheper-ka (mentioned also XIV, 3). Plate II, 2, is spoken of a temple of the goddess Hathor ⟨hieroglyphs⟩, which belongs to Pa Ra-nefer-cheper-ka.[1]

2. *Account of the receipts on flour for baking.*

On the word ⟨hieroglyphs⟩, *vide supra*, Copt. ⲔⲈⲚⲈⳆⲒⲦⲈⲤ, *pistor*, and ⲚⲒ ⲔⲈⲚⲈⳆⲒⲦⲈⲚ, *panes subcinericii* (Peyron *Lex. ling. copticæ*).

3. *Store house of āku loaves by the hand of T'at'a, ground flour sacks 3½, brought by him āku loaves, 168 each of 13½ ten, a tenth[2] of the oven, ten 1½.*

4. *Store house of āku loaves, by the hand of Chara,   ,, sacks 3¼, brought by him āku loaves 156, 5 each of 13 ten, a tenth of the oven, ten 1½, rest of ḥan, ākeku 5 paste ten 3.*

---

[1] That the name of the king is not Ra-nefer-cheper-ka, but Ra-aa-cheper-ka (Tutmes I) Spiegelberg proved, "Commentary," p. 35. When the reading might be doubtful, Pl. XII, 1, it is quite clear on his heliotype of Pl. XIV, 3 (Spiegelberg, Tafel V), where ⟨cartouche⟩ is written. What Pleyte has read as Pa Hathor appears in Spiegelberg, Tafel XV, more as ⟨hieroglyphs⟩ ⟨hieroglyphs⟩ (Spiegelberg ⟨hieroglyphs⟩).

[2] Spiegelberg is in error (Transl., p. 10) in adding the tenth to the foregoing number 13½, as it belongs to the following $\frac{1}{10}$ for baking, *i.e.*, 1½ ten.

5. *Store house of āku by the hand of Nennuamon, ground flour sacks* 3¼, *brought by him āku loaves* 156, *each ten* 13½, *a tenth of the oven, ten* 1½, *together brought on this day loaves* 480, *brought on ḥan* 5, *together* [4] 85.

As is said l. 3–5 the big loaves ⟨glyphs⟩, *ākeku*, differently written from ⟨glyphs⟩ *pa āqu*, XII, 3–13, probably "house of aliments" (Gr. Harris, XVII*b*, XXXV*a*), for big and special kinds of bread had, when baked, a weight of 13 to 13½ ten = 1176 to 1221 grammes, ca. $\frac{5}{4}$ kilo, 2·6 Avoirdupois pounds. The loss of the oven ⟨glyph⟩ (perhaps ⟨glyphs⟩, Gr. Harris, XVII*b*, 10, XXXV*a*, 3), it is by baking, was the tenth part. Göriz, *Betriebslehre*, II, p. 224, accords the lawful loss in baking to $\frac{1}{9}$. Adding the loss of 1½ ten to the 13½ we get 15 ten (resp. 14½) for the weight of the paste of each bread (*āku*). L. 4 the rest (read ⟨glyph⟩ *ut'a*) of ḥan ⟨glyph⟩ are 5 breads. In the addition, l. 5, these 5 breads are counted extra and then added to the 480 = 485. The meaning of ⟨glyphs⟩ ll. 4, 8, 9 (*Pap. Ebers*, LIII, 18, 19 ⟨glyphs⟩) is probably paste (Copt. ϣⲱϯ, *farinae subactae massa*) or *leaven* (Joachim, *Pap. Ebers*, p. 76, Loret, *Rec.* XI, 131).

6. *Thoth day* 3. *One was in Memphis.*

On *autu* (one) = the king's household and the king himself, see above.

7 *Store house of aliments through the hand of T'at'a, ground flour tep sacks* 3½, *brought by him ākeku bread* 168, *each of* 13½ *ten, one-tenth of the oven ten* 1½.

8. *Store house of aliments through the hand of Chara,* „ „ *sacks* 3¼, *brought by him ākeku bread* 151 10·6, *each of* 12½ *ten, one-tenth for the oven* 1½ *ten, rest ten* 1, *makes in ākeku bread* 10, *leaven ten* 6 . . . . . 6.

9. *Store house of aliments through the hand of Nennuamon,* „ „ *sacks* 3¼, *brought by him ākeku bread* 156, 5 *each of* 13 *ten, one-tenth for the oven* 1½ *ten, rest* ½ *ten, makes in ākeku* 5, *leaven* 3 *ten, together this day loaves* 480, *brought of ḥan* 15, *together* 495.

The original has also here (ll. 7–9) not Pleyte's $\frac{1}{20}$ but $\frac{1}{10}$. In ll. 8 and 9 we find a more complete account of the ⏉ ~~~ ⚏ *ut'a en ḥan* (see above p. 97). The 10 additional loaves (*ākeku*) in l. 8 and the 5 additional loaves in l. 9 are without doubt what is called in l. 4 *ut'a en ḥan*. We see that in the addition were these 15 additional loaves are called *en ḥan*. But their number is derived from a rest l. 8 of 1 ten, l. 9 of $\frac{1}{2}$ ten, and besides that is a weight of

⚏ ⚊ , l. 8 of 6 ten, l. 9 of 3 ten adjoined, which must refer to that additional number of loaves, because their weight 6 and 3 corresponds with the numbers of the rest and the loaves : l. 8, rest 1 ten, loaves 10, šeṭu 6 ; l. 9, rest $\frac{1}{2}$ ten, loaves 5, šeṭu 3 ; the last correspondence between loaves and šeṭu is also l. 4, loaves 5, šeṭu 3.

The meaning of this *šeṭu* seems to me to be :

L. 4. Because the ākeku had only $12\frac{1}{2}$ ten, instead of $13\frac{1}{2}$, there remained 1 ten of dough from each of the 156 (so probably we must read the number), 156 ten are sufficient for 10 ākeku, which are added and it remains a rest of 6 ten. $156 = 10 \times 15 + 6$.

L. 8. As *supra* l. 4, from 156 ākeku, which had 13 ten instead of $13\frac{1}{2}$ of dough, remained $\frac{1}{2}$ ten of each of the $156 = 78$. As 5 ākeku demanded only $5 \times 15 = 75$ ten, there were remaining 3 ten of dough. This small rest does not enter into the summation.[1]

L. 8 the second 6 is added, with the 10 additional loaves, to the number of loaves which the scribe did not do with the first 6 and 3 in l. 9, because this was only the rest in paste, see supra.

L. 9 we have, also, XI, 3 ⚏ *θes*, better ⌂ = ⚏ , *Pap. Ebers*, in the meaning of loaves (Pleyte, p. 17 pièce).

The sign ⋀ which is found throughout in the papyrus means the produce (le rendement). I translated it, Pl. V–IX, with *gives* here with *brought*.[2]

---

[1] Spiegelberg, *Comment.*, p. 43, feels unable to explain ll. 7 and 8.

[2] Spiegelberg translates ⋀ "es gingen von ihm ein." In the leather roll published by Virey (*Étude sur un parchemin, Mission archéol.*, Tome I, 3), treating of the accorded supply of materials, especially bricks, for the restoration of the decayed royal stables, the number of the bricks delivered is always preceded by the above sign ⋀ there entered, were delivered.

10. *Thoth day* 4, *one was in Memphis.*

11. *Store house of aliments through the hand of T'at'a, ground
    flour tep sacks* $3\frac{1}{2}$, *brought by him ākeku* 167, *each of* $13\frac{1}{2}$
    ten, $\frac{1}{10}$ *for baking* $1\frac{1}{2}$ *ten, rest ākeku* 1.

12. *Store house of aliments through the hand of Chara* ,,
    sacks $3\frac{1}{4}$, *brought by him ākeku* 145^{16}, *rest ākeku* 11, *rest of
    ḥan* 5, *each of* 13 *ten,* $\frac{1}{10}$ *for baking* $1\frac{1}{2}$ *ten.*

13. *Store house of aliments through the hand of Nennuamon baking
    sacks* $3\frac{1}{4}$, *brought by him ākeku* 156, *each of* 13 *ten,* $\frac{1}{10}$ *for
    the oven ten* $1\frac{1}{2}$, *rest of ḥan* 5, *together this day loaves* 479,
    brought of ḥan 5, *together* 484.

14. *Sum ground flour, tep sacks* 30, *brought in big ākuu* 146c,
    each of 15, *finished* $13\frac{1}{2}$ *ten in coming from the oven.*

The number of ākeku bread in l. 12 is $145 + 16$. The
additional 16 (as above l. 8) is the sum of the two rests $11 + 5$.
We should expect each of 13 ten, as usually, direct after the
number 145; perhaps this is an error of the scribe. In the addition at the end of l. 13, wrongly given by Pleyte, the original has
479, and only 5 $\wedge \sim\sim\sim$ ⁇, though we have in each of ll. 12
and 13 this sum. The original clearly gives 484 as the whole sum.
Before *ra pen* this day is not $\wedge$ but ⊂⊐ together or $= \sim\sim\sim$ of
that day.

The addition of l. 14 gives properly 30 sacks. $3 \times 3\frac{1}{2} =$
$10\frac{1}{2} + 6 \times 3\frac{1}{4} = 19\frac{1}{2} = 30$. The number of 1460 ākuu results from
the adding of the given numbers, 168, 156, 156, 168, 151, 156^5, 167,
145^{11}, 156 $= 480 + 480 + 479 = 1439$. The wanting 21 are given
by the rest of ākuu $5 + 10 + 1 + 5 = 21$. On *ḳerḥ* to between
numbers, l. 14. The original has *ua neb* ⟨⟩, not *neb* and not $\cap$ I,
but 15.

As we said above, Pl. XIII and Pl. X contain the continued
series of the reception in the magazine of the court, which is called
pa ut'a en chennu. The
bread is taken from (*vide* also Pl. XIV, 5, XVIII,
5, 6) the bakehouse, after Brugsch, *Wörterb.*, continuation, pp. 745
and 653, the royal palace, the Königshalle. This bakehouse stood

under the superintendence of a high functionary, the chief
Neferhotepu of Memphis.   From that bakehouse the loaves of
bread are received in the magazine of the court.   This reception
is executed by some scribes, two scribes of the sacrifices, Hui and
Sakaȧn, and some other scribes, Rameŝu and Necht (Pl. XIII),
Thothmesu and Paharpet (Pl. X).   All these belong to the *ut' a en*
chennu, called (l. 4) ut'a uab ⌐⌐⌐, holy magazine.[1]   Only l. 3
refers to the reception of big loaves (ākeku), all the others to the
smaller keleŝta.

(To be continued.)

THE LAY OF THE THRESHERS.

By Sir P. le Page Renouf.

All those who are interested in Egyptology are familiar with the *Lay of the Threshers*, which was discovered by Champollion at El Kab in the tomb of Paheri, over the picture which it accompanies as its appropriate text.   And those who are old enough may remember the scepticism with which the discovery was greeted, and made its way even into such books as Dr. Craik's *History of English Literature*.

Those days are now past: the Song has been published by Champollion, Rosellini and Lepsius and most recently by the Egypt Exploration Fund in its eleventh Memoir (*Ahnas el Medineh and the Tomb of Paheri at El Kab*).   And no great amount of hieroglyphic knowledge is necessary to qualify one for verifying the accurate meaning of the ancient lay.

> " Thresh ye for yourselves,
> Thresh ye for yourselves, ye oxen !
> Thresh ye for yourselves,
> Thresh ye for yourselves,
> The straw for eating :
> And the corn for your masters.'

But I am not aware that any Egyptologist or Folk-Loreist has yet called attention to the fact that these words form part of a song sung to this very day by the peasants of Corsica.

> Tribia tu, chi tribia anch' ellu,
> Mascarone e Cudanellu . . . . .
> Ohi   tribiate, o boni boi !
> A tribiallu voi e noi !
> Chi lo granu tocchi a noi
> E la paglia tocchi a voi.

The Corsican lay is somewhat longer than the Egyptian, but the editor Tommaseo (*Canti Popolari Toscani Corsi Illirici Greci*, Vol. II, p. 300) already in 1841 recognised the resemblance.

We are happily in possession of evidence (*e.g.* in the *Tale of the Two Brothers*) that the Egyptian oxen were not fed upon straw only, and the picture in the tomb of Paheri which accompanies the Lay exhibits, as Mr. Griffith has observed, the mouths of the oxen *unmuzzled*, in conformity with the righteous precept of Deuteronomy xxv, 4, which was not yet written.

The next Meeting of the Society will be held at 37, Great Russell Street, Bloomsbury, W.C., on Tuesday, 6th April, ·1897, at 8 p.m., when the following Paper will be read :—

E. J. Pilcher : " The Date of the Siloam Inscription."

THE FOLLOWING BOOKS ARE REQUIRED FOR THE LIBRARY OF THE SOCIETY.

Members having duplicate copies, will confer a favour by presenting them to the Society.

ALKER, E., Die Chronologie der Bucher der Könige und Paralipomenōn im Einklang mit der Chronologie der Aegypter, Assyrer, Babylonier und Meder.

AMÉLINEAU, Histoire du Patriarche Copte Isaac.

——————— Contes de l'Égypte Chrétienne.

——————— La Morale Egyptienne quinze siècles avant notre ère.

AMIAUD, La Légende Syriaque de Saint Alexis, l'homme de Dieu.

·——————— A., AND L. MECHINEAU, Tableau Comparé des Écritures Babyloniennes et Assyriennes.

——————— Mittheilungen aus der Sammlung der Papyrus Erzherzog Rainer. 2 parts.

BAETHGEN, Beitrage zur Semitischen Religiongeshichte. Der Gott Israels und die Götter der Heiden.

BLASS, A. F., Eudoxi ars Astronomica qualls in Charta Aegyptiaca superest.

BOTTA, Monuments de Ninive. 5 vols., folio. 1847–1850.

BRUGSCH-BEY, Geographische Inschriften Altaegyptische Denkmaeler. Vol. I—III (Brugsch).

——————— Recueil de Monuments Égyptiens, copiés sur lieux et publiés pas II. Brugsch et J. Dümichen. (4 vols., and the text by Dümichen of vols. 3 and 4.)

BUDINGER, M., De Colonarium quarundam Phoeniciarum primordiis cum Hebraeorum exodo conjunctis.

BURCKHARDT, Eastern Travels.

CASSEL, PAULUS, Zophnet Paneach Aegyptische Deutungen.

CHABAS, Mélanges Égyptologiques. Séries I, III. 1862–1873.

DÜMICHEN, Historische Inschriften, &c., 1st series, 1867.

——————————————————— 2nd series, 1869.

——————— Altaegyptische Kalender-Inschriften, 1886.

——————————————— Tempel-Inschriften, 1862. 2 vols., folio.

EBERS, G., Papyrus Ebers.

ERMAN, Papyrus Westcar.

Études Égyptologiques. 13 vols., complete to 1880.

GAYET, E., Stèles de la XII dynastie au Musée du Louvre.

GOLÉNISCHEFF, Die Metternichstele. Folio, 1877.

——————— Vingt-quatre Tablettes Cappadociennes de la Collection de.

GRANT-BEY, Dr., The Ancient Egyptian Religion and the Influence it exerted on the Religions that came in contact with it.

HAUPT, Die Sumerischen Familiengesetze.

HOMMEL, Dr., Geschichte Babyloniens und Assyriens. 1892.

JASTROW, M., A Fragment of the Babylonian "Dibbarra" Epic.

JENSEN, Die Kosmologie der Babylonier.

JEREMIAS, Tyrus bis zur Zeit Nubukadnezar's Geschichtliche Skizze mit besonderer Berucksichtigung der Keilschriftlichen Quellen.

JOACHIM, H., Papyros Ebers, das Àlteste Buch über Heilkunde.

JOHNS HOPKINS UNIVERSITY. Contributions to Assyriology and Comparative Semitic Philology.

KREBS, F., De Chnemothis nomarchi inscriptione Aegyptiaca commentatio.

LEDERER, Die Biblische Zeitrechnung vom Auszuge aus Aegypten bis zum Beginne der Babylonische Gefangenschaft mit Berichsichtignung der Resultate der Assyriologie und der Aegyptologie.

LEDRAIN, Les Monuments Égyptiens de la Bibliothèque Nationale.

LEFÈBURE, Le Mythe Osirien. 2me partie. "Osiris."

LEGRAIN, G., Le Livre des Transformations. Papyrus démotique du I ouvre.

LEHMANN, Samassumukin König von Babylonien 668 vehr, p. xiv, 173; 47 plates.

LEPSIUS, Nubian Grammar, &c., 1880.

MARUCHI, Monumenta Papyracea Aegyptia.

MÜLLER, D. H., Epigraphische Denkmäler aus Arabien.

NOORDTZIG, Israèl's verblijf in Egypte bezien int licht der Egyptische outdekkingen.

POGNON, Les Inscriptions Babyloniennes du Wadi Brissa.

RAWLINSON, CANON, 6th Ancient Monarchy.

ROBIOU, Croyances de l'Égypte à l'époque des Pyramides.

———— Recherches sur le Calendrier en Égypte et sur le chronologie des Lagides.

SAINTE MARIE, Mission à Carthage.

SARZEC, Découvertes en Chaldée.

SCHAEFFER, Commentationes de papyro medicinali Lipsiensi.

SCHOUW, Charta papyracea graece scripta Musei Borgiani Velitris.

SCHROEDER, Die Phönizische Sprache.

STRAUSS and TORNEY, Der Altägyptishe Götterglaube.

VIREY, P., Quelques Observations sur l'Épisode d'Aristée, à propos d un Monument Égyptien.

VISSER, I., Hebreeuwsche Archaeologie. Utrecht, 1891.

WALTHER, J., Les Découvertes de Ninive et de Babylone au point de vue biblique. Lausanne, 1890.

WILCKEN, M., Actenstücke aus der Königl. Bank zu Theben.

WILTZKE, De Biblische Simson der Ägyptische Horus-Ra.

WINCKLER, HUGO, Der Thontafelfund von El Amarna. Vols. I and II.

———— Textbuch-Keilinschriftliches zum Alten Testament.

WEISSLEACH, F. H., Die Achaemeniden Inschriften Zweiter Art.

WESSELEY, C., Die Pariser Papyri des Fundes von El Fajum.

Zeitsch. der Deutschen Morgenl. Gesellsch., Vol. I, 1847; Vols. IV to XII, 1850 to 1858, inclusive; Vol. XX to Vol. XXXII, 1866 to 1878.

ZIMMERN, H., Die Assyriologie als Hülfswissenschaft für das Studium des Alten Testaments.

ut, so that; so also X, 5. — 16: **ביראת אלהיך** v. III, 19. —
בקריאת הגבר cockcrowing. Postbiblical.

VII, 17: שמחה = וישמחו בשמחה.

VIII, 9: זכרה נא לנו לחסדיך (construed with ל, so also
v. 10, and similarly יאמינו הלבבות. — 15: לבלתי לנגוע = נגוע).
— 19: בכל הקמים cf. Deut. 6, 22.

XI, 3: לבו = ושמח בלבו. — 6: אל = ובאה את אביך.
9: לה' = וישתחו אל ה'.

XII, 2: מחצית כל = כל מחצית. — 10: חרפתך: the reproach
with which thou hast been reproached and so ibid. חורפתה.

XIII, 11: ברוך שאכלנו משלו.

אביך ואת אמך בצער גדול · ועתה נלך אנחנו לפנות הבית ותבא אשתך
אחרינו · וילכו שניהם · אמ' רפאל לטוביה כשתבא לבית אביך קח המרה
מן הדג וישם (ושים.l) בעיני אביך וירפא · ויעש כן ואמר טובי לבנו סיפר(!)
לי כל מה שעשית ויספר לו · ואמר ברוך י״י ששלח מלאכו עם בני
והצלח דרכו ורפא שני עינים כמונו · לאחר ימים ברך אלהים לטוביה
על שקיים מצות אביו ויתן מעשר מכל אשר לו · הא למדנו כח הצדקות
והמעשרות כמה גדול על שעשה טובי צדקות והפריש מעשרותיו כראוי
מה שלם לו הבֹהֵ ולפי שהיו יודעין אבות העולם כח הצדקה והמעשרות
היו זהירין בהן · לכך הזהיר משה עשר תעשר את כל תבואת זרעך:

Peculiar forms and constructions in the Hebrew Text A. of Tobit, some of which are postbiblical.

I, 6: וישפך לבו עליו (v. VIII, 4. cf. Lament. 2, 19. Ps. 62, 9). — 10: בא במדי (similar forms with ב: III, 11 ותעל בעלייה; IX, 2 הרגו סנחריב בניו: 17 — .(אל = לבא בשמחה).

II, 2: כי אחד מבני ישראל ראה. cf. V, 2: אחד נאמן. — הרבה יראתי :7 (cf. Eccl. 1, 16. Ezra 10, 1. Nehem. 2, 2.). — 17: אגמול חסד עם המתים neologism. Biblical is: עשה חסד (v. Ruth I, 8). — 14: חיי העולם הבא (postbiblical). — 15: ותעש לרבים (= worked for many). — 17: פן גניבה (Conj. before a noun, not biblical).

III, 7: אוי לך ולמזלך (postbiblical idea of: luck). — 9: לא גומל לחייבים טובות. — 15: נכונו אליה (cf. v. 19. Nehem. 8, 10). — 21: והצדקה תעביר רוע הגזירה (later paraphrase of Prov. 10, 2. v. XII, 7).

IV, 1: מתחנן על נפשו instead of: וישאל את נפשו (I Kgs. 19, 4. Jonah 4, 8). — ויקרא לבנו לאמור = spake.

V, 2 s. II, 2. — 12: אל ירע לפני (biblical: בעיני cf. Gen. 21, 12). — 17: ושלח Perfect instead of Imperfect so also v. 19 ולא תאכל cf. X, 2 ויהיו. והיו = ותן and ונתת = VIII, 11 (ויתן =) ונתן = ולא אכלה. — 20: למהר לשוב cf. Exod. 12, 33.

VI, 1: לפי תומו = suddenly. Postbiblical. — 2: ... עוד יהיו = אשר יצאו. — 15: יורשת בכל = כל. — 7: לרפואה (cf. V, 24).

55 קרוב והרי מתו בעדי שבעה אנשים ולמה יש לי חיים עוד· ואם לא
ייטב בעיניך להרוג אותי רחם עלי ולא אשמע חרפה עוד. אמרו חז"ל
כי ביום הזה קבל הב"ה תפלתם· ושלח למלאך רפאל לרפאת את
שניהם את טובי מעורון עיניו ואת שרה ליתן לטוביה בן טובי לאשה
ולהסיר ממנה אשמדאי מלך השדים· IV. באותה שעה זכר טובי את
60 הכסף שהפקיד ביד גבאל· ויקרא לטוביה בנו ואמר לו· בני כל ימיך
את י"י אלהיך תירא ועשה צדקה כל ימיך ולא תלך עם איש גנב ונואף
והפריש מעשרותיך כראוי והב"ה יתן לך עושר רב· ועתה בני דע כי
עשר· ככר כסף הפקדתי ביד גבאל ולא ידעתי יום מותי· תלך אליו
V. והוא יתן לך הכסף· ויען טוביה אל אביו כל אשר צויתני אעשה
65 אבל איך אוכל לקחת הכסף מיד גבאל הוא לא מכיר לי ואני לא מכיר
אותו· אמר לו אביו קח הטבעת הזאת שנתן לי· וטבעתי נתתי לו·
ועתה בני בקש איש נאמן שילך עמך ואתן לו שכרו· מיד יצא
טוביה לבקש איש נאמן שילך עמו ומצא את המלאך רפאל עומד ולא
הכירו כי מלאך י"י הוא· שאל לו מנין אתה· אמ' לו מבני ישראל· אמר
70 לו ידעת להלוך למדי· אמר לו הן· אמר לו טוביה אמתין (המתן 1.) לי ואגיד
לאבי· הלך טוביה ויגד לאביו· אמר לו קרא אותו· אמר לו טובי בני
רוצה להלוך למדי רוצה אתה להלוך עמו· אמ' לו הן · מיד קרא טובי
לבנו ואמר לו התקן עצמך ותלך עם האיש הזה ואלהי השמים יצליח
דרככם ושבתם בשלום· מיד הלכו שניהם בדרך ויבואו עד הנהר פרת
VI. וילינו שם · VI. וירץ טוביה אל הנהר לשתות ויצא דג ואכל לחמו
75 ויצעק· ואמר רפאל לטוביה לך ואחוז את הדג ולא תעזוב אותו· הלך
טוביה ותפש אל (את 1.) הדג ויוציא אותו ליבשה· אמר לו רפאל בצע אותו
באמצע· וקח לבו והוא טוב להקטיר ממנו לפני כל איש שיש בו רוח
שדים שיברחו ממנו· וקח המרה והיא טובה למשוח ממנה העינים
80 שיש בהם עורון וירפאו· עשה כן טוביה כאשר צוה לו רפאל וילכו עד
מדי· ואמר רפאל לטוביה· אחי לבית רעואל תבא שהוא איש זקן ולו
בת אחת יפה עד מאד ושמה שרה ואמור לו שיתן אותך לו (אותה לי 1.) לאשה·
אמר לו טוביה שמעתי שהיא נשאת לשבעה אנשים וימותו בטרם
שיבואו אליה· אמר רפאל לא תירא כאשר תהיה בחדר עמה קח לב
VII. הדג וקטר אותה תחת בגדיו (בגדיה 1.) והשד מריח ויברח· VII. אמר רפאל
85 לרעואל תן בתך לטוביה לאשה אמר לו הנני· ויקח רעואל את שרה
בתו ויתן לה לטוביה לאשה· אמר רעואל לאשתו אתקיני אדרון בית
משכבא ויבואו שמה טוביה ושרה אשתו· מיד זכר טוביה את דברי
רפאל ויקח לב הדג וישם על המחתה ויקטר תחת בגדי שרה ואשמדאי
90 קבל הריח וברח· מיד התפללו שניהם להב"ה שרפא אותה· למחר אמר
טוביה לרפאל לך לגבאל ויתן לך העשרה ככרי זהב· מיד הלך רפאל
והביא. את הכסף ואמר רפאל לטוביה אחי אתה ידעת איך הנחת את

ירא מן הָבֻה בכל לבו ועל זאת נתן לו אלהים חן וחסד בעיני

שלמנאצר המלך ויפקוד אותו על כל אשר לו עד יום מותו• ובעת

ההיא צוה טובי ביד גבאל קרובו עשר ככרי זהב• ואחר שמת שלמנאצר

20 המלך מלך סנחריב בנו תחתיו• ובימי סנחריב היה עושה טובי חסדים

רבים לעניים• והיה נותן לחם לרעבים וליתומים וכשהיה רואה הרוג

נופל בארץ מן היהודים היה קובר אותו• וישב סנחריב בחפזון מיהודה

והלך לנינוה בחימה גדולה על עשר השבטים והרג מהם רבים והיה

נבלתם מושלכים בארץ ואין היה קובר אותם• וכשראה טובי כך חרה

25 אפו ויקם בלילה וקבר אותם וכזאת עשה פעמים רבות• פעם אחד שאל

סנחריב את פגרי ההרוגים ולא מצא אתהם. ויאמרו אנשי נינוה למלך

טובי קבר אותם בלילה ויצו המלך להרוג אותו• וכששמע טובי כן

ברח• ויצו המלך לשלול את ביתו ויתחבא מלפניו מ״ה ימים עד כי

אדרמלך ושנאצר(!) בניו הרגו אותו בחרב לסנחריב(!) וימלוך אסרחדון בנו

30 תחתיו• ויפקוד המלך לאקנקר על כל אשר לו• ודבר אקנקר דברים

II. טובים על טובי וישיבהו לנינוה• II. וכשהגיע חג שבעות עשה אשתו

ארסטוון רב• וכשהיה יושב על השולחן אמר לטוביה בנו לך והבא

לי מאחינו העניים מיראי אלהים לאכול עמנו• וילך טוביה ומצא איש

אחד מת מושלך בדרך ויגד לאביו• מה עשה אביו קם מן השולחן וילך

35 אתו ויקח אותו מן רחוב העיר ויביא אותו בבית אחד עד בא השמש

שיוכל לקברנו וישב אל ביתו ויאכל לחמו באבל• ואמר אוי לנו שיקים

בנו והפכתי חגיכם וכל שיריכם לאבל• ויבך בכי גדול וכשבא השמש

הלך וקבר אותו וישב אל ביתו וישכב על מטתו ופניו גלויות וגפל

עפר מן הכותל על עיניו• ובבקר היה הולך לרופא לעשות רפואה בעיניו

40 ולא הועיל לו כלום עד שעור משני עיניו והיה עוד ד' שנים• ואקנקר

אוהבו היה מפרנס אותו• לימים רבים חנה אשתו היה עושה מעשה

לנשים ונתנו לה גדי אחד בשכרה וטובי שמע הגדי זועק בבית• ושאל

לה מנין לך הגדי הזה אולי גנבת אותו• אמרה חנה אשתו בשכר מעשה

ידי נתנו לי שלא גנבתיהו• ולא האמין טובי לה ויריבו שניהם על

45 הגדי• אמרה חנה לטובי אן טובך וזכוותך וקלנך אתגלי לכולא•

III. III. כששמע טובי כך חרה אפו ויבך והתפלל להבה בצרת נפשו ואמר

רבשׁעֹ קח את נפשי ממני כי טוב מותי מחיי ולא אשמע חרפה עוד•

וביום ההוא שרה בת רעואל שהיתה באגבתנים בארץ מדי שמעה

חרפה גדולה לפי שנשאת לשבעה אנשים לאשה• ואחד מהם לא בא

50 כדרך כל הארץ ואמרה לה שפחתה את היא שהרגת את האנשים

האלה שנשאת להם ואחד מהם לא בא אליך שאתה מלקה אותם•

ויהי כאשר שמעה שרה את דברי שפחתה ותבך בכי גדול ותעל אל העלייה

להתפלל שם בצרת נפשה• ואמ' רבשׁעֹ אתה ידעת כי טהורה אני ולא

נטמאתי עם אדם• ואני יחידה לאבי ואין לו בן לרשת נחלתו ולא

9 והחסד לאוהביך ולשומרי בריתך: ויאמר טובי אל בנו ואל שרה אשתו·
הודו ליהוה קראו בשמו הודיעו בעמים עלילותיו·[1] כי הפליא לעשות
עמנו ויהפך אבלנו· לשמחה ואת יגונינו למחול וליום טוב·[2] ויענו כל העם·
10 אמן: ויאמר טובי אל טוביה בנו ברוך אלהינו שאכלנו (משלו) ובטובו
חיינו· ויענו כל העם· ברוך הוא אלהינו שאכלנו משלו ובטובו חיינו:[3]
11 ויקומו ויברכו את טובי ואת אשתו וטוביה בנו וכלתו· ויאמרו לטוביה·
יהי ביתך כבית פרץ· ויענו· אמן· וילכו איש לאוהליו שמחים וטובי לב:

XIV. ויהי טובי אחרי האירו עיניו תשע וארבעים שנה· ויהיו ימי חייו
מאה ושבעים שנה: וימת ויאסף אל עמיו בשיבה טובה בעיר ננוה:
2 ויתר מעשיו (אשר עשה?) באהבת יהוה בשמחת לבב· וברוב כל· וליראה
את יהוה ולדבקה בו·[4] ויהי לפני מותו ויאמר אל בנו לאמר גשה אלי
3 בני אל תעמד כי איעצך לפני אלהים לפני·.......

חֲזָק

[ליום שני של שבועות·]

עשר תעשר את כל תבואת זרעך היוצא השדה שנה שנה ואכלת
לפני י״י אלהיך במקום אשר יבחר לשכן שמו שם מעשר דגנך ותירושך
ויצהרך ובכורות בקרך וצאנך למען תלמד ליראה את י״י אלהיך כל
הימים· אמרו חז״ל עשר תעשר· עשר בשביל שתתעשר· תעשר שלא
5 תתחסר· רמז למפרשי ים להוציא אחד מעשרה לעמלי תורה· אם תעשר
דגנך· ואם לאו דגני· שנא׳ לכן אשוב ולקחתי דגני בעתו· זכיתם
תירושך· ואם לאו תירושי· ר׳ לוי אמ׳ נבהל להון איש רע עין ולא
ידע כי חסר יבואנו· זה הפסוק אמ׳ כזה שאינו מוציא מעשרותיו
כראוי· דאמ׳ ר׳ לוי··· מעשה באחד שהיה מוציא מעשרותיו כראוי·
I. לפי׳ משה מזהיר לישראל עשר תעשר· I. מעשה שהיה באיש אחד
10 ושמו טובי משבט נפתלי· וכל ימיו הלך בדרך ישר והיה עושה עם אחיו
חסדים רבים לאשר עמו היו בגלות בנינוה· והוא נשאר יתום מאבין ויגדל
(ותגדל 1.) אותו דבורה אם אביו והיא נהג אותו בדרך ישר· וכאשר היה
איש נשא אשה מזרעו וממשפחתו ושמה חנה ותלד לו בן ויקרא שמו
15 טוביה· וכאשר היה בגולה בעיר נינוה כל אחיו וקרוביו היו מטמאין
נפשם ואוכלים לחמם מן בני האומות· והוא לא היה אוכל מפני שהיה

---

[1] Ps. 105, 1. [2] cf. Jerem. 31, 13. [3] Formula of Grace, Talmud
Berachoth f. 49b and 50a. [4] cf. Deut. 11, 22.

13 ישראל אשר נחם אותנו ויגדל לנו חסדו׃ ויהי אחר מלאת שבעת

הימים׃ ותבא שרה וכל המקנה והטף והגמלים והבהמה אשר נתן לה

14 רעואל אביה׃ ויספר טוביה לאביו את כל הקורות אותו ואת כל

XII. אשר עשה לו המלאך ואשר הצליחו האלהים׃ XII. ויאמר טובי אל

1 בני· במה נכבד את האיש? כי כל הבא אליך בגללו· ויהרג את הרשף

2 והרבה נפלאותיו עמך׃ ועתה בני קרא אותו· ולקח כל מחצית רכושך

3 אשר הבאת׃ וישמע אל אביו ויקרא אל המלאך ויחל את פניו ויאמר

אחלי נא לפני אדני[1] איש האלהים· הנה ברכני יהוה בגללך[2] עתה בחר

4 לך מכל הנמצא לי קח מחצית הכל· ויאמר· לא אקח דבר· אך עבדו

את יהוה ביראה והשתחוו לו וברכו את שם קדשו· כי הוא ישלם לאיש

5 כפעלו׃ והנה ברוך יהוה אשר נתן לך שכרך אשר פעלת עם המתים

6 חסד ואמת[3]· ונצח ישראל לא ישקר[4] ולא ידבר כזב כי אמת הוא׃

7 8 וצדקה תציל ממות[5]׃ והאלהים נסה אותך ויבא עליך הצרות האלה

9 ויצרף אותך ככסף וישמע את תפילתך׃ וישלחני אני רפאל המלאך

אחד מן שבעה השרים המשרתים ראשונה את פני המלך[6] יהוה צבאות׃

10 ויצו עלי לרפאות אותך ולהצילך ולהוליך את בנך ולהשיבהו· וישמע

11 את תפילתך וחרפתך עם תפלת שרה וחרפתה׃ ויהי כשמעם את

12 דבריו ויתמהו איש אל רעהו[7] ויפלו על פניהם׃ ויאמר להם אל תיראו·

כי בדבר יהוה באתי· ובמצותו עשיתי את כל הדברים האלה· כי לא

מלבי· והנה למראה עיניכם נראתי אוכל ושותה אבל לחם לא אכלתי

13 ומים לא שתיתי׃ ויקומו ויברכו את יהוה ויפרד המלאך והם לא

XIII. ידעו· כי יראו פן ימותו· כי מלאך יהוה צבאות ראו עיניהם׃ ויקומו

1 ויברכו את יהוה אלהיהם· ויאמר טובי· גדול אתה יהוה וגדולים מעשיך[8]

2 ותמלוך עלינו לעולם ועד[9]· כי לך המלוכה מוריד שאול ויעל[10]· מוחץ

3 וידיו תרפינה· ואין מידו מציל[11]· הודו ליהוה כי טוב כי לעולם חסדו[12]׃

4 מי ימלל גבורות יהוה ישמיע כל תהילתו כי לו דומיה תהילה[13] ברכו

5 נפשי את יהוה יהוה אלהי גדלת מאד הוד והדר לבשת[14]· ברוך יהוה

6 אלהי ישראל מהעולם ועד העולם· ואמר כל העם· אמן[15]· ויהי טרם כלו

לאכול ויוגד לטוביה הנה אשתך באה עם המקנה והצאן ויקומו וילכו

7 לקראתם בתופים ובמחולות· ויביאם הביתה בשמחה ובשירים[16]׃ וימלאו

ימי המשתה ויברכו את יהוה קול גדול· יודו ליהוה חסדו[17] על כל

8 הטובות והנפלאות אשר פעל לנו יהוה׃ ויאמר טובי· ברוך אתה יהוה

אלהי ישראל אשר לא מנעת חסדך ואמיתך מעמנו שומר הברית

---

[1] II Kings 5, 3.   [2] Gen. 30, 27.   [3] cf. Ruth 1, 8.   [4] I Sam. 15, 29.

[5] Prov. 10, 2.   [6] Esther 1, 13, 14.   [7] Gen. 43, 33 cf. Is. 13, 8.

[8] cf. Ps. III, 2.   [9] cf. Exod. 15, 18.   [10] I Sam. 2, 6.

[11] Deut. 32, 29.   [12] Ps. 106, 1—2.   [13] Ps. 65, 2.   [14] Ps. 104, 1.

[15] I Chr. 16, 36.   [16] Gen. 31, 27.   [17] Ps. 107, 8.

בני בני מדוע בושש אתה לבא ומדוע אחרו פעמיך¹ כה משפטו כל

2 3 הימים: ותבך חנה ולא תאכל כי רבות היו אנחתה ולבה דוי²· ותאמר

אל אישה· אבל אשם אתה כי הבאת עלינו הצרה הגדולה הזאת³:

4 ותשלח את בנינו שמחת לבבינו המכלכל את שיבתנו אשר בצילו

5 נחיה בגוים⁴· ויען לה טובי· אל תיראי אחותי· כי בחסדי אלהי במחתי

אשר ישיבהו בשלום· כי האיש ההולך עמו נאמן מאד· ומלאך יהוה

6 צבאות הוא· לכי נא החוצה אחותי וראי· אולי יאבה יהוה בכל

צדקותיו· ובשרתני ושמחת את לבבי הדוה· כה משפטו כל ימי היות בנו

7 החוצה: וגם טוביה היה מחשב בלבו ואומר אל רעואל חתנו· למה

תאחר אותי ויהוה הצליח דרכי⁵· והנה אבי ואמי נדדה שנתם ולא ינוחו

8 ולא ישקוטו עד יום שובי בשלום: ויאמר לו רעואל לחתנו· הואל נא

9 ושב אתי ומלא שבועים אלה ואשלחך בשמחה ובשירים⁶: ויען לו

טובי(ה)· לא אדני שמעני· שלחני ואלכה (אל) ארצי ואשתי עמי:

10 וירא רעואל כי לא יכול לו וישלחהו ואת אשתו שלח עמו בכסף

11 ובזהב ובמגדנות⁷ ומקנה ועבודה רבה⁸ ובשמחה..גדולה: ויברך

רעואל את בתו ויאמר· יהוה אלהי ישראל יתן לך זרע אנשים ויהוה

XL יצליח דרכיך: XI. וישלחו אותו ואשתו· וכל קרוביו ואהביו ומיודעיו

1 הלכו עמו דרך יום אחד· ויתנו לו מנות· איש נזם זהב וקשיטה

2 ואגורה⁹· וישובו נגוה העירה: ויהי כאשר קרבו העיר· ויאמר מלאך

[אחד]⁹ᵃ יהוה אל טוביה· הנה ידעת כי ארכו לנו הימים¹⁰ אשר

3 התפרדנו מאביך· ועתה שים לדרך פעמיך¹¹ ומהר ובאה את אביך·

4 ואני אתנהלה לאט לרגל אשתך ולרגל המקנה¹²: ויאמר לו טוביה

טוב הדבר אשר דברת· וימהר טוביה ויחבש את חמורו ויקם וילך:

5 ויצו המלאך את טוביה בבואך הבית שים ליהוה תודה וברכהו·

6 ובא לפני אביך ונשקתו· ואת מרת הדג אשר הנחתה למשמרת קח

7 לך ומשח עיני אביך· וראך ושמח בלבו· וילך מאתו טוביה ויבא

8 העירה· ויהי בבאו ותראהו אמו ותרץ ותבשר את אישה: וישמח טובי

מאד ויקם מעל¹³ ממתו· ויבקש לרוץ לקראת בנו· ויגף באבן רגליו ויפל

9 ארצה· כי כהו עיניו: וימהר טוביה וירד מעל החמור· ויקם את אביו

מעל הארץ וישקהו· ויבכו וישתחו אל יהוה ויהללוהו ויברכוהו בקול

10 גדול: ויקח טוביה את מרת הדג וימשח בה את עיני אביו· ותפקחנה

עיני אביו ויפל הלובן אשר כסה [אשר כסה] את עיניו· וישמח מאד:

11 12 ותרא חנה כי ראה אישה וישתחו (!) ליהוה· ותאמר· ברוך יהוה אלהי

---

1 cf. Judg. 5, 28.   2 Lam. 1, 22.   3 cf. Gen. 42, 21.

4 Lam. 4, 20.   5 Gen. 24, 56.   6 Gen. 31, 27.   7 2 Chr. 21, 3.

8 cf. Job. 1, 3.   9 Job 42, 11.   9ª So and sign of del. in MS.

10 Gen. 26, 8.   11 Ps. 85, 14.   12 Gen. 33, 14.

13 מ added afterwards over the word.   14 Ps. 91, 12.

תפילתי לרצון לפניך · ואהיה ראויה לאישי הלז ומברכותיך תשלח לנו :

23 ויגער יהוה בשטן אשר לא יגע באדני זלא זלא יעמד על ימינו לשטנני :

24 על כן נודך יהוה אלהינו על כל ניסיך ונפלאותיך כי רבות המה · כי
השמים ושמי השמים לא יכלכלוך[2] אף כי בני האדם לחקור אחת

25 מהם : ומי ימלל את גבורותיך וישמיע כל תהילותיך[3] ? ואתה הוא

26 המתנשא לכל לראש ומרומם על כל ברכה : ויהי בחצי הלילה בקריאת
הגבר · ויקרא רעואל לאנשיו · קומו מהרו לחצוב קבר לטוביה · כי

27 ידעתי כי קרהו אסון כאשר לשבעת האנשים אשר התחתנו בי : ויהי
ככלותו לחצוב הקבר · וישב רעואל אל ביתו ויאמר לאשתו · שלחי לי את

28 האמה וראתה והתבוננה אם הבחור חי או מת : ותלך האמה · והנה
שניהם חיים שוכבים וישינים במטתם · ותשב ותבשרם בשורה טובה

29 וישמח לבבם : ויברכו את יהוה ויאמרו · ברוך יהוה אלהי ישראל אשר
הטיב עמנו ומפליא לעשות[5] · ויגער בשטן אשר לא יכול להרע לנו
ולבנינו · עד עולם וידעו כל הגוים אשר שמך נקרא עלינו[6] · ויצו רעואל

30 וימלאו את הקבר פה לפה : ויצו ויכינו טבח ויקרא אל כל שכיניו ·

31 ויאכלו וישתו ויכרו כירה גדולה[7] : ויבקש רעואל פני טוביה לשבת

32 אתו עד שבועים : ויתן לו מחצית רכושו הונו ואוצרותיו וצאאנו[8]
ואלפיו ושורו ועבודתו ובכל (וּמכל .l) אשר ימצא לו יתן לו (מחצית)
בחייו · ואחרי מותו יקח הכל : IX. ויאמר טוביה אל המלאך בי

1 אדני · אל יחר אפך בי · אך הפעם הואלתי דבר[9] והטבת חסדך

2 האחרון מן הראשון[10] : והלכת לי אל גבאל (!) אל המדינה (....)
והאותות האלה. קח בידך וקבל מאתו הכסף · ובקש ממנו לבא
בשמחה ולשמוח עמנו · כי לא אוכל להפרד מזה עד מלאת שבועיים

3 תמימות ימי המשתה : ואתה ידעת כי לא ישקוט אבי ולא ינוח עד

4 שובי בשלום : וישמע לו המלאך · ויקח ארבעה מעבדי רעואל ושני
גמלים אתו · ויבא דאגי ויתן אל גביאל האות · ויקח את הכסף מידו :

5 ויגד לו את כל אשר לטוביה בן טובי ואשר בקש ממנו לבא לשמוח

6 עם הקרואים ביום. חתונתו וביום שמחת לבו[11] : ויקם גבאל (!) ויחבש

7 את גמלו וילך · אתו : ויהי בבא ביתה רעואל וימצאהו וטוביה עמו

8 יושבים על הלחם ויפל על צוארו וישקהו ויבך : ויברכהו ויאמר יברכך
יהוה וישמרך[12] כי בן איש טוב וישר אתה · ירא אלהים וסר מרע[13] :

9 יהי ביתך כבית פרץ אשר הוליד את חצרון[14] · ויענו כל העם · אמן ·

X.
1 ויאכלו וישתו וישמחו : X. והנה טובי סר וזעף ויתעצב אל לבו ויאמר

---

[1] Zech. 3, 1.   [2] I Kings 8, 27.   [3] Ps. 106, 2.   [4] I Chr. 29, 11.
[5] Judg. 13, 19.   [6] Jerem. 14, 9.   [7] II Kings 6, 23.
[8] So Ms. on א a stroke i. e. deletur.   [9] Gen. 18, 30.   [10] Ruth 3, 10.
[11] Song 3, 11.   [12] Numb 6, 24.   [13] Job 1, 1.   [14] cf. Ruth 4, 12.

8 אלוה על כל· בורא הכל· גדול על כל· דורש הכל· הוא כל יכול·
מרום על כל· זמר יתנו לו כל· חק ומצוה לכל· טוב לכל· ישר וצדיק
לכל· כל יכול· מורה לכל· נותנין לו שבח הכל· סומך הכל· עונה לכל·
פודה שבויי כל· צדיק וחסיד לכל· קרוב יהוה לכל· רחום יהוה
9 ורחמיו על כל· שירה יתנו לו כל· תומך שמו הכל: אלהי האלהים
ואדני האדנים [רחום] רחום נקרא שמך מעולם. זכרה נא לנו לחסדיך
10 ורחמיך כי מעולם המה[2]: וזכרה נא לי לחסדי טובי אבי אשר התהלך
לפניך בחסד ואמת והצילני וגער בשטן לבלתי לנגוע ולהרע לנו:
11 ונתת לי מן האשה הזאת זרע אנשים[3]· והיו צאצאינו יודעי שמך ולומדי
12 תורתך[4]· ונודע בעמים כי אתה אלהים ואין עוד: ואתה השמים תשמע
תפילתי כאשר שמעת את תפילת אבותינו הקדושים את תפילת אברהם
באור כשדים· ותפילת יצחק בהר המוריה· ותפילת יעקב בביתאל·
ותפילת כל הישרים ושימה דמעתי בנאדך[5] יהיו לרצון אמרי פי והגיון
13 לבי לפניך יהוה צורי וגואלי[6]: ותתפלל שרה ותאמר· יהוה יהוה אל
רחום וחנון ארך אפים ורב חסד ואמת נוצר חסד לאלפים לשמרי
14 עדותיו ומצותיו[7]: יהוה אחד לבדך ואין שני עמך· מי כמוך· ומי ידמה לך
15 ומי ישוה לך· אין זולתך ואין בלתך· ואין ערוך אליך[8]: אתה בראת
הכל· ואין לפניך שכחה· לכן יאמינו הלבבות כי אתה אחד ונפלא בכל
דרכיך ונעלם מעין כל· ועין לא תשורך· ואתה היית עד לא היות
16 העולם· ואחרי אובדו תהיה· ושנותיך לא יתמו[9]: הן כל צבא השמים
בדברך נעשו וידך לא הויה בם לבראותם אך קראת ויעמדו יחדו ובידך·
17 הכח והגבורה להחליפם ולהאבידם ולהשיבם לקדמתם: ובידך החיים
והטוב וברואת העולם הזה לבחון בו בני האדם בחקים ובמשפטים אשר
18 צויתם: והעולם הבא בראת לחסדיך לאוהביך ולשומרי בריתך· ומאתמול
19 ערכת תפתה[10] לזרים הבוגדים בך: ואתה הוא האלהים אשר בחרת
בזרע ישרון מכל העמים אשר על פני האדמה· ותעש להם אותות
20 ומופתים בכל הקמים עליהם[11]: ועתה יהוה· מלך מלא רחמים· האזינה
תפילתי ואל דמעתי אל תחרש· כאשר שמעת אל תפילת אמינו שרה
בהתפללה על אודות [הגר] הגר שפחתה· ותפילת רבקה בהתרוצץ
21 הבנים בקרבה: וכתפילת רחל(!) אם הבנים עקרת הבית בעת כעסתה
אחותה ותפתח את רחמה ותלד בנים עומדים בחצרותיך לשרתך(!):
22 וכתפלת מרים הנביאה· וכתפלת אשת אלקנה כעסתה צרתה גם כעס
לבעבור הרעימה[12]· ותעמיד ממנה בן נביא עומד ומשרת לפניך· כן תעלה

---

1 Poem with an alphabetical Acrostic.   2 Ps. 25, 6.   3 I. Sam. I, 11.
4 cf. Daily Prayers, taken from Talmud Tr. Berachoth f. 11b.
5 Ps. 56, 9.   6 Ps. 19, 15.   7 Exod. 34, 6.
8 Liturgy Sabbath morning prayer (Nishmath).   9 Ps. 102, 28.
10 Jes. 30, 33.   11 Deut. 6, 22.   12 I. Sam. 1, 6.

לילה ולילה תבעיר את הלב באש והעלית את עשנו על המטה אשר

15 תשכבו בה וגם הרשף· והיה בלילה הראשון· והזכרת שמות האבות
הקדושים· ובלילה השני התפלל אל אלהיך אשר יצאו מכם אנשים

16 טובים: והיה בלילה השלישי בקריאת הגבר ועשה רצונך בירֹאת אלהיך

VII. ויצליחך: [חצי] VII. ויבאו אל בית רעואל וישמח מאד· וישק אל טוביה

1 ויאמר אל עדנה אשתו· הנה תארו כתואר איש הטוב טובי· ותאמר

2 אשתו· מי אתם· ומאין אתם? ויאמר נפתלי מן השביה אשר

3 בנינוה: ויאמר להם רעואל· הידעתם את טובי אחי? ויאמר המלאך

4 ידענו· וזה הבחור בנו· ושמו טוביה: וילך רעואל ויפל על פניו ארצה

5 וישקהו ויבך על צואריו[2]: ויאמר· ברוך אתה בני ליהוה[2] כי בן איש טוב
אתה· ותבאנה עדנה אשתו (ובתו) ויבכו עליו· ויכינו לו מטבח[3]· וישחטו

6 שעיר עזים וישבו על הלחם[4]: וטוביה אמר אל רעואל· דודי·
שאלה גדולה אנכי שואל מעמך· בי אדני אל נא תשוב (תשיבי [.l]):

7 ועתה הואל נא ותנה לי בתך לאשה· כי טוב תתה לי לאשה מתתה

8 לאיש אחר[5] כי עצמך ובשרך אני[6]: ויבהל רעואל כי ירא פן ימות גם
הוא כשבעה אנשים המומתים על ידה· וישמר (וישם [.l]) לפיו מחסום[7]:

9 ויאמר המלאך· אל תירא כי בא גד[8] ובשם יהוה תנה לו כי לא
נכונה לה וזה נכון· ויען רעואל לו יהי כדברך אדני· ויתן יהוה אלהי

10 ישראל את ביתם כבית פרץ[9]· וימלא את משאלות לבם ותאותם
למובה· ואלהי אברהם יצחק ויעקב אבתינו יהיה עמהם ויצוה ברכתו

11 על שניכם (שניהם [.l])[10]: ויאספו זקני העיר שם ויכתבו את הדברים·
ויברכו את האלהים והחתן והכלה· ויאכלו וישמחו בשמחה גדולה:

VIII. ויהי אחרי כן ויבאו שניהם החדרה הפנימית: ויזכר טוביה את

1 2 דברי המלאך· ויקח את הכבד· ויתן על גחלי אש· ויעל עשנו· ויקח המלאך

3 את הרשף ויאסרהו· וישלחהו המדברה אשר על פני מצרים: ויאמר
טוביה אל שרה· קומי והתפללי אל יהוה אלהינו הלילה גם בלילה
השני· והיה בלילה השלישי נתחברה יחדו כי בני קדושים אנחנו ולא

4 נלך בחקות הגוים אשר סביבותינו: ויקומו שניהם ויתפללו באימה

5 לפני יהוה· וישפכו את לבם להפיל תחנתם לפניו: ויאמר טוביה· ברוך
אתה יהוה אלהינו מלך העולם אשר ברא ששון ושמחה חתן וכלה:

6 ברוך אתה יהוה אלהינו מלך העולם אשר ברא את האדם בצלמך

7 ובתבניתך[11]· ונתת לו מכח גבורתך לדעת דעתך ולעבדך· ונתת לו עזר
כנגדו· וצוית להם לפרות ולרבות ולהרבות צאצאיהם בקרב הארץ:

[1] Gen. 46, 29.   [2] cf. Judg. 17, 2.   [3] cf. Is. 14, 21.
[4] cf. Gen. 37, 25.   [5] I. Kings 2, 16.   [6] cf. Gen. 29, 14. 19.
[7] Ps. 39, 2.   [8] Gen. 30, 11.   [9] cf. Ruth 4, 12.   [10] cf. Deut. 28, 8.
[11] cf. Wedding Ritual; v. Talmud Ketuboth fol. 8a.

15 המלאך הנני· אלך עמו : ויאמר לו טובי· הגידה לי מה שמך ומאיזה

16 משפחה ושבט אתה?· ויען המלאך ויאמר· שמי עזריה בן חנניה הגדול·

17 ממשפחה גדולה אני· ויאמר טובי· אל יחר בעיניך והגדת לי מאיזו משפחה

אתה? ויאמר משבט .... ויאמר לו טובי· האלהים יהיה עמכם ושלח

18 מלאכו לפניכם· ויכינו צדה לדרך וילכו שניהם יחדו: ותלך חנה אמו

19 מחוץ לעיר הלוך ובכה: ותאמר אליהם· האלהים יהיה עמכם ונתן

20 לכם חסד ורחמים לפני יושבי הארץ: ועתה הכן פעמיך למהר לשוב

21 אלינו לראות פנינו טרם מותינו (והורדנו) ביגון שאולה: ויהי בשובה לביתה

ותאמר אל טובי מה זאת עשית כי שלחת את בנך את יחידך אשר

22 אהבת מעליך?: והיה אם יקראנו אסון והורדנו את שיבתינו ביגון

23 שאולה¹: כי בעוד בנינו אתנו היה לנו למשיב נפשינו ולכלכל את

24 שיבתינו²: ויען לה· אל תיראי אחותי· כי שלח יהוה מלאכו עמו והצליח

VI. את דרכו והוא ישיבהו עוד : וילך טוביה עד הנהר חדקל וישב

1 שם· וירד לרחוץ את רגליו· והנה דג גדול יוצא לקראתו לפי תומו

לבולעו· וירא ויקרא בקול גדול ויאמר· אדני הצילני מן הדג הגדול הזה:

2 ויאמר לו המלאך· קרעהו והוצאת לך לבו ומרירתו וכבדתו ושים לך

למשמרת· כי עוד יהיו לך לרפואה: ויקח את הדג ויבתר אותו בתוכו³·

3 ויאכלו את הבתר האחד· והשיני הצטיידו לדרך עד באם אל דאגי אשר

4 במדינת מדי: וישאל הנער את איש האלהים· מה משפט הלב והכבד

5 והמרה אשר הנחנו למשמרת?· ויען לו· הלב קח לך⁴ להוציא שדים מאיש

6 או מאשה כי תשרפנו באש: וישאלהו הנער· אנא נלין הלילה? ויאמר

7 לו· בדאגי העיר: והנה בעיר איש טוב ושמו רעואל ממשפחת אביך·

ואין לו בן או בת⁵ רק בת אחת והיא יורשת בכל אשר לאביה· ובבאך

9 שם תשאלנה ממנו· כי לא ימנענה ממך: ויען טוביה ויאמר שמעני

10 וישמע לך האלהים: והנה לשמע אזן שמעתיה ותרגז בטני⁶· כי שמעתי

רבים מוציאי דבה· כי נתנה לשבעה אנשים ויהי בלילה הראשון לשכבם

11 יחד ויבא אשמדאי מלך השדים בחצות הלילה ויהרגם: ועל כן זחלתי

ואירא⁷ פן ישים נפשי כאחד מהם· והנה אני כמוה רך ויחיד לאבי ולאמי·

12 והיה אם יפגע בי (אסון) והורדתי את שיבתם בדם שאולה: ויאמר לו המלאך·

אל תערץ ואל תחת ואל ירך לבבך כי אודיעך במה תוציאהו מעליך:

13 ואתה דע לך· כי כל האנשים הממתים לא היו ראוים לה וליצא מהם

זרע אנשים על כן המיתם הרשף: ואתה עשה לך כאשר אצוך· והיו

14 יחד בחדר אחד שלשת ימים לילה ויום ואליה לא תקרב: והיה מדי

15

---

¹ cf. Gen. 42, 38.   ² Ruth 4, 15.   ³ Gen. 15, 10.
⁴ The reading of these two words is uncertain; In the MS. it looks
like זחלך which has no meaning.
⁵ cf. Judg. 11, 34.   ⁶ Habk. 3, 17.   ⁷ Job 32, 6.

טובי כי יחד התפללו• ותעל שוועתם לפני האלהים וישלח מלאכו

IV. רפאל לרפאותם ולהצילם מצרתם: IV. והנה טובי מתחנן על נפשו

1 למות• ויקרא לבנו טוביה לאמר: שמע בני מוסר אביך ותורת אמך

2 לא תטש[1] והיה מוסרם ענוד על לבבך[2]• ובקחת אלהים את נפשי

3 ונשאתני וקברתני בקבורת אבותי• ואת אמך כבד כל ימי חייך:

4 וזכרת הצרות אשר עברו עלינו ועליה מדי יום יום• ובמלאת ימיה

5 וקברת אותה בכבוד אצלי• וכל ימי חייך זכור בוראך[3] והשמר מחטוא

6 ומצות האלהים תשמר ותורתו• ופתוח תפתח לעני ידך• וכי תראה ערום

7 וכסיתו: הלא פרוש לרעב לחמך[4] ועיניך אל תעלים• מהם ויברכך האלהים

בכל מעשה ידיך ויפתח לך את אוצרו הטוב[5]• כי לא יועיל הון ביום

8 עברה וצדקה תציל ממות[6]: ואת האלהים ירא בכל נפשך ובכל מאדך•

9 ואל תתחבר לעושי עולה• ואל תשב במושב לצים: והשב לאיש פעלו

שכרו ביומו.תתן• ואל ילין עמך שכר שכיר: ואהבת לרעך כמוך[7]• ועצת

10 צדיקים תדרוש: ועתה בני• לך לך ובקש ככרי הכסף אשר לי ביד

גביאל בעיר דאגו• והא לך האות אשר נתתי לו זכרון לכסף• ואל תירא

11 כי עמך האלהים בכל אשר תלך אם תשמר מצותיו• ואל יבהלוך הצרות

הגדולות אשר עברו עלינו• כי בטחתי [בבראת] בבראת האלהים כי עוד

V. תהיה לנו ישועה גדולה ורוח• על כן בני אל תירא: V. ויען טוביה

1 אל אביו ויאמר כל אשר תאמר• אלי אעשה• אך הוריני והדריכני בדרך

2 זו אלך• כי אני יחיד ואיככה אלכה לבדי להביא את הכסף: ויאמר לו

לך ובקש לי אחד נאמן בחוץ ואתן לו שכרו בעודני חי• והוא ילך עמך

3 לבקש הכסף: ויצא טוביה ביום ההוא וילך ויבקש בשוקי העיר איש

4 נאמן: ויצא לקראתו רפאל המלאך אשר שלחו האלהים להיות לו לעזר•

5 ולא ידע הנער כי מלאך האלהים הוא: וישאל לו הנער לשלום ויאמר

6 לו מי אתה אדני• ויען לו• מבני יהודה אני: ויאמר לו טוביה• הידעת דרך

7 ארץ נפתלי (!) ויאמר לו• ידעתי כל גבולי הארץ והמדינות: ומכיר אני את

גבאל איש משבטי והוא יושב בדאגי העיר אשר במדי בעיר נגוה(!) בהר

8 אבתנים (אגבתנים.l): ויאמר לו טוביה• אל יחר בעיניך אדני אלכה לאבי

9 ואשובה: וילך טוביה ויגד לאביו• וישלח טובי אחרי האיש ויבא לפני

10 טובי וישאל לו לשלום: ויאמר לו המלאך• ששון ושמחה ישיגוך[8]• ויאמר

11 לו• איזה שמחה תבא לי ואנכי יושב במחשכים כמתי עולם ואור השמש

12 אינני רואה: ויאמר לו• אל ירע לפני אדני כי קרובה ישועתך לבא

13 וראית ושמח בלבך: ואמר לו טובי• הלא קראתי לך ללכת עם בני (אל)

14 גבאל היושב בדאגי במדינת מדי• ובשובך אתן לך שכרך: ויאמר לו

---

[1] Prov. I, 8.   [2] Prov. 6, 21, 22.   [3] cf. Eccles. 12, 1.   [4] Jes. 58, 7. 8.
[5] cf. Deut. 28, 12.   [6] Prov. 11, 4.   [7] Levit. 19, 18.
[8] Jes. 51, 11.

אתה וישר משפטיך ואורחותיך חסד ורחמים ואמת ומשפט[1] : ועתה יהוה 2
זכריני לטובה· ופקדיני בישועתיך[2] · ואל תזכר לי עונות אבותי ומהר עניני
וחטאות אבותינו אל תזכר לי[3] : כי על לא שמרנו מצותיך ותורתך היינו 3
למשל ולשנינה בכל הגוים אשר הבאתנו שמה[4] · ועתה יהוה גדולים 4
מעשיך · והישר בעיניך עשה · והצור תמים עשה לי כחסדך חסד ואמת
ולקחת את נפשי כי טוב מותי מחיי: בעת ההיא ותהי שרה בת רעואל 5
אחי טובי מתפללת ליהוה במדי : כי שמעה נאצות ובוזות ותקל בעיני 6
שפחה אחת לבית אביה : וכעסתה גם כעס[5] מדי יום יום לאמר · אוי לך 7
ולמזלך · כי שבעה אנשים נתנו לך וימותו כל אחד ואחד בלילה הראשונה
אשר באו אלייך בכשפייך : ואיך נשאת עין ותרימי ראש לדבר אלי 8
קטנה או גדולה ואנכי טובה ממך · והנה שקר בפיה כי לא היתה ידה 9
במעל[6] · אך אשמדאי מלך השדים היה הורגם בלילה הראשונה על אשר
(לא) נכונו אליה: ובכל יום ויום היתה אומרת אליה· הנה אינך ראויה לאיש 10
ולהיות לך זרע על הארץ והנה את חושבת להרגני כאשר הרגת אתהם:
ויהי היום ותעל בעליה· ותעמד שם שלשה ימים לילה ויום· לחם לא 11
אכלה ומים לא שתתה· ותעמד לפני יהוה בתפילה ובתחנונים להנקם מן
האמה ההיא המחרפת אותה: ותחשב להמית את עצמה לולי כי 12
יראה פן תורד שיבת אביה ביגון שאולה ופן יאמרו קמיהם לשמצה· בת
אחת היתה לו יחידה ותמת את עצמה: ויהי כאשר תמו שלשת הימים 13
ותפל ותתחנן לפני יהוה ותאמר: ברוך יהוה אלהים אלהי ישראל שומר 14
הברית והחסד לשמרי בריתו ולאהבי מצותיו[7] : אתה הוא העונה בעת 15
צרה פודה ומציל ומושיע· גומל לחייבים טובות : אליך נשאתי עיני 16
היושבי בשמים· כי ידעתי כי עפר אנכי ואל עפר אשוב· והנה 17
אנכי מתפללת לפניך ומפלת תחנתי (על?) אשר חרפוני חנם : והנה ידעת 18
את לבבי כי לא חמדתי איש· וטהורה אנכי בעמדי לפניך: במושב 19
לצים לא ישבתי · ועם משחקים לא באתי · ועם פעלי און לא הלכתי· ולא 20
חפצתי איש כי אם ביראתך (!) · ואנכי לא הייתי נכונה להם: ואני ידעתי
כי איש אחד הת..ת(!) לי והוכחת לי· ואם רצונך שלחיהו לי· כי זאת 21
תורת האדם העובדך באמת ואחריתו תקוה: (.1 לתת לו אחרית ותקוה)[8]
ובבא עליו צרה וצוקה והצלתו בצדקתך · כי לא תחפוץ במות המת כי 22
אם בשובו מדרכו וחיה[9]· והצדקה תעביר רוע הגזירה: יהי שמך 23
מבורך מעולם ועד עולם אמן[10]· בעת ההיא נשמע צעקתה עם צעקת

---

[1] cf. Zech. 7, 9. Ps. 25, 10. [2] cf. Ps. 106, 4 and The additional
service for New Moon in the Liturgy. [3] cf. Ps. 77, 8. [4] cf. Deut. 28, 37.
[5] I. Sam. 1, 6. [6] Ezra 9, 2. [7] Deut. 7, 9.
[9] Liturgy of the Day of Atonement; v. Ezek. 18, 33 and 33, 11.
[10] cf. Ps. 113, 2.

יהודה בבשת פנים על המכה אשר הכהו אלהים• על אשר חירף וגידף•

15 ויכנע סנחריב• ויך רבים מישראל• וטובי היה קוברם: ויוגד למלך• ויצו

16 המלך להרוג אותו ולשלול כל אשר לו: ויברח טובי הוא ואשתו ובניו וילכו יחפים וערומים בלי כסות בקרח ובלי מחיה. ובכל(!) אשר הלך מצא

17 אוהבים רבים: ויהי מקץ ארבעים וחמשה ימים הרגו סנחריב בניו

II. אסרחדון(!) ושראצר• וישמע טובי וישב אל ביתו וכל שללו הושב לו: II. ויהי

1 אחריכן ויהי חג י"י• ויעש טובי סעודה גדולה בביתו: ויאמר אל טוביה

2 בנו• בני לך והבא לנו אנשים ממשפחתינו יראי אלהים ויאכלו עמנו:

3 וילך טוביה. וישב ויגד לאביו• כי אחד מבני ישראל ראה הרוג ומושלך

4 בחוץ: ויקם טובי מכסאו ויעזב הסעודה ולא אכל• וילך אל המת וישאהו

5 בסתר אל ביתו• ובבא השמש קברהו• ואחר אכל באבל וערדה: ויזכר את הדבר אשר ביד עמוס הנביא• והפכתי את חגיכם לאבל ושיריכם

6 לקינה¹: ויריבו אותו קרוביו לאמר הנה ידעת כי צוה המלך להרג על אשר קברת המתים ותברח ותנצל נפשך• ועודך מחזיק בתומתך²:

7 ויאמר• הנה הרבה יראתי את אדני האדנים מיראתי את המלך קרוץ

8 מחומר³ כמוני: וטובי היה הולך ושוב אחרי ההרוגים• ובסתר היה מביאם

9 וקוברם בחצות הלילה: ויהי היום ויעף טובי מקבור אותם• ולא טבל

10 ידיו ובמים לא שטפם אחרי קוברו אותם: וישכב על המטה אצל הקיר וישן• והנה קן צפור דרור ויפל על עיניו צאתם ותכהין עיניו ולא ראה.

11 ולבעבור נסותו עשה לו האלהים כל זאת כאשר עשה לאיוב• וטובי היה ירא את יהוה מנעוריו• וכל (ובכל I.) זאת לא נתן טובי תפלה לאלהים⁴

12 וידבק באלהי ישראל ויבטח בחסדו: ויבאו לפניו ריעי איוב אליפז התימני ובלדד השוחי וצופר הנעמתי• ויהיו כולם מלעינים עליו לאמר• (איה) צדקתך אשר בטחת בה לאמר• צדקתי ואקבר את המתים ואגמול להם חסד⁵?:

13 ויגער בהם טובי ויאמר• אמנם זך וחף אנכי וצדקתי תענה בי⁶• והנה גם הרע וגם הטוב נקבל באהבה ובשמחת לבב⁷• כי כל משפטי יהוה ישרים⁸:

14 כי כל אשר אמונתו שלימה לא ימיר ולא יחליף• ונתן לו אלהים חיי

15 העולם הבא: ותהי אשתו חכמת לב לעשות כל מלאכת מחשבת•

16 ותעש לרבים ותכלכל אישה במעשה ידיה: והנה בכל(!) יום קבלה שעיר

17 עזים אחד בשכרה ותביאהו אל הבית• והשעיר הולך וגעה בבית: וישמע טובי קול השעיר ויאמר לה• ראה פן גניבה אתך• השב תשיב אותו לבעליו•

18 כי כן צונו אלהינו ולא נוכל להלינו בביתינו ולקחת לנו: ותען ותאמר• אם צדיק אתה כדבריך• מדוע קראתך כל הצרה הזאת? כה משפטה כל הימים

III. לדבר אתו קשות עד כי קץ בחייו: III. ויהי כשמע טובי הנאצות האלה

1 ויאנח וישבר לבו וישם פניו• אל הקיר ויתפלל בדמעות• ויאמר• יהוה צדיק

---

¹ Amos 8, 10. ² Job 2, 9. ³ Job 33, 6. ⁴ Job 1, 22.
⁵ cf. Job 33, 9. ⁶ Gen. 30, 33. ⁷ Job 2, 10. ⁸ cf. Nehem. 9, 13.

HISTORY OF TOBIT.

(BRIT. MUSEUM ADD. 11.639 f. 736 — 753.)

A.

I. **טוביה:** דברי טובי בן טוביאל בן חנגאל בן עשאל בן גבתיאל I.
ממשפחת נפתלי בגליל על פישן אחרי דרך מבוא השמש ¹אשר ¹
בשמאל (!) והעיר שפת שמה: וטובי הגלה ונשבה בימי שלמנאסר מלך 2
אשור. ועודו בשבי ודרך אמת לא פרץ• וכל אשר יקנה יתן חלק כתלק
לאחיו השבויים. ויהי עבד לכל מטה נפתלי ולא נתן כתף אחד (1.סוררת?)
במלאכה²: ובשבת ישראל על אדמתם ויתעו ויעבדו עגלי הזהב אשר 3
עשה ירבעם בן נבט. והאיש טובי היה הולך וזובח זבחים בבית יהוה
ויהי מתפלל שם לאלהי ישראל: וכל בכורי אדמתו ומעשרותיו באמונה 4
היה מביא בית יהוה אל היכלו בשנת השלישית שנת המעשר• גם
מנעוריו שמר דרכי יהוה ומצותיו: ויהי כי גדל טובי ויקח אשה משבטו 5
ושמה חנה. ותהר ותלד בן• ותקרא את שמו טוביה: וישפך טובי את 6
לבו עליו וילמדהו דרכי יהוה: וילך בדרכי אביו מנעוריו• וישתמר מכל
עון³: ובא הוא ואשתו ובנו אל ארץ אשור בננוה(!) העיר הגדולה עם כל 7
מטה נפתלי• ויהי כולם מתגאלים במאכלי הגוים• רק טובי לבדו לא
התגאל⁴: ויעבד את יהוה בכל לבבו ויתנהו אלהים לחסד ולרחמים לפני 8
שלמנאסר המלך• וימשילהו בכל אשר יחפוץ• ויצו לעשות רצונו בכל
המלכות: ויתהלך בכל הערים ובכל המבצרים לראות השביה ולשאול 9
ולדרוש שלומם⁵: ויהי כאשר בא במדי• ויהי בידו הון גדול אשר נתן 10
לו המלך אלף ככרי כסף• ויאסף יהודים רבים ממטהו• ויפקד את הכסף
ביד גביאל• ויראו ויהיו עדים• ויתן אות להיות זכרון לכסף: ויהי ימים 11
רבים וימת שלמנאצר מלך אשור• וימלוך סנחריב בנו תחתיו• וירע לבני
ישראל: וטובי היה מפזר הונו ונותן לבני עמו וינחם אותם: ויתן 12
להם לכל אחד ואחד כפי אשר תשיג ידו• ערומים היה מלביש• ורעבים 13
היה משביע: ומתים הרוגים היה קובר: ויהי בשוב סנחריב מארץ 14

---

1 Deut. 11, 30.   2 Zech. 7, 11.   3 cf. Ps. 18, 24.   4 cf. Dan. 1, 8.
5 cf. Ezra 9, 12. Jer. 28, 4.

SOCIETY OF BIBLICAL ARCHÆOLOGY PUBLICATIONS.

n 8 Parts. Price 5s. each. The Fourth Part having been issued, the Price is now Raised to £5 for the 8 Parts. Parts cannot be sold separately.

THE EGYPTIAN BOOK OF THE DEAD.

Complete Translation, Commentary, and Notes.

BY SIR P. LE PAGE RENOUF, KNT. (*President*);

CONTAINING ALSO

𝔄 𝔖𝔢𝔯𝔦𝔢𝔰 𝔬𝔣 𝔓𝔩𝔞𝔱𝔢𝔰 𝔬𝔣 𝔱𝔥𝔢 𝔙𝔦𝔤𝔫𝔢𝔱𝔱𝔢𝔰 𝔬𝔣 𝔱𝔥𝔢 𝔡𝔦𝔣𝔣𝔢𝔯𝔢𝔫𝔱 𝔠𝔥𝔞𝔭𝔱𝔢𝔯𝔰.

he Bronze Ornaments of the Palace Gates from Balawat.

[SHALMANESER II, B.C. 859–825.]

Parts I, II, III, and IV have now been issued to Subscribers.

In accordance with the terms of the original prospectus the price for ach part is now raised to £1 10s. ; to Members of the Society (the original rice) £1 1s.

Price 7s. 6d. Only a Limited Number of Copies will be Printed.

THE PALESTINIAN SYRIAC VERSION OF THE HOLY SCRIPTURES.

Four Recently Discovered Portions (together with verses from the Psalms and the Gospel of St. Luke). Edited, in Photographic Facsimile, rom a Unique MS. in the British Museum, with a Transcription, Transla ion, Introduction, Vocabulary, and Notes, by

REV. G. MARGOLIOUTH, M.A.,

Assistant in the Department of Oriental Printed Books and MSS. in the British Museum ; formerly Tyrwhitt Hebrew Scholar.

Subscribers' names to be Addressed to the Secretary.

SOCIETY OF BIBLICAL ARCHÆOLOGY.

COUNCIL, 1897.

President.

SIR P. LE PAGE RENOUF, KNT.

Vice-Presidents.

THE MOST REV. HIS GRACE THE LORD ARCHBISHOP OF YORK.
THE MOST NOBLE THE MARQUESS OF BUTE, K.T., &c., &c.
THE RIGHT HON. LORD AMHERST OF HACKNEY.
THE RIGHT HON. LORD HALSBURY.
THE RIGHT HON. W. E. GLADSTONE, M.P., D.C.L., &c.
ARTHUR CATES.
F. D. MOCATTA, F.S.A., &c.
WALTER MORRISON, M.P.
SIR CHARLES NICHOLSON, BART., D.C.L., M.D., &c.
ALEXANDER PECKOVER, LL.D., F.S.A.
REV. GEORGE RAWLINSON, D.D., Canon of Canterbury.

Council.

REV. CHARLES JAMES BALL, M.A.
REV. PROF. T. K. CHEYNE, D.D.
THOMAS CHRISTY, F.L.S.
DR. J. HALL GLADSTONE, F.R.S.
CHARLES HARRISON, F.S.A.
GRAY HILL.
PROF. T. HAYTER LEWIS, F.S.A.
REV. ALBERT LOWY, LL.D., &c.

REV. JAMES MARSHALL, M.A.
CLAUDE G. MONTEFIORE.
WALTER L. NASH, F.S.A.
PROF. E. NAVILLE.
J. POLLARD.
EDWARD B. TYLOR, LL.D., F.R.S., &c.
E. TOWRY WHYTE, M.A., F.S.A.

Honorary Treasurer—BERNARD T. BOSANQUET.

Secretary—W. HARRY RYLANDS, F.S.A.

Honorary Secretary for Foreign Correspondence—REV. R. GWYNNE, B.A.

Honorary Librarian—WILLIAM SIMPSON, F.R.G.S.

HARRISON AND SONS, PRINTERS IN ORDINARY TO HER MAJESTY, ST. MARTIN'S LANE.

PROCEEDINGS

OF

THE SOCIETY

OF

BIBLICAL ARCHÆOLOGY.

⁂

VOL. XIX. TWENTY-SEVENTH SESSION.

Fourth Meeting, April 6th, 1897.

CONTENTS.

⁂

PUBLISHED AT

THE OFFICES OF THE SOCIETY,

37, GREAT RUSSELL STREET, BLOOMSBURY, W.C.

1897.

[No. CXLV.]

SOCIETY OF BIBLICAL ARCHÆOLOGY,

37, GREAT RUSSELL STREET, BLOOMSBURY, W.C.

TRANSACTIONS.

	To Members.	To Non-Members.		To Members.	To Non-Members.
		s. d.			s. d.
Vol. I, Part 1 ... 10 6	... 12 6	Vol. VI, Part 1 ... 10 6	... 12 6
,, I, ,, 2 ... 10 6	... 12 6	,, VI, ,, 2 ... 10	... 12 6
,, II, ,, 1 ... 8 0	... 10 6	,, VII, ,, 1 ... 7	... 10 6
,, II, ,, 2 ... 8 0	... 10 6	,, VII, ,, 2 ... 10	... 12 6
,, III, ,, 1 ... 8 0	... 10 6	,, VII, ,, 3 ... 10	... 12 6
,, III, ,, 2 ... 8 0	... 10 6	,, VIII, ,, 1 ... 10	... 12 6
,, IV, ,, 1 ... 10 6	... 12 6	,, VIII, ,, 2 ... 10	... 12 6
,, IV, ,, 2 ... 10 6	... 12 6	,, VIII, ,, 3 ... 10	... 12 6
,, V, ,, 1 ... 12 6	... 15 0	,, IX, ,, 1 ... 10 6	... 12 6
,, V, ,, 2 ... 10 6	... 12 6	,, IX, ,, 2 ... 10 6	... 12 6

PROCEEDINGS.

Vol.				To Members.			To Non-Members.
Vol. I,	Session	1878–79	...	2 0	...	...	2 6
,, II,	,,	1879–80	...	2 0	...	...	2 6
,, III,	,,	1880–81	...	4 0	...	...	5 0
,, IV,	,,	1881–82	...	4 0	...	...	5 0
,, V,	,,	1882–83	...	4 0	...	...	5 0
,, VI,	,,	1883–84	...	5 0	...	...	6 0
,, VII,	,,	1884–85	...	5 0	...	...	6 0
,, VIII,	,,	1885–86	...	5 0	...	...	6 0
,, IX,	,,	1886–87	...	2 0 per Part	...	2 6
,, IX,	Part 7,	1886–87	...	8 0 ,, ,,	...	10
,, X,	Parts 1 to 7,	1887–88	...	2 0 ,, ,,	...	2 6
,, X,	Part 8,	1887–88	...	7 6 ,, ,,	...	10 6
,, XI,	Parts 1 to 7,	1888–89	...	2 0 ,, ,,	...	2 6
,, XI,	Part 8,	1888–89	...	7 6 ,, ,,	...	10 6
,, XII,	Parts 1 to 7,	1889–90	...	2 0 ,, ,,	...	2 6
,, XII,	Part 8,	1889–90	...	5 0 ,, ,,	...	6 0
,, XIII,	Parts 1 to 7,	1890–91	...	2 0 ,, ,,	...	2 6
,, XIII,	Part 8,	1890–91	...	5 0 ,, ,,	...	6 0
,, XIV,	Parts 1 to 7,	1891–92	...	2 0 ,, ,,	...	2 6
,, XIV,	Part 8,	1891–92	...	5 0 ,, ,,	...	6 0
,, XV,	Parts 1 to 7,	1892–93	...	2 0 ,, ,,	...	2 6
,, XV,	Part 8,	1892–93	...	5 0 ,, ,,	...	6 0
,, XVI,	Parts 1 to 10,	1893–94	...	2 0 ,, ,,	...	2 6
,, XVII,	Parts 1 to 8	1895	...	2 0 ,, ,,	...	2 6
,, XVIII,	Parts 1 to 8	1896	...	2 0 ,, ,,	...	2 6
,, XIX,	In progress	1897				

A few complete sets of the Transactions still remain for sale, which may be obtained on application to the Secretary, W. H. RYLANDS, F.S.A., 37, Great Russell Street, Bloomsbury, W.C.

PROCEEDINGS

OF

THE SOCIETY

OF

BIBLICAL ARCHÆOLOGY.

TWENTY-SEVENTH SESSION, 1897.

Fourth Meeting, 6th April, 1897.

REV. JAMES MARSHALL, M.A.,

IN THE CHAIR.

————✵————

The following Presents were announced, and thanks ordered to be returned to the Donors :—

From Prof. Maspero :—M. de Rochemonteix. *Œuvres.* Le Temple d'Edfou, publié d'après les estampages par Émile Chassinat. Avant-propos. Folio. Paris. 1897.

The following Candidates were elected Members of the Society, having been nominated on March 2 :—

Miss Jane Alice Weightman, Fern Lea, Seaforth, W. Liverpool.
Mrs. Peirson, the Haven, Saltwood, Hythe, Kent.

A Paper was read by Mr. E. J. Pilcher, entitled "The Date of the Siloam Inscription," which will be published, with illustrations in a future part of the *Proceedings*.

Remarks were added by the Rev. R. Gwynne, Rev. Dr. Löwy, Rev. James Marshall, and Mr. J. Offord.

The thanks of the Meeting were returned for this communication.

BOOK OF THE DEAD.

By Sir P. le Page Renouf.

CHAPTER CXXXIII.

Book whereby the Deceased acquireth Might (1) *in the Netherworld in presence of the great Cycle of the gods.* [*Said on the first day of the Month*]. (2)

Rā maketh his appearance at the Mount of Glory, with the Cycle of gods about him : the Strong one issueth from his hidden abode.

The Twinklers (3) fall away from the Mount of Glory at the East of Heaven, at the voice of Nut as she buildeth up the paths of Rā, before the Ancient one who goeth round.

Be thou lift up, O Rā who art in thine shrine ; breathe thou the breezes, inhale the north wind . . . . (4) on the day when thou discernest the Land of Maāt.

Thou dividest them that follow; the Bark advanceth and the Ancient ones step onwards at thy voice.

Reckon thou thy bones, and set thy limbs, and turn thy face towards the beautiful Amenta.

For thou art the golden Form, (5) with a couch of the heavenly orbs, with the Twinklers amongst whom thou goest round, and art renewed daily.

Acclamation cometh from the Mount of Glory, and greeting from the lines of measurement. (6)

The gods who are in heaven, they see the Osiris *N*, they present to him their adorations as to Rā.

He is the Great one, who seeketh the Crown and reckoneth up that which is needful.

He is the One, who cometh forth this day from the primeval womb of them who were before Rā, and his coming forth taketh place upon earth and in the Netherworld.   His coming forth is like Rā daily.

Without haste, but unresting, is the Osiris *N* on this Land of Eternity.

Twice blessed is he that seeth with his eyes and heareth with his ears.

Right, right is the Osiris *N*: and his future, his future, (7) is in Annu.

His oars are lifted as in the service of Nu.

The Osiris *N* hath not told what he hath seen ; he hath not repeated what he hath heard in the house of the god who hideth his face.

There are hailing and cries of welcome to the Osiris *N*, the divine body of Rā, on traversing the Nu, and whilst the *ka* of the god is being propitiated, according to his pleasure.

The Osiris *N* is the Hawk, rich in variety of Forms.

The Deceased acquireth might with Rā, and is enabled to possess power among the gods, for the gods are made to regard him as one of themselves, and when the Dead ones see him they fall upon their faces.   He is seen in the Netherworld even as the beams of Rā.

Said over a Boat of four cubits in length, painted green.   And let a starry sky be made, clean and purified with natron and incense. And see thou make an image of Rā upon a tablet of light green colour at the prow of the Boat.   And see thou make an image of the Deceased whom thou lovest, that he may be made strong in this boat, and that his voyage be made in the Bark of Rā, and that Rā himself may look upon him.   Do not do this for any one except for thine own self, thy father and thy son.   And let them be exceedingly cautious for themselves.   The Deceased acquireth might with Rā, and made to possess power among the gods, who regard him as one of themselves, and when men or the Dead see him they fall upon their faces.   He is seen in the Netherworld as the image of Rā. (8)

NOTES.

The earliest known text of this chapter is that of the Tomb of Amenemhait at Thebes (*Ta*), of the time of Thothmes III.   It is almost as inaccurate as that of Nebseni (*Aa*), or the Brockelhurst *Ax*.   Nor is the text of Ani of any use towards clearing up any of the difficulties.

1. *Acquireth Might.* [glyph] does not signify *wise*, nor has it anything to do with *instruction* or *perfection*, as supposed by other translators. As an adjective it is used to qualify not only animate but inanimate things, such as an *egg*, *beer*, and *incense*. The well-known expressions [glyph] and [glyph] exactly correspond to the Hebrew מְאֹד עַד and מְאֹד. The notion implied, as in the Hebrew אוּר, is that of *strength*.

I [glyph], in the Prisse Papyrus, is not a *wise* man, but a *powerful* one, *a man of rank or influence*, δυνάμενος, δυνατός.

This is the meaning of the word in such passages as [glyph] [glyph] (Rougé, *Inscr. hier.*, 80) [glyph] (*Inscr. of Una*, repeatedly) [glyph] (*Pap. Prisse* 17, 1). These expressions are the exact equivalents of the Greek δυνάμενος παρὰ τῷ βασιλῆϊ, Herodot. 7, 5.

The might acquired by the deceased is stated in the final rubric and in all the titles of the chapter in the later recensions to be [glyph], with reference to Rā.

2. *Said on the first day of the Month.* These words first appear on the Papyrus of Ani.

3. *The Twinklers.* The oldest texts in this place have [glyph] [glyph], though the equivalent and corresponding word a little further on is [glyph], which is the usual reading here in the later recensions. The same meaning may be made out of both groups. The stars are manifestly alluded to, as being made to disappear when the Sun makes his appearance. [glyph], or in reduplicated form [glyph] is the pupil of the eye; [glyph] is to *ogle*, *far l'occhiata*. [glyph] on the other hand signifies the *little tremblers*, "tremulo fulgore micantes." The glance of the eye is [glyph].* The stars are here considered as so many eyes, characterised by their tremulous motion.

---

* The Egyptian word signifying *tremble* is written either with [glyph] or with [glyph].

4. The true text is here quite lost.   Some sense might be restored, if we might read ⊿ 𓄿𓏭 ℮ 𓏴 instead of 𓂝 ⊿ 𓊹 𓆓 𓏴. The latter word is absolute nonsense in this place, whatever determinative it may have, but the former is the well known name of a tree held sacred at various places in Egypt.   The whole passage then might mean " Enjoy the north wind, and may the Kabasu trees of thine abode refresh thee."

5. *The golden Form.* The whole of this passage will become clear after reading the final rubric and examining the Vignettes of the chapter.

6. *Line of measurement,* 𓈖𓂉 𓊵 𓅱 𓊹 𓏤𓏥. An explanation of this will be found in the pictures and text of the *Book of Hades.* In Bonomi's *Sarcph.,* Plates VII and VIB, twelve personages are represented in the act of acclamation, and twelve others carry the line 𓈗 𓂉 𓊹 𓏭 𓈖𓂉 𓊵 𓅱 𓊹 ℮.   The use intended for the line is stated in the text.   " The bearers of the line are those who settle the fields of the Chu, 𓉻 𓅯 𓏤𓏤𓏤 𓅃 𓂝 𓊹 𓏥 𓈖 𓅜 𓏤."   They are called upon to take their line and to fix the 𓂝 𓏏𓏏 𓅃 𓂝𓊹, ϲⲉⲑⲓⲟϩⲓ, ἄρουρα, the *arable land* of each allotment.   Rā expresses his satisfaction at the measurement, and tells the gods and the Chu that their domains are theirs, and that he provides their food.

7. *His future* 𓊨 𓅃 𓂋, 𓊨 𓅃 𓅱 𓏏 𓏤𓏤𓏤.

8. The rubric is taken from *Ax.*

CHAPTER CXXXIV.

Chapter whereby the Deceased acquireth might.

Hail to thee who art in the midst of thine Ark, Oh rising Sun who risest, and declining (1) one who declinest : at whose will millions spring forth, as he turneth his face to the unborn generations of men : Chepera in the middle of his Bark, who overthroweth Apepi.

Here are the children of Seb who overthrow the adversaries of Osiris and destroy them from the Bark of Rā.

Horus cutteth off their heads in heaven when in the forms of winged fowl, their hinder parts on earth when in the forms of quad-rupeds or [in the water] as fishes.

All fiends, male or female, the Osiris N destroyeth them, whether descending from heaven or coming forth upon the earth, or issuing out of the water or travelling along with the Stars.

Thoth slaughtereth them, the Son of the Rock, proceeding from the place of the Two Rocks. (2)

The Osiris N is dumb and deaf (3) for the Strong one is Rā, the puissant of stroke, the Almighty one, who washeth in their blood and walloweth in their gore.

The Osiris N destroyeth them from the Bark of his father Rā.

The Osiris N is Horus : his mother Isis bringeth him forth, and Nephthys nurseth him, as they did to Horus, who repelleth the dark ones of Sutu : who, when they see the Crown fixed upon his brow, fall upon their faces.

Osiris Unneferu is triumphant over his adversaries in heaven and on earth, and in the cycle of each god and goddess.

Said over a Hawk in a Boat, with the White Crown upon its head, and the figure of Tmu, Shu, Tefnut, Seb, Nut, Osiris, Isis, Sutu, (4) Nephthys, painted yellowish green on a fresh papyrus placed in this Boat, together with the figure of the Deceased, anointed with the Heknu oil. Let there be offered to them incense burning and roast fowl. It is the adoration of Rā, and his voyage, for it is granted to him to make his appearance each day with Rā, whithersoever he journeyeth ; and it is the Slaughter of the adversaries of Rā; positively and undeviatingly for times infinite.

NOTES.

1. *Declining* ▭ ⊙ . This word frequently occurs in contrast with 🖐] ⊙ . I understand the latter in all such cases to signify the shining of the sun on his rising, and the former to signify the shining of the sun in his afternoon course.

2. *The son of the Rock, proceeding from the place of the Two Rocks.* The only explanation I can think of is derived from the identification (in chapter 62) of Thoth with the Nile, 🖼 . From this point of view the god is both the son of the Rock and

issues from the place of the Double Rock, ⟨𓉔⟩, or of the two Rocks, called in the time of Herodotus Krophi and Mophi.

3. *Dumb and deaf,* 𓉔. It is strange that this meaning of the passage has so long been misunderstood. The sense of the first word has long been recognised, and 'deaf' is the meaning rightly assigned to ⟨𓉔⟩ in Birch's Dictionary. One instance like the following (from *Unas,* 608) is sufficient to settle the question— 𓉔, "He is not so deaf that he should not hear thy voice."

That the subject of these attributes is the Osiris is seen by reference to *At,* where instead of 'the Osiris' the deceased speaks in the first person, 𓉔, "I am dumb, I am deaf."

4. *Sutu.* This divine name occurs in the text of Amenhait in the reign of Thothmes III. And I have noted another instance where the name is written 𓉔. Dr. Birch called the papyrus Miss Brockelhurst's. It cannot however be the *Ax* of M. Naville, which does not contain the chapter.

The disappearance of the god's name from all other documents is a fatal argument against their claims to high antiquity.

CHAPTER CXXXV.

Another chapter recited when the Moon renews itself on the first day of the month.

Osiris is enveloped in storm and rain : he is enveloped : but the fair Horus lendeth succour daily, the Lord of high attributes . . . (1) he driveth off the storm from the face of the Osiris *N*.

Behold him coming : he is Rā on his journey : he is the four gods who are over the upper region.

The Osiris *N* arriveth at his own time : and by means of his lines is brought to the light of day.

If this chapter be known he becometh a Chu of Might in the

Netherworld ; he dieth not a second time, in the Netherworld ; but he eateth by the side of Osiris.

If it be known upon earth he will become like Thoth, so as to be worshipped by the living : he will not fall a victim to a king's wrath (2) or to the fierce heat of Basit, but will be made to advance to a most blissful old age.

NOTES.

This chapter is not found in the papyri of the older period.

1. The words *Offerings of* (or *to*) *the Moment* have the appearance of an interpolated rubrical direction. *See* next note.

2. *A king's wrath* in the cases of gods and men is an impulse which cannot be stopped, but carries everything before it.

TWO ARCHAIC AND THREE LATER BABYLONIAN TABLETS.

By Theophilus G. Pinches.

Having received permission from the owner, Mr. A. B. Ebbs, to publish some Babylonian tablets in his possession, I give them herewith, accompanied by translations or descriptions, hoping that they may be acceptable to scholars, and help to fill gaps or illustrate obscure passages, notwithstanding that one of them is itself not by any means clear, and another a mere fragment.

No. 1.

The first, which is of unbaked clay, is about $1\frac{1}{2}$ in. square, slightly higher, however, on the right-hand side than on the left, The lower part of the reverse and the edge are broken, rendering the twelfth and following lines, containing the date, incomplete. The tablet is difficult to read, cylinder-seals having been rolled over the surface, flattening down the characters. The text is as follows :—

TRANSCRIPTION.	TRANSLATION.
Baru šiķli kaspi	$\frac{1}{2}$ shekel of silver
a-na D.P. êṣidi	for the reaper
3. itti I-na-E-sag-ila-zēru, rê'u,	from Ina-Ésagila-zēru, the shepherd
mâr Arad-i-li-šu	son of Arad-îli-šu
⚊ Ba-ši-ilu mâr Sin-i-din-nam	Baši-îlu, son of Sin-idinnam
6. ilķī	has taken.
Ina ûmi êburi	At harvest-time
D.P. êṣidu i-il-la-ak	the reaper shall come
9. U-ul i-il-la-ak-ma	If he do not come (it shall be)
ki-ma ṣi-im-da-at šar-ri	like a decree of the king.

No. 1.

Obv.

Left-hand Edge.

3.

6.

Edge.

Rev. 9

12.

Edge.

TABLET BELONGING TO A.B EBBS, ESQ.

Maḫar Arad- D.P. Ul-maš-ši-	*Before Arad-Ulmaššitu^m, son*
tu^m mâr Ib-ku-An-nu-ni-tu^m ;	*of Ibku-Annunitu^m*
12. Maḫar [Ta]-ri-bu mâr Gab-ba-a.	*Before Taribu son of Gabbâ.*

Kunuk Ta-ri-bu	*Seal of Taribu.*
. . . . ûmu šalâšēru	. . . . . *13th day,*
. . . .	*[year]* . . . . . *[the king]*
. . . di-di dim (?)-a	. . . .

FREE RENDERING.

"Baši-ilu, son of Sin-idinna^m, has received from Ina-Êsagila-zēru, the shepherd, son of Arad-ili-šu, half a shekel of silver for the reaper

"The reaper shall come at harvest-time—if he do not come, there will be a penalty."

Line 2. The word "reaper" is written ideographically, ⟨cuneiform⟩ ⟨cuneiform⟩ ⟨cuneiform⟩ ⟨cuneiform⟩, "grain-cutter," with ⟨cuneiform⟩ as determinative prefix instead of ⟨cuneiform⟩, which, later, is exclusively used. The question naturally arises whether ⟨cuneiform⟩ may not have indicated, in these texts, that the noun following referred more to a slave than to a free man. In the tablet recording the sale of "fair Gutian slaves" (Meissner, *Altbabylonisches Privatrecht*, no. 4), the seller, ⟨cuneiform⟩ ⟨cuneiform⟩ ⟨cuneiform⟩, *Utul-Ištar*, is called ⟨cuneiform⟩ ⟨cuneiform⟩ ⟨cuneiform⟩ ⟨cuneiform⟩, *a-bi ummanati*, "father (?=owner) of the men," or, perhaps, simply "slave-owner."

Line 6. The word *ilḳî*, "he has taken," is expressed by the Akkadian šu-*ba-an*-TI, as is commonly the case.

Line 7. Here, also, an Akkadian expression, û-EBUR (?)-KU, is used for *ina umi eburi*. W.A.I., II, 14, 17*a* has û-EBUR-KA. The third character, ⟨cuneiform⟩, *ku*, is doubtful, the traces being more like those of ⟨cuneiform⟩, *ki*.

Lines 8, 9. *I-il-la-ak. U-ul i-il-la-ak-ma*, "He shall come. If he do not come." *Âlâku*, Heb. הָלַךְ, means "to come," as well as "to go." This phrase occurs on the tablet V.A.Th. 630 in the Berlin Museum (Meissner, *Privatrecht*, no. 22; Peiser, *Texte juristischen und geschäftlichen Inhalts*, 38, I), and elsewhere.

Line 10. The full phrase should probably be *kima ṣimdat šarri izzaz*, "it shall stand, like a decree (?) of the king" (*cf.* Bu. 88–5–12, 234, Meissner, no. 3). Both Meissner and Peiser translate *ṣimdat* by "yoke" (Gespann)—the usual meaning—but this does not quite satisfy the context, so I have rendered this phrase in accordance with pl. I. attached to the late George Bertin's paper, "Akkadian Precepts," etc., in the *Transactions* of this Society, Vol. VIII, where we find *ṣimit*[*ta?* *šaḫuzu?*] and *dinu šu*[*ḫu*] *zu* (?), "to cause (any-one) to receive judgment," translating the same Akkadian group ⟨𒌋 𒂊 𒁉⟩, *sa-dibba* (lines 27, 28). I take the most probable meaning to be, "The penalty shall be as if he had contravened a decree of the king," *i.e.*, the slave promised should be entirely at the royal disposition. This seems to be proved by the tablet B. 57 (Strassmaier, *Warka*, no. 30), where Ilu-bani, the adopted son of Sin-magir, claims his adoptive father's plantation as his inheritance, *ana ṣimdat šarri*,* "at the decree of the king," it having been promised to him by Rim-Sin, probably the immediate predecessor of Ḫammurabi (in whose reign the tablet is dated). Ilu-bani successfully contests, in this document, the claim of Sin-mubaliṭ,† who had brought an action to get possession of the plantation.

Line 11. *Arad-Ulmaššitu*ᵐ apparently means "Servant of the Ulmassite goddess," or "of her who is worshipped in the temple Ê-ulmaš." This temple, whose name has hitherto been transcribed Ê-ulbar, was situated in Agadé, as the following extract shows :—

𒂍𒌋𒈠	𒂍 𒌍 𒁹 𒀀 𒂵 𒆠
Ê - ul - maš	Bitu šelašâ - tišû ša A - ga - [de D.S.]
E - ulmaš	*Temple* *39,* *of* *Agade.*

[W.A.I., II, 61, 11 add.]

The goddess Ulmaššituᵐ was probably Istar, who was wor-shipped at Agadé. There was also an Ê-ulmaš at Erech, which was called *Ê-ulbarra*=*bît piristi*, "the house of the oracle." W.A.I., IV, 36, 24*b* (38, 25*b*), which is a geographical list, mentions a place called ⟨𒌋 𒁹 𒂍⟩, *Ulmaš* (D.S.), the name of which immediately precedes that of Agadé. Whether the city was so named from the temple, or the temple (and the goddess) from the city, is doubtful.

The seal-impressions (of which little or nothing can be made out) are of Baši-ilu, the seller, and Arad-Ulmassituᵐ and Taribu, the two witnesses. That of Baši-ilu (*Kunuk Ba-ši-ilu*) is on the left-hand edge, at the top; and that of Arad-Ulmaššituᵐ (*Kunuk Arad*-(D.P.) *Ul-maš-ši-tu*ᵐ) beneath it.

* Not *ṣimdattuš*, as the publication gives.

† It is curious that Sin-mubaliṭ is the name of the immediate predecessor of Ḫammurabi, according to the canon, but this is a coincidence, and nothing more.

No. 2.

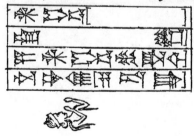

TABLET BELONGING TO A.B. EBBS, ESQ

It will be noticed that the services of the reaper were paid for beforehand, and it is apparently on this account that a penalty was attached to the non-fulfilment of the contract. The "fair Gutian slaves" were also paid for in advance, but in this case their value had to be returned if the contract were not carried out.

No. 2.

The second tablet, which is also unbaked, is $1\frac{9}{16}$ in. square, and practically perfect. Like the first, the text is very difficult to read, in consequence of the cylinder-seal which has been rolled over the whole surface. The text is as follows :—

TRANSCRIPTION.	TRANSLATION.
Esten kaš-baḳ-ḳa ša êllu^m	1 *plot*(?) *of garden-ground* (?)
a-na D.P. Maš-tab-ba	*for the deity Maštabba*
3. ša i-na mu-uḫ-ḫi êḳli šamaš-šame	*which unto the sesame-field*
ša nâri A-ga-ri-in-nu	*of the river Agarinnu*
in-na-ad-nu.	*has been added.*
6. Mu-kin	*Witness :*
⌐ Amel-Mer-ra D.P. rikkü	*Amel-Mera, the planter* (?)

Araḫ Ululi, ûmu ḫamšu	*Month Elul, day 5th*
šattu Am-mi-za-du-ga šar-e	*year Ammi-zaduga the king*
. . . . . gal-la-ni	*was* (?) . . . . .

FREE RENDERING.

"(This refers to) one plot (?) of garden-ground (?), which has been added to the sesame-field of the river Agarinnu, for the deity Maštabba. Witness: Amel-Mera, the planter.

"Month Elul, day 5th, year when Ammi-zaduga, the king, was . . . . . ."

The first line of this text is of considerable difficulty, and the rendering here given, though one that seems to be required by the context, is therefore very doubtful. The first word after the numeral ⌐ (bi-ḫu-ḳa, or, better, bi-baḳ-ḳa or kaš-baḳ-ḳa) seems not to occur elsewhere. The last character but one is doubtful—it may be really two characters, ⟨cuneiform⟩ ⟨cuneiform⟩, *bi-si;* but in view of the group ⟨cuneiform⟩ ⟨cuneiform⟩ in line 7, the reading I have adopted, ⟨cuneiform⟩ ⟨cuneiform⟩, RIG-BI, is probably the best. This group is explained in W.A.I., V. 52, 52*b* by the Semitic Babylonian *ellu*[m], and with ⟨cuneiform⟩, *zi*, or ⟨cuneiform⟩ ⟨cuneiform⟩, *zi-da*, etc., added, means, according to Delitzsch, "an enclosure," hence my conjectural rendering of "garden-ground." As, however, ⟨cuneiform⟩ forms part of certain words which are names of trees, ⟨cuneiform⟩ ⟨cuneiform⟩ may be one of these, but in this case the prefix for "wood," ⟨cuneiform⟩, would be expected.

Line 2. ⟨cuneiform⟩, D.P. *Maštabba.* This is the original Akkadian transcription of the name of a deity apparently meaning "the double god," and the word forms part of the groups used for the great and the little Twins (*Maštabba-galgala* and *Maštabba-turtura*), names of two Babylonian constellations, or portions of constellations. The Semitic transcription of *Maštabba* is *îlu kilallan,* "the double god" (W.A.I., III, pl. 68, 68*b*), whose component persons seem to have borne the names of *Birdu* and *Šarrapu,* and whose "messenger" was named ⟨cuneiform⟩, *Ḫar.* See my note upon these in the *Babylonian and Oriental Record* for Feb., 1887, p. 55.

Line 3. The use of the character ⟨cuneiform⟩ for *uḫ* is common at the period of this tablet.

Line 4. The river Agarinnu was probably one of the numerous canals with which the country was covered. It is apparently from the Akkadian *agarin,* "mother," and the river, or canal, was probably so called as the nourisher of the land.

Line 5. The verbal form *innadnu* (for *innadinu*) is aor. niphal,— a form which does not occur in the dictionary. The form without the final *u* (*innadin*) occurs in Sp., II, 28, l. 8, etc.

Line 7. Besides Amel-Merra, the forms *Lu-Murra* (Akk.), and *Amel-Rammāni,* or *Amel-Addi* (Semitic Babylonian), are also possible. For the value *mur,* see W.A.I., III, 68, 51*e,* and for *mer,* see the *Transactions of this Society* for 1880 (Vol. VII), pp. 114, 115; *Proceedings* for Feb. 6, 1883, p. 73; and *Transactions,* Vol. VIII, p. 352 (Tukulti-Mer). As one *r* may be written instead of two, the best transcription is probably that given in the translation, namely, Amel-Mera. This man was probably the gardener, or guardian, of the place referred to on the tablet, his title being ⟨cuneiform⟩ ⟨cuneiform⟩, probably to be read D.P. *rikku,* he who looks after the green stuff.

The brevity of the text leaves room for considerable speculation as to what it really refers to, but it may be conjectured that it records the gift, by an anonymous donor, of a plot of ground, to the temple of the deity Maštabba, for the services of the twofold god, and the use of the priests, who were, naturally, materially enriched thereby. From the nature of the inscription it may be conjectured that the expression *ina muḫḫi nadānu*, lit., "in over to give," or "unto to give," is an idiom meaning "to add to" a thing, and this is the rendering adopted here. The portion added must have adjoined the "sesame-field of the Agarinnu river," belonging to the deity Mastabba, referred to in the text.

As has been already stated, the name of the giver does not occur in the text, but it may be conjectured that it is his seal of which traces are to be found rolled over the surface of the tablet. The inscription on this, as far as it is readable, is as follows :—

D.P. Marduk		*Marduk* . . . .
dup	- šar	*the scribe,*
mâr D.P. Marduk-mu-ša[-lim].		*son of Marduk-mušalim.*
ârad Am-mi-[za-du-ga]		*servant of Ammi-zaduga.*

Like many other seals of the same nature, it probably bears testimony to the deification of the king during his lifetime, traces of the figure of a divine attendant in an attitude of adoration before the name of Ammi-zaduga being also visible.

No. 3.

The following text belongs to the late period, probably, judging from the traces in line 15, of the time of Artaxerxes. It is of unbaked clay, and is very mutilated. The height is $1\frac{3}{4}$ in. and the width nearly 2 in.

OBVERSE.

Edge. [cuneiform signs]

Reverse.

9. [cuneiform signs]

12. [cuneiform signs]

Edge. 15. [cuneiform signs]

Transcription.

. . . . ḫuraṣi (?) bab-ba-ni-tu^m
makkur Bêl ina muḫḫi Bêl-âḫu-šu

3. mâru ša Nergal-iddina ina araḫ Nisanni
šattu irbittu bil-tu^m-am
ribuṭ ina-an-din e-lát (?) . . . . . .

6. ri-šu-u . . . .
ina pân Bêl (?) ša . . . .
û abu (?). . . . .

9. D.P. Mu-kin-nu D.P. Marduk · · · ·
mâru ša Aḫu-u-nu Nabû (?) · · · · ·
mâru ša Ana-Bêl-balaṭu (?) · · · · ·

12. Nabû-na-ṣir (?)- · · · rittu (?) mâru ša
. . . . šir
. . . . Tebetu, ûmu êšru-ḫamšu (?).

15. . . . . tak (?)-ša (?)-as (?)-su (?)
. . . . mâtâti

* Seems to be erased.   † Or [cuneiform].
‡ Or *irbit*.

TRANSLATION.

.... *consecrated* (?) *gold* (?)
the property of the god Bel unto Bêl-uṣur-šu
3. *son of Nergal-iddina. In the month Nisan,*
year 4th, by talents (?)
a fourth* he shall give, besides (?)
6. *the possession* ....
(which is) with Bel-ša .....
and [his?] father (?) ......
9. *Witnesses: Marduk-* .....
son of Aḫûnu; Nabû (?)- ...
son of Ana-Bêl-balaṭu (?).

12. *Nabû-naṣir* (?)- ..., *scribe, son of*
.... *-šir.*
.... *[Month] Tebet, day 10th,*
15. *[year]* ..., *[Ar]taxerxes* (?)
[king of Babylon, king of] countries.

The mutilation of the tablet renders the translation exceedingly uncertain, and it is impossible, therefore, to discuss satisfactorily the unusual words that the text contains. It need only be noted that the presence of 𒐕𒐕𒐕 𒐕𒐕 𒐕 𒐕, *biltuᵐ-am*, in line 4, suggests that the word 𒐕𒐕𒐕 𒐕𒐕, *biltuᵐ*, may have been present in line 1—". . . talents of . . . ." If this restoration be correct, the reading of the first word of which traces remain as *ḫuraṣu*, "gold," is still more doubtful than is here indicated.

No. 4.

This is a tablet of unbaked clay, of late date, $3\frac{1}{8}$ in. high by $2\frac{7}{8}$ in. wide. It contains a list of amounts paid.

OBVERSE

3.

* Or "four."

6.

9.

12.

REVERSE.

15.

18.

21.

24.

27.

TRANSLATION.

. . . . . -*Merodach, the* . . .

. . . *Balaṭu*

3. . . . [*Li*]*šir, son of A-*-su* (?)

. . . [*Li*]*šir, son of Na-**

. . . . *Nergal-iddina*

6. 60 *ḳa Nabû-âḫê-išallim*

60 *ḳa Nabû-êṭir-napšāti*

60 *ḳa Nabû-zêr-ukîn, son of Bêl-uballiṭ*

9. 60 *ḳa Eriba-Marduk, the builder*

60 *ḳa Rêmut-Bêl*

60 *ḳa Bêl-aḫê-eriba, the* GAL-DU

12. 60 *ḳa Nadin,*   do.

. . . *Lišir,*   do.

REV.   . . . *Ibnâ, the* GAL-DU

15. [60 *ḳa*] *Šamaš-êṭir,* do.

60 *ḳa Bêl-ikîša, the fisherman*

60 *ḳa Bêl-âḫê-eriba*

18. 60 *ḳa Nabû-âḫê-iddina, the linen-weaver*

60 *ḳa Bêl-šunu*

60 *ḳa the field-labourer*[*s*]

21. 60 *ḳa Šamaš-pir'a-uṣur*

60 *ḳa Mušêzib-Nergal* (?), *son of Ṣilli* (?)-*Bêl*

90 *ḳa Pir'u, Silim-Bêl, and Mušêzib-Addu*

24. [60 *ḳa*] *Arad-âḫê-šu*

. . . . *Šamaš-ibnî, Šamaš-zêr-ibnî,*

and Zêrîa

27. . . . . . *palace-servants.*

. . . . *carpenters* (?)

. . . . *s*

As it is apparently stated, in the last three lines, that it is a list of palace-servants and others, it may be supposed that the amounts placed before their names were paid to, not by, these people.

The text is important for the word ⟶ 𐎠 ⟶, read by Delitzsch *rab-bânê*, and translated "architect" (Baumeister). It is difficult, however, to imagine any palace-staff as containing only one working-builder (l. 9) and no less than five architects (ll. 11–15). I have always regarded the ⟶ 𐎠 ⟶, *Galdu*, as a class of priests, and this conjecture is supported by S. +, 334, where 𒐀𒐀𒐀𒐀𒐀, *Galdu ša Šarrat*, "the *Galdu* of the goddess Šarrat" is spoken of, though against this has to be set A.H., 83–1–18, 245, which refers to "iron trowels for brick-laying" (*ana liben ša. libnāti*), given by Nadin the *galdu* ([𒐀] 𒐀 𒐀).

No. 5.

Central right-hand upper portion of a large tablet of late date. Size 2⅞ in. by 2⅞ in. Unbaked clay. The reverse is uninscribed. This fragment represents about one-fifth of the whole.

The above text is only of value in that it may contain part of an inscription to which other tablets may refer, or of which the remainder, or a duplicate, may possibly come to light. It is dated in the 2nd year of Artaxerxes (l. 1), and refers to a certain congrega-

* Or 𒐀.

tion, or assembly (l. 3). Three persons are mentioned: . . -nu, Nabû-iddina, and Bêl-šunu, the shepherd (l. 6), and in the next line (l. 7) the city of the temple of the "alone-great-one"* (*âl Bêt Ušum-gallu,* 𒂍 𒁁 𒂍 𒃲) is spoken of. The doubtful character before 𒂍 in lines 2 and 8 seems to be 𒆧, *kiš,* and, if so, the city Kêš, now represented by the mounds of Hymer, near Babylon, is referred to. The words *išaalu iktabi-ma,* "he asked, he answered and" (l. 8), imply that the text referred to some ceremony, legal or otherwise, in which answers to certain questions were required before the people assembled. The meaning of *šamarri* (or *ša marri*) *šindu'* in lines 5 and 9 is uncertain. The text is in a very bad condition, and many of the characters are doubtful.

---

* A title applied to " the queen of heaven and earth," and to Merodach.

The Society is indebted to Mr. Walter L. Nash, F.S.A., and the President for the two following notes, which may be taken in continuation of those printed with illustrations in Volumes VI and VII of the *Proceedings*.

W. H. R.

The Grange,
Northwood,
Middlesex.
11<i>th March</i>, 1897.

My dear Rylands,

I send you photographs (front and back) of an Hypocephalus that I recently bought in Egypt. It is made of linen, covered over with stucco, and the characters are painted in black on a pale buff-coloured ground. It is eight and a half inches in diameter. I obtained it from the British Consul at Luxor, who found it with a mummy which he unrolled about three years ago.

Yours sincerely,

WALTER L. NASH.

46, Roland Gardens.
19<i>th March</i>, 1897.

Dear Mr. Rylands,

Hypocephalus Plate 1 is the picture of a cow at rest. It has the solar disk between the horns and, as the inscription above it says, is Hathor the Mistress of the divine Netherworld . The divine Cow is protecting her son Rā, the Sun-god, at his setting (*Todt.*, 162, 9).

Plate 2 has its central part divided into four compartments the lowest of which is inverted.

The figure which occupies the middle of the first compartment, a sitting human form with four heads of rams, "four faces on one neck," as it is called in Dendera, is the symbol of the 'god of many names.' "He rises up," says the Mendesian Tablet, "from the Solar Mount, with four heads, lighting up heaven and earth with his rays, and he cometh as the Nile to give life to the universe,"* etc. At Esneh he is said to unite in himself the four living Souls (or active Forces) of Rā, Shu, Osiris and Seb.

He is represented in the picture at the top of the Metternich Tablet as filling the whole of the Solar Disk, as it rises in the morning and is saluted by eight cynocephali. The inscription over this picture is "Adoration to Rā Horus of the Solar Mount, great god, Lord of Heaven, the giver of Light, issuing from the Solar Mount."

These details have not been given in previous descriptions of hypocephali which have appeared in our *Proceedings.*

Behind the god on this hypocephalus are the words "King for ever and ever" ⟨hieroglyphs⟩. The crouching figure in front of the god might be taken on the photograph for a horned quadruped. But it is apparently meant for the hawk crouching on a boat.

In compartment 2 the solar deity, seated on a throne with his flail over his shoulder, is saluted by two cynocephali in front and two behind. And behind the latter are the 'Horus-children,' Amset, Hapu, Tuamautef and Kebhsenuf.

In compartment 3 are two boats, one bearing a Scarab within the Solar Disk and the other a Ram. The latter represents the Sun during the night. Both the Scarab and the Ram are sometimes, as in the Royal Tombs, pictured together within the Solar Disk.

Compartment 4, which is inverted, has the picture of a person in a boat and the inscription is "Osiris the good [or beautiful] god" ⟨hieroglyphs⟩.

The circular inscription consists of an *unfinished Suten-hotep-tā.*

---

* Brugsch (in the *Zeitschr.,* 1871, 84, note) called attention to the words immediately preceding ⟨hieroglyphs⟩ 'of gods and men,' for the sake of the word signifying *men.* But I think that ⟨hieroglyph⟩ here used instead of ⟨hieroglyph⟩, an early Ptolemaic variant, is worth quite as much notice.

"A royal table of offerings grant Osiris, presiding in Amenta, the good god, Lord of Restatit, Sekaru Osiris, the good god, the great god .... Bast, Isis, the great one ..... and Anubis, the Lord of Tat'eserit; may they grant bread, beer, ... wine and milk."

Here the inscription stops for want of room, for it has returned to the place from which it started, and we have no means of learning in whose behalf the petition is made.

Some parts of it are so effaced that I have not ventured to fill up any place on mere conjecture. The goddess mentioned before Isis is probably Bast.* ⌂⌐ is a mistake for ⌂⌐ .

Believe me to be,

Ever yours faithfully,

P. LE P. RENOUF.

* She is very frequently associated in such inscriptions with Nephthys and Isis, who are in fact identical with her.

I cannot remember that any one has noted that at Abydos (Mariette, I, 30, 6) Anubis is called the son of Bast,  .

PLATE I.

Proc. Soc. Bibl. Arch., April, 1897.

HYPOCEPHALUS IN THE COLLECTION OF WALTER L. NASH, ESQ., F.S.A.

PLATE II.

Proc. Soc. Bibl. Arch., April, 1897.

HYPOCEPHALUS IN THE COLLECTION OF WALTER L. NASH, ESQ., F.S.A.

THE ROLLIN PAPYRI AND THEIR BAKING CALCULATIONS.

[*Continued.*]

By Prof. Dr. August Eisenlohr.

(Sent in 1 *November*, 1895. ·

Plate XIII.[1] Translation and Commentary.

1. *Thoth 7.   One was travelling on the western road.*[2]

2. *Reception of the āku loaves of the bakehouse, which is under the chief Neferhotepu of Memphis in the magazine of the court.*

3. *This day received in the magazine of the court by the hand of the scribe of the altar Hui, the controller (?)[3] scribe of the altar Sakaan of the palace Rames, 1800 each of 13½ ten makes on ten 21600.*

I doubt if I have properly understood the hieratic signs by the controller. As we must read , *rāmes* instead of Pleyte's ākeku, a different writing of Rāmessu (l. 4), we seem to have noted only

---

[1] Spiegelberg, Tafel VI.

[2] Spiegelberg reads not *ḥir*, "road," but *rut*, "district, province." I think he is right, and as he translates, not in the western but in the eastern district.

[3] Spiegelberg better Hui, "son ( ) of Pahu," both names with the same title, "cup bearer;" Lieblein, *Dict. de Noms*, 974, not scribe of the altar, but of the drink table. If sakaan is a title, the name of the man is , *rāmes*. Spiegelberg, p. 45, made of this group a kind of cake (!).

two scribes, the first Hui, the second Rāmessu. In this case

⌷ 𓏏 𓂝 ⌷ 𓀀 *sakaān* must not be a proper name, but a function.

We find a ▭ ⌷| ▭ ⌣ 𓀀 *hir saketu* in the Pap. Bologna
1086, l. 17, what Chabas, *Mélanges*, III a, p. 232, has translated, "chef
des mariniers," because the slave reclaimed from the *hir saketu* is said
to be among the slaves of the conductors of ships ▭▭ ▭ ▭ 𓅨 |I|
(ib. l. 10). Perhaps we should refer to the Hebrew שָׁקָה, the
Arabic سَقَى, to drink and give to drink. The numbers of the
original give 1800, but it ought to be 1600, because only then we
get multiplied with $13\frac{1}{2} = 21600$. This same number, 21600 (not
21800, Pleyte), recurs, Pl. XI, l. 3, as the weight of 1800 ▭
loaves. Probably we have there the reckoning to XIII. 3.

> 4. *Thoth day* 11, *received in the magazine of the court by the hand*
> *of the scribe Ramessu (of) the holy magazine, the scribe*
> *Necht, keleŝta* 6000, *makes in ten* 18,000, *in rest*[1] *keleŝta* 10,
> *makes in ten* 30.

pa ut'a uab (also X, 2) is surely only a variant of *pa ut'a en*
chennu. If we try to search for these keleŝta in Pl. V and VI, we
find it difficult to bring them out. (Pl. VI, ll. 14–17), which is of
the corresponding date (Thoth 10) gives added more than 7000
keleŝta.

> 5. *Thoth day* 15, *received in the magazine of the court through his*
> *hand   ,,   ,,   kelesta* 2400, *makes in*
> *ten* 7440, *in rest*[2] *keleŝta* 10, *makes in ten* 31.

> 6. *Thoth day* 16, *received in the magazine of the court through his*
> *hand   ,,   ,,   keleŝta* 1400, *makes in*
> *ten* 4690,[3] *in rest keleŝta* 10, *makes in ten* $33\frac{1}{2}$.

---

[1] Spiegelberg reads 𓅨 ▭ 𓊪, but on his photo. (Tafel VI, ll. 3, 4) the
group is not clear enough. Pleyte's text gives ▭ 𓊪 " rest " so the original,
VI, 4. I incline to Spiegelberg's view (*Comment.*, p. 45) that there is expressed
the proportion of keleŝta to ten, l. 5 10 : 31, l. 6 10 : $33\frac{1}{2}$, l. 7 10 : 35

[2] Proportion.

[3] Spiegelberg, 4590, the proportion 10 : $33\frac{1}{2}$ wants 4690.

The proportion of kelešta to ten, *i.e.*, the weight of the kelešta, does not remain the same.   L. 4 the proportion was 1 : 3, l. 5, 1 : 3,1, ll. 6 and 7, 1 : 3,35, so for the chief number of kelešta as for the rest.

7. *Thoth day* 18, *received in the magazine of the court through his hand (of the scribe Ramessu, etc.)*   „   „ (*kelešta*) 2790, *makes in ten* 9765, (*rest kelešta*) 10' *makes ten* 35.

8. *Thoth day* 21, *received in the magazine of the court through his hand*   „   „   *kelešta* 2[2]90,[1] *makes in ten* 8155. *It was wholly consumed.*

9. *Thoth day* 22, *received in the magazine of the court through his hand* . . .   „   „   *kelešta* [2]200, *makes in ten* 7800. *It was wholly consumed.*

10. *Thoth day* 25, *received in the magazine of the court through his hand*   „   „   *kelešta* [2]600,[2] *makes in ten* 9453. *It was wholly consumed.*

11. *Thoth day* 28, *received in the magazine of the court through his hand*   „   „   *kelešta* [1]168, *makes in ten* 3800.[3] *It was wholly consumed.*

12. *Paophi* 1, *day of travelling of his majesty to the South* (?). *Received into the magazine of the court by the hand of his scribe Necht,* (*kelešta*) 3[9]05,[5] *makes in ten* 13,745.

13. *Paophi day* [4], *received in the magazine of the court by his hand*   „   (*kelešta*) [4]100, *makes in ten* 13,680.[6]

14. *Paophi day* 8, *received in the magazine of the court by his hand*   „:   (*kelešta*) 3 [.]25,[7] *makes in ten* 17,880.

---

[1] Spiegelberg, 1000x + 80, the photo. shows clearly 90.

[2] Spiegelberg, 1000x + 600 ; the proportion wants 2600.

[3] 13,800, surely after the photo., so not 1,000, but 3,000 or 4,000 kelešta. Spiegelberg 1000x + 668.

[4] Spiegelberg, *nach Theben*, "without reason."

[5] Spiegelberg, 3710.

[6] Spiegelberg, 13,580, but the photo. clearly 680.

[7] Spiegelberg, 37(?)1(?)5.

15. *Paophi day 9, received in the magazine of the court by his hand   „   „   (kelešta) 12 . . , makes in ten* 4200.

16. *Paophi day 12, received in the magazine of the court by his hand   „   „   (kelešta) 3 . . . , makes in ten* 10,230.

17. *Paophi day 15, received in the magazine of the court by his hand   „   „   (kelešta) 4 . . . , makes in ten* 15,300.[1]

18. *Paophi day 20, received in the magazine of the court by his hand   „   „   (kelešta) 4 . . . , makes in ten* 13,260.

19. *Paophi day 22, received in the magazine of the court by his hand   „   „   (kelešta) 3 . . . , makes in ten* 1c,000.

20. *Paophi day 26, received in the magazine of the court through his hand   „   „   (kelešta) 3820, makes in ten* 12,421.[2]

21. *Paophi day 29, received in the magazine of the court through his hand   „   „   (kelešta) 3870, makes in ten* 12,550.

22. *Athyr day 2, received in the magazine of the court through his hand   „   „   (kelešta) 3843, makes in ten* 12,700.

23. *Athyr day 6, received in the magazine of the court through his hand   „   „   (kelešta) [4]3,986,[3] makes in ten* 16,350, *together* 705.

PLATE X.[4]

1. *Athyr day 8, received into the magazine of the court through the hand of the scribe Necht. Good bread, kelešta* 2390, *makes in ten* 7870.

2. *Athyr day 10, received into the magazine of the court through the hand of the scribe Necht of the holy[5] magazine, (kelešta)* 2440, *makes in ten* 8050.

---

[1] Spiegelberg, 700 dubious.   [2] Spiegelberg, 13, 421 after the proportion.
[3] The 4 is clear in the photo.   [4] Spiegelberg, Tafel II.
[5] Spiegelberg, reines Magazin.

3. *Athyr day* 14, *received into the magazine of the court through his hand* ,, ,, ,, (*kelešta*) 3790, *makes in ten* 12,630.

4. *Athyr day* 16, *received into the magazine of the court through his hand* ,, ,, ,, (*kelešta*) 2300, *makes in ten* 7850.

5. *Athyr day* 19, *received into the magazine of the court through his hand* ,, ,, ,, (*kelešta*) 2880, *makes in ten* 9500.

6. *Athyr day* 22, *received into the magazine of the court through his hand* ,, ,, ,, (*kelešta*) 2600, *makes in ten* 8900.

7. *Athyr day* 27, *received into the magazine of the court through his hand* ,, ,, ,, (*kelešta*) 5266, *makes in ten* 17,440.

8. *Choiak day* 6, *received into the magazine of the court through the hand of the scribe Thothmesu,* (*kelešta*) 11,072, *makes in ten* 37,220.

9. *Choiak day* 13, *received into the magazine of the court through the hand of the scribe Necht,* (*kelešta*) 4205, *makes in ten* 16,350.[1]

10. *Choiak day* 17, *received into the magazine of the court through his hand* ,, ,, (*kelešta*) 1000, *makes in ten* 3710.

11. *Last* (*Choiak*), *received into the magazine of the court through the hand of the scribe Paharpet,* 1001, *makes in ten* 3090.[2]

Pl. XIII, l. 8. The second figure in the number of kelešta (the hundreds) has faded away. We restore the number to 2290 to get a convenient proportion (1 : 3,56) between kelešta and ten. The word ![glyph] *chaï* has here doubtless the meaning of *consumed*, as the same word as malady means consumption (see Brugsch, *Wörtb.*, Continuat., p. 884). There was no rest on this and the following days. L. 9. We restore 2000 before 200, equally l. 10 before 600. The restoration of the kelešta (ll. 11–19) is doubtful, we can only approximately deduct their number from the number of ten with the proportion of *ca.* 3, 5 : 1.

[1] Spiegelberg, 18,350 ; the photo. indistinct.

[2] Between ll. 4 and 5 of Pl. X the photo. (Spiegelberg, Tafel II) lets see "together 6171" which belong to Tafel III (Pleyte's Pl. XI).

L. 12 is of the second month, the Paophi. Pleyte is right in translating (p. 20), "jour du voyage de sa majesté vers le sud." The sign after the gap is ⟨glyph⟩ *kemat*, and not ⟨glyph⟩. Pleyte's number of kelešta 3205 being too low on account of the number of ten, it may be easily corrected into 3905. L. 13. The real number 13,680 wants more than 4000 kelešta. The date must be between 1 and 8 Paophi, so we supplied the 4. L. 14. The number of hundreds is not to be now seen, but distinctly 25. From the number of ten 17,880 we should expect 5000 and not 3000 kelešta in the proportion of $3\frac{1}{2}:1$. L. 23 the number of ten 16,350 wants not 3986 but 4986.[1]

The last number at the end of Pl. XIII which looks like an addition, probably 705, cannot be the sum of the rests (?) above; this would be only $129\frac{1}{2}$; perhaps it remained from the former manuscript. Pl. X is only the continuation of Pl. XIII, no void being between them, as Pl. XIII closes with 6 Athyr, and Pl. X begins with the 8th of the same month. It is to be noticed that Pl. X–XII is written on a papyrus sheet which was used before, what is called palimpsest. ⟨glyph⟩ *ta nefer*, "good breads," are often mentioned in the great Harris, XVII*a*, 7, XXXV*a*, 1, etc., combined not only with ākuu, XVII*b*, 8, but also with kelešta, XVII*b*, 15 (*cf.* Piehl, *Dict.*, p. 102).

PLATE XI.[2]

*a*1. 1601.   392,325,
  2. *together bread* 107,893 *makes in ten* 364,371
  3. *bread* 6171 *loaves* (θes) 1800 *makes in ten* 21,600
  4. *together* 385,871 [3]
  5. *rest* 6354.
*b*1. *quantity of maize sacks* 1601 *makes in bread* 112,090
  2. *makes in ten* 392,306
  3, 4. *brought to the magazine bread* 114,064 [4] *makes in ten* 385,971
  5. *rest bread*   *ten* 6335 *makes in bread* 1815.[5]

---

[1] So also the photo.

[2] Spiegelberg, Tafel III, before the text of Pl. XII, but very indistinct.

[3] Spiegelberg, 971. The photo. too indistinct to decide.

[4] Spiegelberg could not recognise the number; he reads 80 instead of the apparent 60.

[5] Spiegelberg, 1825.

We have here a double account of the same quantity of *boti* 〰, so has the original, Pl. XI*b*, l. 1, not Pleyte's flour. *Boti* is probably spelt or maize, Indian corn, *vide* p. 94, Greek ὄλυρα. The quantity is in both accounts 1601 sacks; these are calculated in ten and in bread.

a. First account 1601.   392,325.

These 392,325 ten consist of two sorts :—

1. loaves 107,893, which give ten 364,371
2.   „   6121 θes 1800   „   21,600

                                    ─────────
                                    385,971
                          Rest   6354
                                    ───────── If we add these last
numbers we get the number above. 392,325

The likeness of the hieratic signs for 20 and 70 makes this account rather uncertain. After the signs in the original, we could read l. 1, 392,375, and l. 2, 364,321, but for the additional sum compare the above reading. The relation of loaves to ten $\frac{364,371}{107,893}$ = 3,377 proves that the loaves are kelešta. This seems also the case with the 6121 relation 1 : 3, 5, but the second number θes 1800, the 1800[1] loaves, if it is not displaced and belongs to the rest (l. 5), are bigger loaves (ākuu). If we divide 21,600 by 1800 we get 12½, which is XII, 8, the weight of an ākuu bread.

A probably corrected and better account is the second of Pl. XI. Here the sum of loaves is 112,090 in ten 392,306 (only 15 less than in the first account). From these were brought into the magazine 114,064 = 385,971 ten. As rest is noted 1815 loaves = 6335 ten, together 115,879 loaves = 392,306 ten.

If we compare the 114,064 delivered loaves to this of the first account, we get the same number if we add to 107,893 (l. 2),

                                    6,171 (l. 3)
                                    ─────────
                          (l. 1), 114,064

The number of ten in the second account (385,971) disagrees by a hundred with the number of the first account. This all demonstrates that our calculator was a rather careless man.

It is to be noted that we have here not, as in Pl. V–IX and

─────────
[1] See XIII, 3, where we corrected 1,800 to 1,600 à 13½ ten = 21,600.

Pl. XII, a calculation of tep sacks of flour, but of sacks of *boti* (Indian corn or spelt); these sacks of spelt or maize must have been considerably smaller than those tep sacks of flour, because we have seen above, p. 96, that a tep sack of flour was calculated to give 720 ten = 65 kilogr. of bread, whilst here a sack of *boti* is supposed to give only $\frac{392325}{1601}$ = 245 ten or 22 kilogr. of bread. In this manner would be the proportion between sacks of corn and sacks of flour as 22 : 65. In Pl. XVIII, $7\frac{1}{2}$ sacks of flour correspond to $18\frac{3}{4}$ tep sacks of *boti*, i.e. $1 : 2\frac{1}{2}$, a somewhat different proportion from that here, 22 : 65 = 1 : nearly 3. I confess that there is a difficulty in accepting two different measures of flour and of corn with the same name *tep* 𐦥𐦤, but it is nearly impossible to think that the same volume of corn and flour could produce bread, the first only in the weight of 22 kilogr. (245 ten), the other in the weight of 65 kilogr. = 720 ten, even if the first one would be reckoned in ears not skinned. We cannot arrive at the *real* weight of a sack of boti, because we are not certain if this boti is spelt or maize. I draw from a good manual of agriculture (Göriz, *Betriebslehre*, Vol. II, p. 221 ff.) the following information :

100 pounds of corn (*Roggen, Secale cereale*) give 85 pounds of flour, and these, 115-120 pounds of bread.

100 pounds of wheat (*Triticum vulgare*) give 84 pounds of flour, and these, 100-106 pounds of bread.

100 pounds of spelt grains (*Dinkel, Triticum spelta*) give 83-90 pounds of flour, and these, 100-108 pounds of bread.

or from 100 pounds of flour ca. 130 pounds of bread $\left\{ \begin{array}{l} \text{corn, 100 give 133-150} \\ \text{wheat, 100 give 126-133} \\ \text{spelt, 100 give 122-150} \end{array} \right.$

From the same source (Göriz, I, 139) I draw the average weight of a hektolitre of winter wheat from 71 to 76 kilogr.,

„   „   winter corn (*Roggen*) from $68\frac{1}{2}$ to 71 kilogr.,

„   „   maize from 60,6 to $68\frac{1}{2}$ kilogr.

To this section belongs also the Papyrus 1883 = 209,[1] not published by Pleyte, dated the second year of Seti I, who sojourned at

---

[1] Spiegelberg gives the Papyrus 209 in *extenso*, Tafel IX and Tafel X. Text, p. 20 *ff.* Of this text, which contains, besides Seti I, the names of King Rameses I, Amenophis I, and Haremheb, only a small part, recto Col. I, verso Cols. II—III, belongs to the baking accounts.

hat time at Heliopolis (*àutu em* *àn*). On this very corroded heet, nearly unrecognisable, which was written on both sides, we ncounter the same personalities we have met in the two first sections, he scribe [1] *Hui*, of the ,

Pa Ramenpehti (Ramses I), and a scribe of *perait*[2] ,

lso the baker T'at'a receiving sacks of flour (*annu*), whom we met o often, Pl. V–IX and Pl. XII.

---

[1] Not in Spiegelberg.

[2] Spiegelberg reads this word *petaï*, and translates it "cultus, worship."

The next Meeting of the Society will be held at 37, Great Russell Street, Bloomsbury, W.C., on Tuesday, 4th May, 1897, at 8 p.m., when the following Paper will be ead :—

THE HON. MISS PLUNKET: "The Median Calendar."

NOTICES.

SUBSCRIPTIONS to the Society become due on the 1st of January each year. Those Members in arrear for the current year are requested to send the amount, £1 1s., at once to Messrs. Lloyds Bank, Limited, 16, St. James's Street, S.W.

PAPERS proposed to be read at the Monthly Meetings must be sent to the Secretary on or before the 10th of the preceding month.

Members having NEW MEMBERS to propose, are requested to send in the names of the Candidates on or before the 10th of the month preceding the meeting at which the names are to be submitted to the Council.

A few complete sets of the publications of the Society can be obtained by application to the Secretary, W. HARRY RYLANDS, 37, Great Russell Street, Bloomsbury, W.C.

The LIBRARY of the Society, at 37, GREAT RUSSELL STREET, BLOOMSBURY, W.C., is open to Members on Monday, Wednesday, and Friday, between the hours of 11 and 4, when the Secretary is in attendance to transact the general business of the Society.

As the new list of members will shortly be printed, Members are requested to send any corrections or additions they may wish to have made in the list which was published in Vol. IX of the *Transactions*.

THE FOLLOWING BOOKS ARE REQUIRED FOR THE LIBRARY OF THE SOCIETY.

'embers having duplicate copies, will confer a favour by presenting them to the Society.

I.KER, E., Die Chronologie der Bücher der Könige und Paralipomenōn im Einklang mit der Chronologie der Aegypter, Assyrer, Babylonier und Meder.

MÉLINEAU, Histoire du Patriarche Copte Isaac.

————— Contes de l'Égypte Chrétienne.

————— La Morale Egyptienne quinze siècles avant notre ère.

MIAUD, La Légende Syriaque de Saint Alexis, l'homme de Dieu.

——— A., AND L. MECHINEAU, Tableau Comparé des Écritures Babyloniennes et Assyriennes.

—— Mittheilungen aus der Sammlung der Papyrus Erzherzog Rainer. 2 parts.

AETHGEN, Beiträge zur Semitischen Religiongeshichte. Der Gott Israels und die Götter der Heiden.

LASS, A. F., Eudoxi ars Astronomica qualis in Charta Aegyptiaca superest.

OTTA, Monuments de Ninive. 5 vols., folio. 1847-1850.

RUGSCH-BEY, Geographische Inschriften Altaegyptische Denkmaeler. Vols. I—III (Brugsch).

————— Recueil de Monuments Égyptiens, copiés sur lieux et publiés par H. Brugsch et J. Dümichen. (4 vols., and the text by Dümichen of vols. 3 and 4.)

UDINGER, M., De Colonarium quarundam Phoeniciarum primordiis cum Hebraeorum exodo conjunctis.

URCKHARDT, Eastern Travels.

ASSEL, PAULUS, Zophnet Paneach Aegyptische Deutungen.

HABAS, Mélanges Égyptologiques. Séries I, III. 1862-1873.

ÜMICHEN, Historische Inschriften, &c., 1st series, 1867.

—————————————— 2nd series, 1869.

——— Altaegyptische Kalender-Inschriften, 1886.

————————— Tempel-Inschriften, 1862. 2 vols., folio.

BERS. G., Papyrus Ebers.

RMAN, Papyrus Westcar.

tudes Égyptologiques. 13 vols., complete to 1880.

AYET, E., Stèles de la XII dynastie au Musée du Louvre.

OLÉNISCHEFF, Die Metternichstele. Folio, 1877.

————— Vingt-quatre Tablettes Cappadociennes de la Collection de.

RANT-BEY, Dr., The Ancient Egyptian Religion and the Influence it exerted on the Religions that came in contact with it.

AUPT, Die Sumerischen Familiengesetze.

OMMEL, Dr., Geschichte Babyloniens und Assyriens. 1892.

JASTROW, M., A Fragment of the Babylonian "Dibbarra" Epic.

JENSEN, Die Kosmologie der Babylonier.

JEREMIAS, Tyrus bis zur Zeit Nubukaḍnezar's, Geschichtliche Skizze mit besonderer Berücksichtigung der Keilschriftlichen Quellen.

JOACHIM, H., Papyros Ebers, das Älteste Buch über Heilkunde.

IOHNS HOPKINS UNIVERSITY. Contributions to Assyriology and Comparative Semitic Philology.

KREBS, F., De Chnemothis nomarchi inscriptione Aegyptiaca commentatio.

LEDERER, Die Biblische Zeitrechnung vom Auszuge aus Aegypten bis zum Beginne der Babylonische Gefangenschaft mit Berichtigung der Resultate der Assyriologie und der Aegyptologie.

LEDRAIN, Les Monuments Égyptiens de la Bibliothèque Nationale.

LEFÈBURE, Le Mythe Osirien. 2me partie. "Osiris."

LEGRAIN, G., Le Livre des Transformations. Papyrus démotique du Louvre.

LEHMANN, Samassumukin König von Babylonien 668 vehr, p. xiv, 173. 47 plates.

LEPSIUS, Nubian Grammar, &c., 1880.

MARUCHI, Monumenta Papyracea Aegyptia.

MÜLLER, D. H., Epigraphische Denkmäler aus Arabien.

NOORDTZIG, Israël's verblijf in Egypte bezien int licht der Egyptische outdekkingen.

POGNON, Les Inscriptions Babyloniennes du Wadi Brissa.

RAWLINSON, CANON, 6th Ancient Monarchy.

ROBIOU, Croyances de l'Égypte à l'époque des Pyramides.

———— Recherches sur le Calendrier en Égypte et sur la chronologie des Lagides.

SAINTE MARIE, Mission à Carthage.

SARZEC, Découvertes en Chaldée.

SCHAEFFER, Commentationes de papyro medicinali Lipsiensi.

SCHOUW, Charta papyracea graece scripta Musei Borgiani Velitris.

SCHROEDER, Die Phönizische Sprache.

STRAUSS and TORNEY, Der Altägyptische Götterglaube.

VIREY, P., Quelques Observations sur l'Épisode d'Aristée, à propos d'un Monument Égyptien.

VISSER, I., Hebreeuwsche Archaeologie. Utrecht, 1891.

WALTHER, J., Les Découvertes de Ninive et de Babylone au point de vue biblique. Lausanne, 1890.

WILCKEN, M., Actenstücke aus der Königl. Bank zu Theben.

WILTZKE, Der Biblische Simson der Agyptische Horus-Ra.

WINCKLER, HUGO, Der Thontafelfund von El Amarna. Vols. I and II.

———— Textbuch-Keilinschriftliches zum Alten Testament.

WEISSLEACH, F. H., Die Achaemeniden Inschriften Zweiter Art.

WESSELEY, C., Die Pariser Papyri des Fundes von El Fajum.

Zeitsch. der Deutschen Morgenl. Gesellsch., Vol. XX to Vol. XXXII, 1866 to 1878.

ZIMMERN, H., Die Assyriologie als Hülfswissenschaft für das Studium des Alten Testaments.

SOCIETY OF BIBLICAL ARCHÆOLOGY PUBLICATIONS.

n 8 Parts. Price 5s. each. The Fourth Part having been issued, the Price is now Raised to £5 for the 8 Parts. Parts cannot be sold separately.

THE EGYPTIAN- BOOK OF THE DEAD.
Complete Translation, Commentary, and Notes.

By SIR P. LE PAGE RENOUF, KNT. (*President*);

CONTAINING ALSO

𝕬 𝔖eries of 𝔓lates of the 𝔙ignettes of the different ℭhapters.

The Bronze Ornaments of the Palace Gates from Balawat.

[SHALMANESER II, B.C. 859–825.]

Parts I, II, III, and IV have now been issued to Subscribers.

In accordance with the terms of the original prospectus the price for each part is now raised to £1 10s. ; to Members of the Society (the original price) £1 1s.

Price 7s. 6d. Only a Limited Number of Copies will be Printed.

THE PALESTINIAN SYRIAC VERSION OF THE HOLY SCRIPTURES.

Four Recently Discovered Portions (together with verses from the Psalms and the Gospel of St. Luke). Edited, in Photographic Facsimile, from a Unique MS. in the British Museum, with a Transcription, Translation, Introduction, Vocabulary, and Notes, by

REV. G. MARGOLIOUTH, M.A.,

Assistant in the Department of Oriental Printed Books and MSS. in the British Museum ; formerly Tyrwhitt Hebrew Scholar.

Subscribers' names to be Addressed to the Secretary.

SOCIETY OF BIBLICAL ARCHÆOLOGY.

COUNCIL, 1897.

President.

SIR P. LE PAGE RENOUF, KNT.

Vice-Presidents.

THE MOST REV. HIS GRACE THE LORD ARCHBISHOP OF YORK.
THE MOST NOBLE THE MARQUESS OF BUTE, K.T., &c., &c.
THE RIGHT HON. LORD AMHERST OF HACKNEY.
THE RIGHT HON. LORD HALSBURY.
THE RIGHT HON. W. E. GLADSTONE, M.P., D.C.L., &c.
ARTHUR CATES.
F. D. MOCATTA, F.S.A., &c.
WALTER MORRISON, M.P.
SIR CHARLES NICHOLSON, BART., D.C.L., M.D., &c.
ALEXANDER PECKOVER, LL.D., F.S.A.
REV. GEORGE RAWLINSON, D.D., Canon of Canterbury.

Council.

REV. CHARLES JAMES BALL, M.A.
REV. PROF. T. K. CHEYNE, D.D.
THOMAS CHRISTY, F.L.S.
DR. J. HALL GLADSTONE, F.R.S.
CHARLES HARRISON, F.S.A.
GRAY HILL.
PROF. T. HAYTER LEWIS, F.S.A.
REV. ALBERT LÒWY, LL.D., &c.

REV. JAMES MARSHALL, M.A.
CLAUDE G. MONTEFIORE.
WALTER L. NASH, F.S.A.
PROF. E. NAVILLE.
J. POLLARD.
EDWARD B. TYLOR, LL.D., F.R.S., &c.
E. TOWRY WHYTE, M.A., F.S.A.

Honorary Treasurer—BERNARD T. BOSANQUET.

Secretary—W. HARRY RYLANDS, F.S.A.

Honorary Secretary for Foreign Correspondence—REV. R. GWYNNE, B.A.

Honorary Librarian—WILLIAM SIMPSON, F.R.G.S.

HARRISON AND SONS, PRINTERS IN ORDINARY TO HER MAJESTY, ST. MARTIN'S LANE.

PROCEEDINGS

OF

THE SOCIETY

OF

BIBLICAL ARCHÆOLOGY.

——❦❦——

VOL. XIX. TWENTY–SEVENTH SESSION.

Fifth Meeting, May 4th, 1897.

———❦❦———

CONTENTS.

———❦❦———

PUBLISHED AT

THE OFFICES OF THE SOCIETY,

37, GREAT RUSSELL STREET, BLOOMSBURY, W.C.

——

1897.

No. CXLVI.] -

SOCIETY OF BIBLICAL ARCHÆOLOGY,

37, GREAT RUSSELL STREET, BLOOMSBURY, W.C.

TRANSACTIONS.

	To Members.	To Non-Members.		To Members.	To Non-Members.
		s. d.			s. d.
Vol. I, Part 1 ...	10 6	... 12 6	Vol. VI, Part 1 ...	10	... 12 6
,, I, ,, 2 ...	10 6	... 12 6	,, VI, ,, 2 ...	10	... 12 6
,, II, ,, 1 ...	8 0	... 10 6	,, VII, ,, 1 ...	7	... 10 6
,, II, ,, 2 ...	8 0	... 10 6	,, VII, ,, 2 ...	10	... 12 6
,, III, ,, 1 ...	8 0	... 10 6	,, VII, ,, 3 ...	10	... 12 6
,, III, ,, 2 ...	8 0	... 10 6	,, VIII, ,, 1 ...	10	... 12 6
,, IV, ,, 1 ...	10 6	... 12 6	,, VIII, ,, 2 ...	10	... 12 6
,, IV, ,, 2 ...	10 6	... 12 6	,, VIII, ,, 3 ...	10	... 12 6
,, V, ,, 1 ...	12 6	... 15 0	,, IX, ,, 1 ...	10 6	... 12 6
,, V, ,, 2 ...	10 6	... 12 6	,, IX, ,, 2 ...	10 6	... 12 6

PROCEEDINGS.

				To Members.		To Non-Members.
Vol. I,	Session	1878–79	...	2 0	... ...	2 6
,, II,	,,	1879–80	...	2 0	... ...	2 6
,, III,	,,	1880–81	...	4 0	... ...	5 0
,, IV,	,,	1881–82	...	4 0	... ...	5 0
,, V,	,,	1882–83	...	4 0	... ...	5 0
,, VI,	,,	1883–84	...	5 0	... ...	6 0
,, VII,	,,	1884–85	...	5 0	... ...	6 0
,, VIII,	,,	1885–86	...	5 0	... ...	6 0
,, IX,	,,	1886–87	...	2 0 per Part	...	2 6
,, IX, Part 7,		1886–87	...	8 0 ,, ,,	...	10 6
,, X, Parts 1 to 7,		1887–88	...	2 0 ,, ,,	...	2 6
,, X, Part 8,		1887–88	...	7 6 ,, ,,	...	10 6
,, XI, Parts 1 to 7,		1888–89	...	2 0 ,, ,,	...	2 6
,, XI, Part 8,		1888–89	...	7 6 ,, ,,	...	10 6
,, XII, Parts 1 to 7,		1889–90	...	2 0 ,, ,,	...	2 6
,, XII, Part 8,		1889–90	...	5 0 ,, ,,	...	6 0
,, XIII, Parts 1 to 7,		1890–91	...	2 0 ,, ,,	...	2 6
,, XIII, Part 8,		1890–91	...	5 0 ,, ,,	...	6 0
,, XIV, Parts 1 to 7,		1891–92	...	2 0 ,, ,,	...	2 6
,, XIV, Part 8,		1891–92	...	5 0 ,, ,,	...	6 0
,, XV, Parts 1 to 7,		1892–93	...	2 0 ,, ,,	...	2 6
,, XV, Part 8,		1892–93	...	5 0 ,, ,,	...	6 0
,, XVI, Parts 1 to 10,		1893–94	...	2 0 ,, ,,	...	2 6
,, XVII, Parts 1 to 8		1895	...	2 0 ,, ,,	...	2 6
,, XVIII, Parts 1 to 8		1896	...	2 0 ,, ,,	...	2 6
,, XIX, In progress		1897				

A few complete sets of the Transactions still remain for sale, which may be obtained on application to the Secretary, W. H. RYLANDS, F.S.A., 37, Great Russell Street, Bloomsbury, W.C.

PROCEEDINGS

OF

THE SOCIETY

OF

BIBLICAL ARCHÆOLOGY.

TWENTY-SEVENTH SESSION, 1897.

Fifth Meeting, *4th May*, 1897.

THE REV. JAMES MARSHALL, M.A.,

IN THE CHAIR.

————✵❦✷————

The following Presents were announced, and thanks dered to be returned to the Donors :—

From the Secretary of State for India in Council:
The Sacred Books of the East :—
Vol. XXXVIII, Vedânta-Sûtras, with Sankara's Commentary. Part II. Translated by George Thibaut.
Vol. XLII, Hymns of the Atharva-Veda, together with extracts from the Ritual Books and Commentaries. Translated by Maurice Bloomfield.
Vol. XLV, Gaina Sûtras. Translated from Prakrit by Herman Jacobi. Part II.
Vol. XLVI, Vedic Hymns. Translated by Hermann Oldenberg. Part II. 8vo. 1895–6–7. Oxford.

From Professor Russell Martineau :—

————— Zeitschrift für die Kunde des Morgenlandes. Vol. I, 1837 ; Vol. II, 1839 ; Vol. III, 1840 ; Vol. IV, 1841. 8vo. Gottingen.

——————————— Bd. 5, Heft 2. Bonn. 1844. Bd. 6, Heft 1. Bonn. 1844. Heft 2. Bonn. 1845. Bd. 7, Heft 1. 8vo. Bonn. 1846.

————— Jahresbericht der Deutschen Morgenländischen Gesellschaft für das Jahr 1845. Leipzig. 1846. Für das Jahr 1846. Leipzig. 1847.

——————— Zeitschrift der D. M. Gesellschaft, Vol. I. Leipzig. 1847 ; Vol. IV, 1850 ; Vol. V, 1851 ; Vol. VI, 1852 ; Vol. VII, 1853 ; Vol. VIII, 1854 ; Vol. IX, 1855 ; Vol. X, 1856 ; Vol. XI, 1857 ; Vol. XII, 1858.

——————————— Register zu Band I–X. 8vo. Leipzig. 1858.

From the Author :—Professor Karl Piehl. Mélanges and Notices of Books (10 8vo. Papers).

————— Réponse à M. Gaston Maspero à propos de son avant-propos du " Temple d'Edfou." 8vo. Upsala. 1897.

————— Notes de Léxicographique Égyptienne. Texte Provenant du Grand Temple d'Edfou. Extraits, Congrès Intérnat. des Orient. Genève. 8vo. 1894. Leide. 1896.

————— Sur une nouveau paradigme en Égyptien.

————— Quelques Textes Égyptiens empruntés à des monuments conservés au Musée de Stockholm. Rémarques générales sur le dictionnaire hiéroglyphique. Observations sur quelques signes et groupes hiéroglyphiques. Quelques Mots sur la vie et les œuvres de l'illustre orientalisté suédois. J. D. Akerblad.

Extraits : 8 Cong. des Orientalistés. Stockholm. 8vo. 1889. Leide. 1891.

————— Deux déesses Égyptiennes. Leide. 4to. Extrait des Mélanges Charles de Harlez.

From R. A. Rye :—The Dawn of Civilization ; Egypt and Chaldea.
By G. Maspero. Edited by A. H. Sayce. Translated by
M. L. McClure. 8vo. London. 1894.

From the Author, Captain H. G. Lyons, R.E. :—A Report on
the Island and Temples of Philæ, with introductory note by
W. E. Garstin, C.M.G. Printed by order of H. E. Hussein
Fakhri Pasha, Minister of Public Works. Fol. London.
[1897.]

A special vote of thanks was given to Prof. Russell
Martineau for his donation to the Library.

A Paper by the Hon. Miss Plunket was read : entitled
" The Median Calendar," which will be printed, with illustrations, in a future part of the *Proceedings*.

Remarks were added by Mr. Joseph Offord, Miss Plunket,
and the Chairman.

BOOK OF THE DEAD.

By Sir P. Le Page Renouf.

CHAPTER CXXXVIA.

Chapter whereby one is conveyed in the Bark of Rā.

Lo the Light (1) which riseth up in Cher-āba. (2)
He is born, he of the strong cord, (3) his cable (4) is at an end, and his rudder (5) hath been taken in hand.

I poise the divine machinery (6) by which I raise up the Bark to the cord above head, by means of which I come forth into Heaven, and am conveyed to Nut.

I am conveyed by it along with Rā. I am conveyed by it like the Kaf. (7)

I stop the path at the Uārit of Nut, at the staircase where Seb and Nut bewail their hearts.

CHAPTER CXXXVIB.

Chapter whereby one is conveyed in the Great Bark of Rā to pass through the orbit of flame.

O bright flame which art behind Rā, and dividest his Crown !
The Bark of Rā feareth the storm.
Ye* are bright and ye are exalted.

I come daily with Sek-hra (8) from his exalted station, so that I may witness the process of the Maāt (9) and the lion-forms (10) which belong to them . . . . so that I may see them there.

* *Sic.*

We are rejoicing: their great ones are in jubilation, and their smaller ones in bliss.

I make my way at the prow of the Bark of Rā, which lifteth me up like his disk.

I shine like the Glorious ones, whom he hath enriched with his wealth, holding fast like a Lord of Maāt.

Here is the Cycle of the gods, and the Kite of Osiris.

Grant ye that his father, the Lord of them, may judge in his behalf.

And so I poise for him the Balance, which is Maāt, and I raise it to Tefnut that he may live.

Come, come, for the father is uttering the judgment of Maāt.

Oh thou who callest out at thine evening hours, grant that I may come and bring to him the two jaws of Restau, and that I may bring to him the books which are in the Annu and add up for him his hosts.

And so I have repulsed Apepi and healed the wounds he made.

Let me make my way through the midst of you.

I am the Great one among the gods, coming in the two Barks of the Lord of Sau, the Figure of the great saluter, who hath made the Flame.

Let the fathers and their Apes make way for me, that I may enter the Mount of Glory, and pass through where the Great ones are.

I see who is there in his Bark, and I pass through the orbit of Flame which is behind the Lord of the Side-lock, over the serpents.

Let me pass: I am the powerful one, the Lord of the powerful.

I am the Sāhu, the Lord of Maāt, the creator of every Dawn. (11)

Place me among the followers of Rā: place me as one who goeth round in the Garden of Peace of Rā.

I am a god greater than thou art.

Let me be numbered in presence of the Divine Cycle when the offerings are presented to me.

NOTES.

The two chapters which are numbered by M. Naville as 136A and 136B are represented in the later recensions by a single chapter, which has been made out of them. There is very much obscurity in the ancient texts though the MSS. containing them are numerous, and the more recent versions are quite as difficult to understand. We must be satisfied for the present by a strict literal and grammatical translation, wherever this amount of success is attainable. The royal sarcophagus 32 of the British Museum gives the latest form of 136A.

1. *Light* 〔hieroglyphs〕✕. A common noun signifying *lamp*, but the determinative here shows that a heavenly body is meant. The sun is here spoken of exactly in the same poetical way as when Antigone (879) speaks of τόδε λαμπάδος ἱερὸν ὄμμα, or Virgil of the *Phœboea lampas.*

2. The later recension speaks of "the Lamp in Annu and the Hammemit in Cherāba. This reading is already found in a few of the Theban texts. The royal sarcophagus 32 of the British Museum gives the important variant 〔hieroglyphs〕 = 〔hieroglyphs〕, whence it follows that 〔hieroglyph〕 is phonetically = 〔hieroglyph〕. The latter sign has only two known values 〔hieroglyph〕 *āḥā*, and 〔hieroglyph〕 *āba*. That the latter is the true equivalent of 〔hieroglyph〕 is certain, in consequence of the complementary vowels 〔hieroglyph〕, which commonly accompany that sign, whether in the word signifying *battle*, or in the name of a place. It is *impossible* that 〔hieroglyph〕 should be the right reading, and no one has a right to convert 〔hieroglyph〕 into a simple 〔hieroglyph〕.

The well known word 〔hieroglyph〕, "strike," takes the prothetic 〔hieroglyph〕, and is found under the form 〔hieroglyph〕, in the name of one of the hours of the night.* No fresh information is derived from the discovery by M. Daressy of the same word under the form 〔hieroglyph〕, that is 〔hieroglyph〕, as it should be corrected if cited. To *strike* and

---

* To press the identity of 〔hieroglyph〕 and 〔hieroglyph〕 in the name of this hour is to forget that its variants would equally prove that 〔hieroglyph〕 = 〔hieroglyph〕 = 〔hieroglyph〕.

fight are different words, though they may often be used synono-
usly, and admit of being substituted one for the other.*

3. *He of the strong cord,* ⟨glyph⟩. This is grammatically the subject
the verb *is born,* and I consider it as a compound expression in
ich the adjective precedes the substantive, as in longimanus.
nderstand ⟨glyph⟩ as = ⟨glyph⟩ (see *Zeitsch.,* 1868, p. 70, and 1870,
154, 155). In the later recessions (*e.g.,* Todt. 136, and B.M. 32)
s omitted in this place, but not in the passage which follows.

4. *His cable,* ⟨glyph⟩. See Bonomi, *Sarc.* 8 D, and *cf.* a
ssage in the Pyramid Texts (*Pepi* I, 413, *Merenrā* 590) which
ers to this or a similar voyage. M. Maspero thus translates it :—
"ais amener à Pepi ta barque sur laquelle naviguent tes purs el
and tu auras reçu ta libation d'eau fraiche sur cette CUISSE DES

DESTRUCTIBLES (the Uārit ⟨glyph⟩ of the Circumpolar
rs), fais naviguer Pepi dans cette barque avec ce cable d'étoffe
te et blanche par lequel l'Œil d'Hor est remorqué," &c. The
irit, or *Leg* (on which see Ch. 74, Note 1) of Nut is mentioned at
: end of this chapter.

---

* See *P.S.B.A.* IX, p. 313, and two previous articles of mine there referred to.
e corrections I have to make are the following :—I wrongly assumed that the *fish*
ich in hieratic papyri crosses the foot of the sign ⟨glyph⟩ in the variants of ⟨glyph⟩
s the same fish as we find in the group ⟨glyphs⟩
e fishes are different. On referring to M. Naville's *Festival Hall of Osorkon II,*
18, pictures will be found of the ⟨glyph⟩ and the ⟨glyph⟩. The
t of these is clearly the fish in ⟨glyph⟩, *ḥem-reu,* and the corresponding sign
the variant is to be read ⟨glyph⟩, *ḥem,* in harmony with the other evidence
duced by W. Max Müller (*Recueil,* vol. IX). The picture of it does not
ble one to determine its species. The pictures at Babastis of the ⟨glyph⟩
m to indicate the *Synodontis,* but a picture found by Petrie (*Medum,* pl. 12)
ws an immense fish which has been identified with the *Latus* or *Perca
lotica.* This being of the Acanthopterygian family is of course a very
nidable *warrior,* like our own small perch, which, as Mr. Ward says, "does
: yield its life without endangering the person of its captor, for the formidable
s of spinous rays belonging to the first dorsal fin have wounded the hands of
ny an incautious angler."

5. *Rudder* [hieroglyphs] or [hieroglyphs].

6. *Machinery* [hieroglyphs]. The word has disappeared from the later texts and been replaced by various conjectural emendations of the scribes.

7. *The Kaf,* [hieroglyphs], one of the divinities in form of apes. Etymologically the word signifies "the *hot* one."

8. *Sek-ḥra,* [hieroglyphs] is the more common reading, but [hieroglyphs] also occurs and so does [hieroglyphs]. I cannot remember where I found [hieroglyphs] (*P.S.B.A.* VI, 191) which would identify this divinity with Thoth.

9. *The Maāt,* the series of phenomena occurring in strict conformity with Law, that is with the laws of Nature.

10. *Lion forms,* [hieroglyphs], phonetically [hieroglyphs], in most of the papyri. Some of the words which follow are evidently in very corrupt condition.

11. *Every Dawn,* [hieroglyphs].

THE DATE OF THE SILOAM INSCRIPTION.

By E. J. PILCHER.

In the month of June, 1880, a sharp-eyed pupil of Dr. Schick detected the letters of an inscription upon the wall of a rock-hewn channel which conveys water from the Virgin's Spring to the Pool of Siloam, at Jerusalem. Professor A. H. Sayce, of Oxford, in February, 1881, made the first intelligible copy; and the following is his latest revised translation of his restoration of the inscription.

Line 1. "(Behold) the excavation! Now this is the history of the excavation. While the excavators were lifting up

Line 2. The pick each towards his neighbour, and while there were yet three cubits (to excavate there was heard) the voice of one man

Line 3. calling to his neighbour, for there was an excess in the rock on the right hand (and on the left). And after that on the day

Line 4. of excavating, the excavators had struck pick against pick, one against the other,

Line 5. the waters flowed from the spring to the pool for a distance of 1,200 cubits. And a

Line 6. hundred cubits was the height of the rock over the head of the excavators."*

This inscription was carefully and artistically engraved upon the *lower half* of a niche, or tablet, cut in the rock; the upper half being left blank. This seems to indicate that the notice was intended to be bi-lingual; but, for some reason, the other language was never added. In 1890 an attempt was made to steal the inscription by cutting it out of the rock; but the only result was to break it in pieces, and the fragments are now preserved in the

---

* *The Higher Criticism and the Verdict of the Monuments*, by the Rev. A. H. Sayce. (London, 1894), p. 379. See also an account of the inscription, with facsimile plate, *Proceedings*, Vol. IV, 68.

Royal Museum at Constantinople. A cast of it, as it appeared in its original condition, may be seen at the offices of the Palestine Exploration Fund.

As the inscription contains no historical statement, its interest is purely paleographical; and its date is uncertain.

Mr. Shapira, of Jerusalem, asserted that he could read the name of Uzziah upon it, and that it must therefore be attributed to that monarch. As, however, no one else could find the name, this theory has been dropped.

Professor Sayce, upon its discovery, somewhat hastily assumed the language of the inscription to be Phœnician; and its date to be of the time of Solomon. Although he quickly discovered that the language was Hebrew, he still maintained the Solomonic date in 1883. In his latest work, however, he assigns it to Hezekiah, because 2 Kings xx, 20, happens to mention that Hezekiah made a conduit. Dr. Neubauer suggested that when Isaiah viii, 6, mentioned "the waters of Shiloah that go softly," the prophet referred to the Siloam tunnel; and that therefore the latter was in existence, if not made, in the time of Ahaz. These theories seem to rest merely upon the assumption that the Siloam tunnel is one of the watercourses mentioned in the Old Testament, of which assumption there is of course no proof. Dr. Schick in 1891 announced in the *Quarterly Statement* of the Palestine Exploration Fund that he had partly explored the remains of another conduit running along the ancient surface of the ground from the Virgin's Spring to the Pool of Siloam. Seeing, therefore, that other aqueducts exist, it would be premature to identify the rock-hewn channel with any passage of Scripture.

Canon Isaac Taylor, in his work on *The Alphabet* (p. 236), assigns the Siloam inscription to the reign of Manasseh. After giving it as his opinion that it cannot be earlier than the eighth, or later than the sixth century B.C., he says :—

"But these limits of date may to some extent be further narrowed. It has been shown (p. 201) that the chief paleographic test which distinguishes the two great epochs of the Phœnician alphabet consists in the change in the forms of the two letters *mem* and *shin*. During the first part both letters have the zigzag form. In the second epoch they have a horizontal bar and cross stroke. The transition took place in the seventh century, when there was a short period during which the letter *mem* exhibits the new form, while *shin*

remains unchanged. It is precisely to this transitional period that
the Siloam Inscription must be referred."

Canon Taylor, however, does not appear to have noticed that
the Old Hebrew Alphabet *never* passed this "transitional period,"
and never adopted the barred *shin*. The coins of Bar-Cochab,
A.D. 135, still exhibited the barred *mem* and the zigzag *shin*.
Consequently Canon Taylor's inferior limit of date cannot be
sustained.*

Scholars, therefore, being at variance as to the exact date of the
inscription, and, moreover, having no definite grounds for the
opinions they express as to its date, it is proposed to examine the
alphabet of the Siloam Inscription in the light of our knowledge of
other inscriptions in the Old Hebrew character.

The fact that the Siloam inscription is in Hebrew, and in the
Old Hebrew character, gives us no clue to its date; because we do
not know when Hebrew ceased to be spoken at Jerusalem, or when
the use of the Old Hebrew alphabet was finally abandoned.

There are ancient Hebrew inscriptions in the square character
near Jerusalem; but there is no proof that any of them are earlier
than the time of Constantine the Great, when the edicts of Hadrian
were revoked, and the Jews were once more allowed to settle in the
city. On the other hand, whenever the Jews struck national
coins they always used the Hebrew language and the Old Hebrew
character, even in the time of Hadrian. Just as upon the Sidonian
bronze coins of the Seleucids we find the Phœnician inscription
לצדנם, and occasionally longer inscriptions in the same language
and character. We can hardly imagine that Bar-Cochab, and his
associate Eleazar, would have had their names and titles put upon
their coins in characters that no one could read; or that they would
have taken the trouble to make such announcements as : "First year
of the redemption of Israel," in a language and script that was
utterly unintelligible to the Israelites of that period. When, moreover, we find upon the coins statements of value, such as "half,"
and "quarter," it is evident that the people who used this money
were expected to read it. The capital of Amwas is another proof
that the Old Hebrew character was intelligently employed at a very

---

* We should not forget the valuable work done by Herren Guthe, Kautzsch,
Socin and other German and French scholars, more especially in the elucidation
of the text of the inscription. As, however, they have not developed theories
differing from the above, it is not necessary to mention them specifically.

late period. This monument is the capital of a pillar, of a debased
Ionic form, found at Amwas (Emmaus Nicopolis), between Joppa
and Jerusalem. Upon one side it bears the Greek inscription
Εἰς θεός, upon the other the words *Beruk shemo l'olam* in the Old
Hebrew character ; the letters being of the same shape as upon the
coins of Bar-Cochah. Under the capital is the Latin letter *S.* The
Greek and Hebrew are evidently intended to be read consecutively
as "(There is) One God, blessed be His Name for ever." M. Clermont
Ganneau ascribes this capital to the fourth century of the Christian
era ; but this seems partially founded upon his idea that it came
from a Christian church. If, as is far more probable, it came from
a Jewish synagogue, it may be a century or so earlier. In any case
it is a proof of the use of the Old Hebrew character at a late date.
As M. Clermont Ganneau points out, the shapes of the letters, and
more especially the *Vau*, show that the inscription is not a Samaritan
one, but that it is in the genuine Old Hebrew character.*

Our knowledge of the Old Hebrew alphabet is derived from two
sources, coins and gems. The coins of the Jews may be divided
into three well-defined classes :—

1. The bronze pieces of the Hasmonean princes.

2. The silver shekels and half-shekels bearing on the obverse a
cup, or chalice; and upon the reverse a triple lily, with the legend
Yerushalaim ha-qedoshah, "Jerusalem the Holy."

3. All other Jewish silver and bronze coins bearing inscriptions
in the Old Hebrew character.

All these coins are fully illustrated and described in Mr. F. W.
Madden's great work, *Coins of the Jews* (London, 1881); which
book will be referred to as "Madden."

(1.) There can be no question as to the date of the coins of
Class 1, as they all bear the names of the princes who struck them,
from ·John Hyrcanus, 135 B.C., to Antigonus, 37 B.C. They thus
cover the period of a century; and it is important to observe that
the Jewish alphabet did not remain stationary during this period.
It was not a fossil, but a living alphabet. The letters at the
beginning of the Hasmonean century have a strong resemblance to
those upon the sarcophagus of Eshmunazar, and the contemporary
Phœnician coins; the chief exceptions being the *He* and the *Vau*.
But at the close of the century the coins of Antigonus give us an

---

* *Survey of Western Palestine* vol. iii, "Judæa" (London, 1883), pp. 64-81.

PLATE I.

CAPITAL OF AMWAS.

GREEK INSCRIPTION— Εἷς Θεός.

OLD HEBREW INSCRIPTION—בָרוּך שְׁמוֹ לְעוֹלָב׃

alphabet almost exactly like that found upon the *Yerushalaim qedoshah* shekels.

(2.) The *Yerushalaim qedoshah* shekels form a clearly marked type. They are well-designed, though somewhat rudely executed, and the lettering upon them is regular and correct, except upon the half-shekels, where the *Qoph* is often defective, and the *He* slightly distorted. The alphabet upon them differs materially from that of John Hyrcanus, and agrees with that of Antigonus. The coins of Hyrcanus and his successors are not dated till we come to the time of Antigonus, who uses *Aleph* and *Beth* to denote the first and second years of his reign. The years of issue of the *Yerushalaim qedoshah* shekels are denoted in the same way, from שא to שה, *i.e.*, "Year 1" to "Year 5." Three opinions have been expressed as to their epoch.

(*a.*) M. de Saulcy ascribed these shekels to Ezra, on the strength of Ezra vii, 18; but this verse says' nothing whatever about coining money. Further, from a numismatic point of view it is almost impossible to assign these Jewish shekels to so early a date. When we examine the coins of the fifth century B.C., we find them nearly invariably with an incuse square upon the reverse; whereas these shekels possess a good reverse type. The word *Shanah* (year) does not occur upon Phœnician coins till 238 B.C., and the title "Holy" does not appear upon them until 176 B.C.*

(*b.*) The *Yerushalaim qedoshah* shekels have been ascribed to Simon Maccabeus on the strength of 1 Maccabees xv, 6, 7; and this view is adopted by Mr. F. W. Madden. But 1 Maccabees does not say that Simon actually struck coins; and it adds that Antiochus VII (Sidetes) revoked the edict directly afterwards. The shekels are dated in *five* years, and Simon only lived *three* after the accession of Antiochus VII.

(*c.*) Ewald, in 1855, suggested that the *Yerushalaim qedoshah* shekels were struck during the revolt of the Jews under Nero, A.D. 66–70; and this view has been supported by Professor Emil Schürer (*History of the Jewish People*, vol. ii, pp. 378–383) and Theodore Reinach (*Les Monnaies Juives*, Paris, 1888).

As the Hasmonean bronze pieces present us with the only undisputed dated series of Jewish coins, it becomes necessary to

---

* *A Guide to the Principal Gold and Silver Coins of the Ancients*, by Barclay V. Head (London, 1889), p. 93.

enquire to which end of the series the shekels belong : whether they
were struck before or after. If they were struck immediately before
the accession of John Hyrcanus, we ought to find upon them exactly
the same alphabet as is used by that prince. But the silver shekels
are strikingly different in fabric, type, and alphabet, from the bronze
coins of Hyrcanus. This seems fatal to their Maccabean authorship.
On the other hand, when we examine the large bronze coins of
Antigonus at the other end of the Hasmonean series, likenesses at
once become apparent. The alphabet employed is almost identical
with that of the shekels ; and the year of issue is denoted by letters
of the Old Hebrew alphabet. It is not impossible that the cup or
chalice upon the shekels was suggested by the form of the cornucopiæ on the coins of Antigonus : at any rate the date occupies
much the same place in both. The issue of *silver* coins was equivalent to a declaration of independence ; and if the *Yerushalaim
qedoshah* shekels were struck after the time of Antigonus, we cannot
suppose any earlier date than the period of the Neronian revolt,
A.D. 66–70. As this rebellion broke out on the 17th of Iyyar,
A.D. 66, when the Roman Governor was chased out of Jerusalem,
and terminated on the 8th of Elul, A.D. 70, when the last quarter of
the city was captured by Titus, it follows that it lasted four years
and four months, which exactly corresponds with the fact that the
Yerushalaim qedoshah shekels are struck in the years 1, 2, 3, 4,
and 5. It is therefore evident that these shekels must be assigned
to the revolt of A.D. 66–70.

(3.) The remaining silver and bronze coins with Old Hebrew
inscriptions bear dates in four years upon their reverses. They
have a multiplicity of types ; and the names of Simon, or Simon,
Prince of Israel, and Eleazar ha-Kohen. The alphabet employed
is that of the *Yerushalaim qedoshah* shekels ; but as a rule the
letters are carelessly formed, occasionally distorted, and sometimes
upside down. Madden (p. 205) even shows a coin with the letters
linked together, as in the Nabathean inscriptions. And most of the
bronze coins of Eleazar have his name written backwards, as though
the die-engraver were a Greek, who did not know that Semitic
writing was read from right to left. The Hasmonean bronze coins
exhibit several cases of careless lettering, but they are not so per-
sistent as in the coins of this series. If Gentiles were employed
as die engravers, this might be explained. The language upon
the coins is Hebrew, but the letters of the names are often mis-

placed. That Simon and Eleazar were contemporaries, is proved not only by their issuing coins with the same types or devices, but by the existence of coins bearing the name of Eleazar on one side, and Simon on the other (Madden, p. 201). The date of the coins is proved by the fact, that some of them are struck upon denarii of the Roman Emperors Vespasian, Titus, Domitian, Trajan, and Hadrian, portions of the old devices showing through. We can, therefore, only assign these coins to the period of the second Jewish revolt under Bar-Cochab, A.D. 132-135. This revolt broke out in the spring of A.D. 132, and was finally quelled in August, 135, thus lasting three years and a half. This agrees exactly with the fact that the coins bear dates in *four* years; the rebellion ending in its fourth year. It is generally held by numismatists that the Simon whose name appears upon the coins is the same individual as is known in history by his surname of Bar-Cochab, and that Eleazar ha-Kohen was his uncle, Eleazar of Modeïn. Bar-Cochab did not have the treasures or the resources of a city like Jerusalem at his disposal, and that will account for his striking his devices over the Roman denarii. There are also indications that some of the bronze pieces were struck over Roman coins, and his shekels upon Greco-Roman tetradrachms.

The different theories promulgated about the coins of Class 3 will be found stated in Mr. Madden's great work. Mr. Madden assigns the coins of the fourth year of Bar-Cochab to Simon Maccabeus, and divides the others between the first and second revolts, though he candidly admits, that there are enormous difficulties in this division of the series, and quotes the opinions of Von Sallet and De Saulcy to the effect that they must all belong to one and the same period. If the *Yerushalaim qedoshah* shekels be admitted to belong to the first revolt, there should be no object in dividing the later bronze and silver pieces; which can all be assigned to Simon Bar-Cochab in accordance with the evidence of their style and lettering, and the fact of some of them being struck over Roman coins.

It therefore appears from the above remarks that the Jewish coins can be arranged in a series which gives us dated specimens of the Old Hebrew alphabet as used from 135 B.C. to A.D. 135, a period of 270 years.

Our second source of information regarding the Old Hebrew Alphabet is the inscriptions upon engraved gems used as seals.

Among these there is only one which can be definitely proved to be
Jewish, and which can be definitely dated.   This is the seal of
" Haggai ben Shebaniah," in the possession of the Palestine
Exploration Fund.   This gem was discovered by Sir Charles
Warren in 1868, among the foundations of Herod's temple at
Jerusalem, at a depth of twenty-two feet from the present surface of
the ground.*   Its discoverer describes it as bearing " the name
engraved in Hebrew of the transition period, supposed to be at
least as old as the time of the Maccabees."   Seeing, however, that
the Temple of Herod was completed in 17 B.C., we are at least
justified in assigning the seal to that date.   This gem is very
important for the present study, because the lettering upon it, as
far as it goes, agrees exactly with the lettering of the Siloam
Inscription.

Having now indicated the sources of our information, it remains
to describe the

TABLE SHOWING THE PROGRESS OF THE OLD HEBREW ALPHABET
AFTER 135 B.C.

Col. 1 shows the alphabet employed upon the statue of Hadad
erected by Panammu bar Qarrul, King of Samala, and discovered
by Dr. F. von Luschan in 1890 upon the mound of Gerjin, near
Zenjerli.   This monarch is mentioned upon the inscription of Bar-
Rekub (whose alphabet is shown in column 2) about 730 B.C.; and
as he was at least the grandfather of the latter, his date may safely
be placed about 800 B.C.   The inscription of Panammu I, is
therefore only removed from the Stela of Mesha by about half a
century, and it is important to observe that the alphabet employed
is almost identical with that of the Mesha Stela.   This shows us
that in the ninth century B.C. precisely the same alphabet was in use
over the whole of the western Semitic area.

Col. 2 shows the alphabet employed upon the statue of
Panammu II, erected by his son Bar-Rekuh, and discovered at
Zenjerli by the German Expedition in 1889.   As this inscription
mentions that Panammu II died at Damascus, while serving in the
army of Tiglath-pileser III of Assyria, who thereupon created
Bar-Rekub king of Samala, the monument can be confidently dated
730 B.C.   It will be noted that this alphabet differs very slightly

* *Survey of Western Palestine*, vol. vi, "Jerusalem" (London, 1884), p. 170.

PLATE II.

Table showing the Prog

		2	3	4	5

Proc. Soc. Bibl. Arch., May, 1897.

Alphabet after 135 B.C.

from that of column 1, and in the case of *Kaph*, *Mem*, and *Nun* it is more like the lettering of the Mesha Stela than column 1.

Col. 3 gives a list of letters from the Assyrian lion-weights. They have been taken from the tables of Canon Taylor, in "The Alphabet," p. 227. They do not represent the characters upon any single inscription; but have been specially chosen to show those forms which correspond most closely to the forms of the Siloam inscription, in order to favour the latter as much as possible. The only letters of importance, however, are the *Vau* and the *Tau*. These lion-weights are valuable on account of their definite dates, ranging from 745 B.C. to 681 B.C. On comparing the alphabets of this and the two preceding columns with the alphabet of the Siloam inscription, it will be seen that the צנמוא and ק differ very materially. As there are only twenty letters in the Siloam inscription, these six represent a very large proportion. In other words, *thirty per cent. of the letters of the Siloam inscription present forms which were unused and unknown in the seventh and eighth centuries* B.C.

Col. 4 gives the alphabet upon the well known sarcophagus of Eshmunazar, king of Sidon. This inscription is now assigned to the time of the Ptolemies, about 300 B.C., or slightly later. The great inscription of Yekhaumelek, king of Gebal (280 B.C.), is in the same character, which also agrees closely with the lettering of the Cyprian inscriptions of the third and fourth centuries B.C., in the British Museum.*

Col. 5 shows the alphabet employed upon the coins of John Hyrcanus and Judas Aristobulus, 135–78 B.C. This is the earliest Jewish alphabet to which a date can be definitely assigned. It agrees generally with that of Eshmunazar. The *He* and *Vau*, however, have peculiar forms of their own; the *Vau* resembling that upon the capital of Amwas, mentioned above. The *Kaph* and *Mem* are the same as upon the contemporary Phœnician coins.

Col. 6 shows the alphabet employed by Alexander Janneus and his successors, 78–40 B.C. In this alphabet the *He* of column 5 is still retained; but the *Vau* has the shape of a cross with the head inclined to the left. The Z headed–*Vau* of Hyrcanus, however, appears in some cases; and Madden (p. 88) figures a coin with *both* varieties upon it. It would therefore seem that in the time of

* *Sechs Phönikische Inschriften aus Idalion*, von Dr. Julius Euting. Strassburg, 1875.

Alexander Janneus the fashion of the *Vau* was just changing from the Z head to the cruciform shape. The *Kaph* and *Mem* only differ from column 5 by having tails; but the *Nun* has an entirely fresh shape, unknown to the Phœnician inscriptions, and apparently modelled from the form of the *Mem*. Among his series of uncertain Jewish coins Mr. Madden figures two which he supposes to have the name of Alexander in Hebrew characters upon them. These coins, however, are hardly legible; and the inscriptions, as reproduced, give forms of letters unknown to Semitic caligraphy; we cannot, therefore, admit any of the characters copied from them, in the absence of better preserved specimens.

Col. 7 shows the alphabet employed upon the large bronze coins of Antigonus (40–37 B.C.). Here the F shaped *Aleph* appears for the first time, and remains constant in the rest of the columns. This shape does not appear to be older than the fourth century B.C., when it appears upon the Phœnician coins. Hyrcanus (135–105 B.C.) still employs the old bull-headed form, as shown in column 5, so that it would appear that the F shape was only adopted by the Jews in the first century B.C. At any rate, the first *dated* instance of its use is the coin of the first year of Antigonus, 40 B.C. The *He* of columns 5 and 6 is also abandoned, and we now have the standard Phœnician form with three bars. The *Kaph*, *Mem*, and *Nun* have the same forms as upon the coins of Hyrcanus, except that they now have a horizontal stroke at the foot of the letter. This bottom stroke appears sporadically at an earlier period; but after the time of Antigonus it became an essential part of the letter, as may be seen in columns 10 to 13. These forms of course took their rise in the curved tails which we see in the same letters upon the coins of Alexander Janneus.

Col. 8 contains the letters found upon the seal of Haggai ben Shebaniah (B.C. 17), these are שנגליהחגב. The other letters have not been chosen on account of their resemblance to the characters upon the Siloam Inscription, but the object has been to complete the alphabet from as few, and as late seals as possible. They are, with the exception of the *Pe*, derived from gems figured by Dr. M. A. Levy;* three of which are engraved in the plate accompanying this paper, and are described in detail later on. מו and ק are taken from the gem in pl. III, fig. 2; בזר and ע from fig. 3, צדא and

---

* *Siegel und Gemmen* (Breslau, 1869), Tafel III.

Proc. Soc. Bibl. Arch., May, 1897.

PLATE III.

Fig 1.

Fig 2.

Fig 3.

Fig 4

Fig 5.

Fig 6.

Fig 7.

Fig 8.

ה are from Dr. Levy's Taf. III, fig. 5, a gem which belongs to the period when the bull-headed *Aleph* was being replaced by the F form (*i.e.*, about 100 B.C.), because both letters appear in it. The *Pe* is taken from the seal of Shekharkhor ben Zephaniah figured by Professor Wright.* This last gem has the Z headed *Vau* of Hyrcanus; and is probably also about 100 B.C. It would have been an easy matter to compile an alphabet from the gems, agreeing in every essential particular with that of the Siloam Inscription, as only the *Zain* and *Qoph* used in the latter present any novel features. The letter *Teth* is not given in this column, because it does not occur upon the gems. Dr. Levy figures a seal, which he reads as "of Sariah, son of Ben-Samerner;" and calls attention to the two *Samekhs* upon it as giving the form of the Old Hebrew *Samekh*. As however this inscription is plainly in the Aramean character, and not in the Old Hebrew alphabet at all, we cannot admit these two letters, although they are copied into the great table of Jewish alphabets contributed by Dr. Julius Euting to Chwolson's *Corpus Inscriptionum.*† The letters upon the seal of Haggai are exactly the same as those of the Siloam Inscription. The *Nun* is particularly noticeable, as it has a special form. The *He* upon this seal has no tail, owing to its cramped position at the end of the line; but normally the letter has a short tail. The form of the *Zain* in column 8 should be specially noted. It has one hook at the end, instead of the two hooks of the Siloam letter. The *Mem* in this column is not figured as the closest known to the Siloam form, but because it occurs on the gem in pl. III, fig. 2. Th tables of the Duc de Luynes‡ show that this is an earlier form than that of the Siloam *Mem*.

Col. 9 gives the alphabet found upon the Siloam Inscription. The alphabets usually figured are mostly inaccurate, having been taken from printed copies, and not from casts of the actual inscrip-

---

* *Proc. Soc. Bibl. Arch.*, Vol. IV, p. 54.

† *Corpus Inscriptionum Hebraicarum*, von D. Chwolson. (St. Petersburg. 1882.) In the *Babylonian and Oriental Record* (Vol. I, p. 194) Professor Sayce figures a seal containing a genuine Old Hebrew *Samekh*. The gem seems to be a Phœnician imitation of late Persian work; and would therefore belong to the fourth century B.C., which is too early for our column. The *Samekh* has the shape shown in our column 2. There is a very similar gem in the British Museum, with the legend "Hodu the Scribe."

‡ *Essays on Indian Antiquities*, by James Prinsep (London, 1858), Vol. II, p. 166. Essay by the Duc de Luynes on "L'Alphabet Phénicien."

tion.   The real forms of the letters can be seen in Professor Wright's photograph in the *Proc. Soc. Bibl. Arch.*, Vol. IV, pp. 68, 69.

The Siloam *Aleph* has the F shape, as first used upon the coins of Antigonus, 40 B.C. ; instead of the older bull-head form which was in use as late as the time of Hyrcanus.

Beth has the same shape as upon the seal of Haggai ; this is the ordinary Phœnician form.

Gimel is like that of Haggai ; the top bar not so sloping as upon the Hasmonean coins, and not straight as upon the shekels.

Daleth is normal.

He has the normal Phœnician form ; and is quite unlike the oldest dated Jewish *He* upon the coins of Hyrcanus.

Vau deserves special mention.   This form occurs upon the lion-weights of Sargon (705 B.C.), and upon Jewish seals of apparently early date ; but, as we have seen, it was not used by Hyrcanus, and first appears on the Jewish coins of Alexander Janneus.   Exactly the same form is employed upon the *Yerushalaim qedoshah* shekels, as may be seen by examining a good specimen.   It is therefore certain that this particular form was in general use when the shekels were struck ; and it was the immediate parent of the modern Samaritan letter.

Zain, it will be observed, has each of the horizontal strokes ending in a hook ; but the *Zain* in column 8 has only one hook. Column 11 shows the letter with the hooks exaggerated, and explains the genesis of the modern Samaritan form.   Dr. Levy, of Breslau, in 1869, drew attention to the hooked *Zain* of the gem in pl. III, fig. 3, and pointed out that this was evidently the ancestor of the form on the coins of Bar-Cochab, and in the modern Samaritan alphabet.   The discovery of the Siloam Inscription proves the contention of Dr. Levy to be right ; for it supplies the missing link in the shape of the double-hooked letter.   This *Zain*, therefore informs us that the Siloam Inscription is earlier than Bar-Cochab ; but later than the gem in pl. III, fig. 3, which gem, as we shall see presently, is admitted by M. Joachim Menant to be of very late date.

Kheth resembles the *Kheth* of Haggai on the one hand, and the same letter on the Nablus inscription on the other.

Teth does not occur.

Yod has the ordinary Phœnician form.

Kaph resembles the same letter upon the seals. On the Phœnician coins we sometimes find it with one stroke in the head, sometimes two; so that this does not appear to be a matter of much importance.

Lamed is curved, as on most of the seals; instead of being angular, as upon nearly all the coins. Madden (p. 90) figures a coin of Alexander Janneus in which the *Lamed* has the curved form, which is sufficient proof of the use of the curved form at a late date. The difference between the curved and the angular *Lamed* seems merely to be due to whether they are begun from the bottom or the top. Both forms are found at all periods.

Mem. The tables of the Duc de Luynes show that the *Mem* used in the Siloam Inscription does not appear upon the Phœnician coins before B.C. 312. The *Mem* in our column 8 is used from 331 to 324 B.C., and is then succeeded by the Siloam type.

Nun has a peculiar form, evidently modelled from that of the *Mem*. The Phœnician *Nun* never appears in this shape, but to the last retains the zig-zag form of our column 4. It will be observed that the seal of Haggai presents the same *Nun* as the Siloam Inscription.

Samekh does not occur.

Ain is not round like the early Phœnician form, but is shaped like an almond, as in column 8. This almond-shape eventually resulted in the triangular *Ain* of the modern Samaritan alphabet.

Pe has much the same shape as upon the gems.

Sade deserves special attention; because it is a link in the chain which shows how the Phœnician *Sade* became the modern Samaritan letter. Column 8 shows us the Phœnician form. This, like the *Zain*, had a hook attached to its extremity, as may be seen in the seal of Shekharkhor figured by Professor Wright. The left-hand stroke then became shortened to a mere hook; and in this modified form appears at Siloam. Exactly the same shape is used upon the *Yerushalaim qedoshah* half-shekels; but in the coins of Bar-Cochab the left-hand stroke has disappeared altogether. The ancient Samaritan *Sade* of column 12 is evidently an ornamental modification of the Bar-Cochab letter; and it is then but a step to the modern Samaritan of column 13.

Qoph also calls for special mention. In the gems, as shown in column 8, the letter is shaped like a cross-bow. On the *Yerushalaim qedoshah* shekels it is somewhat like the Roman P. The Siloam letter is exactly intermediate between the two, and explains how the cross-bow attained the P shape, so characteristic of the modern Samaritan.

Resh has its normal form.

Shin has its usual Jewish form. The Phœnician letter was modified at an early date, as shown in column 4.

Tau is in the shape of an X instead of being like a ✚, as in the coins of Alexander Janneus. The Siloam *Tau* is not exactly square, *i.e.*, the limbs are not of equal length, but the lower left-hand stroke is a trifle elongated. This modification was probably made for the sake of ornament.

It will be observed that the characters of the Siloam Inscription are carefully and ornamentally written, though the ornamental writing nowhere interferes with the standard shape of the letter. The letters נמלכ and פ are written with elegant double curves, as is the case with כב and פ in the modern Samaritan character.

Col. 10 shows the alphabet of the *Yerushalaim qedoshah* shekels. As before remarked, the *Vau* on these coins has the exact shape of the Siloam letter. Mr. Madden's table does not show this, but it is evident to anyone who examines the *Vau* upon a clear and well-preserved coin. The *Yod* often inclines on its face; but this does not alter the shape of the letter. The *Mem* has a bottom bar, which should prove these coins later than the time of Hyrcanus, who uses the form shown in column 5. The *Sade* has the Siloam form.

Col. 11 gives the alphabet of the Bar-Cochab coinage, which does not differ from that of column 10. The *Vau* has each of its limbs of equal length, but if the bottom stroke be lengthened, it will be seen that the letter is of the same cruciform shape as the preceding columns, though without the initial tick of Siloam, and the shekels. The *Z* headed *Vau* is confined to the coins of the fourth year. For the *Zain*, see Madden, p. 200, and the remarks on our plate, figs. 7 and 8. The *Kaph* introduces a new form, which, however, is supported by the Samaritan letter. The *Nun* occurs in two forms; the most frequent being that of Antigonus, the other (occurring on the coins of Janneus) is probably due to Aramean influence. As a rule the variations in the forms of the letters on the Bar-Cochab coins are more due to carelessness than ignorance. It is evident that the alphabet of Bar-Cochab is not an artificial archaism, but that it exhibits the genuine transition from the Old

Hebrew to the Samaritan character, and stands midway between the two.

Col. 12 gives the alphabet of the well known Samaritan inscription of Nablus, which contains the Ten Commandments, and has been built into the wall of a church founded by the Emperor Justinian, who came to the throne in A.D. 527. As will be seen, this alphabet agrees almost exactly with that of the Siloam inscription as far as *Kheth*. The *Teth* is added from another source.

Col. 13 shows the Samaritan alphabet as printed in modern books.

DESCRIPTION OF PLATE.

Fig. 1. Jewish seal, inscribed לחגי בן שבניה "of Haggai, son of Shebaniah." This has already been described.

Fig. 2. Seal, inscribed לעשיו בן יוקם "of Asayu, son of Yoqim." On the reverse is the device of Harpocrates seated on the lotus. The original is engraved upon rock-crystal, and is preserved in the British Museum (Semitic Room, Table-case B, No. 1025). It was acquired from the Pollini collection at Florence. The name *Asayu* is related to the form "Asaiah" of 2 Kings xxii, 12. The full form of both would be "Asa-Yahu"—made by Yahveh. *Yoqim* appears in the same form as on the gem in 1 Chron. iv, 22. It is a contraction of "Yeho-yaqim" (2 Kings xxiii, 34)—Yahveh sets up. The words are divided from one another by a short shallow stroke (omitted in the engraving for the sake of clearness). Both the *Yods* have hooked tails. The *Vaus* have the characteristic cruciform shape. The *Qoph* is formed like a crossbow, and the *Mem* has the shape of the letter upon the Phœnician coins of Alexander the Great.

Fig. 3. Seal, inscribed לזכרהושע "of Zekarhoshea." This looks a strange name ("Memorial of Deliverance"), but is formed in the same way as the biblical Zechariah. The original gem is in the British Museum (Semitic Room, Table-case B, No. 1043). It is a green jasper, in scarabæus form. From the shape of the letters M. de Vogüé considered this seal to have been engraved in the reign of Titus : but M. Joachim Menant * thinks this is exaggerated, although he admits that it belongs to a very late period. The chief feature of the lettering is the hooked *Zain*. The *Vau* resembles the

---

* "Recherches sur la Glyptique Orientale," par M. Joachim Menant. (Paris, 1886.) Second Partie, p. 236.

Siloam, but is not cruciform. It will be noted in these two gems that there was a tendency to add hooks to the end strokes of the letters at this period; just as we find them in the Siloam *Zain* and *Sade*.

Fig. 4. Obverse of bronze coin of John Hyrcanus (weight 31 grains). Within a wreath is the inscription—

יהוחנן הכהן הגדל ראש וחבר היהדם

"Yehokhanan, the High Priest, Chief, and *Khaber* of the Jews." This coin shows the alphabet employed by the Jews in the second century B.C. The *He* and *Vau* are peculiar, and the *Aleph* has not the F shape of later times.

Fig. 5. Reverse of bronze coin of Antigonus (weight 186 grains). Around a double cornucopia מתתיה כהן גדל חבר יד" "Mattathiah, High Priest, *Khaber* of the Jews." Between the cornucopiæ שא—"first year." The letter preceding the *Aleph* is an Aramaic form of the *Shin*, and probably adopted here for the sake of distinction, just as we find upon Greek coins the sign L preceding dates. The *Yods* on this coin are inverted; but this mistake is corrected in the subsequent issues of Antigonus. The difference between the alphabet of this coin and that of fig. 4 will be marked.

Fig. 6. Obverse of silver shekel of the *Yerushalaim qedoshah* type (weight 219 grains). In the centre is a chalice surrounded by the words שקל ישראל "Shekel of Israel," and surmounted by שה for "Year 5." If a century had not separated these two coins, we might have suspected that the chalice of the shekel had been suggested by the Seleucid cornucopiæ of the bronze pieces of Antigonus. There is certainly a superficial resemblance, and the year of issue occupies much the same place in both. A shekel of the year 5 has been chosen for illustration, because the obverse presents us with both א and ה which may be compared with those upon the coin of Antigonus, as contrasted with the lettering of Hyrcanus.

Fig. 7. Obverse of bronze coin of Eleazar (weight 99½ grains). A palm tree with the inscription אלעזנר הכה ; evidently meant for "Eleazar ha-Kohen;" but the *Nun* has been misplaced; and the *Kaph* has had two bars of the preceding *He* attached to it by the ignorance or carelessness of the engraver. This is like the coin illustrated by Madden, p. 200; and it is engraved here through the courtesy of Sir John Evans, F.R.S., who has kindly supplied the writer with an impression. The bronze coins of Eleazar occur in two forms : one with the name reversed, and the other with the name in the proper direction ; although both bear the same types of a palm tree, copied from the coins of the Roman Procurators, Coponius and Annius Rufus. The coin in the possession of Sir John Evans has the name in the right direction, and, being well struck, and in excellent preservation, gives the true form of the *Zain* of the time of Bar-Cochab. Mr. Madden's illustration is not quite correct in the shape he gives to this letter. Some other coins of the same class are illustrated in Madden, p. 199; but, being probably badly preserved specimens, they do not exhibit the letters so clearly.

Fig. 8. Obverse of bronze coin of Eleazar (weight 93 grains). A palm tree with the reversed inscription אלעזר הכהן "Eleazar ha-Kohen." This is the class usually illustrated ; and the incorrect form of the *Zain* upon it is the one generally ascribed to Bar-Cochab. The same form appears upon the silver pieces.

The earliest inscription of Zenjerli, and the Mesha Stela prove to us that in the ninth century B.C. the same alphabet was in use in Northern Syria and in Southern Palestine. The letters of the second Zenjerli inscription (730 B.C.) do not differ very materially ; and we may assume that the Jewish alphabet of the eighth century B.C. closely resembled it. But on comparing it with the Siloam inscription we find most serious divergences. If the Siloam alphabet is really to be dated 700 B.C., we are compelled to assume that at that period the Jewish alphabet exhibited forms which did not develope in the Phœnician till centuries later ; and other forms which never developed in the closely related Phœnician alphabet at all. We are also compelled to assume that, after this early advance, the Jewish alphabet reverted to the Phœnician type as shown on the Hasmonean coins, and then suddenly re-developed the Siloam peculiarities at the beginning of the Christian era, and passed these peculiarities into the Samaritan alphabet. Such assumptions are of course absurd; and the only other alternative is to admit that the Inscription of Siloam is much later than 700 B.C.

Our table of alphabets shows that paleographically the Siloam Inscription falls somewhere near the beginning of the Christian era. The tunnel of Siloam can only have been executed by some person of authority ; and the same remark applies to the inscription. The latter is not a mere *graffito*, but an elegantly engraved piece of sculpture, set out by a skilful writer. It is carved upon the *lower half* of a tablet specially cut in the rock. The upper half was evidently intended to bear a Greek translation. If this Greek portion had been cut, as in the bi-lingual Amwas capital, it would have saved a great deal of discussion; but for some reason it was never added. As the lettering of the Siloam Inscription is so like that upon the seal of Haggai, found among the foundations of the Temple of King Herod, the most likely hypothesis is that both the Siloam tunnel and the inscription were the work of Herod. The death of the king was most probably the cause of the sudden cessation of the work, and the reason why the tablet was only half completed. This would make the true date of the Siloam Inscription to be the year 4 B.C., as Herod the Great died in that year

---

The Society has been indebted to the Palestine Exploration Fund for permission to reproduce the capital of Amwas; and to Mr. E. J. Pilcher for the illustrations of this paper.

A COPTIC SPELL OF THE SECOND CENTURY.

By F. LEGGE.

The great magic papyrus of the *Bibliothèque Nationale* contains a spell or formula of exorcism, written partly in Greek and partly in Coptic words expressed in Greek characters, which seems to have more interest for archæologists than most of these relics of superstition. Dr. Karl Wessely gave an English version of part of it in the *Expositor* of 1886 (Series 3, Vol. IV, pp. 194 *sqq.*), and transcribed the whole text in his *Griechische Zauberpapyrus von Paris und London* (Wien, 1888, pp. 75, 76). In his preface to the latter, he also gave a French version of part of the Coptic words by M. Revillout. Unfortunately, it was so badly revised for the press that M. Revillout's transcription of the Coptic agrees neither with the original nor with his own translation. As reproduced by Wessely, the spell runs thus :—-

1227 πραξις γενναια εκβαλλουσα δαιμονας
λογος λεγομενος επι της κεφαλης αυτου
βαλε εμπροσθεν αυτου κλωνας ελαιας
1230 και οπισθεν αυτου σταθεις λεγεις
χαιρε φνουθι π̄ αβρααμ · χαιρε πνου
τε π̄ ϊσακ χαιρε πνουτε π̄ ϊακωβ
ϊησους π χρηστος πι αγιος π̄ πνευμα
ψιηρινφιωθεθσαρηϊ π̄ ισασφε
1235 εθσαχουν π̄ ισασφι · ˉ ενα ιαω σα
βαωθ μαρετετεν ϭομ σωβις α
βολ απο του ⳨ * σατετεννουσθ παϊ
π ακαθαρτος π̄ δαιμων πι σαδανας

* The usual sign for the person in whose behalf the spell is said. This and the three preceding words have apparently got out of place.

εθηϊωθφ* εξορκιζω σε δαιμον

1240 εcτινεcτιντοτουνει† κατα τουτου
του θεου σαβαρβαρβαθιωθ σαβαρ
βαρβαθιουθ · σαβαρβαρβαθιωνηθ
σαβαρβαρβαφαϊ εξελθε · δαιμον
οστις ποτ ουν ει και αποστηθι απο του ✝

1245 αρτι αρτι ηδη-εξελθε δαιμον
επει σε δεσμευω δεσμοις αδαμαντινοις
αλυτοις και παραδιδωμι σε εις το με
λαν χαος εν ταις απωλιαις : ποιησις
ζ κλωνας ελαιας αρας τας μεν εξ

1250 δησον ουραν και κεφαλην εν καθ εν
τω δε ενι δερε εξορκιζων κρυβε
επραχθη εκβαλων περιαπτε τον
✝ φυλακτηριον οπερ τῖθησιν ο καμνω—
μετα το εκβαλειν τον δαιμονα επι

1255 κασσιτερινου πεταλου ταυτα
βωρ φωρ φορ βαφορ φορβα
βες χαριν βαυ βωτε φωρ βωρφορ
βα· φορβαβορβαφορβα φαβραιη
φωρβα φαρβα φωρ φωρ φορβα ·

1260 βωφορφορβα φορφοφορβα ·
βωβορβορβα παμφορβα φωρ
φωρφῶρβα φυλαξον τον ✝ και
αλλο εχει φυλακτηριον οπου το ση
μειον τουτο χ . . . . (nine lines blank).

I propose to restore this as follows :—

Πρᾶξις γενναία ἐκβάλλουσα δαίμονας.

Λόγος λεγόμενος ἐπὶ τῆς κεφαλῆς αὐτοῦ. Βάλε ἔμπροσθεν

* This seems to be ⲈⲐⲱ�ⲩ = Αἰθίοψ. So, in the *Pistis Sophia* (p. 367 Copt.), the fiend who presides over one of the hells is called *Ethiopian* Ariuth.

† Evidently a mistake of the scribe's. The proper phrase is used four lines later.

αὐτοῦ κλῶνας ἐλαίας καὶ ὄπισθεν αὐτοῦ σταθεὶς λέγεις
ⲬⲀⲒⲢⲈ ⲠⲚⲞⲨⲦⲈ Ⲡ̅ ⲀⲂⲢⲀⲀⲘ ⲬⲀⲒⲢⲈ ⲠⲚⲞⲨⲦⲈ Ⲡ̅ ⲒⲤⲀⲔ
ⲬⲀⲒⲢⲈ ⲠⲚⲞⲨⲦⲈ Ⲡ̅ ⲒⲀⲔⲱⲂ ⲒⲎⲤⲞⲨⲤ ⲠⲬⲢⲎⲤⲦⲞⲤ ⲠⲒ
ⲀⲄⲒⲞⲤ Ⲡ̅ ⲠⲚⲈⲨⲘⲀ ⲠϢⲎⲢⲒ Ⲛ̅ⲪⲒⲰⲦ ⲈⲦⲤⲀⲒ̈ⲢⲎⲒ Ⲡ̅ ⲒⲤⲀⲤⲠⲈ
ⲈⲦⲤⲀⲒ̈ϨⲞⲨⲚ Ⲡ̅ ⲒⲤⲀⲤⲠⲈ ⲈⲠⲀ ⲒⲀⲰ ⲤⲀⲂⲀⲰⲐ ⲘⲀⲢⲈⲦⲈⲚ-
ⲈⲠⲤ̅ⲞⲘ ⲤⲰⲂⲒ ϢⲀⲦⲈⲦⲈⲚⲠⲞⲨⲬ ⲈⲂⲞⲖ ⲀⲠⲞ ⲦⲞⲨ
ⲆⲈⲒⲚⲀ ⲠⲀⲒ Ⲡ ⲀⲔⲀⲐⲀⲢⲦⲞⲤ Ⲡ̅ ⲆⲀⲒⲘⲰⲚ ⲠⲒ ⲤⲀⲦⲀⲚⲀⲤ
ⲈⲐⲰϢ. Ἐξορκίζω σε, δαῖμον, ὅστις ποτ' οὖν εἰ, κατὰ
τουτοῦ τοῦ θεοῦ σαβαρβαθιωτ σαβαρβαθιουθ σαβαρ-
βαθιωνηθ σαβαρβαφαι. Ἔξελθε, δαῖμον, ὅστις ποτ'
οὖν εἰ, καὶ ἀπόστηθε ἀπὸ τοῦ δεῖνα. Ἄρτι, ἄρτι, ἤδη
ἔξελθε, δαῖμον, ἐπεὶ σε δεσμεύω δεσμοῖς ἀδαμαντίνοις
ἀλύτοις καὶ παραδίδωμι σε εἰς τὸ μέλαν χάος ἐν ταῖς
ἀπωλείαις.

Ποιήσις.

ζ κλῶνας ἐλαίας ἄρας· τὰς μὲν ἔξ δῆσον οὐράν καὶ
κεφαλήν ἕν καθ' ἕν· τῷ δὲ ἑνὶ, δέρε ἐξορκίζων κρυβῇ.
Ἐπράχθη ἐκβάλων. Περίαπτε τὸν δεῖνα φυλακτήριον
ὁπὲρ τίθησιν [ἐν] ᾧ κάμνον μετὰ τὸ ἐκβάλειν τὸν δαίμονα
ἐπὶ κασσιτέρινου πέταλου ταῦτα. Βωρ φωρ κ. τ. λ.
Φυλάξον τὸν δεῖνα καὶ ἀλλὸ ἐχεῖ φυλακτήριον ὅπου τὸ
σημείον τοῦτο . . . .

which may be thus translated :—

" Famous process for casting out spirits.
" A spell to be said over his (*i.e.*, the patient's) head.

" Strew olive-branches before him, and taking up your station
behind him, say :—Hail, God of Abraham ! Hail, God of Isaac !
Hail, God of Jacob ! Jesus the Merciful, the Holy Spirit, the Son of
the Father who is below Lo-she-hath-been who is within Lo-she-
hath-been-and-will-be, Jaho Sabaoth, may your Power laugh at you
until you have cast forth from such-an-one this unclean spirit, this
Ethiopian Satan. I adjure thee, spirit, whoever thou art, by this
God Sabarbathiot, etc. Come forth, spirit, whoever thou art, and
keep thou far from such-an-one ! At once ! At once ! Come forth,

O spirit, even now, for I bind thee with adamantine bonds never to be loosed, and I deliver thee to the black Chaos among the lost!

" Ceremony.

"Join together seven olive-branches. Bind the six root to tip one by one, but thrash* with the remaining one, exorcising the while under your breath. Here ends the casting-out. Tie on the patient when they are in place an amulet, on which engrave after the spirit has been cast out these words . . . . 'Baubo, nourisher of oxen, nourisher of all things . . . . protect such-an-one!' And have another amulet when this sign . . . ."

The spell appears to have been copied with some care, and the instances of iotacism are not very numerous. Why a solitary π should have been placed before the word ἀκάθαρτος is not easy to see. Otherwise, the rendering of the Coptic words by Greek letters comes out pretty much as might be expected, the ⲡ̄ and the ⲋ being apparently the only two sounds that the scribe found the Greek alphabet unable to represent. The word "Isaspe," which has not, I think, been met with elsewhere, seems capable of being decomposed into ⲉⲓⲥ: *Ecce*, ⲁⲥ (Fem. Pref. 3 sing. first Perf.), and ⲡⲉ: *esse*, and I have so treated it. The word "Isaspe-ena," from the middle of which something seems to have been omitted seems to be the same word, with the sign of the Second Future added. "Isaspe" is (if I am right in my guess) a phrase made into a divine name in the manner of those in the *Book of the Dead*. One is tempted to see in it the *EIEAZEREIE* (אהיה אשר'אהיה) of Exod. iii, 14, so frequently met with in Ceremonial Magic, or the ὁ ὢν καί ὁ ἦν καί ὁ ἐρχόμενος of Rev. i, 4, a name which is perhaps compounded and declined in the same way. But it should not be forgotten that the statue of Isis at Sais bore, according to Proclus (in Tim. i, 30 D), an inscription to the effect that the goddess was all that had been, was, and would be (τὰ ὄντα καὶ τὰ ἐσόμενα καὶ τὰ γεγονότα ἐγώ εἰμι), and it is probable that it is this which is referred to. Of the four divine names all beginning with the dissyllable SABAR, I can make nothing, nor do I know to what language they can be referred. The words written on the amulet are, however, a reproduction of an invocation to Hecate to be found in another part of the same papyrus, although they have here been so much corrupted that only the words Βαυβώ,

---

* The use of the stick as a remedy for demoniac possession, or in other words hystero-epilepsy, is well-known among savages, and is said to be efficacious.

βουφορβή, πάμφορβη, can be distinguished.   The reference to the "Power" of Jesus seems to refer to the gospel of Peter, where the words of Mark xv, 34, are altered into "My Power! My Power! Why hast thou forsaken me!"

The papyrus is, according to Wessely, to be attributed to the "very earliest years" of the fourth century, and he thinks the spells it contains are at least a century earlier.   The one in the text can hardly have been composed after the time of Tertullian, for the confusion of the Second with the Third Person of the Trinity, an error of which Clement of Alexandria has been accused, was at an end in his day, as may be gathered from his treatise against Praxeas (c. I, t. ii, p. 164 Migne).   The author was certainly a professional exorcist, or his spell would hardly have found its way into what is practically a book of magical recipes.   The words "God of Abraham," etc., give us no clue to his nationality, since we know from Origen (cont. Celsus IV, c. 33) that these words were used not only by the Jews, but by "almost all those who busy themselves with incantations and magical rites."   Such spells as these are often called Gnostic, but there is nothing in our text to connect it with any of the Gnostic sects described by the Fathers.   The irreverent tone of the adjuration to Jesus would certainly not have been employed by any Christian Gnostic, while it rather suggests the imprecations which the Egyptian magicians are said by Porphyry to have used to their gods.   It is therefore most probable that the author was an Egyptian, and the date not later than 200 A.D.

In this connection, the use as an amulet of an invocation to Hecate is extremely suggestive.   In the longer invocation from which it is apparently copied, Hecate is addressed as φρουνή or "she-toad."   Miller (*Mélanges de Littérature Grecque*, Paris, 1868, pp. 442, 460), sees in this an allusion to the attitude in which the Eleusinian Baubo* is sometimes represented.   But it should not be forgotten that the Egyptian goddess Hek-t was represented with the head of a frog or toad, and it is possibly she who was introduced into the Eleusinia under the name of Hecate.   No really satisfactory etymology of the name of Hecate has yet been given, and it may be that it was only a Græcised form of the word Hek-t.   If this be so, the patron goddess of sorcery, as she appears in Macbeth, would seem to have had an Egyptian origin.

---

* In all the spells of the Post-Christian Magic Papyri, Baubo and Hecate are treated as the same person.

YOUNG AND CHAMPOLLION.

The substance of a paper read on Tuesday, June 2nd, 1896.

By Sir P. le Page Renouf.

Is it necessary, or even desirable, in this last decade of the century, to take serious notice of attacks directed against a name so imperishable as that of the founder of Egyptian Philology and Archæology?

It is most natural that the question should be asked, but there are imperative reasons for answering it in the affirmative.

The policy of silent contempt is too often of no avail in opposition to the potent vitality of a lie or mendacious insinuation, put forth on what is ignorantly supposed to be respectable authority. And such lies cannot be too vigorously stamped out. The grossest, though perhaps not most offensive, form of the recent attack upon Champollion proceeds indeed from anonymous journalism, but it was suggested by a book issuing from a press justly supposed to be of great authority,* and my attention to it was first called by the plaintive expostulation of a French Egyptologist, who actually seemed to acknowledge "les défaillances du maitre"!

Few men of the present generation have read either Young's writings or the earlier ones of Champollion. It is only at second

---

* On opening this book, which at best is a mere *crambe repetita* of what others have rightly or wrongly said, my eyes fell upon an Egyptian list of Roman Emperors with transcriptions. These transcribed names are followed by *netχ*, or *netiχ*, as English names are by *Esq.* No explanation is given of this mysterious word except in dots (. . . . .). The original consists of *two* easy and very common Egyptian Words, ⟨hieroglyphs⟩ *enta ḥau,* 'who protecteth,' or "the Protector." ⟨hieroglyphs⟩ is the Egyptian for Σωτήρ in the title of the first Ptolemy. The author confounds two words into one which is not Egyptian, and cannot recognize the ideographic sign ⟨hieroglyph⟩.

[I take the liberty of reading the sign \\ as = *a*, as the Egyptians did, *e.g.,* in the names of Vespasian and Nerva, in the titles *Autokrator* (Hadrian) and *Kaisar* (Trajan), and in the verb ⟨hieroglyphs⟩ *ḥau,* as it is written with the name of Hadrian.]

188

hand that most people know anything about the history of hieroglyphic discovery; and this secondhand information is generally
most inaccurate.   I hope, therefore, that the present Essay may be
of use in correcting misstatements or misconceptions.

Most of the attacks upon Champollion belong to an early period,
that is before the revival under M. de Rougé, and therefore before
one could guess what a splendid future lay before the science.
Even Klaproth's "Examen" was published before the appearance
of Champollion's Grammar.   George Long did not believe that with
Champollion's theory of the combination of phonetic and symbolic
signs it would ever be possible to make out the meaning of a single
text.   Mr. Leitch, to whom English readers are indebted for the
translations of two important works of Karl O. Müller, published
in 1852 the works of Dr. Young.   The third volume of this
publication contains Young's writings on hieroglyphics and some
correspondence of his upon the subject.   The text is accompanied
throughout with notes containing the most virulent accusations and
special pleadings against Champollion, whose most innocent sayings
and doings are preposterously interpreted.   Mr. Leitch deals with
Champollion as Mr. Serjeant Buzfuz dealt with the "systematic
villainy" of Mr. Pickwick.   And this volume is the quarry whence
recent detractors have gathered stones or pellets, wherewith to
assault the memory of a great man.

All the accusations hang together, and they depend upon the
altogether imaginary hypothesis that Champollion was a lying sneak,
an infamous scoundrel, a "systematic villain," and a pitiful scholar
who could not get on by himself.   " He took years to arrive at the
position occupied by Young in a few months," * "he appropriated
Young's discoveries," "he appropriated. of course without acknowledgment, the enchorial discoveries of Akerblad." "Nothing can
exceed his effrontery." " His charlatanerie and literary dishonesty
are acknowledged by the most eminent of his countrymen, such as
de Sacy and Letronne." " If Young had taken the trouble of
getting his essay printed as a separate publication, there would have
been less doubt in the minds of scholars as to the good work
which he did, and *results borrowed from it* by Champollion would
have been more easily identified."   A full acknowledgment by

---

* We are here reminded of the fable of the Hare and Tortoise, with the
curious additional facts that on being distanced the Hare became paralysed,
whilst the Tortoise acquired more than a fifty-Hare-power of speed.

Champollion of what Young had done (that is, *in sensu auctoris*, what Champollion had borrowed from Young), " would have in no way injured or lessened his own immortal fame."

Champollion of course never acknowledged that he had borrowed from Young ; and there must be a very peculiarly delicate sense of honour in a writer who thinks that immortal fame may be acquired by one who has done the shameful things (lying, for instance) laid to the charge of Champollion. We have all been taught that "the name of the wicked shall *rot !*"

It is right to say that Young is not accountable for these calumnies. He may be quoted in disproof of many of them. He claimed *priority* of publication, but did not accuse Champollion of borrowing or of anything dishonourable. And if he thought Champollion did not do sufficient justice to him, this is because he never understood the essential difference between their modes of operation. He considered it a question of less or more. It was a question of "quomodo ?"

The real difference is most felicitously expressed by Champollion's bitter personal enemy. After mentioning Young's success with reference to the names of Ptolemy and Berenice, Klaproth proceeds to say :—

"La sagacité du savant anglais n'alla pas au delà de cette *rencontre heureuse*, et il laissa à son compétiteur en France la gloire qui peut s'attacher à *une découverte raisonnée et soumise à la démonstration*."

And this essential difference was at once seen by such acute men of science as Young's two friends Silvestre de Sacy and Arago.

Champollion's process is strictly demonstrative, but it has no sense whatever unless the steps of the process are taken in the order in which they are described by the discoverer himself. And the very first step of the process is acknowledged as unassailable by Young himself. It was not one of which he could claim to be the discoverer. No one who understands the process and sees the conclusions to which it necessarily leads can dream of such nonsense as the charge of plagiarism.

Plagiarism is a very base and dishonourable thing, and it is the more detestable when it is united with habits of evil speaking, lying and slandering, envy, hatred, malice, and all uncharitableness. It is not however in Champollion that we have to look for the impersonation of all these unenviable habits.

When a schoolboy is suspected of having "borrowed" his neighbour's "results," it is only fair to ask if he was unable to arrive at these results independently, and also to see whether he has copied the neighbour's *mistakes* as well as the right results. No intelligent schoolmaster would condemn a boy who had worked a sum correctly, because some of his figures (which were right) were the same as those of a neighbour, all whose other figures were wrong. A plagiarist never fails to copy the mistakes.

Which of Young's mistakes has Champollion copied?

Young had thoroughly satisfied himself, he tells us, of Champollion's capability to arrive at independent results, by his decipherment of the name of Cleopatra, and of Apollonius and the other witnesses to the 'Casati Contract,' names corresponding to those in the Greek translation which Champollion had not seen, but which came through Mr. Grey into the hands of Young. All these names, through his long and accurate study of the three different kinds of Egyptian writing, Champollion was able to transcribe into hieroglyphic.

His method of decipherment is in fact as rigorously apodeictic, step by step, as that of any mathematical demonstration that can be named. No one who understands it can possibly talk about "borrowed results." It is a method which no more admits of "borrowing" than the binomial theorem or the extraction of the cube root. And it is only a quack who at the present day can write that if Young had "taken the trouble of having his article [EGYPT] printed as a separate publication, there would have been less doubt in the minds of scholars as to the good work which he did, and results borrowed from it by Champollion would have been more easily identified."

What is the "good work" done by Young? To what has it led?

"Le peu de place que sa méthode tient dans la science hiéroglyphique se prouve clairement par sa *stérilité*; elle ne produisit pas la lecture d'un seul nom propre nouveau [or of any other word], et l'on peut affirmer hardiment que tous les sceaux du livre mystérieux étaient encore fermés lorsque Champollion étendit la main pour les briser." This judgment of M. E. de Rougé * will certainly not be questioned by any competent person.

Young's "work" lay not in decipherment but in conjectural

* *Discours à l'ouverture du cours d'Archéologie Egyptienne, au Collège de France*, 19 *Avril*, 1860, p. 12.

identification. His decipherment is only identification of letters instead of words. This process of identification will, I think, be made intelligible by its application to another kind of writing than the Egyptian.

A person wholly unversed in the language of China might easily discover the name of *Abraham* in a Chinese New Testament. It occurs in the first verse of St. Matthew, and again in the following verse. The only group of Chinese characters corresponding to it must be 亞 伯 拉 罕. There can be no doubt whatever on the subject, and fifty persons or five hundred might independently arrive at the same inevitable conclusion. No one but an ignoramus could venture to assert that one of these must have borrowed from another, even if one of them had first proclaimed his discovery. It is in the same way demonstrable that the Chinese 生 throughout the chapter corresponds to "begot." All the proper names in the chapter may in like manner be identified, and there is no difficulty in determining the Chinese words for 'husband' 'wife,' 'mother,' 'son,' 'angel of the Lord,' 'fourteen generations' and others. A close inspection might also enable one to detect certain grammatical forms, such as 的 as a sign of the 'genitive,' or as the termination of an adjective. All this may be done by a person unable to read a word of the language, and it may be done by ever so many independent enquirers, who might, if they thought it worth their while, draw up the "Rudiments of a Chinese Vocabulary" just as Young drew up the "Rudiments of a Hieroglyphical Vocabulary" in the famous article EGYPT in the *Encyclopædia Britannica*. But rash persons might easily commit themselves to faulty identifications.

Identification as I have just described it is not *decipherment.*

Silvestre de Sacy pointed this out to Young in a letter written in January, 1816 :--

"Je crois bien que l'on peut souvent déterminer, comme vous l'avez fait, la place qu'occupe dans l'inscription Egyptienne alphabétique (he means the demotic) tel mot de l'inscription Grecque comme on le ferait pour une inscription purement hiéroglyphique ; mais indiquer ensuite la valeur des lettres dont le mot se compose, en fixer la lecture, le présenter en tout autre caractère, *hic labor, hoc opus est.*" *

* This was the view of Champollion. "Pour quelq'un qui aurait fait une longue étude du texte *démotique* de Rosette, il ne pouvait rester douteux, à la première inspection du texte hiéroglyphique que le cartouche renfermait le nom de

Akerblad wrote to Young, as we shall see shortly, very much to the same effect; and the criticism of these two scholars may be applied to the "Specimens of Hieroglyphics," which in the year 1823 Young reprinted from his article EGYPT, as Appendix II to his *Discoveries in Egyptian Literature*. Of these "Specimens" most are composed of ideographic signs; none of these have been *deciphered*, all have been *identified*, with more or less success. The identifications are sometimes so true that a dabbler in hieroglyphics might be tempted to say, "Dear me! Champollion must have borrowed *this*." But the dabbler who so judges cannot be aware of the enormity of his own dullness. The true identifications are extremely easy and could hardly be missed by any one of average skill. If Young had been wise he would have confined his attempts to cases where success was certain. But it is noteworthy and significant that he breaks down most thoroughly where 'alphabetic' characters form part of the word. ⟨glyph⟩ is "Cteristes (or Cerberus")," while ⟨glyph⟩ is "Anubis," ⟨glyph⟩ (*sic*) is "Tetrarcha," ⟨glyph⟩ is "Greek," ⟨glyph⟩ is "respectable," ⟨glyph⟩ is "father," and out of ⟨glyph⟩ he makes out ⟨glyph⟩ "loving" and ⟨glyph⟩ "Ptah." The secret of his success and of his failure is plain enough. He worked mechanically, like the schoolboy who finding in a translation that *Arma virumque* means "Arms and the man," reads *Arma* "arms," *virum* "and," *que* "the man." He is sometimes right but very much oftener wrong, and no one is able to distinguish between his right and his wrong results until the right *method* has been discovered.

Out of all Young's *identifications* of the royal names only two are *exceptions* to the general failure. It is only in consequence of Champollion's successful method that we can point out exactly what is right and what is wrong in what Young says about these names.

Ptolemy is the only royal name in the hieroglyphic text of Rosetta, and there could be no difficulty about its identification. It is not

Ptolémée. Mais une découverte véritable, ce serait d'avoir réellement *lu* ce nom hiéroglyphique, c'est-à-dire, d'avoir fixé la valeur propre à chacun des caractères qui le composent, et de telle manière que ces valeurs fussent applicables partout où ces mêmes caractères se présentent." *Précis*, p. 22.

Champollion only, but Klaproth who says, " Tout le monde avait reconnu dans cette inscription la place qu'occupait le nom de Ptolémée ; et on avait indiqué de même sur d'autres monuments les cadres ou *cartouches* qui devaient contenir ceux de Bérénice et Arsinoé."

But it does not follow that because we know that a certain Egyptian group represents the name of Ptolemy, we can at once infer the value of the letters. Each sign is like one of the unknown quantities in an equation, and its value has to be *proved*. The Chinese name of Abraham, as I have said, is most easily discovered, but no one could possibly guess that the characters of which it is composed are *Ia-peh-la-han*. Reference to a Syriac lexicon will show that such names as Scopas, Sparta, Strato and Stephen do not necessarily begin with an S. The Arabic name of Plato does not begin with a P. Moreover Πτολεμαῖος is a significant name, derived from πτόλεμος. What antecedent proof have we that the Egyptian name is not a translation of the Greek one ? At all events Young has to prove that the first sign □ of the Egyptian name of Ptolemy is P.

His only proof is that it "answers invariably in all the manuscripts" to the character resembling the P of Akerblad, derived from the beginning of the enchorial name. *But this is really not the case.* Young's mistake may be called a lucky one, but a mistake it is undeniably.

On the other hand, how does Young read the ⧠, which he rightly (though with wrong reason) reads as PT in Ptolemy, when they occur in other words?

We have just seen that he identified □ 𝟟 with the sense of 'loving.' He says "The square block, the semicircle, and the chain are employed very clearly in the sense of LOVING, or beloved ; the Coptic ⲙⲁⲓ." Even as late as the end of 1827, Young was reluctant to admit Champollion's reading.

The royal name ⬭ he interprets as *Nechao*.

If he knew the true values of □, ⌒ and 🦉, how came he to read the royal name □⌒🦉 as *Sesostris?*

Here then we have in the same essay *four* different values

assigned to the ' square block ' □, and *three* different ones to the semicircle ◠. And how can Young be said to have demonstrated any one of these values, or indeed to have any notion of a *phonetic system* ?

So much for the first two signs of the name of Ptolemy. He broke down upon the third sign ⚱, which he says is "not essentially necessary, being often * omitted in the sacred characters and always in the enchorial." He is here again entirely wrong, and only shows that he was unable to decipher the " enchorial," which *never* omits the sign.

The last mistake compelled him to break down again on the next sign ⬲, which corresponds to the enchorial sign rightly read by Akerblad.

Young's analysis of the name Berenice is not more successful. The first sign 🐝 (*ba*) he recognises as " precisely of the same form with a basket, represented at Byban el Molouk .... and a basket in Coptic is BIR." The second sign ⬭ (*r*) he reads *e*: the " little footstool," ⊿ (= *q*), " seems to be superfluous " ! like the ⚱ in the name of Ptolemy. Instead of the eagle 🦅 (*a*) he reads 🦆 (a goose) and transcribes it KE or KEN, a value which he defends upon very ridiculous grounds. It is hardly possible to imagine a more complete failure in the decipherment of a name already known with certainty.

An equation containing several unknown quantities cannot be solved without the help of other equations in which the same unknown quantities are involved, and the values obtained for each unknown must satisfy each of the equations. This is an elementary principle in all decipherment, but it is not recognised by Young in his attempts upon the names of the royal personages of the Egyptian inscriptions. It was not until Champollion had an abundant supply of the necessary equations, that he published his letter to M. Dacier, and convinced all competent judges of the correctness of his method of decipherment.

The truth is, that in his Essay Young has no notion of a real phonetic system, nor does he profess to have one. Under the title " Sounds ? " he gives a table affording " something like a hieroglyphic alphabet, which *however* is merely collected as a specimen of the

* It is *once* omitted, through an oversight, in the Rosetta inscription.

mode of expressing sounds in *some particular cases*, and *not as having been universally employed when sounds were required.*" And the title which he puts over a list of demotic signs is SUPPOSED ENCHORIAL ALPHABET. As a whole it had, long before he began his speculations, ceased to be hypothetical. The greater part of it had been fully demonstrated. It is idle to speak of such a writer as having demonstrated anything, or having a system however imperfect: all is hypothesis, conjecture, guesswork, as far as hieroglyphics are concerned. No one could learn anything from his famous Essay, for even the true things contained in it are *logically* undistinguishable from the false.

Young was in the habit of calling Champollion's discoveries an *extension* of his own. * But the difference was not one of quantity but of quality. A man who sometimes hits upon the right answer to an arithmetical problem is not on the same level as one who knows the rule for working all such problems.

I now proceed to notice the charges of plagiarism which ignorance and malevolence have brought against Champollion.

1. The first which has to be dealt with implies such an amount of stupidity on the part of its authors that we can only wonder at its ever being repeated. "We know that a printed copy of Young's paper on the Rosetta Stone had been put into Champollion's hands by De Sacy!"

This is not quite accurate, but sufficiently so as to furnish a pretext for the insinuation. But the question is, what did the paper consist in? What could Champollion possibly learn from it?

It consisted † of a "Conjectural Translation of the Egyptian [demotic] Inscription printed side by side with [Mr. Gough's] Translation of the Greek Inscription copied and corrected by Porson." There is not the least attempt at decipherment in it, unless we apply that term to the transcription of the proper names, which had already been made out by Akerblad and was as familiar to Champollion as to Young.

* He ludicrously speaks of Champollion as having added *three* new letters to *his* phonetic alphabet, whereas the phonetic values of at least seventy signs were demonstrated in the *Lettre à M. Dacier.*

† "I sent him a copy of my conjectural translation of the inscriptions, as it was inserted in the *Archæologia.*" Young, *Discoveries in Hieroglyphical Literature,* p. 40. Let the reader take down the 17th volume of the *Archæologia,* and see for himself the absolute worthlessness of the essay, and the absence of anything which could help an enquirer.

Akerblad himself writes to Young (Leitch, III, p. 72), "As for your conjectural translation of the Egyptian inscription, I really do not conceive the purpose of it, as the question is to discover the alphabet, and consequently to separate and read the Egyptian words, not merely to make out the meaning of the inscription, which is undoubtedly the same as in Greek."

Does the insinuation imply anything more than that in the author's experience an English crib is more intelligible than the authentic Greek? But he is bound to point out the particulars in which Champollion took advantage of the English crib in preference to the Greek. And he certainly is unable to do so.

The late Mr. Sharpe published a "conjectural" translation of the Rosetta Stone long before M. Chabas. Is M. Chabas in any way liable to the suspicion of having borrowed from Mr. Sharpe, whose translation he had certainly seen in a volume frequently quoted by him?

2. But Champollion "appropriated, of course without acknowledgment, the enchorial discoveries of Akerblad." So says Mr. Leitch, and his sapient follower joins him in this impudent imputation. "It is now time to ask how much he [Ch.] was indebted to Akerblad's letter for ideas and results."

I call the imputation an impudent one, and it is an impudent *falsehood* to say that Champollion "appropriated without acknowledgement" the enchorial discoveries of Akerblad. "Les travaux si connus de MM. Silvestre de Sacy et Ackerblad *démontrèrent* que ce texte renfermait des noms propres grecs écrits en caractères égyptiens alphabétiques ; notion précieuse qui est devenue en quelque sorte le *germe véritable de toutes les découvertes faites depuis sur les écritures égyptiennes.*" So writes Champollion, and he tells us (what is undeniable) that his own labours on the demotic text of Rosetta had enabled him to augment and on certain points to rectify the alphabet of Akerblad. He never for an instant claimed to be its discoverer.*

With this acknowledgment of Akerblad's merits it is well to contrast the utterance of Mr. Leitch's hero.

Akerblad had written to Young (Leitch, p. 72), "By your third letter to M. de Sacy, I learn that you have adopted almost the

---

* And Champollion-Figeac in the *Journal Asiatique* (July, 1823, p. 39) speaks of "l'alphabet de cette écriture [démotique] complété et publié par mon frère, *après les travaux de* MM. Silvestre de Sacy et Ackerblad."

whole of my alphabet and most part of the readings which I propose in my printed letter."

To this Young replies (Leitch, p. 81), "You must not expect me to allow, that my adoption of the principal part of the readings which you proposed in your first letter, depended on any disposition to acquiesce in the result of your labours, rather than to conduct the investigation on independent grounds; the fact is, that the three names most easily identified were discovered without difficulty by Mr. de Sacy, the sixteen or eighteen other words which you pointed out in your letter were also amongst the most prominent; and it was natural that most of them should have occurred both to you and to me, even if I had never heard of the existence of your letter."

If it was natural that they should occur "both to you and to me," why not also to Champollion? But Champollion does not take this ground. What would Mr. Leitch have said if he had done so?

Champollion's words are perfectly true and unassailable when he says : " Feu Ackerblad essaya d'étendre ses lectures hors des noms propres grecs, et il échoua complètement." But his recent assailant quotes these words as proving that Champollion (like Young) did not give sufficient credit to Akerblad for what he accomplished. Champollion, on the contrary, gave the fullest credit to Akerblad for what he accomplished, and only declined to follow him where he had failed.

3. There is a self sufficient ignorance as well as stupidity in the observation (implying that Champollion was a liar) "that Champollion should not have known of Young's article EGYPT is *a thing not to be understood*, especially as advance copies were sent to Paris and elsewhere as early as 1818." "Young's article in the *Encyclopædia Britannica* obtained great celebrity in Europe, and was reprinted by Leitch in the 3rd vol. of the Works of Dr. Young."

Leitch's reprint was executed many years after the death of Champollion. It is not true that the article obtained great celebrity either in England or in Europe till after the discoveries of Champollion, and the efforts of his enemies to convict him of plagiarism. Then, indeed, it was a good deal talked about rather than read, but it had previously only attracted the attention of Young's private friends.

It is easy enough, at the present day, at the British Museum or at the University libraries, to obtain the sight of any of the noted works published in any part of the world. But it is a thing to be understood by any intelligent person that in the first quarter of this century, long before the time of railways or that of cosmopolite public libraries, a young man living at Grenoble, a town of not more than 20,000 inhabitants, more than 350 miles south of Paris, had not the same opportunities as we now have of knowing what is being published abroad.

There is abundance of evidence in Mr. Leitch's volume showing that Young's article was not so very accessible, even to his own friends.

Sir William Gell writes from Rome on May 25, 1821 :— "Whether your book or pamphlet or dissertation on Egyptian hieroglyphics be published, or whether it be only presented to your particular friends, I have never been able to discover ; but after repeated trials *in London*, I could not procure it through my bookseller. You have, as my friend Dodwell informs me, made a present of it to the Library of the Vatican ; but whether it be there or not, a public library is always so difficult to get at, and so very useless to the public that," etc.

Letronne writes from Paris in June, 1824, to excuse himself for not having quoted an opinion of Young similar to his own, and of which Young claimed the priority. "N'ayant pas sous les yeux votre article 'EGYPT' dans l'Encyclopédie, *et ne pouvant me le procurer*, je ne puis vérifier si c'est là que vous en avez parlé."

It may however be suggested that Young had sent Champollion a copy. But Young himself tells us that this was not the case. "Mr. Champollion," he says in his *Discoveries in Hieroglyphical Literature* (p. 41), "continued to reside at Grenoble till the beginning of 1821. I had not a convenient opportunity of sending him any of my later papers, and it was not till after he had left Grenoble, that he read the article EGYPT in the Supplement of the Encylopædia, into which their contents were condensed. He had been devoting himself in the meantime to the uninterrupted study of the enchorial inscription," etc.

Champollion had, in fact, as Young himself states, a few lines after those just quoted, been devoting himself to something even more important than the enchorial inscription. "He had taken the trouble to copy at length, with the permission of their various possessors," "*a multitude of Egyptian papyri*," hieroglyphic, hieratic and demotic, and from the study of all these documents he had discovered the equivalence of the hieroglyphic signs with the cursive forms (hieratic and demotic) derived from them.

The equivalence of the hieratic and hieroglyphic was demonstrated in the plates of his work, *De l'Ecriture Hiératique des anciens Egyptiens*, printed at Grenoble in 1821. His memoir on the Demotic was read before the *Académie Royale des Inscriptions*.

4. It is with reference to his work on the hieratic character that the most odious of all the charges against Champollion has been propagated.

It is not known how many copies were issued, but very few are known to exist, and only one or two have the introductory text. It has been asserted that Champollion suppressed this text, for the purpose of concealing the fact that as late as 1821 he had spoken of the hieratic characters, and of the hieroglyphs from which they were derived as *signs of things and not of sounds*. It has been asserted therefore that between the date of this work, in 1821, and that of the letter to M. Dacier, in 1822, he had learnt from Young's EGYPT a new and more correct theory on the subject, and did his utmost to destroy all traces of the old one.

To those who have never seen the letter to M. Dacier the charge may seem plausible, but those who repeat the charge after reading the letter are utterly without excuse. How can anyone be fool enough to believe that if Champollion wished to destroy all traces of his old theory, he would have *repeated it in the very same words* in the letter to Dacier the whole of which presupposes the old theory, and is consistent with it throughout?

When, in my Hibbert Lectures of 1879, I pointed out the manifest absurdity involved in the charge, I was not aware that I had been forestalled by no less an authority than Young himself.

" The French translator of Mr. Browne's ingenious article," he writes, " has certainly gone a good deal out of his way to find matter of accusation against Mr. Champollion. He quotes the text of a memoir published in 1821, and afterwards suppressed .... But the translator might have found in the beginning of the letter to Mr. Dacier, dated in 1822, the same opinion respecting these systems of writing : that is the *hieratic* and *demotic*, which he says are not alphabetic, but *ideographic* like the hieroglyphs themselves, expressing ideas and not sounds. *Nothing can possibly agree better than this with the opinion which Dr. Young had long before published ; and which he has since confirmed in his octavo volume.*"

The present generation of readers may have a difficulty in understanding how Young, after phonetically reading the names of

Ptolemy and Berenice, or Champollion, after reading so many Greek and Roman names and such titles as *Autokrator, Kaisar, Sebastos,* and *Sebaste,* could still talk of hieroglyphs "expressing ideas not sounds."

The explanation of this mystery is nevertheless simple enough, if we only try to understand these words in the sense in which they were written; that is, according to the phraseology then current in Chinese philology. The analogy between Chinese and Egyptian modes of writing had long been universally admitted, and strong assertions had even been made as to the identity of the two systems. As early as the 7th August, 1810, Champollion, in a memoir read before the *Society of Science and Arts* at Grenoble, showed the impossibility of explaining the Egyptian by means of the Chinese signs, and this essay contains a number of very important observations. The analogy of Chinese practice, for instance, suggests that the names of the Egyptian kings being mostly derived from the religious worship, might easily be expressed by significant symbols; but that India, Arabia and other countries involved in war with Egypt, having names foreign to the language and religion of Egypt, necessarily required phonetic signs for their transcription. He continues: "L'inscription de Rosette présente les noms grecs de Ptolémée, Bérénice, Arsinoé, Pyrrha, d'Aréïa, de Diogène, d'Aétès, d'Alexandre, etc; *ils ne pouvaient être exprimés dans la partie hiéro- glyphique de ce monument si ces hiéroglyphes n'avaient, comme nous l'avons dit, la faculté de produire des sons.*" *

The problem here stated was solved in the letter to M. Dacier, the theory of which is, that Egyptian hieroglyphs like the Chinese are not alphabetic but *essentially ideographic,* though under the exceptional condition of transcribing *foreign* words they like the Chinese (under the same condition) conventionally become *phonetic;* that is to say, *letters* or *syllables, void of meaning.†*

* See *Revue Archéologique,* 1857.

† " Les Chinois pour écrire un mot étranger à leur langue, ont tout simplement adopté les signes idéographiques dont la prononciation leur parait offrir le plus d'analogie avec chaque syllable ou élément du mot étranger qu'il s'agit de transcrire. On conçoit donc que les Égyptiens voulant exprimer, soit une voyelle, soit une consonne, soit une syllabe, d'un mot étranger se soient servis d'un signe hiéroglyphique *exprimant* ou réprésentant un objet quelconque dont le nom, en langue parlée, contenait ou dans son entier, ou dans sa première partie, le son de la voyelle, de la consonne ou de la syllabe qu'il s'agissait d'écrire."

And Klaproth wrote, after Champollion's death,—" Les Chinois ont aussi

In Chinese every sign expresses 'an idea not a sound' *; it is not a letter nor a syllable. It is a complete word in itself with determinate significance and pronunciation. No word can normally be written in Chinese which is not the expression of *native* Chinese thought.

But when *foreign* names and words have to be transcribed, as in the translations of Indian Buddhist literature, the signs with which these words are written lose their ideographic character altogether, and are used (*but then only*) with purely phonetic values. M. Stanislas Julien in his *Méthode pour déchiffrer et transcrire les noms sanscrits qui se rencontrent dans les livres chinois*, has described the laborious process by which he succeeded in solving a problem which had baffled even such scholars as Abel Rémusat and Klaproth,† who knew Chinese but not Sanskrit.

At the time of the publication of his *Lettre à M. Dacier*

une *manière phonétique* d'écrire les noms propres [étrangers] qu'ils entourent souvent d'un cartouche comme les Egyptiens. La seule différence entre leurs système phonétique et celui des bords du Nil est que chez eux, les caractères idéographiques, employés phonétiquement, ne deviennent pas des lettres alphabétiques, mais qu'elle réprésentent la syllabe entière qu'ils expriment dans leur usage ordinaire."

* See Rémusat's inaugural discourse, 16 Jan., 1815.

"Croirait on l'écriture chinoise plus difficile à apprendre, parcequ'elle réprésente les idées, au lieu de figurer des sons." . . . . "Cette nature singulière de la langue chinoise qui consiste à réprésenter immédiatement les idées par des symboles convenus, au lieu de les rappeler à la mémoire par l'intermédiaire des sons, leur appartient exclusivement, depuis que les hiéroglyphes égyptiens ont cessé d'être en usage, et c'est un des rapports sous lesquels elle peut d'avantage piquer la curiosité." *Mélanges Asiatiques*, II, pp. 12 and 13.

In Morrison's Chinese " Introduction to a Knowledge of Letters of the Kingdom of England " in his English-Chinese Dictionary (Macao, 1822), the same view is taken. Writing represents either (1) the sense of words, or (2) their sounds. Of the latter kind are those of the Sanskrit, the Mandshu, and the English and other European languages. Of the former are the ancient characters of Egypt and those of China.

Similarly Young himself in the article LANGUAGES, written for the supplement to the *Encyclopædia Britannica*, Vol. V, 1824, and repeated by him from earlier publications—"The Chinese . . . . is distinguished from almost all others by a more marked peculiarity, which is, that its written characters *instead of depicting sounds, are the immediate symbols of the objects or ideas.* . . . And in this point of view the Chinese will require to be classed with old Egyptian only."

† " On sait que dans ces transcriptions, le caractère symbolique de l'écriture chinoise disparaît totalement, et que les signes au lieu d'être des images, destinées à éveiller la pensée, ne sont plus que des articulations qui doivent frapper l'oreille." Landresse, in his "Introduction" to Rémusat's translation of the *Foĕ Kouĕ Ki*, p. lx.

Champollion did not suppose that he had done more than solve the problem, which he had already before him in 1810, of discovering the key to reading the Greek and Roman names in Egyptian hieroglyphs, just as Stanislas Julien at a later period found the key to reading Sanskrit names in Chinese literature.

We are now in a position to form a true estimate of this abominable accusation.

Instead of suppressing the opinion expressed in the work on Hieratic, Champollion repeated it *totidem verbis* in the letter to M. Dacier, and Young, so far from being startled by it, claims it as identical with his own,* and needing no correction.

Champollion did not mean by it that foreign names could not be written hieroglyphically when necessity required it. This obvious necessity he had pointed out as early as 1810, some years before Young had begun his Egyptian studies. Still less did he mean, as some foolish people have imagined, that because signs represented ideas and not sounds, they were not sounded when read.

The accusation then is simply a *lie*, and those who, like Messrs. Long and Leitch, continued to circulate it ought to have been ashamed of themselves for having failed to recognize it as such.

The most criminal of all is Klaproth, who, as a Chinese scholar, thoroughly understood Champollion's meaning.

The discovery announced in the letter to M. Dacier was indeed a memorable one, but it was almost immediately followed by a second not less memorable. The letter was no sooner published than Champollion discovered that his phonetic alphabet was a key not only to the transcription of Greek and Roman names but to the language of Egyptian inscriptions of every period. This discovery was communicated to the Academy in the April of 1823, and in a letter to Young of the same year he announces the approaching publication of his Essay (the *Précis du Système Hiéroglyphique*). In this letter he states his new conviction, "qu'une très grande partie des signes employés dans les inscriptions *hiératiques* et *hiéroglyphiques* de tous les âges ne sont autre chose que des signes *de son* ainsi que la plus grande partie de tout texte *Démotique* ou *enchorial*."

---

* In the principle both men undoubtedly agreed, but they differed greatly in its application. As all the "ideographical" signs in Demotic which were used phonetically in proper names became alphabetic, Champollion argued that such necessarily was the case with the hieroglyphic signs. But there were other and more serious differences.

Leitch, in a footnote (p. 367) upon this letter, observes—"It is curious to contrast Champollion's opinions upon this subject in the above letter with those which he entertained two years before, when he published his memoir 'De l'Ecriture Hiératique." It is very much more curious a circumstance that Mr. Leitch, in order to insinuate that Champollion had borrowed from Young, should wantonly ignore the theory of the letter to Dacier so recently published, which is identical with that of the Grenoble publication, and that he should fail to see that the new theory was more removed than ever from any approximation to Young's views. The old theory was abandoned simply because it was too narrow to account for all the new facts which had come within the observation of Champollion since he published his letter to Dacier, or for the new light now thrown upon old facts.

These two memorable stages of progress and the necessary passage from one to other have never been sufficiently distinguished.

5. Were it not for an unguarded and most inaccurate statement of so eminent a man as Dr. Birch, that Young "traced the name of Ptolemy up in his own way, from the demotic into hieratic, into the hieroglyphs," it would hardly be worth while to say that Young never knew what Dr. Birch called 'demotic, hieratic and hieroglyphic.' What Young called hieratic is *linear hieroglyphic.* He would have been surprised at the sight of the Rhind papyri, presenting a hieratic text with a version in demotic writing. Under the name of 'cursive' or 'enchorial,' Young confounded hieratic and demotic. And where had Young ever seen the name of Ptolemy in hieratic? He had certainly come to the conclusion (which is obvious enough to any one possessed of eyes) that the cursive forms were derived from the hieroglyphic, but he had not verified it in minute detail like Champollion, who knew all the equivalences, sign by sign, of the three kinds of writing. The demotic name of Cleopatra on the Casati papyrus* was easily read back letter by letter into hieroglyphics, and

* The importance of this discovery, which he calls "a great event in Egyptian literature," is fully acknowledged by Young (*Discoveries*, p. 56), who also speaks in the highest terms of Champollion's skill in enchorial decipherments.

It ought never to be forgotten by those who talk about the matter, that Champollion did not start with the names of Ptolemy and Berenice but with that of Cleopatra, which was of great service in deciphering that of Ptolemy, but even these names would not have led him very far, if he had not already accumulated an immense mass of other material, and had a scientific method to guide him in dealing with it.

the obelisk of Philæ, which contained both that name and the name of Ptolemy, came at the opportune moment to crown the efforts of the enquirer with success. Cleopatra was the name first read with absolute certainty, and from the hieroglyphic □ of that name Champollion obtained with certainty the P of Ptolemy. The ◠ of course was known from a large number of equations.

The ⚵ and the ⚏ of Ptolemy corresponded to the o and the L of Cleopatra; the ⋀ is proved to be s by many names so ending. The long array of royal Greek and Roman names and titles was made out with equal certainty, and if some errors can be occasionally detected, it was Champollion himself who furnished the tests by which they could be detected, no less than the method by which they could be corrected.

6. "His charlatanism and literary dishonesty are acknowledged by some of the most eminent of his countrymen such as de Sacy and Letronne"! Is this true?

It is well to observe the categories. When, where, how, under what circumstances did M. de Sacy utter so terrible a judgment? Was it in public? Was it after Champollion had published his discoveries? Did M. de Sacy think Champollion had borrowed from Young? Did he include no one else in the same censure? And did he never alter his opinion? All these are very important considerations.

M. de Sacy uses the word "charlatanisme" as applied to Champollion in two private letters to Young of which the dates are noteworthy. In 1815 Champollion had not published any of his discoveries. "J'ai bien peur que ce ne soit là que du charlatanisme." This term in French usage does not necessarily imply what it would mean if I used it in reference to certain impostors. The term is applied in the *Mémoires de Madame de Larochejacquelin* to an officer highly esteemed by everybody in the Vendean army for his good qualities. It need mean nothing more than 'brag.' M. de Sacy's expression is applied in this letter to Akerblad and Quatremère as well as to Champollion. He had worked at the Rosetta inscription with some success, and was not eager to admit that others had succeeded where he had failed. There is here no "*acknowledgment of literary dishonesty*," but only a caution to Young not to be too liberal in communicating his discoveries. But there is no doubt that Sacy was deeply irritated against Champollion, as we can see from his second letter.

The first letter is dated 20 July, 1815, about a fortnight after the allied troops had entered Paris. Silvestre de Sacy was devotedly attached to the royal family of France, and had in deference to his undisputed rank as an orientalist been allowed, in 1795, to continue in his professorship after refusing to take the oath of hatred against royalty, then exacted from all professors. He bitterly resented the political conduct of Champollion "*pendant le règne de trois mois d'Ahriman*" (Leitch, p. 51): Champollion had, like so many others of his countrymen, and of his townsmen * in particular, taken part with the Corsican usurper. We may sympathize (and I do most thoroughly) with the political feelings of the old royalist, but we must make allowance for them in judging of somebody else, in a question which has nothing to do with politics.

But is it a right action to quote these private letters, written in times of political irritation, without quoting the mature judgment of the great orientalist after he had seen and read Champollion's discoveries? This is what he writes of Champollion in the *Journal des Savans* in March, 1825.

"Il a à mon avis complètement démontré que malgré quelques légers point de contact entre les résultats des conjectures de M. le Docteur Young et ceux qu'il a d'abord obtenus de la découverte dont l'honneur lui est dû, leurs manières de procéder sont essentiellement différentes, l'une de l'autre; et qu'en adoptant pour base du déchiffrement, les idées fondamentales de M. Young, on se serait égaré dans une fausse direction, et on n'eut fait qu'augmenter le nombre des conjectures hazardées dont les hiéroglyphes ont été l'objet. Nous croyons que ce jugement sera confirmé par tous les savans de quelque nation que ce soit, qui examineront avec impartialité les droits respectifs de M. Young et de M. Champollion à l'honneur d'avoir découvert la route qui peut conduire à l'intelligence des anciens monuments écrits de l'Egypte."

So much for Silvestre de Sacy. The other eminent countryman of Champollion, Letronne, does not say a word about 'charlatanism' or 'literary dishonesty,' but only implies that Champollion is jealous of intruders into what he considers his own domain. Letronne's own judgment on the respective merits of the two scholars was identical with that of Silvestre de Sacy. Mr. Leitch acknowledges this, and ascribes it to national partiality. And he

* Grenoble was the first French town which opened its gates to Bonaparte on his return from Elba.

accuses Arago, one of the most enthusiastic friends of Young, of the same national sin, because he happened to say " que la France n'est pas cosmopolite." But Arago, a most thoroughly scientific man, was an admirable judge of the merits of a question depending on demonstrative proof; and had a full right to glory in the nationality of the candidate who had established his claim by incontrovertible arguments.

It is not right to leave this part of the subject without touching on one of the most interesting traits in Champollion's character. Young had been cautioned against being too liberal in communicating his discoveries to him. Champollion, on the other hand, was most liberal to Young, and the latter acknowledges with gratitude the important communications which he received from him.

Sir William Gell writes (Leitch, p. 431), " I beg to state that so far from hiding his new discoveries, the said Champollion has given me so many things not published, that if I were inclined, I could pretend I was the inventor of as much again as he is. I have the whole Rosetta Stone from line V divided by him into words, and the Coptic corresponding to every figure under. I have lectured him till I hope he is going to publish what he now knows, which is out of all comparison more than is published."

How thoroughly true this is, is well known to those who have seen the manuscripts he left behind him.

His liberality in lending his manuscripts to Rosellini and to Ungarelli is well known. How shamefully Salvolini abused this liberality is but too well known. And the brood of Salvolini's is not yet extinct.

I must finally protest against that ridiculous table in parallel columns, which is represented as giving the judgments of experts in Egyptology as to the comparative claims of Young and Champollion. Salt is quoted, as if his opinion were of the slightest consequence,[*] and Goodwin and E. de Rougé are names conspicuous by their absence! Yet the most important name of all is that of M. de

---

[*] Sir W. Gell writes (5th Aug., 1826) to Young (Leitch, p. 392): " Salt's claim to originality only fit to set up in the region of Humbugia, for I have myself sent to Egypt all the inventions of yourself and Champollion as fast as they come out. . . . I understand from Mr. Scoles the architect, that Salt went crazy on the subject of *his own inventions,* and told them all that you and Champollion knew nothing about it and that he was only real discoverer. *Wherever Champollion had not published, Salt is generally wrong,* which corroborates the proof of his having seen what was printed : Nectanebus or Nekthanebph for instance."

Rougé, not merely on account of his transcendent merits, but because he has dealt with the matter *judicially ;* his judgment being the result of an accurate and critical survey of all the facts of the case. The only name which from this point of view approaches it in value is that of Lepsius. The very best scholar is, in a matter like this, of no authority unless he has studied the case, and had the facts before him. How do we know if this or that German or Frenchman has ever read a line of Young? Is it justifiable to quote the hasty passage of a scholar who writes as if Young had deciphered the names of Ptolemy and Berenice, letter by letter, without a single mistake? Is there a single Egyptologist who, after testing the facts and arguments of M. de Rougé, would venture to dispute any one of them? And what would M. de Rougé himself have said of this stupid collection of extracts, in which even those statements which might claim to be really of a judicial character are reduced to the appearance of *obiter dicta ?*

Two undeniable facts remain after all that has been written : Champollion learnt nothing whatever from Young, nor did anyone else. It is only through Champollion and the method he employed that Egyptology has grown into the position which it now occupies. It is only by the strictest application of that method that Lepsius, Birch, and de Rougé were able to correct the errors and imperfections adhering to the system founded upon it, but in no way pertaining to its essence.*

The limits of this paper preclude anything more than a passing allusion to such matters. But I ought not to conclude without saying a word about an important element of his system, for which

Salt's official position in Egypt enabled him to secure very valuable antiquities, but that is no reason for giving oneself airs. If I buy a Greek papyrus of the Iliad, or of Plato's Republic, or a lost play of Aeschylus, or even of a version by Manetho of the Book of the Dead, without being able to read a line of the text or translate it when transcribed, are not people fools who praise my sagacity, when my only merit is in knowing that all the libraries in Europe would willingly purchase a document in that special character?

* *E.g.,* insisting on the alphabetical nature of phonetic signs. This error was tempered by explanations which practically corrected it. ⌷ and ⑃ were called *m* and ⑂ *n*, but they were termed *abbreviations of men, mes* and *nefr,* and read as such.

But there is a suggestion in the Letter to Dacier, that the phonetic alphabet was syllabic, that is, consisting of open syllables like *be, re.* And I am convinced that this is more true that the commonly received view in favour of simple consonants.

Champollion was indebted to his studies of Chinese writing, and without which the most perfect phonetic alphabet would have been inadequate for the study of the language.

Words in Chinese signifying *sea, lake, river, canal, rapid, running, deep, flow, rush, bathe, float, trickle, leak, ooze, bubble, weep, wash, refresh, limpid, pure, unsullied, extinguish,* and the like, have in common a sign representing *water,* which accompanies them, as the sign 〰 follows Egyptian words of kindred meanings, as their determinative.

In like manner words implying the notions of *flame, heat, burning, cooking, smoke, candle,* etc., have for determinative a sign signifying *fire,* like the Egyptian 𓊮.

The Chinese sign for *mouth* accompanies words signifying *eat, talk, ask, call, command, sing, boisterous,* etc.

The sign for *heart* accompanies the words for *thought, resolve, will, anger, joy, fear, regret, love, happiness, sadness,* etc.

Every one familiar with Egyptian will at once see what an important step was gained by Champollion's recognition of the analogy between the Chinese and the Egyptian uses of determinative symbols.*   The same sort of symbols have since been discovered in the cuneiform writings, and their existence in Egyptian is by itself conclusive against all attempts to illustrate that writing by inferences from Hebrew, Phœnician, and other Semitic writings.   Egyptian writing is, in its origin, not alphabetic but essentially ideographic like the Accadian, Assyrian, Chinese, and Japanese.†   It is no more tied than they to the expression of *consonantal* ‡ sounds.   The evidence derived from the comparative history of these ancient systems would seem to lead to the inference that in periods anterior to those of the earliest monuments which have come down to us, the Egyptian hieroglyphic system may have very much more nearly resembled the Chinese in principle, than it did in later times.

* These ideograms are in Chinese grammars called "Keys" or "Radicals." The grammarians count 214, under which all the words of the language are arranged in the Imperial Dictionary of Kánghi.

† Klaproth said that the Egyptian system most nearly resembled Japanese. This is certainly truer than he was aware.   I will here only allude to the polyphony of the two systems, and to the phonetic complements which enable one to determine the exact value intended.   The same phenomena are to be found in cuneiform writing, and in all these writings they are to be ascribed to the same cause.

‡ *Cf.* my paper "Are there really no Vowels in the Egyptian Alphabet," in the "Transactions of the Ninth International Congress of Orientalists."

A COPTIC PALIMPSEST.

I. Prayer of the Virgin in " Bartos."
II. Fragment of a Patriarchal History.

By W. E. Crum.

This MS. was acquired by the British Museum a few years ago. It is numbered *Or.* 4714. For the permission to publish it I have to thank Professor Douglas, Keeper of the Oriental MSS. I must also acknowledge the consent of the Rev. George Horner; for though the MS. reached England in his possession, he generously resigned his claims upon its publication to me.

The MS. was obtained at Siut. It consists of six consecutive leaves of coarse vellum, in book form, each now about 6½ in. × 5 in. It is a palimpsest; but the earlier text is so faintly visible, that even had the original leaves not been cut down to accommodate the subsequent scribe, little would now be legible.

I. Prayer of the Virgin in " Bartos."

This is the later text. It is in a single column and in very black ink. The characters are thick, coarsely formed, and incline to the right. None of the published facsimiles have much resemblance to the type exhibited, for they represent almost exclusively the careful literary scripts, while the rougher colophons show only Bohairic hands. Hyvernat, *Album* xii, 3 is a finer and presumably earlier specimen of a somewhat similar style. It may safely be assigned to a date not before the 11th century. The lines in a page vary between 15 and 25. The pages are numbered $\overline{\text{B}}$ — $\overline{\text{IT}}$. The text is that of the magical prayer said to have been made by the Virgin on behalf of S. Matthias in "the city of Bartos," *i.e.*, among the Parthians.[1] It

---

[1] *v.* Guidi in *Soc. as. ital., Giornale*, 1889, 173.

is already known in Ethiopic and Arabic versions, presumably derived from the Coptic. For the Ethiopic version I have used M. Basset's translation ;[1] for the Arabic, the description and excerpts of the Bodleian MS. *Rot. or.* 2,[2] a curious amulet not mentioned by M. Basset. Both these versions, the former especially, appear to be developed to a much greater length than the Coptic which, while retaining signs of a higher antiquity (*e.g.*, the use of the old Gnostic word ἀπολογία), is unadorned by many of the glosses and expansions seen in the others (*e.g.*, the names of the five nails).[3] It is said that this prayer and the consecrated water and oil to which it refers were used in a particular (penitential or exorcising ?) ritual of the Ethiopic church,[4] and its composition is attributed in the Arabic version to Cyril of Jerusalem.

P. ⲃ̅. [ⲉⲓⲙⲏ]ⲧⲉⲓ ⲁⲛⲟⲕ ⲙⲡⲁⲉⲓⲱⲧ ⲙⲡⲡⲉⲡ̅ⲛ̅ⲁ̅
ⲉⲧⲟⲩⲁⲁⲃ ⲡⲁⲣⲁⲛⲡⲉ ⲁⲗⲫⲁ ⲡⲣⲁⲛ ⲙⲡⲁⲉⲓⲱⲧⲡⲉ
ⲁⲣⲱⲙ ⲇⲁⲛⲓⲏⲗ ⲡⲣⲁⲛ ⲙⲡⲉⲡ̅ⲛ̅ⲁ̅ ⲉⲧⲟⲩⲁⲁⲃⲡⲉ
ⲙⲡⲁⲣⲁⲕⲗⲏⲧⲟⲥ ⲁⲛϩⲛⲟⲩⲙⲛⲧⲛⲟⲩⲧⲉ ⲛⲟⲩⲱⲧ
ⲕⲁⲧⲁ ⲧⲕⲉⲗⲏⲧⲥⲓⲥ ⲙⲡⲁⲉⲓⲱⲧ ⲙⲡⲡⲉⲡ̅ⲛ̅ⲁ̅
ⲉⲧⲟⲩⲁⲁⲃ ⲁⲓⲧⲉⲓ ⲙⲙⲱ ⲱ ⲙⲁⲣⲓⲁ ⲧⲁⲙⲁⲩ
ⲭⲉⲕⲁⲥ ⲉⲣⲉⲡⲉⲧϩⲛⲡⲉⲯⲧⲉⲕⲟ ⲉⲓ ⲉⲃⲟⲗ ⲙⲁⲣⲓⲁ ⲇⲉ
ⲁⲥⲁϩⲉⲣⲁⲧⲥ ⲁⲥⲡⲱⲣϣ ⲛⲛⲉⲥϭⲓⲝ ⲉⲃⲟⲗ ⲛⲥⲁ
ⲛⲧⲁⲛⲁⲧⲟⲗⲏ ⲉⲣⲉⲡⲉⲥⲃⲁⲗ ⲣⲓⲕⲉ . . . . ⲧⲡⲉ
ϣⲁⲡⲉ[ⲥϣⲏⲣⲉ] ⲙⲙⲉⲣⲓ[ⲧ 8 or 9 letters]ⲣⲥ
[about 10 letters]

P. ⲅ̅. ⲉⲥⲭⲱ ⲙⲙⲟⲥ ⲭⲉⲁⲛⲟⲕⲡⲉ ⲙⲁⲣⲓϩⲁⲙ ⲁⲛⲟⲕⲡⲉ
ⲙⲁⲣⲓⲁ ⲁⲛⲟⲕⲡⲉ ⲧⲙⲁⲁⲩ ⲙⲡⲱⲛϩ ⲙⲡⲕⲟⲥⲙⲟⲥ
ⲧⲏⲣϥ ⲉⲓⲱϣ ϩⲣⲁⲓ ⲉⲣⲟⲕ ⲡⲁⲛⲟⲩⲧⲉ ⲁⲩⲱ ⲡⲁϣⲏⲣⲉ
ⲁⲩⲱ ⲡⲁⲙⲉⲣⲓⲧ ⲁⲩⲱ ⲡⲁⲣⲣⲟ ⲁⲛⲟⲕⲡⲉ ⲙⲁⲣⲓⲁ
ⲧⲉⲕⲙⲁⲁⲩ ⲉⲓⲱϣ ϩⲣⲁⲓ ⲉⲣⲟⲕ ⲭⲉⲕⲁⲥ ⲉⲕⲉⲥⲱⲧⲙ

---

[1] *Les Apocryphes éthiopiens* V. Paris, 1895.

[2] *v.* Uri-Nicholl's Catalogue, II, 482. But this is now numbered *Marsh. or.* 131 (R).

[3] For this curious palindrome " Sator areto tenet otera rotas," *v.* besides the citations in Heim, *Incantamenta*, Krall in the Rainer *Mittheilungen* V, who regards it as probably not older than the 8th century.

[4] *v.* Basset, p. 7.

ⲉⲡⲁϩⲣⲟⲟⲩ ⲛⲅⲧⲛⲛⲟⲟⲩ ⲛⲁⲓ ⲙⲡⲟⲩⲟⲉⲓⲛ ⲛⲛⲁⲧ-
ⲡⲁⲙⲓⲥ ⲧⲏⲣⲟⲩ ⲛⲙⲡⲏⲧⲉ ⲛⲁⲅⲅⲉⲗⲟⲥ ⲙⲛⲛⲁⲣ-
ⲭⲁⲅⲅⲉⲗⲟⲥ ⲛⲓ[ⲭⲉⲣ]ⲟⲩⲃⲓⲛ ⲙⲛⲛⲓⲍⲉ[ⲣⲁⲫⲓ]ⲛ
ⲙⲛⲛϭⲟⲙ ⲧⲏ[ⲣⲟⲩ ⲙⲙⲡⲏ]ⲧⲉ ⲛⲥⲉ[about 10 letters]
ⲉⲃ[ⲟⲗ]

P. ⲇ. ⲛⲛⲉⲧϩⲙⲡⲁϩⲏⲧ ⲙⲛϩⲱⲃ ⲛⲓⲙ ⲉⲃⲟⲗ
ϩⲓⲧⲟⲟⲧⲟⲩ ⲉⲓⲧⲉ ⲡⲉⲑⲟⲟⲩ ⲉⲓⲧⲉ ⲡⲉⲧⲛⲁⲛⲟⲩⲩ
ϫⲉⲡⲉⲕⲣⲁⲛ ⲉⲧϣⲟⲟⲡ ⲛⲁⲓ ⲡⲃⲟⲏⲑⲟⲥ ⲙⲡⲉϩⲟⲟⲩ
ⲙⲛⲧⲉⲩϣⲏ ⲁⲧⲱⲛⲁⲓ ⲡⲱⲛⲉ ⲙⲁⲣⲉϥⲡⲱⲱⲛⲉ
ⲙⲁⲣⲉϥⲡⲱϩ ϩⲁⲧⲉϥϩⲓⲏ ⲙⲡⲓⲙⲟⲟⲩ ⲙⲡⲡⲉⲓⲛⲉϩ
ⲙⲁⲣⲉⲙⲡⲉⲛⲓⲡⲉ ⲃⲱⲗ ⲉⲃⲟⲗ ⲡⲣⲟ ⲉⲧϣⲱⲧⲙ
ⲁⲩⲱ ⲉⲧϩⲏⲡ ⲙⲁⲣⲟⲩⲟⲛ¹ ⲛⲁⲓ ⲧⲁⲭⲏ (ταχύ)
ⲛⲉϩⲟⲩⲥⲓⲁ ⲙⲡⲕⲁⲕⲉ ⲙⲁⲣⲟⲩⲁⲛⲁⲭⲱⲣⲓ ⲛⲁⲩ
ⲡⲥⲁⲃⲟⲗ ⲛⲓⲙ ⲩ̅ⲧ̅ⲥ̅ (υἱός) ⲛⲛⲓⲙ

P. ⲉ. ⲏ ⲙⲁ ⲛⲓⲙ ⲉⲧⲟⲩⲛⲁϫⲱ ⲛϩⲏⲧϥ ⲛⲧⲡⲣⲟⲥⲉⲩⲭⲏ
ϫⲉⲧⲛⲁⲟⲩⲱ ⲧⲛⲁⲧⲱⲟⲩⲛ ⲛⲛⲁⲩ ⲛϣⲱⲣⲡ ⲧⲁⲭⲟⲥ
ⲛⲧϩⲉ ϫⲉⲭⲉⲣⲉ (χαῖρε) ⲡⲉⲓⲱⲧ ⲛⲁⲅⲁⲑⲟⲥ ⲡⲉⲛ-
ⲧⲁϥⲧⲛⲛⲟⲟⲩ ⲛⲁⲓ ⲙⲡⲉϥⲁⲅⲅⲉⲗⲟⲥ ⲅⲁⲃⲣⲓⲏⲗ
ⲁϥⲉⲓⲛⲉ ⲙⲡϣⲉⲙⲛⲟⲩⲃⲉ ⲛⲁⲓ ϫⲉⲭⲉ² ⲡⲉⲑⲣⲟⲛⲟⲥ
ⲙⲡⲉⲟⲟⲩ ⲉⲧⲉϥϩⲙⲟⲟⲥ ϩⲓϫⲱϥ ⲭⲁⲓⲣⲉ ⲧⲉϭⲣⲏⲡⲉ
[ⲉ]ⲧϩⲓϫⲛⲧⲉϥⲁ[ⲡⲉ 2 or 3 letters]ⲧϣ ⲭⲁⲓⲣⲉ

P. ⲋ. ⲡⲥⲁϣϥ ⲛⲣⲁⲛ ⲉⲧϩⲏⲡ ⲛϩⲏⲧϥ ⲉⲧⲉⲛⲁⲓⲡⲉ
ⲁⲉⲏ[ⲓ]ⲟⲩⲱ ⲭⲁⲓⲣⲉ ⲡⲥⲁϣϥ ⲛⲕⲁⲧⲁⲡⲉⲧⲁⲥⲙⲁ
ⲉϥⲥⲏⲣ ⲉⲧⲉϥⲥⲕⲏⲛⲏ (σκηνή) ⲉⲧⲟⲩⲁⲁⲃ ⲭⲁⲓⲣⲉ
ⲡⲥⲁϣϥ ⲛⲥⲧⲗⲗⲟⲥ (στῦλος) ⲉⲧⲁϩⲉⲣⲁⲧⲟⲩ ϩⲓϫⲱϥ
ⲭⲁⲓⲣⲉ ⲡϣⲟⲣⲡ ⲛϣⲁϫⲉ ⲛⲧⲁϥⲉⲓ ⲉⲃⲟⲗ ϩⲣⲟϥ
ⲙⲡⲉⲓⲱⲧ ⲁϥϫⲟⲟⲩ ⲛⲅⲁⲃⲣⲓⲏⲗ ϫⲉⲁϫⲓⲥ ⲙⲙⲁⲣⲓⲁ.

P. ⲍ. ϫⲉⲉⲓⲥ·ⲡⲁϣⲏⲣⲉ ⲛⲏⲩ ϣⲁⲣⲟ ⲭⲁⲓⲣⲉ ⲡⲁϣⲏⲣⲉ
ⲙⲙⲉⲣⲓⲧ ⲭⲁⲓⲣⲉ ⲡⲣⲣⲟ ⲙⲙⲉ ⲭⲁⲓⲣⲉ ⲡϣⲉⲣⲡⲙⲙⲓⲥⲉ ⲙⲡⲉϥⲉⲓⲱⲧ ⲁⲩⲱ ⲡϣⲉⲣⲡⲙⲙⲓⲥⲉ ⲛϩⲏⲧ
ⲭⲁⲓⲣⲉ ⲡⲓⲑⲣⲟⲛⲟⲥ ⲉⲧⲉϥϩⲙⲟⲟⲥ ϩⲓϫⲱϥ ϩⲓⲧⲟⲩ-

---

¹ For ⲙⲁⲣⲟⲩⲟⲩⲟⲛ.   ² For ⲭⲉⲣⲉ.

ⲛⲁⲙ ⲙ̅ⲡⲉϥⲉⲓⲱⲧ ⲭⲁⲓⲣⲉ ⲧⲧⲁⲡⲣⲟ ⲛ̅ⲧⲁⲥ-
ⲭⲓⲉⲣⲱⲧⲉ ⲟⲛ̅ⲡⲁⲉⲕⲓⲃⲉ ⲙⲡⲁⲣⲑⲉⲛⲓⲕⲟⲛ ⲭⲁⲓⲣⲉ
ⲧⲟ̄ⲓⲝ ⲛ̅ⲧⲁⲥⲡⲗⲁⲥⲥⲉ ⲛⲁⲁⲙ ⲡⲡⲉⲓⲱⲧ ⲭⲁⲓⲣⲉ
ⲛⲟⲧⲉ-

Ρ. ⲏ̅. ⲣⲏⲧⲉ ⲛ̅ⲧⲁⲙⲟⲟϣⲉ ⲟⲙ̅ⲡⲡⲁⲣⲁⲍⲓⲥⲟⲥ ⲛⲟⲁⲟ
ⲛⲥⲟⲡ ⲭⲁⲓⲣⲉ ⲡⲗⲟⲅⲟⲥ ⲡⲓⲱⲧ [1] ⲟⲉⲛⲟⲩⲙⲉ ⲭⲁⲓⲣⲉ
ⲡⲛ̅ⲧⲁϥⲭⲟⲥ ⲛⲁⲓ ⲭⲉⲁⲓⲧⲉⲓ (αἰτεῖν) ⲙⲙⲟ[ⲓ] ⲱ
ⲧⲁⲙⲙⲁⲧ ⲙ̅ⲡⲉⲧⲣⲟⲩϣϥ [2] ⲧⲁⲧⲁⲁϥ ⲡⲉ ⲁⲓⲁⲓ†
ⲛ̅†ⲡⲣⲟⲥⲉⲧⲭⲏ ⲭⲉⲕⲁⲥ ⲣⲧⲁⲗⲟ⳿ [3] ⲛ̅ⲛⲉⲧϣⲱⲛⲉ
ⲛⲟⲏⲧⲥ ⲙ̅ⲡⲉⲧⲥⲣⲙ [4] ⲙ̅ⲡⲉⲧⲣ̅ⲟⲣⲟⲟ ⲟⲛ̅ⲛⲉϣ-
ⲧⲉⲕⲟ ⲙ̅ⲛⲟⲩⲟⲛ ⲛⲓⲙ ⲉⲧⲟⲗⲓⲃⲉ (θλίβειν) ⲟⲛ̅ⲛⲉⲡⲛ̅ⲁ
ⲛⲁⲕⲁⲑⲁⲣⲧⲟⲛ ⲛ̅ⲅⲃⲱϣ ⲛⲁⲛ ⲛⲁⲓ

Ρ. ⲑ̅. ⲍⲉ ⲉⲥⲭⲱ ⲙ̅ⲙⲟⲟⲩ ⲛ̅ϭⲓ ⲧⲡⲁⲣⲑⲉⲛⲟⲥ ⲁⲥϭⲱϣⲧ
ⲟⲓⲟⲩⲛⲁⲙ ⲙ̅ⲙⲟⲥ ⲉⲥⲛⲁⲧ ⲉⲙⲓⲭⲁⲏⲗ ⲙ̅ⲛ̅ⲧⲁⲃ-
ⲣⲓⲏⲗ ⲟⲓⲟⲃⲟⲩⲣ ⲙ̅ⲙⲟⲥ ⲁⲥϣⲧⲟⲣⲧⲣ̅ ⲛ̅ⲧⲉⲩⲛⲟⲩ
ⲡⲉⲭⲉ ⲅⲁⲃⲣⲓⲏⲗ ⲛⲁⲥ ⲭⲉⲙ̅ⲡⲣ̅ⲟⲟⲧⲉ ⲱ ⲙⲁⲣⲓⲁ
ⲁⲛⲟⲕⲡⲉ ⲅⲁⲃⲣⲓⲏⲗ ⲡⲉⲛⲧⲁϥⲉⲓⲛⲉ ⲡ̅ϣ̅ⲙ̅ⲛⲟⲩⲃⲉ
ⲙ̅ⲡⲟⲩⲣⲏⲛⲉ [5] ⲛ̅ⲧⲁⲉⲓ ϣⲁⲣⲱ ⲧⲁⲭⲱⲕ ⲉⲃⲟⲗ
ⲙ̅ⲡⲟⲩⲁⲓⲧⲏⲙⲁ ⲙ̅ⲡⲉⲧⲣ̅ϣⲓⲛⲉ ⲛ̅ⲥⲱϥ ⲡⲉⲭⲉ
ⲙⲁⲣⲓⲁ ⲭⲉⲛⲓⲙ̅ⲡⲉ ⲡⲁⲓ ⲉⲧⲉⲣⲉⲡⲉⲟⲣⲁⲃⲧⲟⲥ
(ῥάβδος) ⲛ̅ⲛⲟⲃ [6] ⲉⲟⲛ̅ⲧⲉϥϭⲓⲭ ⲡⲉⲭⲁϥ ⲛⲁⲥ
ⲭⲉⲛⲁⲓⲡⲉ ⲙⲓⲭⲁⲏⲗ ⲛ̅ⲛⲟϭ ⲟⲛ̅ⲧⲁⲛⲕⲉⲗⲕⲉ
(ἀγέλη ?) [7] ⲧⲏⲣⲥ ⲛ̅ⲛⲁⲅⲅⲉⲗⲟⲥ ⲛ̅ⲧⲟⲥ ⲍⲉ

Ρ. ⲓ̅. ⲁⲥϭⲓ ⲛⲁⲥ ⲛⲟⲩⲥⲙⲏ ⲉⲥⲟⲟⲗϭ ⲡⲉⲭⲁⲥ ⲭⲉ[†]ⲧⲁⲣⲕⲟ
ⲙⲙⲟⲕ ⲙ̅ⲡⲟⲟⲩ ⲙⲓⲭⲁⲏⲗ †ⲱⲣⲕ ⲉⲣⲟⲕ
ⲙ̅ⲡⲁϣⲏⲣⲉ ⲡⲉⲛⲧⲁϥϥⲓ ⲙ̅ⲡⲉⲟⲣⲁⲃⲧⲟⲥ ⲟⲛ̅ⲧϭⲓⲭ

---

[1] For ⲙ̅ⲡⲉⲓⲱⲧ.   [2] For ⲟⲩⲱϣϥ.

[3] For ⲉⲣⲉⲣⲧⲁⲗϭⲟ.   [4] For ⲥⲟⲣⲙ.

[5] ? For ⲙ̅ⲡⲟⲩⲉⲓⲣⲏⲛⲏ.   [6] For ⲛⲟⲩⲃ.

[7] Or ἀγγελική. Cf. BUDGE, *St. Michael*, 116, where †ⲁⲅⲅⲉⲗⲓ
ⲧⲏⲣⲥ = جميع اسكر الملائكة (v. Guidi in *L'Oriente* II, 83).

ⲙⲙⲁⲥⲧⲏⲙⲁ¹ ⲁⲩⲧⲁϥ ⲉⲧⲟⲟⲧⲕ ⲁⲩⲕⲱ ⲛϩⲏⲧⲕ
ⲛⲟⲩⲣⲁⲛ ⲛⲥⲟⲉⲓⲧ ϯⲱⲣⲕ ⲇⲉ ⲉⲣⲟⲕ ⲁⲩⲱ ϯⲉⲓⲣⲉ
ⲙⲙⲟⲕ ⲛⲣⲧⲙⲉϩⲉ ⲁⲛ ϣⲁⲛⲧⲉⲕϫⲱⲕ ⲛⲁⲓ ⲉⲃⲟⲗ
ⲛⲛⲁⲡⲟⲗⲟⲅⲓⲁ ⲧⲏⲣⲟⲩ ⲙⲡⲁⲗⲁⲥ ⲉⲧⲉⲡⲓⲙⲟⲟⲩ ⲡⲁⲓ
ⲙⲛⲡⲓⲛⲉϩ, ⲛⲁⲓ ⲉⲧⲕⲏ ϩⲣⲁⲓ ⲙⲡⲁⲙⲧⲟ ⲉⲃⲟⲗ
ⲉϥⲉϣⲱⲡⲉ ⲛⲧⲁⲗϭⲟ ϩ[ⲛ about 9 letters]

P. ⲓ̄ⲁ̄. ⲛⲛⲓⲙ ⲧ̄ⲥ̄ (υἱός) ⲛⲓⲙ ⲉϥⲟ ⲛⲑⲉ ⲛⲟⲩⲕⲉⲛⲏ (καινή)
ϩⲛⲡⲉϥⲕⲉⲉⲥ ⲉϥϥⲓ ⲉⲃⲟⲗ ⲙⲙⲟϥ ⲛϣⲱⲡⲉ ⲛⲓⲙ
ϩⲓϩⲓⲥⲉ ⲛⲓⲙ ϩⲓⲗⲟϭⲗⲉϭ² ⲛⲓⲙ ϩⲓⲉⲡⲓⲃⲟⲩⲗⲉⲧⲉ
(ἐπιβουλή?) ⲛⲓⲙ ⲛⲧⲉ ⲡⲁⲛⲇⲓⲕⲓⲙⲉⲛⲟⲥ (ἀντικεί-
μενος)³ ⲙⲁⲣⲟⲩⲁⲛⲁⲭⲱⲣⲓ ⲛⲁⲩ ⲛⲥⲁⲃⲟⲗ ⲛⲟⲩⲟⲛ
ⲛⲓⲙ ⲉⲧⲛⲁϫⲱⲕⲙ ϩⲙⲡⲓⲙⲟⲟⲩ ⲙⲡⲛⲓⲛⲉϩ,
ϩⲓⲧⲛⲧϭⲟⲙ ⲡⲛⲟⲩⲧⲉ⁴ ⲡⲉⲓⲱⲧ ⲡⲡⲁⲛⲧⲟⲕⲣⲁⲧⲱⲣ
ⲙⲁⲣⲟⲩⲥⲁϩⲟⲟⲩ ⲉⲃⲟⲗ ⲙⲙⲟϥ ⲛϭⲓ ⲡ̄ⲛ̄ⲁ̄ ⲛⲓⲙ
ⲛⲁⲕⲁⲑⲁⲣⲧⲟⲛ ⲉⲧⲉⲡⲟⲩⲁⲡⲟⲩⲁ ⲃⲱⲕ ⲉⲡⲉϥⲙⲁ
ϩⲓⲧⲛⲧϭⲟⲙ ⲛⲧⲛⲡⲣⲟⲥⲉⲩⲭⲏ ⲉⲧⲟⲩⲁⲁⲃ

P. ⲓ̄ⲃ̄. ϯⲧⲁⲣⲕⲟ ⲙⲙⲟⲕ ϩⲟⲕ ⲱ ⲅⲁⲃⲣⲓⲏⲗ ⲡⲛⲧⲁϥ-
ⲛϣⲙⲛⲟⲩϥⲉ ⲛⲁⲓ ⲛⲧϭⲛϣⲩⲡⲟ⁵ ⲙⲡⲁϣⲏⲣⲉ
ϯⲧⲁⲣⲕⲟ ⲙⲙⲟⲕ ⲁⲩⲱ ϯⲱⲣⲕ ⲙⲙⲟⲕ ⲁⲩⲱ ⲉⲓⲉⲓⲣⲉ
ⲙⲙⲟⲕ ⲛⲣⲉⲙϩ[ⲉ ⲁ]ⲛ ϣⲁⲛⲧⲉⲕϫⲱⲕ ⲛⲁⲓ ⲉⲃⲟⲗ
ⲛⲛⲁⲁⲡⲟⲗⲟⲅⲓⲁ ⲧⲏⲣⲟⲩ ⲙⲡⲁⲗⲁⲥ ϫⲉⲕⲁⲥ ϩⲛⲧⲉⲧ-
ⲛⲟⲩ ⲉⲧⲛⲁϫⲱⲕⲙ ϩⲙⲡⲓⲙⲟⲟⲩ ⲙⲡⲛⲓⲛⲉϩ, ⲁⲛⲟⲕ
ⲛⲓⲙ ⲧ̄ⲥ̄ (υἱός) ⲛⲛⲓⲙ ⲧⲱⲕⲙ ⲛⲧⲉϥⲥⲛϥⲉ ⲉⲥⲧⲏⲙ
ⲉⲥⲧⲱⲕⲓ (διώκειν) ⲛⲥⲁⲇⲓⲙⲱⲛⲓⲟⲛ ϩⲙⲡⲙⲁ

---

¹ = מַשְׂטֵמָה v. Dillm. Lex. 177, ⲙⲏ̄ⲧ̄ⲟ̄. Occurs as the name of one of
the chiefs of the evil angels in the *Bk. of Jubilees.* Cf. Rönsch, *B. der Jub.* 107,
418. The Greek form is Μαστιφάτ or Μανσημάτ. The Latin, Mastima. The
Ethiop. text appears, according to Basset and the only MS. I have seen (Brit.
Mus. *Or.* 564, f. 20b), to substitute ⲍⲛ̄ⲗ ⲗⲛ̄ⲧ̄ *the Evil doer,* while the
Arabic has باغض الخيرات الذى هو الشيطان.

² = ⲗⲟⲭⲗⲉⲭ, v. Peyr. *Lex.* 85.

³ Cf. a Berlin papyrus, *A.Z.* xxxiii, 44.

⁴ For ⲙⲡⲛⲟⲩⲧⲉ.   ⁵ For ϭⲓⲛϫⲡⲟ.

ⲉⲧϣⲟⲟⲡ ⲛϩⲏⲧϥ ⲧⲏⲩ[1] ⲉⲣⲑⲉ ⲛⲟⲩϣⲟⲉⲓϣ ⲛ[ⲕ]ⲁϩ
ⲛⲟⲩⲧⲏⲧ ⲧⲱⲣⲕ ⲉⲣⲟⲕ ⲙⲡⲟⲩ ⲛⲓⲃⲧ ⲛⲧⲁϩⲟⲩ[2]
ⲉⲡⲉⲕⲥⲱⲙⲁ ⲉⲧⲟⲩⲁⲁⲃ ϩⲓⲡⲉⲥϯⲟ̄ⲥ̄ (σταυρός)
ⲭⲉⲕⲁⲥ ⲉⲕⲉⲭⲟⲟ[ⲩ 1 or 2 letters] ⲛ [11 or 12 letters]

P. ⲓ̄ⲍ̄. ⲛⲁⲅⲅⲉⲗⲟⲥ ⲛⲥⲉⲁϩⲉⲣⲁⲧⲟⲩ ⲛⲙⲙⲁⲓ ϣⲁⲧⲉ[3]
ⲡⲉⲧϩⲙⲡⲁϩⲏⲧ ⲭⲱⲕ ⲉⲃⲟⲗ ⲉⲧⲉⲡⲓⲙⲟⲟⲩ ⲡⲁⲓ
ⲙⲛⲡⲓⲛⲉϩ ⲉⲧⲕⲏ ϩⲣⲁⲓ ⲙⲡⲁⲙⲧⲟ ⲉⲃⲟⲗ ⲙⲁⲣⲉϥ-
                                                          sic
ϣⲱⲡⲉ ⲛⲟⲩⲙⲟⲟⲩ ⲛⲧⲁⲗϭⲟ ϩⲙⲡⲥⲱⲙⲁ ⲛⲛⲓⲙ
ⲭⲉⲕⲁⲥ ϩⲛⲧⲉⲩⲛⲟⲩ ⲉϥϣⲁⲛⲭⲱⲕⲙ ⲛϩⲏⲧϥ
                                          sic
ⲛⲥⲉⲡⲱⲧ ⲙⲙⲟϥ ⲛϭⲓ ⲡⲛ̄ⲁ̄ ⲛⲓⲙ ⲛⲛⲁⲕⲁⲑⲁⲣⲧⲟⲛ
ⲁⲩⲱ ⲉϣⲱⲡⲉ ⲁⲩⲣϩⲱⲃ ⲉⲣⲟϥ ⲙⲁⲣⲉϥⲕⲧⲟϥ
ⲉⲭⲛⲧⲁⲡⲏ ⲙⲡⲉⲛⲧⲁϥⲥϩⲁⲓⲥⲟⲩ ϩⲓⲧⲉⲧϭⲟⲙ
ⲙⲡⲉⲕⲣⲁⲛ ⲭⲱⲣⲉ ⲓ̄ⲥ̄ ⲡⲉⲭ̄ⲥ̄ ⲡⲁϣⲏⲣⲉ ⲙⲙⲉⲣⲓⲧ
     sic
ⲙⲁⲣⲉⲛⲓⲙ ⲧ̄ⲥ̄ ⲛⲡⲛⲓⲙ ϣⲱⲡⲉ ⲉϥⲉⲧϩⲁⲛ[ⲉ](αὐξάνειν)
                                              ?
ⲙⲉⲛⲧⲉϥⲯⲩⲭⲏ ⲙⲛⲡⲉ [1 or 2 letters] ⲛⲉϥⲣⲟⲉ
ⲙⲡⲉϩⲟⲟⲩ ⲛⲧⲁⲩⲭⲡⲟϥ ⲛϩⲏⲧϥ ⲭⲉⲁⲛⲟⲕⲡⲉ
ⲙⲁⲣⲓⲁ ⲧⲉⲕⲙⲁⲩ ⲉⲓⲡⲁⲣⲁⲕⲁⲗⲉⲓ ⲙⲙⲟⲕ ⲓ̄ⲥ̄
[ⲡ]ⲁϣⲏⲣⲉ ⲁⲩ[9 or 10 letters]ⲉ ϯⲧ [8 or 9 letters].

P. ⲕ̄. ["No one knows this prayer except] me and my Father
and the Holy Spirit. Alpha is my name; the name of my Father
is Arôa Daniel;[4] the name of the Holy Spirit, the Comforter —?
We are in one divinity, according to the command of my Father
and the Holy Spirit. I send (*lit.* give) thee Maria, my mother, that
those that are in prison may come forth."

---

[1] ? For [ⲛ]ⲧⲉⲩ-, a rare form of Sa'id. conjunctive.

[2] For ? ⲛⲧⲁⲩⲧⲟⲕⲥⲟⲩ.   [3] For ϣⲁⲛⲧⲉ.

[4] *Cf.* F. Rossi, *Trattato Gnostico* (Mem. Acad. Torino, ser. II, xliii),
f. 17, where in certain mystical, "holy names of the Father" the name
Daniel is declared to be hidden; ⲡⲁⲓ ⲉⲣⲉⲁⲁⲛⲓⲏⲗ ϩⲏⲡ ⲛϩⲏⲧϥ
(*l.* ϩⲏⲧⲟⲩ). The Eth. and Ar. versions have Ala and Ô for the Father's,
Arâdyâl for the Holy Spirit's name. Perhaps therefore read ⲱ ⲁⲣⲁⲁⲛⲓⲏⲗ.

Then (δέ) Maria stood and stretched forth her hands [to] the
eastern side, while her eyes were turned toward heaven, to her
beloved son . . . . (p. Ῑ) and she said, "I am Mariham (Μαριάμ),[1]
I am Maria, I am the mother of the Life of the whole World! I cry
aloud to Thee, my God and my Son and my Beloved and my King,
I Maria, Thy mother, do cry aloud to Thee, that Thou mayst hear
my voice and send to me the light of all the powers of heaven, the
angels and the archangels, the Cherubim and the Seraphim and all
the host of heaven and that they [may fulfil for me all things] (p. Λ̄)
that are in my heart and everything by their means, whether evil or
good. For Thy name it is that is my helper by day and night.
Adonai! Let the stone be overturned, let it break before this water
and this oil! Let the irons be loosed (or melted) from the door
closed and hidden; let them open forthwith to me! Let the powers
depart from NN., the son of NN. (p. Ē) or any place in which this
prayer shall be said; for I will arise[2] early and will say thus; Hail
to the good Father, who sent His angel Gabriel to me and brought
me the good tidings. Hail to the throne of glory on which He sits.
Hail to the diadem which is upon His . . . . head (?). Hail to
the (p. Ϛ̄) seven secret names that are hidden in it, namely
ΑΕΗ[Ι]ΟΤΩ. Hail to the seven veils that are spread upon His
holy tabernacle. Hail to the seven pillars that stand by it (?). Hail
to the first word that came forth from the Father's mouth[3] (as) He
sent Gabriel saying, 'Say to Maria, lo, my son cometh to thee.'
Hail, my beloved Son. Hail, true king. Hail to the first-born of
His Father and the first-born of my womb. Hail to the throne on
which He sits at the right hand of His Father. Hail to the mouth
that took milk from my virgin breasts. Hail to the hand that
formed Adam, our father. Hail to the feet (p. Ῡ) that often walked
in Paradise. Hail to the true Word [of] the Father. Hail to Him
that said to me, 'Ask of Me, oh! My mother, what thou wouldest
and I will give it thee. I have given this prayer that thou mightest
heal by it the sick and those that are gone astray and that are
wretched in the prisons and everyone that is tormented by unclean
spirits.' Relieve us!"[4] (p. Θ̄) But as the Virgin said these [words],

---

[1] A form of the name frequent in the *Pist. Soph.* and *Pap. Bruce.*
[2] *Lit.* I will have already arisen.   [3] *Cf.* Rossi, *l.c.*, f. 14.
[4] *Lit.* conjunctive, apparently after 'Hail,' with ethic dative.

she looked upon her right hand and seeing Michael and Gabriel
upon her left, forthwith was affrighted.   Gabriel said to her, " Fear
not, oh, Maria ! I am Gabriel that brought the good tidings of thy
peace(?), and that came to thee and fulfilled thy request and that
for which thou didst ask."   Maria said to him, "Who is this in
whose hand is the golden staff?"   He said to her, "This is
Michael, the greatest in the whole host of angels."   Then ($\delta\epsilon$) she
(p. $\overline{\iota}$) raised (*lit.* took) a sweet voice and said, " I conjure thee this
day, Michael, and adjure thee by my Son, who took the staff from
the hand of Mastema and gave it to thee and gave thee a famous
name; I conjure thee and will not release thee till thou fulfil for
me all the incantations[1] of my tongue, namely, this water and
this oil that are before me; that they may be for healing in
[the body?] (p. $\overline{\iota\alpha}$) of NN., the son of NN., that he may be as
new in his bones, removing from him every sickness and every
trouble and every infirmity and every plot of the Adversary.   Let
them depart from every one who shall wash in this water and
this oil, through the power of God Almighty.   Let there retire
from him every unclean spirit, each one going to his place through
the might of our holy prayer.   (P. $\overline{\iota\beta}$) I conjure thee, too, Gabriel,
that brought me the good tidings of the birth of my son ; I conjure
thee and adjure thee and will not release thee till thou fulfil for
me all the incantations of my tongue, so that in the hour in which
I shall wash in this water and this oil, I NN., the son of NN. [thou
mayst ?] draw thy (?) sharp sword[2] which pursues the demons in
the place where they are, so that they (?) become like dust of the
earth [in ?] a wind.   I adjure Thee by the five nails that were
fixed in Thy holy body upon the cross, that Thou send [me a
host ?] of (p. $\overline{\iota\gamma}$) angels, that they may stand with me until what is in
my heart be fulfilled, namely this water and this oil that lie in my
presence.   Let them (*MS.* it) become a water of healing in the body
of NN., that in the hour in which he shall wash in it, every unclean
spirit may flee from him, and if he is being (magically) practised

---

[1] Or "charms." Ἀπολογία is a Gnostic term for the phrases, generally ἐφέσια
γράμματα, by the potency of which the supernatural powers could be compelled.
v. Pap. Bruce, ed. C. Schmidt, pp. 127, 215, 478, etc., also *Pist. Soph.,* 291, etc.
This, no doubt, is also the meaning of ⲁⲡⲟⲗⲟ/, so frequent in Rossi's *Trattato,*
and which Amélineau (*Nouv. traité gnost.,* p. 11) does not explain. ⲭⲱⲕ
ⲉⲃⲟⲗ must here mean " conform to."

[2] *Cf. A.Z.* xxxiv, 87.

upon, let it (*i.e.* the spirit) return upon the head of him that invoked
(? *lit.* wrote) it (*lit.* them),[1] through the might of Thy strong name,
Jesus the Christ, my beloved son. Let NN., the son of NN.,
increase in (?) his soul and [his ——?] and become as on the day
on which he was born. For I am Maria, Thy mother. I call upon
Thee, Jesus, my son and (?) . . . ."

II. *Fragment of a Patriarchal History.*

The earlier text with which all six leaves were covered is written
in two columns, in a small sloping hand, of Zoega's 9th class. It is
probably therefore of no great age.

My attention was first attracted by the name of "the Bishop
Zoilus," which shows that the texts relate to that obscure period of
the Monophysite struggle during which Justinian had attempted,
by the deposition of the intractable Jacobite Theodosius[2] and the
appointment of Paul,[3] to restore the Catholic predominance in the
distracted church of Alexandria. Paul's tenure of office was
however short, and in 541 he too was deposed by a synod at Gaza
and succeeded by Zoilus,[4] the Jacobite majority still regarding the
exiled Theodosius as their true patriarch.

What our MS. offers is far too meagre to, be of much assistance
in clearing up obscurities. Most of such sentences as can be
consecutively deciphered are cast in the 1st pers. pl., and appear to
address now one, now several hearers. Of narrative passages almost
nothing remains. Some 30 lines can be counted in the best
preserved pages, with the lower, but never the upper margins. The
speeches which occur are signalized by quotation-marks at each line.
The lacunæ are of too uncertain size to be exactly measured, and
the dots here printed bear no relation to their extent. The readings

---

[1] A tentative translation. The pronouns appear to be confused.

[2] M. Revillout promised a Life of Theodosius years ago (*v. Les Blemmyes* 66),
but has not as yet published it.

[3] There is a confusion in the Arabic texts between Paul of Tanis and of
Tabennese. Those of Severus in the Brit. Mus. (*Or.* 26100, ff. 46, 47 and *Or.*
1338, ff. 49, 50) show complete uncertainty. John of Nikiou (transl. p. 516) has
clearly Tabennese. Eutychius has merely "Paul."

[4] Of Zoilus nothing is known. He came, according to John of Nikiou
(p. 282), from "the town of አክላኝያ" 'Āklanyā. The continuator of
Zacharias Rhetor (Land, *Anecd.* III, 316) calls him a monk, ‏ܐܠ ܝܡܝܢ‎,
whom the members of the Gaza Synod brought from Palestine to Alexandria.
I owe this reference to Mr. E. W. Brooks.

and restitutions are often most questionable. The pages are here indicated by the numbers which they bear referring to the later text (no. I *above*). As to their sequence only so much can be said: that the pairs $\overline{\text{B}}$, $\overline{\text{IΓ}}$ and $\overline{\text{Γ}}$, $\overline{\text{IB}}$; $\overline{\text{IΔ}}$, $\overline{\text{Δ}}$ and $\overline{\text{I}}$, $\overline{\text{E}}$; $\overline{\text{Γ}}$, $\overline{\text{θ}}$ and $\overline{\text{Z}}$, $\overline{\text{H}}$ are in each case *Recto* and *Verso* of a single fol. ; though it may be difficult to decide which are the *Rectos*, which the *Versos*.

A. Pp. $\overline{\text{Γ}}$, $\overline{\text{θ}}$. . . . . ⲟⲩⲫⲁⲛⲧⲁ[ⲥⲓⲁ ⲁⲛ] ⲁⲗⲗⲁ ⲕⲁⲛ
ⲉⲛϣⲁⲛ[ⲙⲟ]ⲩⲧⲉ [ⲉⲣ]ⲟ[ϥ] ⲭⲉⲣⲉϥ[ϣ]ⲙ̅ϣⲉⲉⲓⲇⲱ-
ⲗⲟⲛ ⲡⲉⲓⲉⲧⲟⲩⲙⲉ ⲡⲉⲧⲛϫⲱ [ⲙ̅]ⲙⲟϥ ⲛⲑⲉ ⲅⲁⲣ
ⲛⲛⲉ[ⲧ]ⲙⲙⲁⲩ ⲉⲁⲩⲉⲣⲁⲧⲥⲟ[ⲟⲩ[ⲛ ⲉⲧⲇⲱⲣⲓⲁ
ⲙⲡⲛ[ⲟⲩ]ⲧⲉ . . . . ⲁⲩ[ϣⲙ̅]ϣⲉ ⲛⲛϩⲓⲕⲱⲛ ⲛⲁⲓ-
ⲙⲟⲛⲓⲟⲛ ⲁⲩ[ⲟⲩ]ⲱϣⲧ ⲙⲡⲥⲱⲟⲩⲧ(? ⲥⲱⲛⲧ) ⲛ . . . .
[ⲛⲧⲉ]ⲓϩⲉ ϩⲱⲱⲕ [ⲙ̅]ⲡⲉⲕⲡⲓⲥⲧⲉⲩⲉ ⲉⲧⲙⲛⲧ-
[ⲛⲟ]ⲩⲧⲉ ⲙⲡⲙⲟⲛⲟⲅⲉ[ⲛ]ⲏⲥ ⲉⲁϥⲣⲥⲁⲣⲝ ⲕⲁ . ⲛⲁ
. . . [ⲉϥ]ⲟⲩⲱⲛϩ ⲉⲃⲟⲗ ⲛⲧ[ⲙ̅]ⲛⲧⲟⲩⲁ ⲛⲧⲉⲧⲣⲓⲁⲥ
[ⲉ]ⲧⲟⲩⲁⲁⲃ ⲁⲩⲱ ⲁ . . . . ⲧⲁ ⲙⲙⲟⲕ ⲛⲣⲉϥ[ϣⲙ̅]-
ϣⲉⲣⲱⲙⲉ ⲁⲩⲱ [ⲛ]ⲣⲉϥϣⲙ̅ϣⲉⲛⲟⲩⲧⲉ [ⲁ]ⲛ
ϩⲓⲧⲙ̅ⲛ . . . . ⲡⲉⲭ̅ⲥ̅ [ⲡⲗ]ⲟⲅⲟⲥ ⲙⲡⲛⲟⲩⲧⲉ
ⲙⲛ[ⲧⲉ]ϥⲙⲛⲧⲟⲩⲁ ⲛⲁⲧϣⲁ[ϫⲉ] ⲉⲣⲟⲥ[1] ϩⲣⲁⲓ
ⲛϩⲏⲧⲥ (*margin*) (*col.* 2) . . . . ⲡⲉⲧⲛⲙⲉⲩⲉ ⲉⲡⲉⲭ̅ⲣ̅ⲥ̅
ⲓ̅ⲥ̅ ⲡ[ⲙⲟⲛⲟ]ⲅⲉⲛⲏⲥ ⲛϣⲏ[ⲣⲉ] ⲛⲧⲉ ⲡⲛⲟⲩⲧⲉ ⲡⲁ[ⲓ]
ⲉⲧⲛⲟⲩⲱϣⲧ ⲛ[ⲁϥ] ϩⲛⲟⲩⲡⲣⲟⲥⲕⲩ[ⲛⲏ]ⲥⲓⲥ ⲛⲟⲩⲱⲧ
ⲧⲉϥⲥⲁⲝ ⲟⲩⲣ[ⲱ]ⲙⲉ ⲅⲁⲣ ⲁⲛⲡⲉ [ⲉⲁϥ]ⲙⲟⲩ
ϩⲁⲣⲟⲛ ⲕⲁ[ⲛ] ⲉⲧⲉⲧⲛⲙⲉⲩⲉ ⲉ[ⲣⲟⲥ] ⲱ ⲛϣⲏⲣⲉ
ⲛⲛ[ⲉⲥ]ⲧⲱⲣⲓⲟⲥ ⲛϩⲟⲩⲟ ⲇ[ⲉ] ⲛϣⲏⲣⲉ ⲙⲡⲇⲓⲁⲃⲟ-
[ⲗⲟⲥ ⲁ]ⲗⲗⲁ ⲡⲗⲟ[ⲅⲟⲥ] ⲙⲡⲛ[ⲟⲩⲧ]ⲉ ⲡⲱ[ⲧ]
ⲉⲧϣⲟⲟⲡ ϩⲁⲑⲏ ⲛⲛⲉⲁⲓⲱⲛ ⲧⲏⲣ[ⲟⲩ] ⲡⲉⲛⲧⲁϥⲣ-
ⲣⲱ[ⲙⲉ] ϩⲛⲟⲩⲙⲛⲧⲁⲧ[ⲛⲟ]ⲃⲉ ⲁϥⲣⲣⲱⲙ[ⲉ]
ϩⲛⲟⲩϫⲱⲕ ⲉ[ⲃⲟⲗ] ϩⲛⲟⲩⲡⲛⲁ̅ ⲉϥ[ⲟ] ϩⲙⲙⲁⲣⲓⲁ
ⲧⲉ[ⲡⲁⲣ]ⲑⲉⲛⲟⲥ ⲉⲧⲟⲩⲁⲁ[ⲃ] ⲉⲧⲧⲁⲓⲏⲩ ϣⲁ[ⲉⲛⲉϩ]
ⲁϥϯ ϩⲓⲱⲱϥ [ⲙ̅ⲡ]ⲉⲓⲛ[ⲉ] (*margin*).

" . . . . is no phantasm. And even if we call thee (?) idolater, it is truth that we speak. For like as those, knowing not the gift

---

[1] As in Zoega 605 *inf.*

of God[1] .... served the images of demons[2] and worshipped the creature (?)[3] .... so too thou hast not believed on the Godhead of the only-begotten (Son), who became flesh ...., revealing the unity of the holy Trinity, and .... thee a worshipper of man and not of God through .... the Christ, the Word of God, and His ineffable unity .... that we think of the Christ, Jesus, the only-begotten Son of God, whom we worship in a single adoration (προσκύνησις). For His flesh is not man who (?) died for us, even if ye think it (?), oh, ye children of Nestorius, nay more, children of the Devil! But (He is) the Word of God the Father, who was before all worlds, who became man in sinlessness, and became a perfect man, by (?) a spirit which was in Mary the Virgin, holy and honourable for ever, and took on Himself the likeness .... ”

Pp. $\overline{\zeta}$, $\overline{\text{н}}$, col. I, mostly illegible. The words ⲛⲙⲙⲙⲁⲕ "with thee," ⲛⲁⲛ "to us," are discernible; further on, the important phrase ⲓⲟⲩⲇⲁⲥ ⲛⲃ̅ⲣⲣⲉ "New Judas," يودس الجديد whence we have a clue to the events with which this part at least of the text is concerned. For Severus relates[4] that this was the name given by the hostile Alexandrians to Justinian's nominee, Paul. The foregoing words make it likely that we have here the reproaches or defiance addressed by the people (or perhaps clergy) to Paul, and this may explain also what we read on pp. $\overline{\text{ⲧ}}$, $\overline{\text{ⲑ}}$, where the speakers clearly contrast their (Jacobite) orthodoxy with the heresy of the person they address. Col. II seems also to be in the 1st pers. pl. In it occurs the word ⲛⲕⲁⲗⲭⲓⲧⲟⲛ .... "of Chalcedon."

B. Pp. $\overline{\text{ⲓⲁ}}$, $\overline{\text{ⲗ}}$. .... [ⲟ]ⲧⲙⲁⲛϩⲁⲣⲉϩ ⲁⲧⲱ ϣⲁⲧⲛⲁⲧ
ⲡⲭⲟⲉⲓⲥ ⲕⲛⲁⲛⲟⲩϭⲥ ⲉⲣⲟⲛ ϣⲁⲃⲟⲗ ⲡⲉⲕϭⲱⲛⲧ
ⲛⲁⲙⲟⲩϩ ⲛⲑⲉ ⲛⲟⲩⲕⲱϩⲧ ⲡⲱϩⲧ ⲛⲧⲉⲕⲟⲣⲅⲏ
ⲉⲭⲛⲛϩⲉⲑⲛⲟⲥ ⲉⲧⲉⲙⲛ[ⲟ]ⲩⲥⲟⲩⲱⲛⲅ ⲁⲧⲱ [ⲉ]ⲭⲛ
[ⲙⲙⲛⲧⲉⲣⲟ] ⲉⲧⲉⲙⲛⲟⲩⲉⲡⲓⲕⲁⲗⲉⲓ [ⲉ]ⲡⲉⲕⲣⲁⲛ
ⲭⲉⲁⲩ [ⲟⲩⲱⲙ] ⲛⲓⲁⲕⲱⲃ [ⲁⲧⲱ] ⲁⲩⲣ [ⲡⲉϥ] ⲙⲁ
ⲛⲭⲁⲓⲉ ϩⲉⲛⲕⲟⲟⲩ[ⲉ] ⲟⲛ ⲭⲉⲁⲕⲧⲁⲁ[ⲩ ⲉ]ⲧⲟⲟⲧⲟⲩ
ⲛϩⲉ[ⲛⲣⲱⲙⲙ]ⲉ ⲛⲁⲛⲟⲙⲟⲥ [ⲛⲭⲁⲭⲉ] ⲛⲁⲡⲟⲥⲧⲁⲧⲏⲥ
ⲁⲧⲱ ⲉⲧⲟⲟⲧϥ ⲉⲛⲟⲩⲣⲣⲟ ⲛⲣⲉϥϫⲓⲛϭⲟⲛⲥ ⲁⲧⲱ

---

[1] John iv, 10. [2] Cf. Apoc. ix, 20.
[3] Cf. Rom. i, 25. [4] Renaudot, p. 141.

[ⲙ]ⲡⲟⲛⲏⲣⲟⲥ ⲡⲁⲣⲁ [ⲡ]ⲕⲁϩ ⲧⲏⲣϥ [ⲁ]ⲛⲟⲛ ⲭⲉⲗⲛ
. . . . [ⲡ]ⲭⲟⲉⲓⲥ ⲡⲁⲣⲁ ⲛ[ϩⲉⲑ]ⲛⲟⲥ ⲧⲏⲣⲟⲩ [ⲁⲩ]ⲱ
ⲧⲛⲑⲃⲃⲓⲏⲧ [ⲡⲁⲣⲁ] ⲡⲕⲁϩ ⲧⲏⲣϥ . . . ⲉⲧⲃⲉⲛⲉⲛ-
ⲛⲟⲃⲉ (margin) (col. 2) . . . . ⲟⲩⲇⲉ . . . . ⲟⲩⲇⲉ
ϣⲟⲩϩⲏⲛ[ⲉ] . . . . ⲧⲁⲗ[ⲱⲟⲩ] ⲙⲡ[ⲉⲕ]ⲙⲧⲟ ⲉⲃⲟⲗ
ⲉⲧⲣⲉⲛ . . . . ⲁⲛⲟⲛ . . . . ⲭⲉⲛⲟⲣⲑⲟⲇ[ⲟⲝ]ⲟ[ⲥ
ϩⲛ]ⲟⲩⲡⲁⲣⲏⲥⲓ[ⲁ] . . . . ⲧⲛⲛⲁ . . . . ⲙⲙⲟⲕ . . . .
ⲙⲓϣⲉ ⲙⲛⲡⲛⲟⲩⲧⲉ ⲙⲡⲙⲧⲟ . . . . ⲙⲛⲡⲣⲱⲙⲉ
ⲙⲛ[ⲡⲉϥ]ϣⲙϣⲉ ⲛⲁⲥⲉⲃⲏ[ⲥ] ⲉⲧⲟⲟⲩ ⲃ !ⲧⲉ . . . .
ⲉⲣⲟⲛ ⲁⲛ ⲉⲙⲁⲧⲉ . . . . ⲉⲑⲉⲣⲉⲥⲓⲥ ⲙⲫⲩⲥⲓⲥ ⲥⲛⲧⲉ
ⲧⲁⲓ ⲛⲧⲱⲧⲛ ⲉⲧⲉⲧⲛⲭⲟⲙ[ⲙ]ⲟⲥ (margin).

" . . . . a place to dwell in. And how long, Lord, wilt Thou
be wroth with us for ever? Shall thy fury blaze as a fire? Pour
out Thine anger upon the nations that have not known Thee and
upon the kingdoms that have not called upon Thy name; for they
have devoured Jacob, they have made his place desert.[1]   Others too
hast Thou given into the hand of lawless and apostate hostile men,
and into the hand of a King violent and wicked above all the earth.[2]
As for us, we have . . . . the Lord above all nations, and we are
humbled beyond all the earth . . . . because of our sins . . . . neither
. . . . nor incense offered (?) in Thy presence, that we may . . . . we
. . . . orthodox openly . . . . we will . . . . Thee . . . . contend with
God before . . . . with men and with their evil worship . . . . not to
us only . . . . the heresy of two natures which ye say (?) . . . . "

Pp. Ⲓ̄, Ⲉ̄.   On these nothing can be read.   The prayer of which
the above is a passage is offered by the Monophysites, probably
on account of the unsympathetic treatment they had received at the
Emperor's hands.   The last words seem however to be addressed
to the Catholics; but the reading is very doubtful.

C. Pp. Ⲃ̄, ⲓ̄ⲧ̄. Very little legible at first. . . . . ⲡⲱⲣⲭ
ⲉⲛⲉⲡⲉⲣⲏⲩ ⲭⲉⲛⲛⲉⲧⲉⲓⲙⲉ ⲉⲧⲉ! ⲡⲟⲗⲓⲥ ⲁⲩⲱ ⲡⲭⲟⲓ
                 sic
ⲛⲧⲁⲛⲉⲓ ϩⲓⲟⲩϣ ⲙⲛⲧⲁⲡⲟⲑⲏⲕⲏ !ⲧⲛ . . . . .
ⲉⲧⲟⲟⲧϥ ⲭ[ⲉ]ϩⲟⲧⲁⲛ ⲉⲕϣⲁⲛⲛⲁⲩ ⲉⲣⲟⲛ ⲉⲡⲁ-
ⲙⲁϩⲧⲉ ⲙⲡⲉⲡⲓⲥⲕⲟⲡⲟⲥ ϩⲟⲣⲟⲕ (? for ϩⲱ ⲉⲣⲟⲕ)

[1] Ps. lxxix, 5 ff.   [2] Dan iii, 32 (Song of 3 Child.).

ϣⲁⲛⲧⲛϫⲟⲟⲥ ⲛⲁⲕ ⲙⲛⲛⲥⲁⲟⲩⲕⲟⲩⲓ ϫⲉ ⲉⲧⲉⲥⲟⲩⲥⲛⲁⲩ ⲛⲉⲱⲟⲩⲧⲡⲉ ⲁϥ ⲉⲧⲥⲩⲛⲁⲝⲓⲥ ⲛϭⲓ ⲍⲱⲏⲗⲟⲥ ⲡⲉⲡⲓⲥⲕⲟⲡⲟⲥ . . . .

" . . . . separate ourselves, for they know not the (?) city and the ship upon which we embark and the store . . . . [commanded him] saying, 'When thou seest us laying hold upon the Bishop, wait (?) until we shall tell thee.'" But after a little, namely upon the 2nd of Thoth, the Bishop Zoilus went to the Synaxis . . . . "

Pp. ⲣ̄, ⲓ̄ⲃ̄.   . . . . . ϩⲉⲛⲣⲱⲙⲉ ⲛⲣⲉϥⲣⲛⲟⲃⲉ . . . . ϫⲉ ϩⲛⲧⲡⲓⲥⲧⲓⲥ ⲙⲙⲡⲉⲛϫⲟⲉⲓⲥ ⲓ̄ⲥ̄ ⲡ[ⲉⲭ̄ⲥ̄] ⲡⲁⲓ ⲛⲧⲁϥⲙⲟⲩ . . . .

"sinful men . . . . but in the faith of our Lord Jesus, the Christ, He who died . . . . "

Here the first pair of pages seems to refer to some movement for the seizure presumably of Zoilus, the Catholic patriarch. The second pair may be connected with the texts on pp. ⲓ̄ⲃ̄ ff., and should, if so, preceed pp. ⲣ̄, ⲓ̄ⲃ̄.

Would it be possible by the help of the above data—the day of the month and the celebration of the Communion,—to fix the year for these events?

The next Meeting of the Society will be held at 37, Great Russell Street, Bloomsbury, W.C., on Tuesday, 1st June, 1897, at 8 p.m. when the following Paper will be read :—

Mr. H. Rassam : "Abraham and the Land of his Nativity."

THE FOLLOWING BOOKS ARE REQUIRED FOR THE LIBRARY OF THE SOCIETY.

Members having duplicate copies, will confer a favour by presenting them to the Society.

ALKER, E., Die Chronologie der Bucher der Könige und Paralipomenōn im Einklang mit der Chronologie der Aegypter, Assyrer, Babylonier und Meder.

AMÉLINEAU, Histoire du Patriarche Copte Isaac.

————— Contes de l'Égypte Chrétienne.

————— La Morale Egyptienne quinze siècles avant notre ère.

AMIAUD, La Légende Syriaque de Saint Alexis, l'homme de Dieu.

————— A., AND L. MECHINEAU, Tableau Comparé des Écritures Babyloniennes et Assyriennes.

—————.Mittheilungen aus der Sammlung der Papyrus Erzherzog Rainer. 2 parts.

BAETHGEN, Beiträge zur Semitischen Religiongeshichte. Der Gott Israels und die Götter der Heiden.

BLASS, A. F., Eudoxi ars Astronomica qualis in Charta Aegyptiaca superest.

BOTTA, Monuments de Ninive. 5 vols., folio. 1847–1850.

BRUGSCH-BEY, Geographische Inschriften Altaegyptische Denkmaeler. Vol. I—III (Brugsch).

————— Recueil de Monuments Égyptiens, copiés sur lieux et publiés pas H. Brugsch et J. Dümichen. (4 vols., and the text by Dümichen of vols. 3 and 4.)

BUDINGER, M., De Colonarium quarundam Phoeniciarum primordiis cum Hebraeorum exodo conjunctis.

BURCKHARDT, Eastern Travels.

CASSEL, PAULUS, Zophnet Paneach Aegyptische Deutungen.

CHABAS, Mélanges Égyptologiques. Séries I, III. 1862–1873.

DÜMICHEN, Historische Inschriften, &c., 1st series, 1867.

————————————— 2nd series, 1869.

————— Altaegyptische Kalender-Inschriften, 1886.

————————— Tempel-Inschriften, 1862. 2 vols., folio.

EBERS, G., Papyrus Ebers.

ERMAN, Papyrus Westcar.

Études Égyptologiques. 13 vols., complete to 1880.

GAYET, E., Stèles de la XII dynastie au Musée du Louvre.

GOLÉNISCHEFF, Die Metternichstele. Folio, 1877.

————— Vingt-quatre Tablettes Cappadociennes de la Collection dé.

GRANT-BEY, Dr., The Ancient Egyptian Religion and the Influence it exerted on the Religions that came in contact with it.

HAUPT, Die Sumerischen Familiengesetze

HOMMEL, Dr., Geschichte Babyloniens und Assyriens. 1892.

JASTROW, M., A Fragment of the Babylonian "Dibbarra" Epic.

JENSEN, Die Kosmologie der Babylonier.

JEREMIAS, Tyrus bis zur Zeit Nubukadnezar's Geschichtliche Skizze mit besonderer Berucksichtigung der Keilschriftlichen Quellen.

JOACHIM, H., Papyros Ebers, das Älteste Buch über Heilkunde.

JOHNS HOPKINS UNIVERSITY. Contributions to Assyriology and Comparative Semitic Philology.

KREBS, F., De Chnemothis nomarchi inscriptione Aegyptiaca commentatio.

LEDERER, Die Biblische Zeitrechnung vom Auszuge aus Aegypten bis zum Beginne der Babylonische Gefangenschaft mit Berichsichtignung der Resultate der Assyriologie und der Aegyptologie.

LEDRAIN, Les Monuments Égyptiens de la Bibliothèque Nationale.

LEFÈBURE, Le Mythe Osirien. 2me partie. "Osiris."

LEGRAIN, G., Le Livre des Transformations. Papyrus démotique du Louvre.

LEHMANN, Samassumukin König von Babylonien 668 vehr, p. xiv, 173; 47 plates.

LEPSIUS, Nubian Grammar, &c., 1880.

MARUCHI, Monumenta Papyracea Aegyptia.

MÜLLER, D. H., Epigraphische Denkmäler aus Arabien.

NOORDTZIG, Israèl's verblijf ih Egypte bezien int licht der Egyptische outdekkingen.

POGNON, Les Inscriptions Babyloniennes du Wadi Brissa.

RAWLINSON, CANON, 6th Ancient Monarchy.

ROBIOU, Croyances de l'Égypte à l'époque des Pyramides.

———— Recherches sur le Calendrier en Égypte et sur le chronologie des Lagides.

SAINTE MARIE, Mission à Carthage.

SARZEC, Découvertes en Chaldée.

SCHAEFFER, Commentationes de papyro medicinali Lipsiensi.

SCHOUW, Charta papyracea graece scripta Musei Borgiani Velitris.

SCHROEDER, Die Phönizische Sprache.

STRAUSS and TORNEY, Der Altägyptishe Götterglaube.

VIREY, P., Quelques Observations sur l'Épisode d'Aristée, à propos d un Monument Égyptien.

VISSER, I., Hebreeuwsche Archaeologie. Utrecht, 1891.

WALTHER, J., Les Découvertes de Ninive et de Babylone au point de vue biblique. Lausanne, 1890.

WILCKEN, M., Actenstücke aus der Königl. Bank zu Theben.

WILTZKE, De Biblische Simson der Ägyptische Horus-Ra.

WINCKLER, HUGO, Der Thontafelfund von El Amarna. Vols. I and II.

———— Textbuch-Keilinschriftliches zum Alten Testament.

WEISSLEACH, F. H., Die Achaemeniden Inschriften Zweiter Art.

WESSELEY, C., Die Pariser Papyri des Fundes von El Fajum.

Zeitsch. der Deutschen Morgenl. Gesellsch., Vol. XX to Vol. XXXII, 1866 to 1878.

ZIMMERN, II., Die Assyriologie als Hülfswissenschaft für das Studium des Alten Testaments.

SOCIETY OF BIBLICAL ARCHÆOLOGY PUBLICATIONS.

In 8 Parts. Price 5s. each. The Fourth Part having been issued, the Price is now Raised to £5 for the 8 Parts. Parts cannot be sold separately.

THE EGYPTIAN BOOK OF THE DEAD.
Complete Translation, Commentary, and Notes.

By SIR P. LE PAGE RENOUF, KNT. (*President*);

CONTAINING ALSO

𝔄 Series of Plates of the Vignettes of the different Chapters.

The Bronze Ornaments of the Palace Gates from Balawat.

[SHALMANESER II, B.C. 859–825.]

Parts I, II, III, and IV have now been issued to Subscribers.

In accordance with the terms of the original prospectus the price for each part is now raised to £1 10s.; to Members of the Society (the original price) £1 1s.

Price 7s. 6d. Only a Limited Number of Copies will be Printed.

THE PALESTINIAN SYRIAC VERSION OF THE HOLY SCRIPTURES.

Four Recently Discovered Portions (together with verses from the Psalms and the Gospel of St. Luke). Edited, in Photographic Facsimile, from a Unique MS. in the British Museum, with a Transcription, Translation, Introduction, Vocabulary, and Notes, by

REV. G. MARGOLIOUTH, M.A.,

Assistant in the Department of Oriental Printed Books and MSS. in the British Museum; formerly Tyrwhitt Hebrew Scholar.

Subscribers' names to be Addressed to the Secretary.

SOCIETY OF BIBLICAL ARCHÆOLOGY.

COUNCIL, 1897.

President.

SIR P. LE PAGE RENOUF, KNT.

Vice-Presidents.

THE MOST REV. HIS GRACE THE LORD ARCHBISHOP OF YORK.
THE MOST NOBLE THE MARQUESS OF BUTE, K.T., &c., &c.
THE RIGHT HON. LORD AMHERST OF HACKNEY.
THE RIGHT HON. LORD HALSBURY.
THE RIGHT HON. W. E. GLADSTONE, M.P., D.C.L., &c.
ARTHUR CATES.
F. D. MOCATTA, F.S.A., &c.
WALTER MORRISON, M.P.
SIR CHARLES NICHOLSON, BART., D.C.L., M.D., &c.
ALEXANDER PECKOVER, LL.D., F.S.A.
REV. GEORGE RAWLINSON, D.D., Canon of Canterbury.

Council.

REV. CHARLES JAMES BALL, M.A.
REV. PROF. T. K. CHEYNE, D.D.
THOMAS CHRISTY, F.L.S.
DR. J. HALL GLADSTONE, F.R.S.
CHARLES HARRISON, F.S.A.
GRAY HILL.
PROF. T. HAYTER LEWIS, F.S.A.
REV. ALBERT LOWY, LL.D., &c.

REV. JAMES MARSHALL, M.A.
CLAUDE G. MONTEFIORE.
WALTER L. NASH, F.S.A.
PROF. E. NAVILLE.
J. POLLARD.
EDWARD B. TYLOR, LL.D., F.R.S., &c.
E. TOWRY WHYTE, M.A., F.S.A.

Honorary Treasurer—BERNARD T. BOSANQUET.

Secretary—W. HARRY RYLANDS, F.S.A.

Honorary Secretary for Foreign Correspondence—REV. R. GWYNNE, B.A.

Honorary Librarian—WILLIAM SIMPSON, F.R.G.S.

HARRISON AND SONS, PRINTERS IN ORDINARY TO HER MAJESTY, ST. MARTIN'S LANE.

PROCEEDINGS

OF

THE SOCIETY

OF

BIBLICAL ARCHÆOLOGY.

————✦✦✦————

'

VOL. XIX. TWENTY-SEVENTH SESSION.

Sixth Meeting, June 1st, 1897.

————✦✦✦————

CONTENTS.

————✦✦✦————

PUBLISHED AT

THE OFFICES OF THE SOCIETY,

37, Gʀᴇᴀᴛ Rᴜꜱꜱᴇʟʟ Sᴛʀᴇᴇᴛ, Bʟᴏᴏᴍꜱʙᴜʀʏ, W.C.

——

1897.

SOCIETY OF BIBLICAL ARCHÆOLOGY,

37, GREAT RUSSELL STREET, BLOOMSBURY, W.C.

TRANSACTIONS.

			To Members.		To Non-Members.						To Members.		To Non-Members.
					s.	d.							s.	d.
Vol.	I, Part	1 ...	10	6	... 12	6	Vol.	VI, Part	1 ...	10	6	... 12	6
,,	I, ,,	2 ...	10	6	... 12	6	,,	VI, ,,	2 ...	10	6	... 12	6
,,	II, ,,	1 ...	8	0	... 10	6	,,	VII, ,,	1 ...	7	6	... 10	6
,,	II, ,,	2 ...	8	0	... 10	6	,,	VII, ,,	2 ...	10	6	... 12	6
,,	III, ,,	1 ...	8	0	... 10	6	,,	VII, ,,	3 ...	10	6	... 12	6
,,	III, ,,	2 ...	8	0	... 10	6	,,	VIII, ,,	1 ...	10	6	... 12	6
,,	IV, ,,	1 ...	10	6	... 12	6	,,	VIII, ,,	2 ...	10	6	... 12	6
,,	IV, ,,	2 ...	10	6	... 12	6	,,	VIII, ,,	3 ...	10	6	... 12	6
,,	V, ,,	1 ...	12	6	... 15	0	,,	IX, ,,	1 ...	10	6	... 12	6
,,	V, ,,	2 ...	10	6	... 12	6	,,	IX, ,,	2 ...	10	6	... 12	6

PROCEEDINGS.

Vol.				To Members.					To Non-Members.	
Vol.	I,	Session	1878–79	...	2	0	...	...	2	6
,,	II,	,,	1879–80	...	2	0	...	...	2	6
,,	III,	,,	1880–81	...	4	0	...	...	5	0
,,	IV,	,,	1881–82	...	4	0	...	...	5	0
,,	V,	,,	1882–83	...	4	0	...	,~	5	0
,,	VI,	,,	1883–84	...	5	0	...	..	6	0
,,	VII,	,,	1884–85	...	5	0	...	...	6	0
,,	VIII,	,,	1885–86	...	5	0	...	...	6	0
,,	IX,	,,	1886–87	...	2	0 per l'art	...	2	6
,,	IX,	Part 7,	1886–87	...	8	0 ,, ,,	...	10	6
,,	X,	Parts 1 to 7,	1887–88	...	2	0 ,, ,,	...	2	6
,,	X,	Part 8,	1887–88	...	7	6 ,, ,,	...	10	6
,,	XI,	Parts 1 to 7,	1888–89	...	2	0 ,, ,,	...	2	6
,,	XI,	Part 8,	1888–89	...	7	6 ,, ,,	...	10	6
,,	XII,	Parts 1 to 7,	1889–90	...	2	0 ,, ,,	...	2	6
,,	XII,	Part 8,	1889–90	...	5	0 ,, ,,	...	6	0
,,	XIII,	Parts 1 to 7,	1890–91	...	2	0 ,, ,,	...	2	6
,,	XIII,	Part 8,	1890–91	...	5	0 ,, ,,	...	6	0
,,	XIV,	Parts 1 to 7,	1891–92	...	2	0 ,, ,,	...	2	6
,,	XIV,	Part 8,	1891–92	...	5	0 ,, ,,	...	6	0
,,	XV,	Parts 1 to 7,	1892–93	...	2	0 ,, ,,	...	2	6
,,	XV,	Part 8,	1892–93	...	5	0 ,, ,,	...	6	0
,,	XVI,	Parts 1 to 10,	1893–94	...	2	0 ,, ,,	...	2	6
,,	XVII,	Parts 1 to 8	1895	...	2	0 ,, ,,	...	2	6
,,	XVIII,	Parts 1 to 8	1896	...	2	0 ,, ,,	...	2	6
,,	XIX,	In progress	1897							

irre

had

A few complete sets of the Transactions still remain for sale, which may be obtained on application to the Secretary, W. H. RYLANDS, F.S.A., 37, Great Russell Street, Bloomsbury, W.C.

PROCEEDINGS

OF

THE SOCIETY

OF

BIBLICAL ARCHÆOLOGY.

TWENTY-SEVENTH SESSION, 1897.

Sixth Meeting, 1st June, 1897.

Rev. Dr. A. LÖWY.

IN THE CHAIR.

The Chairman announced with deep regret the irreparable loss the Society, with the world of science, had suffered by the decease, on May the 21st, of Sir A. W. Franks, K.C.B., F.R.S., etc., etc., President of the Society of Antiquaries.

The following Presents were announced, and thanks ordered to be returned to the Donors :—

From the Author :—Dr. Fritz Hommel. The Ancient Hebrew Tradition as illustrated by the Monuments, a protest against the Modern School of Old Testament criticism. Translated into English by Edmund McClure, M.A., and Leonard Crosslé. 8vo. London. 1897.

From the Author :—Dr. A. Wiedemann. Zu dem Thierkult der Alten Aegypter. 4to. Leide. Extr. Mélanges Charles de Harlez.

———— Dr. A. Wiedemann. G. Maspero. Histoire ancienne des Peuples de l'Orient classique. Notice. Neue Phil. Rundschau, Nr. 20. 8vo.

———— G. Margoliouth, M.A. Ibn Al-Hitī's Arabic Chronicle of Karaite Doctors. Edited, translated, and annotated. 8vo. London. 1897. [*Jewish Quarterly Review*.]

———— Arthur Lincke. Kambyses in der Sage, Litteratur und Kunst des Mittlealters. 8vo. Leipsig. 1897. Sep.-Abdr. Aegyptiaca-Festschrift für Georg Ebers, zum 1 März, 1897.

———— Rev. P. A. Cesare de Cara, S. J. Gli Hethei-Pelasgi d'Oriente. Conclusione storico-critiche Estrat. Civilt. Catt. Serie XVI. Vol. X. 8vo. Roma. 1897.

From the Rev. Dr. Löwy :—A Souvenir of the Rev. Dr. A. Löwy's Eightieth Birthday, Speeches on presentation of a congratulatory address, Sunday, December 13th, 1896. 8vo. London. 1896. Reprinted from *The Jewish Chronicle*.

————— Middath Yaménu, The Measure of our Days, A Song of Affection to Brothers and Friends, by the Rev. Dr. Löwy, on his Eightieth Birthday, December 8th, 1896. 8vo. London.

From Walter L. Nash, F.S.A. :—A Series of large Photographs taken by him in Egypt during his recent visit.

————————

A Paper by Mr. H. Rassam was read, entitled : " Abraham and the Land of his Nativity."

Remarks were added by Mr. Theo. G. Pinches, Mr. Rassam, and the Chairman.

Thanks were returned for this communication.

BOOK OF THE DEAD.

By Sir P. le Page Renouf.

CHAPTER CXXXVIIA.

Chapter whereby a Light is kindled (1) *for a person.*

Oh Light! let the Light be kindled for thy Ka, O Osiris Chentamenta. Let the Light be kindled for the Night which followeth the Day: the Eye of Horus which riseth at thy temple (2): which riseth up (3) over thee and which gathereth upon thy brow; which granteth thee its protection and overthroweth thine enemies.

Undefiledly (bis) and successfully (bis):

The light is kindled for Osiris Unnefer: with fresh vases and raiment like the Dawn.

CHAPTER CXXXVIIB.

Chapter whereby a Light is kindled for a person.

The Eye of Horus cometh, the Light one: the Eye of Horus cometh, the Glorious one.

Come thou, propitiously, shining like Rā from the Mount of Glory, and putting an end to the opposition (4) of Sutu.

The prescription (5) of her (6) who hath raised him up, and seized upon the Light for him, and who putteth an end to the troubles against thee, like the Mount of Glory.

NOTES.

The two most ancient authorities for this chapter, as it is found in the Turin *Todtenbuch* and the late recension, are one of the four tablets of the Museum of Marseilles, published by M. Naville (*Les quatre stèles orientées du Musée de Marseille*), and the Berlin papyrus of Nechtuamon. The chapter which M. Naville has published as 137A, in the first volume of his own *Todtenbuch*, and which is taken from the papyrus of Nebseni, is manifestly, I think, not the orignal text, but another edition very considerably revised and enlarged. And, in imitation of the rubric of ch. 64, it concludes with a veracious statement, that it was discovered by Prince Hortatef in a secret chest in the temple of Unnut, and was brought away by the royal carriages.

These texts are found among the texts preserved in the tomb of Petamenemapt (see *Zeitschr.*, 1883, Taf. 1), but with various additions, and have been appropriated by the Ritual of Ammon, published by Dr. O. von Lemm.

The solemn ceremony of Kindling the Light for the dead is repeatedly mentioned in the Siut inscriptions of Hapit'efae.

1. *Kindle* 𓊹 ⸻ conveys the same notion as 𓊹 in the title of 137B. The Ammon Ritual has 𓊹 *strike a Light*. Dr. von Lemm thinks that by a play of words it is implied not only that a light but Sut is struck.

2. *At thy temple* 𓄿𓏛 ⸻ *Ba* and *Marseilles;* 𓄿 in Abydos, *Aa* and *Petamenemapt*.

3. *Riseth up* ⸻, *Ba*, ⸻ *Marseilles;* ⸻ *Aa*, 𓃟 *Petamenemapt*.

4. *Opposition* 𓏥𓏥𓏥, where 𓏥 is = 𓂋 as in the Sallier Calendar. The sense is made clear in the parallel passages ⸻. 𓏥, if not an error of recent transcribers, is a wrong reading for 𓏥, which is very distinctly written in the Nebseni papryus.

PLATE XXXIX.

Proc. Soc. Bibl. Arch., June, 1897.

BOOK OF THE DEAD.

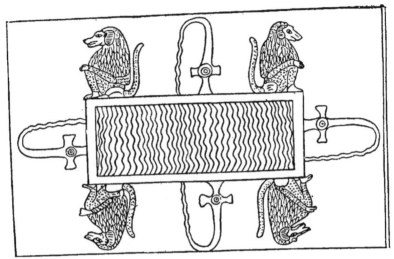

CHAPTER CXXVI. **Papyrus of Ani.**

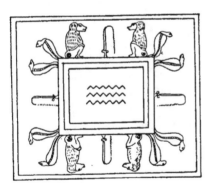

CHAPTER CXXVI.
British Museum Papyrus, No. 9913.

CHAPTER CXXIX.
Musée du Louvre, Papyrus III, 36.

CHAPTER CXXX. **Papyrus, Leyden, VI.**

PLATE XL.
Proc. Soc. Bibl. Arch., June, 1897.

BOOK OF THE DEAD.

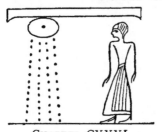

CHAPTER CXXXI.
Papyrus, Musée du Louvre, No. 3079.

CHAPTER CXXXII.
Brit. Mus. Papyrus, No. 9964.

CHAPTER CXXXII.
Papyrus, Brocklehurst, II.

CHAPTER CXXXIII.
Papyrus, British Museum, No. 9900.

CHAPTER CXXXIV. Papyrus of Ani, British Museum.

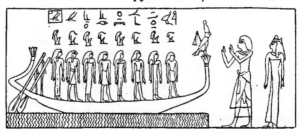

CHAPTER CXXXIV. Papyrus, British Museum, No. 9900.

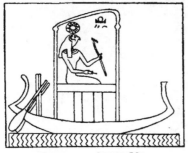

CHAPTER CXXXVI.
Papyrus, Brit. Mus., No. 9913.

CHAPTER CXXXVI.
Papyrus, Brit. Mus., No. 9900.

5. *Prescription* [hieroglyphs] .

6. *Her.* The Vignette in the Nebseni papyrus exhibits the goddess Apit, in hippopotamus form, lighting the light. Over her are the words [hieroglyphs], "Apit, mistress of divine protections."

CHAPTER CXXXVIII.

Chapter whereby one is enabled to enter into Abydos.

Oh all ye gods who are in Abydos, [each one and his] (1) divine circle likewise in its entirety, who are coming with acclamation to meet me: let me see my father Osiris: let me be held as one who cometh forth as of his house (2).

I am Horus, the Lord of Kamit, and the heir of Tesherit,(3) which I have also seized. I, the invincible one, whose eye is potent against his adversaries: who avengeth his father, and is fierce at the drowning of his mother ; (4) who smiteth his adversaries and putteth an end to violence on their part. . . . (5).

Oh thou of the potent Lock, king of hosts, who art seized of the Two Worlds ; whose father's house is seized (6) [by him] in virtue of the writs (7) ; my balance is perfectly even, my voice is law, and I prevail over all mine adversaries. (8)

NOTES.

1. [*Each one and his*]. These words are necessary for the purpose of bringing out the meaning of the text. Every god, it has already been said, has his circle of associates. The feminine suffix [hieroglyph] after [hieroglyphs] shows the concordance with [hieroglyphs], which, like other collective nouns, is of the feminine gender.

2. The exact text here is doubtful, and the sense of [hieroglyphs] depends upon it. [hieroglyphs] or [hieroglyphs] is the well known title of a

priestly official, whose presence was required in the ritual of the dead. He is sometimes in attendance upon royal personages. Here according to its etymological sense the word might simply mean a relative.

3. *Kamit* ⬜🦅⊗, the "Black Land" is Egypt; *Tesherit* ⬜🌀, the "Red Land," is whatever lies beyond the limits of Egypt.

4. *The drowning of his mother* ⌒𓎡𓏭𓈖𓈖𓈖𓆓 . *Drowning* may be too strong a word, but immersion at least is meant. We are at present without any other reference to this incident in the career of the goddess Isis.

5. Here occurs a word, 𓉻𓎯𓅾 or 𓉻𓎿𓅾, of doubtful meaning. As the next word to it begins a sentence, it must be considered as connected with the words preceding it. I am not satisfied that "silently" or "causing silence" would be a grammatical solution of the question.

6. Seized (throughout this chapter) in the juridical sense of *seisin* or feudal possession.

7. *Writs* 𓈖𓏤𓎯𓏦, a reading of three early papyri, which has disappeared in the later ones. The Turin *Todtenbuch* has 𓅃𓏤𓂝, "with his two hands."

8. Here the chapter ends in *Pi*, and even sooner in the later texts. The three older papyri differ as to the words which immediately follow and are certainly corrupt and unintelligible.

CHAPTER CXXXIX

is identical with CHAPTER CXXIII.

THE MEDIAN CALENDAR AND THE CONSTELLATION TAURUS.

By Hon. E. M. Plunkett.

In a former number* of these *Proceedings* we contrasted as follows, what we believed to be the calendar of the Accadians with that of the inhabitants of Lagash :—

" In Accad the calendar makers clung to the originally instituted *star-mark* † for the year, and made it begin with the sun's entry into [the constellation] Aries, therefore by degrees the beginning of their year moved away from the *Winter Solstice*, and in the 1st century B.C. coincided very closely with the *Spring Equinox*.

" In Lagash, on the contrary, the calendar makers clung to the originally established season of the year, and made it begin at the *Winter Solstice ;* therefore by degrees the beginning of their year moved away from the *constellation Aries*, and in Gudea's time [about 2800 B.C.] the new year's festival was held in honour of the goddess Bau = Gula = Aquarius."

We now desire to draw attention to the Median Calendar, which appears to have differed from that used, as above suggested, in Accad or in Lagash ; inasmuch as the beginning of the Median year was not dependent on the sun's entry into the *constellation Aries*, as in Accad ; nor was it fixed to the season of the *Winter Solstice* as in Lagash.

The beginning of the Median year was fixed to the *season of the Spring Equinox*, and remaining true to that season, followed no star mark. The great importance however of Tauric symbolism in Median art seems to point to the fact that *when the equinoctial year was first established* the spring equinoctial point was in the

---

* Feb., 1896, XVIII, 67.

† A star mark, as earlier suggested, first established when the *Winter Solstice* oincided with the sun's entry into the *constellation Aries, i.e.*, about 6000 B.C.

constellation Taurus. Astronomy teaches us that was the case, speaking in round numbers, from 4000 to 2000 B.C.

It is true that we have no documentary proof of the existence of a Median *equinoctial* calendar in the remote past, such as that which we possess in the Babylonian standard astrological works regarding the ancient *sidereal* Accadian calendar. We have however among the modern representatives of the Medes, the Persians, a very distinctive calendrical observance, namely, that of the "Nowroose," or the festival of the new year; and we have the Persian tradition that the institution of this festival was of fabulous antiquity. We quote from Ker Porter's remarks on this subject :—

"The 21st of March, the impatiently anticipated day of the most joyous festival of Persia, at last arrived. It is called the feast of the Nowroose, or that of the commencement of the new year; and its institution is attributed to the celebrated Jeemshid, who, according to the traditions of the country, and the fragments yet preserved of its early native historians, was the sixth in descent from Noah, and the fourth sovereign of Persia, of the race of the Kaimours, the grandson of Noah . . . . But to return to the feast of the Nowroose, it is acknowledged to have been celebrated from the earliest times in Persia, independent of whatever religion reigned there; whether the simple worship of the one great Being, or under the successive rites of Magian, Pagan, or Mahomedan institutions."

This equinoctial and "Solar" year, as the writer proceeds to point out, is adhered to by the Persians, though they, being Mahomedans, also celebrate Mahomedan "lunar" festivals, and for many purposes make use of the Mahomedan "lunar year."

It is easy to see how greatly the Persian Nowroose differs from the purely lunar Mahomedan anniversaries—anniversaries which in the course of about thirty-two and a half years necessarily make a complete circuit through the seasons. The difference, though not so marked, which exists between the purely "solar" Nowroose and all "soli-lunar" festivals such as those of the Babylonians should also be taken note of. These last, like our Easter, were dependent on the phases of the moon, and were therefore "moveable." The Persian Nowroose, like our Christmas Day, is an "immovable" festival—fixed to the day of the Spring Equinox.*

---

* A purely lunar year contains only twelve lunar months or 354 days.

A soli-lunar year contains sometimes twelve and sometimes thirteen lunar months; in some years, therefore, 354 days, in others 383 or 384 days.

Modern tradition concerning the distinctively Persian custom of celebrating the Nowroose would if it stood alone furnish very slight grounds on which to found a far reaching theory; but historical evidence confirms this tradition to a great extent, by teaching us that the Median and Persian worshippers of Ahura Mazda, and of Mithras, certainly under the Sassinide dynasty, and almost with equal certainty under the Achæmenid kings, kept their calendar and celebrated their religious festivals in a manner differing from that of the surrounding nations; their months were not lunar, their years were not soli-lunar but distinctly "solar," and the Spring Equinox was the date to which as closely as possible the beginning of their year was fixed.

In Darmstetter's translation of the Zend Avesta the Persian months are treated of in Appendix C, p. 33, and in Appendix D, p. 37, we read of the Persian years :—

"L'année était divisée en quatre saisons, correspondant aux nôtres; cette division ne parait guère que dans les textes post-avestéens; mais il-y-a dans l'Avesta même des traces de son existence ancienne. La division normale de l'année est, dans l'Avesta, en deux saisons été et hiver: l'été *hama*, qui comprend les sept premiers mois (du 1re Farvardin au 30me Milos, soit du 21 Mars au 16 Octobre .... Cette division a une valeur religieuse non seulement pour le ritual, mais aussi pour les pratiques qui varient selon la saison."

The worship of the Persian sun-god Mithras was introduced into Rome about the time of the fall of the Republic. How far this worship differed from that taught in the Zoroastran writings we need not inquire; however changed it may have been, it was evidently originally derived from a Persian or a Median source. The worship of Mithras, in spite of much opposition, gained many followers in Rome. The birthday of the sun-god was, we read, kept at the Winter Solstice, but the greatest festivities in his honour, "*the mysteries of Mithras," were celebrated on the day of the Spring Equinox*, and were famous even among Roman festivals. Let us

---

A purely solar year has no reference to the phases of the moon, and contains never less than 365 days.

To keep our solar year true to the seasons, one day, at leap year, is added to the ordinary year of 365 days. According to Darmstetter, thirty days were added once in every hundred and twenty years to the ordinary Median year of 365 days.

now turn our attention to the Tauric symbolism so closely connected with Mithraic observances in Rome.

A writer in the *Athenæum* thus describes a Roman Mithræum :—
"Discovery was made during some excavations at Ostia* of a handsome house containing among its various rooms a Mithræum. . . . Into the kitchen opens a narrow and tortuous passage, from which by a small half concealed staircase the Mithræum is reached . . . . it is quadrangular and regular in shape, as is usually the case in buildings of the kind. Almost the whole length of the two lateral walls run two seats, and on the side opposite the door is seen a little elevation, which served as the place for the usual statue of Mithras, in the act of thrusting his dagger into the neck of the mystic Bull. A very singular peculiarity of this little Ostian Mithræum is that it is entirely covered with mosaics—pavements, seats, and walls alike. The various figures and the symbols are splendidly drawn, and all executed in black tesseræ on a white ground. Upon each side of the seats turned to the entrance door is figured a genius bearing a lamp, that of the genius of the Spring Equinox with the face raised, and that of the Autumn Equinox with the face cast down . . . . It is known in fact that the whole myth of Mithras is related to the phases of the sun . . . . hence are represented in the ground below the seats all the twelve signs of the zodiac by means of the usual symbols, but each accompanied by a large star upon the front of the seats themselves."

In the many sculptures of the Mithras group similar to that above described, which have been so well figured in Lajard's "Culte de Mithras," various heavenly bodies are represented. The scorpion (the constellation Scorpio of the Zodiac opposed to Taurus) joins with Mithras in his attack upon the Bull, and always the genii of the Spring and Autumn Equinoxes are present in joyous and mournful attitudes.

In looking at these plates the conviction is clearly forced upon our minds that the bull so persistently, and we may add so serenely, slain by Mithras in these Roman representations is the Zodiacal Bull, overcome, and as it were destroyed or banished from heaven in the daytime by the Sun-god and at night by Scorpio, the constellation in opposition. With almost equal conviction we arrive at the conclusion that this triumph of Mithras was associated traditionally—

---

* *Athenæum*, 1886, Oct. 30 and Nov. 6.

in Roman days it could only have been traditionally—with the occurrence, at a remote date, of the Spring Equinox during the time that the sun was in conjunction with the constellation Taurus.

In the ruins of Persepolis ruins of buildings designed, erected, and decorated by the worshippers of the supreme god Ahura Mazda, and of his friend and representative Mithras, Tauric symbolism abounds.   We do not amongst these ruins find portrayals of Mithras as a Phrygian capped youth "thrusting his dagger into the neck of the mystic Bull," but again and again, in the bas-reliefs adorning the walls, we do find a colossal being "thrusting his dagger into the body of a still more "mystic" creature than the Bull of the Roman sculptures—a creature combining in one instance at least * the attributes of Bull, Lion, Scorpion, and Eagle, and frequently those of two or more of these animals.

Perrot and Chippiez have supposed this constantly repeated scene to represent imaginary contests between the reigning monarch and all possible or impossible monsters, but a very different impression was produced on the mind of Ker Porter by these same bas-reliefs, and though he did not adopt a purely astronomic theory to explain them, he was firmly convinced that the combat depicted was not one waged between an ordinary human being and an ordinary or extraordinary animal, but that it was a symbolical representation of the combat constantly carried on by Ormurzd (Ahura Mazda), and by his representative Mithras against the powers of evil and darkness.†

With the astronomic clue to Persian symbolism put into our hands by the Roman sculptures, of which mention has been made, and by a study of the researches of Lajard, it is not difficult to recognise in the composite animals represented on the bas-reliefs allusions not only to the Zodiacal Bull, traditionally associated with

---

* Plate I.

† " The man who contends with the animals . . . . is represented as a person of a singularly dignified mien, clad in long draperied robes, but with the arms perfectly bare.   His hair, which is long and curled, is bound with a circlet or low diadem ; and his sweeping pointed beard is curled at different heights in the style that was worn by majesty alone . . . .   The calmness of his air contrasted with the firmness with which he grasps the animals and strikes to his aim gives a certainty to his object, and a sublimity to his figure beyond anything elaborate action or ornament could effect.   From the unchanged appearance of the hero, his unvaried mode of attack, its success, and the unaltered style of opposition adopted by every one of the animals in the contests, I can have no doubt that all mean different achievements towards one great aim . . . . "—Ker Porter's *Travels*.

the Spring Equinox, but also to three other constellations which at the same date of the world's history (namely, from 4000 to 2000 B.C.) marked more or less accurately the remaining colures, *i.e.*, the Lion, the Scorpion, and the Eagle.

The constellations of the Lion and the Scorpion, there can be no doubt, were appropriate star marks for the summer and autumn seasons, when the spring equinoctial point was in the Bull;* but as regards the Eagle it must be admitted that though it adjoins the zodiacal Aquarius (the constellation in which the winter solstitial point was then situated), yet its principal stars lie considerably to the north and west of that constellation.

A reason for the substitution of the Eagle (Aquila) for the zodiacal water man or water jar (Aquarius or Amphora) may, however, be found in the fact of the very great brilliancy of the star Altair in the Eagle. It is a star of the first magnitude. In the water man there is no star above the third. The Persians we are told had a tradition that four brilliant stars marked the four cardinal points (*i.e.*, the colures). In Taurus, Leo, and Scorpio we find stars of the first magnitude : there was therefore no temptation for Mithraic calendar makers and mythologists to seek for an extra zodiacal star to mark and represent the spring, summer, or autumn seasons; but for the Winter Solstice the only stars of the first magnitude within at all suitable distance were Aquila, to the north-west, or Fomalhaut, to the south of Aquarius. For a nation dwelling as far to the north as the Medians are supposed to have done, Fomalhaut (when the Winter Solstice was in Aquarius) very far to the south of the equator would have been rarely visible. The choice by a Median astronomer and symbolic artist in search of a very brilliant star mark for the solstice would therefore have been restricted to the constellation of the Eagle, containing the conspicuous Altair, a star of the first magnitude.

The very constant association, not only in Persian and Median, but also in the mythologic art of other nations, of the Lion and the Eagle, seems to confirm the view here put forward, *i.e.*, that the constellations of Leo and Aquila rather than of Leo and Aquarius were sometimes chosen to symbolise the Summer and Winter Solstices.

---

* The solstitial and equinoctial colures were situated, speaking in round numbers, for 2000 years in the constellations Taurus, Leo, Scorpio, and Aquarius.

The Griffin, a fabulous animal sacred to the sun, composed of a *Lion* and an *Eagle*, is a well known figure in ancient classic art.

In Babylonian and Assyrian sculptured and glyptic art Merodach is often represented as in conflict with a griffin. Merodach has been claimed by Jensen and other writers as a personification of the sun of the Spring Equinox. The forever recurring triumph of spring over winter is probably figured in Merodach's triumph over the Griffin.

The association of Eagle and Lion is to be noticed in the arms of the city of Lagash; they were "a double-headed Eagle standing on a Lion or two demi-lions."* In Lagash, as we pointed out in a former paper, the new year's festival appears to have been held at the Winter Solstice : such a supposition would furnish an astronomical interpretation for the arms of Lagash.† Mythologic references to the eagle alone are also to be met with which point to the *Celestial Eagle* (Aquila) marking the Winter Solstice in lieu of the constellation Aquarius.

As for instance the Babylonian legend of the ambitious zu-bird‡ who stole the tablets of destiny, and thus sought to vie in power with "the great gods." Here we may find allusions to the substitution (deemed by some, no doubt, as unauthorised) of an extra zodiacal for a zodiacal constellation.

Again, in Grecian mythology the eagle is sent by Zeus to carry Ganymede up to heaven, and in Grecian astronomy Ganymede is placed in the constellation Aquarius. It does not therefore seem unreasonable to suppose that the eagle associated in the Persepolitan bas-reliefs with the Lion, the Bull, and the Scorpion (as at

---

* Maspero, *Dawn of Civilization*, p. 604.

† In this connection the following passage from Sayce's "Hibbert Lectures," p. 961, is interesting :—

> "Hymn to Bel Merodach, Month Nisan
> . . . . O Zamana[1]
> Why dost thou not take thy seat ?
> Bahu the queen of Kis has not cried to thee."

[1] Zamana was the sun-god of Kis, and was consequently identified with Adar by the mythologists. On a contract stone he is symbolized by an eagle, which is said to be the image of the southern "sun of Kis."

We claimed in a former paper (Feb., 1895), that "*the Southern sun*" was "*the sun of the Winter Solstice*," and that Gula (=Bahu) was the name of the constellation, or of some stars in the constellation *Aquarius*. In these lines *Bahu*, as we have supposed, *Aquarius*, and *Zamana*, symbolised by the *Eagle—the image of the Southern sun or Winter Solstice*, are closely associated.

‡ Maspero, *Dawn of Civilization*, p. 666.

Plate I), is the constellational Eagle, symbolising the Winter Solstice, and that the compound animal is emblematic of the four seasons of the year, and also it may be of the four quarters of the world.

If to the composite monster of the bas-reliefs we ascribe an astronomic motive, we shall be ready to grant the same to other Tauric symbolisms prominent in the Persepolitan ruins.

With full conviction we shall recognise in the demi-bulls which crowned the columns in Persepolis and Susa representations of the demi-bull of the Zodiac. The resemblance is so striking that words are scarcely required to point it out when once the outlines of the two figures have been compared (Plate II). In the spirited description which we quote from Perrot and Chippiez* of these capitals, we mark with italics some lines which might be applied with exactness to the demi-bulls of the Zodiac.

"On ne saurait cependant ne point admirer le grand goût et l'art ingénieux avec lequel, dans ses bustes de taureau, il [l'artiste perse] a plié la forme vivante au nécessités de la décoration architecturale. Il a su la simplifier sans lui enlever l'accent de la vie; les traits caractéristiques de l'espèce sur laquelle s'est porté son choix restent franchement accusés, quoique les menus détails soient éliminés; ils auraient risqué de distraire et de troubler le regard. Les poils de la nuque et du dos, de l'épaule, des fanons, et des flancs sont réunis en masses d'un ferme contour, auxquelles la frisure des boucles dont elles se composent donne un relief plus vigoureux; en même temps le collier qui pend au col, orné de rosaces et d'un riche fleuron qui tombe sur la poitrine, écarte toute idée de réalité; ce sont la des êtres sacrés et presque divins, que l'imagination de l'artiste a comme créés à nouveau et modelés a son gré pour les adapter à la fonction qu'elle leur donnait à remplir. Cependant, tout placé qu'il soit en dehors des conditions de la nature, l'animal n'a pas perdu sa physionomie propre. Dans le mouvement de *la tête légèrement inclinée en avant et sur la côté*, on sent la force indomptée qui anime ce corps ample et puissant. Hardiment indiquées, la construction et la musculature des *membres inférieurs replies sous le ventre*, laissent deviner de quel élan le taureau se lèverait et se dresserait en pied, s'il venait à se lasser de son éternel repos. J'en ai fait plusieurs fois l'expérience au Louvre, devant la parti de chapiteau colossal que notre musée doit à M. Dieulafoy:

* *Histoire de l'Art dans l'antiquité*, Perse, p. 519.

parmi les visiteurs qui se pressaient dans cette salle, parmi ceux mêmes qui semblaient le moins préparés à éprouver ce genre d'impressions, il n'en est pas un qui n'ait subi le charme, qui de manière ou d'autre, n'ait rendu hommage à la noblesse et à l'étrange beauté de ce type singulier."

For the exquisite columns crowned by these tauric capitals the same writers have claimed a distinctively Median origin. This claim they sustain at great length, and with much architectural learning. They show that in their proportions, and in every detail of their ornamentation, the Persepolitan differed from the Ninevite, Grecian, or Egyptian column. They also point out that no where except at Persepolis and at Susa is the demi-bull of the capital to be met with; and yet they express the opinion that this feature, so far as is known proper to Persia, was mainly derived from, or helped, at least, by the models of Assyria.

Very close resemblances can indeed be traced in Medo-Persian to Assyrian art, and as the Medo-Persian buildings whose ruins are at Persepolis and Susa were erected certainly at a later date than the palaces of the Assyrian kings discovered on the site of Nineveh, it is natural to attribute, as Perrot and Chippiez, and nearly all writers on the subject attribute, such resemblances to imitations on the part of the Medo-Persians of Assyrian art and symbolism.

There are however some considerations which make it difficult to adopt this view. In the first place, the symbolism supposed to have been copied by the Medo-Persians was religious symbolism, and the religion of the Aryan Medo-Persians was very[different from that of the Semitic Assyrians.

The Achæmenid kings who built their palaces at Persepolis claimed constantly that they were worshippers of the one great Lord Ahura Mazda, of whom Mithras was the friend and representative; That these kings should have adopted from the polytheistic Assyrians not only the Tauric symbolism we have above described, but also, as it is suggested, the emblem of their one great Lord Ahura Mazda (see Plate III, figs. 1, 2, 3) from that of Assur, would in itself be strange, but that they should have done so when Assur and all his followers had, by the victorious worshippers of Ahura Mazda, been utterly vanquished, seems still more improbable.

From the state in which the ruins of Nineveh were when discovered by Layard, it is easy to see that, from the very day of the sacking of the city, it had for the most part been left just as it fell.   It may have been rifled of its material wealth, but its literary and artistic treasures were left uncared for and undesired.   A few hundred years later the very site of Nineveh was unknown.

With such neglect the great city would not have been treated had the Medo-Persian artists turned to it for inspiration and for themes of symbolic art with which to decorate the palaces of Persepolis.

The resemblance, however, between Medo-Persian and Ninevite art is in many instances so striking that some way of accounting for it must be sought, and those who are dissatisfied with one explanation will naturally seek about to find some alternative suggestion.

The alternative suggestion we would now propose is that *the progenitors of the Assyrians at an early period of the world's history borrowed Tauric and other religious symbolisms from the ancestors of the Medes.*

In support of this alternative suggestion the following considerations are put forward.

Tauric symbolism, if it is at all astronomic, points us back to a very remote date for its first institution, to a date considerably earlier than that at which the existence of the Assyrian people as an independent nation is generally put.   The symbolism we have already discussed must, at the latest, have been originated about 2000 B.C.   Of the Assyrians as a nation we have no monumental proof earlier than 1600 B.C.

But further, in the symbol of Ahura and Assur (see Plate III, figs. 1, 2, 3), we believe an astonomic reference may be traced to the position of the colures, a reference which points us back not merely to a date between 4000 and 2000 B.C., but rather, and with curious precision, to the furthest limit of the time mentioned, namely to 4000 B.C.

To penetrate into the meaning of this symbol of Ahura we must study both the Median and Assyrian representations of the figure presiding over the winged disc, and we may also seek for further light to be thrown upon it by other references in Assyrian art to the god Assur.

Ahura presiding over the winged circle holds in his hand a ring or crown ; Assur in some examples is similarly furnished ; but more often he appears armed with bow and arrows.   In this figure, variously equipped, we believe that the heavenly Archer, the zodiacal Sagittarius, is to be recognised (Plate III, fig. 4).   Sagittarius,

PLATE I.

Proc. Soc. Bibl. Arch., June, 1897.

Proc. Soc. Bibl. Arch., June, 1897.

PLATE II.

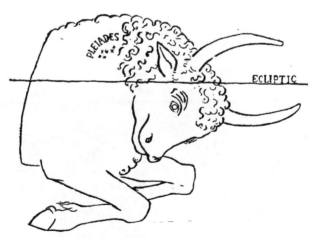

THE CONSTELLATION TAURUS.

PLATE III.

Proc. Soc. Bibl. Arch., June, 1897.

FIG. 1.

FIG. 3.

FIG. 2.

FIG. 4.

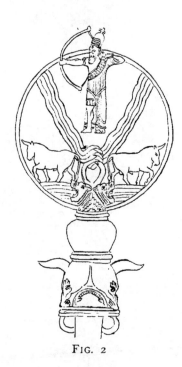

Fig. 2

Proc. Soc. Bibl. Arch., June, 1897.

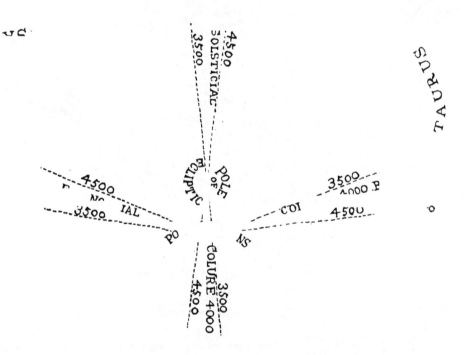

the constellation in which the autumnal equinoctial point was situated, speaking in round numbers, from 6000 to 4000 B.C.

The fact that a crown or wreath or ring often replaces the bow and arrows in the hand of Ahura and of Assur might at first sight make us doubtful as to the connection of the figure with the constellation Sagittarius, but a glance at the celestial globe will rather make this fact tell in favour of our astronomical suggestion; for there we find close to the hand of the archer the ancient Ptolemaic constellation Corona Australis (the Southern Crown), actually incorporated with the zodiacal constellation Sagittarius (Plate III, fig. 4).

Not only do Assur's bow and crown remind us of Sagittarius, but his horned tiara, resembling so closely that worn by the man-headed Assyrian bulls, inclines us to look for some astronomic and Tauric allusion in this Assyrian and Median symbol.

True it is that, speaking generally, "Gemini" and not Taurus is the constellation of the zodiac opposed to Sagittarius, but owing to the irregularity in the shape and size of the portions assigned in the ecliptic to the zodiacal constellations, the extreme western degrees of Sagittarius are opposed to the extreme eastern degrees of Taurus (see Plate IV). Therefore about 4000 B.C. the equinoctial colure passed through the constellations of the Archer and the Bull.

In the Assyrian Standard (depicted in Plate IV, fig. 1) we see the figure of an Archer above that of a galloping bull, and in another Assyrian Standard, that of Sargon II (Plate IV, fig. 2) we find not only the Archer and the Bull, the two constellations which 4000 B.C. marked the *equinoctial* colure, but we may also clearly trace a reference to the two constellations which at the same date marked the *solstitial* colure, namely those of the Lion and the Waterman.

Here the *Archer* dominates over a circle in which symmetrically duplicated *Bulls* appear, and duplicated *Lions'* heads emerge out of what appears to be a hollow vessel resembling a *water jar;* the wavy lines that traverse the disc suggest streams that unitedly pour their waters into this jar. Below the jar again are to be seen halved and doubled heads, partly Lion and partly Bull.

This standard of Assur may (like the Persepolitan monster earlier described) be considered as an astronomic monogram representing the four constellations which marked the four seasons of the year, and the four corners of the earth.

The monogram of the Standard refers us back however to an earlier date for its origin than does the monogram of the composite animal in the Persepolitan bas-relief, for in the Standard the Archer is opposed to the Bull, in the bas-relief the Scorpion takes the place of the Archer, and the Eagle takes the place of the Waterman.

The precession of the Equinoxes advances from east to west amongst the stars. Therefore the Scorpion marked the colure at a later date than did the Archer. The Eagle, as we have already pointed out, is considerably to the west of Aquarius, and could scarcely have been chosen as a substitute for that constellation when the colure was in its extreme eastern degrees.

At Plate V* we give the position of the colures at 4000 B.C.; not much earlier or much later than this date can we place the *origin* of the symbolism in the Standard shown at (Plate IV, fig. 2). Earlier *not* Leo and Aquarius, but Virgo and Pisces would have marked the solsticial colure. Later *not* Sagittarius but Scorpio would have in opposition to Taurus marked the equinoctial colure.

At this date, 4000 B.C., suggested with such curious accuracy by this Assyrian Standard, we have absolutely no trace of the existence of the *Semitic nation of the Assyrians* in northern Mesopotamia. In Babylonia two hundred years later the Semitic Sargon I ruled at Accad. In the astrological work drawn up if not for Sargon yet, as we may judge from internal evidence, for some king of Accad, no mention is made of the Assyrian nation.

The Phœnicians, the Hittites, the Kings of Gutium and the "Uman Manda" are then the dreaded foes of Accad. Of the Manda we read as follows: "The Uman Manda comes and governs the land. The mercy seats of the great gods are taken away. Bel goes to Elam."

Professor Sayce is opposed to the view that the "Manda" are necessarily identical with the Medes; but he admits that Herodotus, following the authority of Medo-Persian writers, claimed as Median the victories of the Manda.†

-If now on the authority of Herodotus and the Medo-Persian writers we assume, at least as a possibility, that these Manda were

* In this diagram the central point is the pole of the Ecliptic; owing therefore to the limitations imposed by the laws of projection, the colures, which on a celestial globe intersect each other at *right angles* at the pole of the Heavens, cannot be correctly represented.

† *Proceedings*, Vol. XVIII, Part 6, pp. 176, 177.

Medes, we should expect to find them worshippers of Ahura
Mazda. Ahura, it is on all hands admitted, is the Iranian
form of the Vedic "Asura," just as Mithras is the Iranian form of
the Vedic Mitra. At whatever date the separation between Iranian
and Vedic Aryans took place, the worship of Ahura (still probably
under the form Asura) must have existed amongst the Iranians;
indeed, many have supposed that the monotheistic reform which
placed one great Ahura or Asura above all other Asuras, and above
the Devas, occasioned the separation of these two great Aryan
races.

It is for the Lord "Ahura," in early times, as we have supposed,
called "Asura" by the Aryan Manda, that we would claim the
astronomical symbol of the Archer presiding over the circle of the
ecliptic, or, in other words, over the circle of the year, and of
a year beginning at the Spring Equinox—a year, as we have already
pointed out, distinctively Median.

According then to our supposition, a powerful Median race was
established in the vicinity of Babylonia early in the fourth mille-
nium B.C.—a race who worshipped one great Lord, first under the
name of *Asura*—afterwards under that of *Ahura*.

It is for these Aryan *Manda* or *Medes* that we would claim, at
the date of 4000 B.C., the original conception of the astronomic
monogram in which so plainly may be read allusion to the four
constellations of the Zodiac, which at that date marked the four
seasons and the four cardinal points, *i.e.*, Sagittarius and Taurus,
Aquarius and Leo. This monogram was used as a standard
thousands of years later by the Semitic Assyrians.

To the *Manda* or *Medes*, also, we would, as we have suggested,
attribute the first imagining of the astronomic emblem common to
Ahura and Assur—that of the divine Being presiding over the
circle of the Ecliptic.

Berosus mentions a Median dynasty as having reigned in
Babylon for one or two hundred years. Let us now suppose that
in this dynasty we are to recognise a temporary supremacy, over the
whole of Babylonia, of the very *Manda* of whom we have been
speaking, and then we may picture to ourselves these Manda being
successfully driven back from Babylonia under the rule of the
powerful Semitic Hamurabi, about 2200 B.C. The tide of conquest
must then, it would seem, have turned in favour of the Semites, for
some few hundreds of years after Hamurabi's date we meet in the

inscriptions, for the first time, mention of the Semitic Assyrians, and we find them established in the region from whence in former times, as it would seem, *the Uman Manda* threatened the inhabitants of Babylonia.

To account for the existence of the Assyrian nation, their close resemblance in language and race to the ruling Semitic class in Babylon, and yet to explain the great difference in the religion of these two peoples, has always been a difficulty.

The Assyrians worshipped, and worshipped with enthusiasm, all the Babylonian gods; but high above the whole Babylonian pantheon they placed as their supreme and great Lord "*Assur*"— Assur whose very name is not to be met with in Babylonian mythology. This difficulty, continuing our suppositions, we would explain in the following manner :

When the Medes had, by Hamurabi or his successors, been driven out of Northern Mesopotamia, they were replaced by Semitic settlers who (like the settlers sent into Samaria more than a thousand years later by a king of Assyria) adopted, to a certain extent, the religion of the nation whom they had dispossessed. In 2 Kings xvii we read that in this parallel instance "the king of Assyria brought men from Babylon and from Cuthah, and from Ava, and from Hamath, and from Sepharvaim, and planted them in the cities of Samaria instead of the children of Israel, and they possessed the cities thereof." Later in the same chapter we read that in order to appease, as they believed, the wrath of the "*God of the land*," these idolatrous settlers, retaining in full the worship of all their own gods, added to it a worship of the Lord of the dispossessed Israelites.

We suppose then that the polytheistic Semites, who after Hamurabi's time settled in Northern Mesopotamia, acted in a similar manner. Coming into a region where for nearly 2000 years the monotheistic Medes or Manda had been established, they, to avert the wrath of the *god of the land*, adopted to a certain extent his worship. In fact, like the Samaritans, "they feared the Lord [Asura], and served their own gods."

This explanation of the difference in religion between the Babylonians and the Assryians seems to yield also an explanation of the resemblances between the Assyrian and Median religions, or rather of the resemblances between the religious art of he two people; and thus we return to the problem which we set ourselves to discuss earlier in this paper, namely, the inadequacy of the generally held opinion which accounts for the resemblances in Persepolitan and Ninevite symbolic art by supposing that the Medes borrowed from the Assyrians.

In support of the alternative suggestion put forward at p. 238, that *the progenitors of the Assyrians at an early period of the world's history borrowed Tauric and other religious symbolisms from the ancestors of the Medes,* we claim that the Assyrians borrowed not only religious symbolisms, but that they borrowed even the very name of their god *Assur* from the Medes. For we look upon *Assur* as a "loan word" adopted from the Aryan *Asura.*

To the Medes or Manda, who were, as we have argued, in power in Northern Mesopotamia about 4000 B.C., we have attributed the *origin* of the astronomic Assyrian and Ahurian emblem. To them also belongs the first imagining of the astronomic Assyrian standard. To them, on the same grounds, we attribute the devising of the man-headed and winged monsters so well known as "Assyrian Bulls," and to them indeed we would leave the honour of having invented and not borrowed the idea of the magnificent Tauric capitals that crowned the columns of Persepolis and Susa.

To all these conclusions we have been led by a consideration of the distinctively equinoctial character of the Median Calendar, taken in connection with the importance given in Median art to the constellation Taurus.

The following has been received from Mr. Offord :—

The evidence of the cuneiform inscriptions has decided beyond doubt that the months of the Babylonians extended, to in every case, thirty days, and were therefore not twenty-eight days, or four weeks, nor, as after the Persian period, were they of twenty-nine, or thirty days' duration alternately.

The proofs of this, both direct and indirect, from cuneiform texts are ample. For instance, Sayce in "Babylonian Astronomy," cites Rawlinson ("Cuneiform Inscriptions of Western Asia"), III, 32, reverse, 37, "twelve months in the year 6 × 60 days in number." Again, Rawlinson, III, 60, says, "In the month Nisan from the first to the thirtieth day;" and Rawlinson, V, 48, 49, gives a Babylonian calendar which apparently assigns thirty days to each month.

Also the Hemerologies in Rawlinson, IV, 32, give thirty days to the month Elul, and in the 1891 edition of Vol. IV, 33, also to Marchesvan, and it is particularly important to notice that on this occasion these two months are referred to as intercalary or duplicate months.

A "portent tablet" states that "from the first to the thirtieth of January if an eclipse happens the altars are destroyed."

The ideograph for month also indicates the truth, being the figure of the sun (which also denotes a day) with the sign for thirty inside it.

Finally, the peculiar difficulty of the nineteenth day of a month being in one case a sabbath, in addition to the seventh, fourteenth, twenty-first, and twenty-eighth (see text in Sayce, "Hibbert Lectures," p. 73), is shown by Jensen to result from its being the forty-ninth day, namely, 7×7 days from the first day of the preceding month.

An indirect proof that Babylonian months were thirty days long, is derived from the certainty that they were not lunar months, proved by the occurrence of lunar eclipses upon any day of the month; so many texts illustrating this are known to scholars and have been quoted in reference to Babylonian astronomy that this need not be dwelt upon.

Dr. Muss Arnolt mentions another fact, that of the variation in the day of the month upon which the vernal equinox took place, showing that whatever length the months were, the multiplication of them by twelve did not coincide with a solar year.

Then as noted already we have direct evidence from the cuneiform tablets that the intercalary months,* of which the names of four are known, were also of thirty days (see Rawlinson, IV, 32 and 33).

Accepting then the thirty-day Babylonian months, leads us to the interesting conclusion that an extra month must have been added to the calendar every sixth year, because years consisting of 12×30-day months would every sixth year become a month too short. This will account for the existence of one of the intercalary months, probably the duplicate, or Ve Adar. It is also indirectly confirmed by the statement of Censorinus, "that every twelfth year was a Chaldean cycle," that being a double period of six years.

---

* In reference to the periods of intercalation of supernumerary months, see E. Mahler, "Der Schaltcyclus der Babylonier," *Zeits. für Assyriologie*, Vol. IX, p. 42, etc.

But three other duplicate month names are known, one of which may be accounted for by the astronomical error being really more in six years by about thirty-five hours than the addition of an extra thirty-day month would rectify. In about one hundred and twenty-four years this error reached thirty days or a month more, and may have been the period when a second Nisan was interpolated. It may here be noted in reference to the changing day of the month for the vernal equinox, that though it occurs on various days in Nisan, it has never yet been found shifted into another month, showing that when the error amounted to a month, either a duplicate Nisan or another intercalary month of another name was at once added to get the year into order again.

As stated we know of two other intercalary months, a second Elul and second Marchesvan; why and wherefore these were used, supposing the mention of them is at the era when only thirty-day months were in use, it is difficult to say. If they were to rectify another small astronomical difference, the periods between their utilisation must have been immense; perhaps they sometimes took the name place of an Adar or Nisan, when they had to be put in for some occult reason.

Epping and Strassmaier in their "Astronomisches aus Babylon," show that in later times there was a year of alternate months of twenty-nine or thirty days (which it is interesting to note is practically a lunar year), and made the error annually six days worse; adding this to the previous five days' error, we get eleven days, or about one hundred and twenty days in eleven years. These authors show, and it is therefore most interesting, that during every eleven years the Arsacidæ and Seleucidæ inserted four additional months, being approximately this very one hundred and twenty days, to rectify their calendar. As shown however in regard to the Babylonian year, the annual error exceeded five days, so the four months every eleven years would not quite correct the calendar, and Epping and Strassmaier show undoubtedly. in connection with this fact we may presume, that besides the four months added during every eleven years an extra one was intercalated every one hundred and thirty-two years.*

---

* It may be that when the equinox error amounted to a month the calendar for other reasons, needed rectification to the extent of a month and so the equinox error was remedied so to speak automatically irrespective of itself.

ADDITIONAL NOTE BY THE HON. MISS PLUNKETT.

The Babylonian years, which Epping and Strassmaier so closely studied, and which are so clearly described in their book, *Astronomisches aus Babylon*, were *Soli-lunar*. The months composing them were *lunar*, and contained sometimes thirty and sometimes twenty-nine days.

The actual time that elapses between new-moon and new-moon, or between full-moon and full-moon, and therefore the mean time between "new-light and new-light" (the starting point and termination of Babylonian months), is twenty-nine days twelve hours forty-four minutes and three seconds. Every second month and sometimes oftener the fractions of a day in the above sum amounted to a thirtieth day.

The Babylonian almanacs commented on by Epping and Strassmaier in the above named work, and also in many articles contributed to the *Zeitschrift für Assyriologie* belong it is true to the last centuries of Babylonian history, that is, to what Mr. Offord describes as the "Persian period." These almanacs, however, show no signs of Persian influence. They are all issued "At the command of my Lord Bel and my Lady Beltis, an edict." The names of the months and all the technical terms employed are decidedly Babylonian. There are moreover very many indications, so many indeed as to amount to actual proof, that the method of reckoning which appears in these tablets was in use before the Persian period.

It is on this basis that not only Epping and Strassmaier discuss earlier dated documents. Mahler, Oppert, and Lehman all adopt the same course.

In the January number for this year of the *Zeitschrift für Assyriologie*, C. E. Lehman translates a very interesting notice of an eclipse of the moon which took place on the 15th *Sabatu* in the time of Samassumkin of Babylon. Oppert in commenting on C. E. Lehman's paper cites other "pre-Persian" eclipses, the dates of which are noted according to a soli-lunar calendar apparently identical with that of the Epping and Strassmaier almanacs.

In favour of the opinion that the Babylonian months were lunar, we may also point to the description of the months in what is called the Fifth Creation tablet, there we read :—

"Nanna the moon was charged to illumine the night, and he caused it to be renewed, to hide the night and to prolong the day; month by month without interruption fill thy disc.   At the beginning of the month the night must prevail.   The horns will be invisible, for the heaven renews itself . . . . ."

That Babylonian months were counted by the phases of the moon before the Persian period is very plain.   But the evidence we as yet possess is perhaps not sufficient to prove that they were counted in the same manner in the very ancient time when the standard astrological works translated by Prof. Sayce, and alluded to by Mr. Offord, were first drawn up; still the identity of the month names, and of many technical terms in the earlier and later astronomical works speak strongly in favour of such a supposition; and the series of dated trade documents which have come down to us from various periods of Babylonian history show us that a well established calendar was long in existence in Babylon and other Mesopotamian cities.

The ancient astrological tablets have not, except in a few instances, so far as we know, been re-translated since the year 1874, when Prof. Sayce contributed his paper on " The Astronomy and Astrology of the Babylonians," to the Transactions of this Society (Vol. III).   Since that date many advances have been made in the identification of planet and constellation names, and also in the right understanding of many technical astronomical expressions. As the work at present stands, it is difficult for those who (like the writer of this paper) are entirely dependent on translations, to form any clear judgment on isolated passages occurring in its text.

Epping in the first chapter of his *Astronomisches aus Babylon*, referring to Profs. Oppert's and Sayce's early astronomical papers, says :   " Wer jedoch diese arbeiten durchliest der wird sich leicht überzeugen, das die angaben der monumente nicht genügen um ein sicheres System zu construiren."

But if from the sources at our command we have not sufficient evidence to prove that the ancient Babylonian months were certainly lunar, neither can it be claimed that the works in question prove " beyond a doubt that the months of the Babylonians extended to in every case thirty days."

Prof. Sayce at p. 160 claims for the Accadians a year of 360 days; but again, at p. 207, he states that the " months were lunar, and were divided into two lunations ; and the days on which the quarters of the moon began, as well as the beginning of the second lunation, were called days of sulum or 'rest,' on which certain works were forbidden."

Now a year counted by lunar months cannot also be described as consisting of 360 days.

If the tablets appear to give evidence of two such contrary methods of counting the year, we must either treat their evidence as unreliable, or we must suppose that in some way the meaning of their evidence has been misunderstood, such for instance may have been the case as regards the following passage quoted by Mr. Offord, "twelve months in the year 6 × 60 days in number."

In Prof. Sayce's *Astronomy and Astrology of the Babylonians*, p. 155, the sentence appears in a slightly different form, "twelve months to each year (6 × 60 =) 360 days in order are recorded....."

The variation of these two renderings, though slight, presents some difficulty in discussing the passage. *Twelve* months, in "the" year referred to, would not contradict the assumption that in some other year there might be *thirteen* months; "the" year is therefore not so much opposed to the theory of a soli-lunar year as are the words twelve months to "each" year. Leaving this point in uncertainty, it is curious to observe that the number of days in the succeeding phrase is given not as "12 × 30" but as "6 × 60." 6 × 60 exactly describes the divisions of the Babylonian day,[*] and one is tempted to suppose that this expression may refer to the divisions of the day and not to the days of the year; or again, the 360 days mentioned may be not real but *fictive* days. The Hindus divide every lunar month into thirty days or " Tithis ;" they do so for purposes of astronomical calculation. The actual days of the month noted in their calendars is however always the true solar day. English astronomers also for purposes of astronomical calculation, make use of a "sidereal day," and count 366 such days to every 365 solar days.

The tablet in which the sentence we have been discussing occurs, contains many very bewildering statements, as for instance that in the immediately following lines : " During the middle of the day a deficiency of the sight of the non-existent star." It is difficult in reading these lines to believe that a full and certain comprehension of what the ancient astronomer here intended to express, has been arrived at.

---

[*] P. 45, *Astronomisches aus Babylon* (Epping).

Some notices of the " occurrence of lunar eclipses on any day of the month" appear among the translations in Prof. Sayce's paper, and as they stand are utterly opposed to the theory of lunar months. Of such is tablet W.A.I. III, 55, i, (p. 222); in it eclipses for each of the first fifteen days of the month Tamuz are suggested.   So contrary however are these exceptional notices to the general drift of the great body of the astronomical texts, that, as in the case of the passage already discussed, it would seem well to wait for the light of further research to be thrown on them before accepting them as conclusive evidence of non-lunar months having held a place in the Babylonian calendar.

Some other points put forward by Mr. Offord as hostile to the lunar theory may be more easily explained.

The mention of thirty days in any month presents no difficulty. In all soli-lunar years six, at least, of the months must contain thirty days.   It is not therefore to be wondered at that the ideograph for a month is "the figure of the sun with the sign for thirty inside it." Prof. Sayce tells us that in the astronomical tablets the moon is generally represented by the symbol XXX.   This fact is in favour rather than in opposition to the theory that the Babylonian months were dependent on the phases of the moon.

NOTE SUR UN LINTEAU DE PORTE DÉCOUVERT EN ASSYRIE PAR GEORGE SMITH.

By Alfred Boissier.

Dans ses *Assyrian Discoveries* George Smith a signalé un monument très curieux. Voici comme il s'exprime à ce sujet (page 146) : "In the south-eastern court (du palais de Sanchérib) I penetrated to the pavement, and in front of one of the entrances on the western side I discovered the lintel of a doorway ; it was formed of a block of stone six feet long, and was sculptured along the face. In the centre was an ornamental cup or vase, with two handles ; on each side of the vase stood a winged griffin or dragon, looking towards the centre, having a long neck and an ornament or collar round it just behind the head. Over the cup and the dragon was an ornament of honeysuckles. This curious lintel is the first Assyrian object of the kind which has been discovered, and I saw it lifted out of the excavation with much pleasure." Si j'ai reproduit textuellement la note de Smith sur ce monument, c'est qu'en effet elle ne parait pas avoir été assez remarquée ; j'ai été aussi très étonné en lisant l'article "Gryps," du dictionnaire de Roscher, de voir que M. Furtwängler n'a pas cru devoir mentionner ce curieux bas-relief. Peut-être les deux animaux fantastiques qui l'ornent n'ont-ils rien à voir avec les griffons ;* mais il me semble qu'il faudrait encore s'en assurer, et c'est pourquoi je me permets de rappeler aux archéologues ce monument remarquable et trop dédaigné jusqu'à présent. L'art babylonien et l'art assyrien ne nous avaient encore rien révélé d'analogue, et il est très probable que ce sont des artistes étrangers à

---

* M. Perrot parle de *dragons ailés*. Le linteau de porte découvert par Smith est reproduit dans les "*Assyrian Discoveries*," page 309, et dans *Perrot* et *Chipiez, Histoire de l'Art*, Tome II, page 248. Voir aussi Meissner Rost : Die *Bauinschriften Sanheribs*, page 29.

l'Assyrie qui ont exécuté le bas-relief en question. L'on sait que Sanchérib et les grands rois qui l'avaient précédé, de même que ceux qui lui succédèrent employèrent à la construction de leurs palais des prisonniers venus de l'occident. Si les deux animaux qui encadrent la coupe ou le vase sont bien des griffons, on leur trouvera une ressemblance assez marquée avec le griffon mycénien, au corps allongé, symbole de l'animal rapide et féroce. Il faudrait examiner si dans les inscriptions cunéiformes il est jamais fait mention d'un être qui se rapproche du griffon. Pour cela l'on cherchera tout naturellement dans la "Grande Epopée Babylonienne de la Création," où sont mentionnés tous les animaux terribles que Tiamat soulève contre Marduk. Quoique plusieurs de ces noms d'animaux ne soient pas expliqués, que nous ignorons absolument quels êtres sont désignés par les *laḫmu*, les *ûmgallu*, les *šidimmu*, etc., il ne me semble guère probable qu'il soit question du griffon dans ces textes et dans l'inscription historique d'Agum. Bérose ne fait aucune allusion au griffon. Dans les monuments archaïques de la basse Chaldée il ne se rencontre pas. Il parait pour la première fois dans les monuments qui datent environ du 9e siècle, a. J.C., d'après Furtwängler et Puchstein. Il est impossible de dire à quel peuple les Assyriens ont emprunté ce symbole, originaire peut-être du nord de la Syrie. Dans la série des monuments de la Chaldée et de l'Assyrie le bas-relief du linteau de porte découvert par Smith occupe une place à part ; il mériterait d'être étudié de plus près par les archéologues ; il nous diront peut-être quelle était la nationalité de ceux qui l'exécutèrent.*

* Nous mentionnerons encore un très beau spécimen de la glyptique orientale qui représente un griffon à corps de cheval. (*Ménant*, catalogue de la collection de Clercq, Vol. II, Pl. IV, No. 90.) On trouvera également un monument fort intéressant reproduit dans le grand ouvrage des Antiquités de la Russie Méridionale publié par Kondakof, Tolstoï et Salomon Reinach, page 272, figure 243. M. Helbig dit que le griffon était un objet de prédilection de l'art phénicien. (Epopée Homérique, traduction française de Trawinski, page 498.)

[*The illustration of this interesting monument will be issued with the next part of the Proceedings.*—W.H.R.]

THE ROLLIN PAPYRI AND THEIR BAKING CALCULATIONS.

[*Conclusion.*]

BY PROF. DR. AUGUST EISENLOHR.

(Sent in 1 *November*, 1895.)

PLATE XIV.[1]

1885 = 206*a*.

This plate, although much later than the latest date of Pl. XIII, and later also than the final date of Pl. XX of the next section (27 Payni), was notwithstanding written on the same sheet as Pl. XIII, filling up the first column, whilst Pl. XIII filled the second.

Translation.

1. *Year 2 Mesori day 23 of the king Ramenmat, Life, Welfare, Health!*
2. *son of Ra, Seti mer en ptah, L.W.H., living for ever to eternity, like his father Ra every day*
3. *this day one was in Memphis in the house of Ra-nefer[2]-cheper-ka*
4. *Register. Received corn (boti) from the granary of the Pharaoh L.W.H., in Memphis*
5. *to make flour in āku bread in the bakehouse, put under the superintendence*
6. *of the chief Neferhoiepu of Memphis ; providing the store house of the Pharaoh, L.W.H.*

This document is dated from Memphis in the same locality as Pl. XII, 1 ; II, 3, the Pa Ra-nefer[2]-cheper-ka, of which nearly unknown king perhaps of sole Lower Egypt we spoke above. I

---

[1] Spiegelberg, Tafel V.

[2] According to Spiegelberg's emendation, Ra-aa-cheper-ka.

think to be right in translating [hieroglyphs], l. 4, *from* the granary, because the corn is given to the bakers out from it. We have to read with the original [hieroglyphs] *boti* and not *nut'* (Pleyte). L. 5, instead of the common word [hieroglyphs], *nut'* (Pl. V–IX), the word [hieroglyphs], which follows generally the first term, stands here alone. Doubtless this is the Coptic CIKE or CIKI, *molere* (Peyron, *Lex. Copt.*) in hieroglyphs written [hieroglyphs], *vide* Brugsch, *Wörtb. Cont.*, p. 1140. We met the word [hieroglyphs] before, Pl. XIII, l. 2. It must be bakehouse, because the bread is there prepared. This bake-house is put, as we heard already at the *loc. cit.*, under the superintendence of a chief $\left(\text{[hieroglyph]} \right)$ called Neferhotep. The aim of this baking was to provide (*suat'*) the store house [hieroglyphs], *ut'a* (see the corrections), of the Pharaoh.

7. *Mesori day 23, corn flour tep sacks* 100.
8. *Mesori day 28, corn flour tep sacks* 250.[1]
9. *Mesori day 28, corn flour tep sacks* 280.[2]
10. *Mesori day 28, corn flour tep sacks* 280.[2]
11. *Mesori day 28, corn flour tep sacks* 290.[3]
12. *Mesori day 28, corn flour tep sacks* 280.[2]
13. *Mesori day 28, corn flour tep sacks* 260.
14. *Mesori day 28, corn flour tep sacks* 280.[4]
15. *Mesori day 28, corn flour tep sacks* 260.

20   1500.[5]

With the original were the numbers in ll. 12 and 14 corrected from 260 to 280. From l. 7 we learn that [hieroglyphs], which was often supposed to be wheat or corn (*Roggen*), is a general expression for every kind of corn, as here the *boti* (spelt). The sum 1500 seems imperfect, as the number of tep sacks added gives more than 2000.

---

[1] Spiegelberg, 150.   [2] Spiegelberg, 180.
[3] Spiegelberg, 190.   [4] Spiegelberg, $x + 180$.
[5] Spiegelberg, 1600¼.   On the heliotype, Tafel V, the number is cut away.

SECTION III.   (PLATE XVII–XX) 1889 = 205.[1]

As the little sketch on p. 93 demonstrates, Pl. XVIII standing above Pl. XVII precedes that plate.   We see that also from the dates, Pl. XVIII dating from Athyr 21 till Choiak 7, whilst Pl. XVII is dated from the 7th Choiak of the 2nd year of Seti I, and Pl. XIX beginning with the same 7th Choiak till to Phamenoth 7, and Pl. XX in continuation from Phamenoth 17 to Payni 27. Pl. XVIII, contemporary with Pl. X of the second section, contains the distribution of flour to the bakers on fifteen consecutive days ($\frac{1}{2}$ month), the amount in mill sacks (for every day $7\frac{1}{2}$ sacks) is transferred into *boti*, spelt, or maize in the probably smaller measure of 𓆓𓆟 tep sacks, which we have already found in the two former sections.   As the relation between the mill sacks of flour and the tep sacks of *boti* is throughout as $7\frac{1}{2}:18$, each mlll sack of flour must have contained $2\frac{1}{2}$ tep sacks of maize.

TRANSLATION OF PLATE XVIII, 1889.

1. *Athyr, day* 21, *given to the bakers flour sacks* $7\frac{1}{2}$, *makes in boti tep sacks* $18\frac{3}{4}$.

2. *Athyr, day* 22, *given to the bakers flour sacks* $7\frac{1}{2}$, *makes in boti tep sacks* $18\frac{3}{4}$.

3. *Athyr, day* 23, $7\frac{1}{2}$, *makes in boti tep sacks* $18\frac{3}{4}$.

4. *Athyr, day* 24, $7\frac{1}{2}$, *makes in boti tep sacks* $18\frac{3}{4}$.

5. *Athyr, day* 25, $7\frac{1}{2}$, *makes in boti tep sacks* $18\frac{3}{4}$.

6. *Athyr, day* 26, $7\frac{1}{2}$, *makes in boti tep sacks* $18\frac{3}{4}$.

7. *Athyr, day* 27, $7\frac{1}{2}$, *makes in boti tep sacks* $18\frac{3}{4}$.

8. *Athyr, day* 28, $7\frac{1}{2}$, *makes in boti tep sacks* $18\frac{3}{4}$.

9. *Athyr, day* 29, $7\frac{1}{2}$, *makes in boti tep sacks* $18\frac{3}{4}$.

[1] Spiegelberg, Tafel IV.

10. *Athyr, day last, given to the bakers flour sacks* 7½, *makes in boti*
    tep sacks 18¾.
11. *Choiak, day 1,*   7½, *makes in boti*
    tep sacks 18¼.
12. *Choiak, day 2,*   7½, *makes in boti*
    tep sacks 18¾.
13. *Choiak, day 3,*   7⅓, *makes in boti*
    tep sacks 18¾.
14. *Choiak, day 4,*   7½, *makes in boti*
    tep sacks 18¾.
15. *Choiak, day 6,*   7½, *makes in boti*
    tep sacks 18¾.

The sum of the mill sacks of flour would be $15 \times 7\frac{1}{2} = 1125$
and the sum of the tep sacks of corn $15 \times 18\frac{3}{4} = 281\frac{1}{4}$. See the
corrections, where you find also the term mill sacks (l. 1) before the
number 7½.

Now would follow the continuation of this register, Pl. XIX
and XX, but the scribe has inserted before a special account over
85 big loaves (ākeku).

Plate XVII. Translation.

1. *Year 2, Choiak day 7 (of) the king Ramenmat, L. W.H.*
2. *Son of Ra, Seti mer en ptah, L. W.H., living for ever to*
   eternity like his father Ra every day.
3. *This day one was travelling in the northern district.*
4. *Account of the taxations of the verificators of the entrances*
   which are under
5. *the royal scribe, Neb nefer, in the bakehouses, to make out of*
   them āku bread.
6. *The bakehouse under (the superintendence) of the chief Nefer-*
   hotepu of Memphis,
7. *verified loaves great* 85 *each ākeku in the proportion* 15
   per 1 *sack*
8. *makes in great ākeku* 85 *makes in* 1 *day*
9. *corn tep sacks* 5⅔, *makes in* 10 *days sacks* 1½, 5⅔.

The object of this plate appears to be the establishment of the proportion between sacks of corn (probably *boti*) and loaves of ākeku bread, which we met before, Pl. XII. It is said that the (daily) production of ākeku is 85 ākeku, and that these ākeku are in the proportion of 15 to one sack. What we translated with proportion is the word 𓎡 *pefsu*, which is very well known, not only from the Medinet Abu accounts, but from the Rhind Mathematical Papyrus (*vide* Eisenlohr, *Mathem. Handbuch*, p. 259, the problems there cited). The *pefsu* indicates how many pieces (here *ākeku* loaves) are made of one measure (here sack of corn). So we must give here another meaning of the word 𓎡, as Pl. XII, where we rendered it by baking, or oven, indicating there the loss of weight by baking the bread in the oven. When 15 bread are made of one sack of corn, the 85 loaves of daily product want $5\frac{2}{3}$ of such sacks, because 85 is $5\frac{2}{3} \times 15$ that will tell l. 9. But we do not understand how that daily product of $5\frac{2}{3}$ sacks can make in ten days only $1\frac{1}{2}$ sack. We would await $56\frac{2}{3}$ sacks. The proportion of $1\frac{1}{2}$ to $5\frac{2}{3}$ is really like 1 : 3, 77, and we would rather believe that it is not a calculation for ten days, but a transposition of corn sacks in another measure, of which an example is found in Pl. XVIII, but there the relation of measures is 1 : $2\frac{1}{2}$ and not 1 : 3, 77.

Of the verbal explanation of this plate, in l. 3 the word 𓊪𓎼𓊪𓂝𓂻, "travelling," which has been already alluded to on XIII, 1, l. 4, the original does not read *hannu*, as supposed by Pleyte, but 𓊪𓎡𓏭 *heterä'*, which word is known from the problems No. 82–84 of the Mathematical Rhind Papyrus. It must have here, as there, the general sense of establishing, determining by some officials, and not the special sense of taxation, or imposing taxes. This duty was fulfilled by a certain kind of officials, whose name is not to be recognised in Pleyte's edition; they were the 𓊪𓄿𓄿𓏭[1] 𓈖 𓅱𓄿𓄿𓂝, *hesuau' en mau*, which new

---

[1] Spiegelberg, Tafel IVa, transcribes 𓈖𓊪𓄿𓄿 *nan nehesiu' en maut*, and translates Text, p. 14 (Tribut) der Neger von Mawet; equally l. 7 𓊪𓄿𓄿 , *Neger*, persons 85. As negroes are mentioned in the Rollin Papyri (Spiegelberg, Tafel X, 209, Col. 2, 4, verso), I think he may be right.

word we understand as the verifiers, though the determinative of *mau* speaks more for a coherence with 〔hieroglyphs〕 *mat*, "shore-land" (Edfu Donation, I, 4) than with 〔hieroglyphs〕 *māt,* "verity." These verifiers were under the care of the royal scribe Nebnefer. On 〔hieroglyphs〕, "the bakehouses," see *supra* to Pl. XIV. These bakehouses stood under another chief Neferhotepu of Memphis, whom we met XIV, 6. It is dubious how we ought to read the first word of l. 7; probably it is 〔hieroglyphs〕 *ḥestu*, the action of the above *ḥesu*, verified, and not *ástu*, "look." The 〔hieroglyph〕,[1] ll. 7 and 8, are the great loaves, the *ákeku*, l. 9, 〔hieroglyphs〕, tep sacks, and not, as Pleyte's supposes, 15, but $5\frac{2}{3}$ in red we must read before the repeated $5\frac{2}{3}$, 〔hieroglyphs〕 sacks $1\frac{1}{2}$).

PLATES XIX–XX.

After the protocol of Pl. XVII, dated from the 7th. Choiak of the second year, the journal of deliveries to the bakers, contained in Pl. XVIII, is here continued, and begins with the same date as the protocol of Pl. XVII, and a day later than the last entry of Pl. XVIII. We said above that according to time the entries of Pl. XVIII coincide with the entries of Pl. X, the third of the second section of the Papyrus; but we must not forget that the register in Pl. XII, XIII, X treats of the reception of bread into the magazine of the court, whilst the entries of Pl. XVIII, XIX and XX, deal with the dispensing of *flour* and corn (*boti*) to the bakers. As Pl. XVIII is beginning with a much later date than Pl. XII, XIII and X, we must acknowledge that a good part of the journal foregoing Pl. XVIII ff has been lost. Whilst Pl. XVIII contains the dispensing of flour to the bakers, the amount of which is only translated in the much smaller ($1 : 2\frac{1}{2}$) sacks of corn, Pl. XIX and XX give us the entries only of the receipt of corn (boti), if we correctly understand the term 〔hieroglyphs〕 *šet*, Pl. XIX, 1, which we translate with Loret (*Rec.*, XI, 131) *enlever, tirer, i.e.,* "to draw,

---

[1] Spiegelberg, 〔hieroglyph〕 *sà*, "persons."

receive." This corn is drawn from , a magazine , at Memphis, the designation of which I do not quite understand; perhaps we may read the signs ,[1] so that it would be a house of beating, *i.e.*, threshing-floor.

Translation.

1. *Year 2 Choiak 7.   The day of taking the corn* (boti) *from the threshing-floor at Memphis for making . . .*

[The end of the phrase, probably *hotep',* "bread," or *ākuu,* has been cut by the binder, who pasted the sheet on cardboard.]

2. *This day, corn, tep sacks* $2\frac{1}{2}$ $54\frac{2}{3}$
3. *Choiak, day* 14, *corn, tep sacks* $2\frac{1}{2}$ $54\frac{2}{3}$
4. *Choiak, day* 24, *corn, tep sacks* $2\frac{1}{2}$ $54\frac{2}{3}$
5. *Tybi, day* 4, *corn, tep sacks* $2\frac{1}{2}$ $54\frac{2}{3}$
6. *Tybi, day* 14, *corn, tep sacks* $2\frac{1}{2}$ $54\frac{2}{3}$
7. *Tybi, day* 24, *corn, tep sacks* $\frac{3}{4}$ $16\frac{1}{4}$
8. *Tybi, day* 27, *corn, tep sacks* $2\frac{1}{2}$ $54\frac{2}{3}$
9. *Mechir, day* 7, *corn, tep sacks* $2\frac{1}{2}$ $54\frac{2}{3}$
10. *Mechir, day* 17, *corn, tep sacks* $2\frac{1}{2}$ $54\frac{2}{3}$
11. *Mechir, day* 27, *corn, tep sacks* $2\frac{1}{2}$ $54\frac{2}{3}$
12. *Phamenoth day* 7, *corn, tep sacks* $2\frac{1}{2}$ $54\frac{2}{3}$.

We have in this journal the entries of 11 days in the series from ten to ten, ten of which note the drawing of $2\frac{1}{2}$ tep sacks of corn, only one of a $\frac{3}{4}$ sack, after the correction according to the original. Under this corn we have to understand the *boti* (spelt or durra) of l. 1. Regarding the register of Pl. XVIII, where the flour sacks are transferred into the smaller measure (tep sacks) of corn, we must also here presume these smaller sacks, which are not giving 720

---

[1] Spiegelberg reads (Tafel IV, 6) as name of this magazine, but the hieratic sign is quite another than that for or ᛆ which we found in Pl. XIII, 3, in the name of Hui.

ten = 65 kilogr. of bread, but only 245 ten or 22 kilogr. of bread (*vide* p. 96).   Now it will be without question that the following red ciphers $54\frac{2}{3}$ (once $16\frac{1}{4}$) [Pleyte's sign for $\frac{2}{3}$ must be corrected after the original] are loaves of bread.   If we divide $2\frac{1}{2} \times 245 = 612$, 5 ten by $54\frac{2}{3}$, we get for each loaf 11, 2 ten not much under the weight of an ākeku (Pl. XII) of $12\frac{1}{2}$—$13\frac{1}{2}$.   The next plate (XX) exhibits—of $2\frac{1}{2}$ tep sacks of corn—only 50 loaves ;. that would augment the weight of each loaf to $12\frac{1}{4}$ ten, still nearer to the normal weight.   The somewhat indistinct traces of the product in l. 7 we fix by the proportion $2\frac{1}{2} : 1\frac{3}{4} = 54\frac{2}{3} : 16\frac{1}{4}$.

PLATE XX

Joins, according to time, to Pl. XIX with the same intervals of 10 days for each entry, and differs only in the quantity of the product, as here are reckoned for $2\frac{1}{2}$ tep sacks of flour not $54\frac{2}{3}$, but only 50 (loaves of bread).

Translation.

1. *Phamenoth, day* 17, *day of making bread by the chief of bakers sacks* $2\frac{1}{2}$ .... 50.

To transfer ⬯⬯ ⚏□ "making bread" is not uncertain, but Pleyte's reading of the following was erroneous.   There is no trace of ⬯, but the calf-head ⬯ of *chent* with its complements and the small ball not uncommon with this word (see Brugsch, *Dictionary*, 948) so we must read ⬯⬯ *chenti* or *chentu*, "the bakers." It is the chief of the bakers, who takes charge of the corn to dispense it to his bakers for making bread.   Perhaps it was here the charge of the bakers also to grind the corn, whilst they received also (Pl. V, IX, XII) the flour already ground.

2. *Phamenoth, day* 27, *corn, tep sacks* $2\frac{1}{2}$ .... 50.

The original has 27 not 26 in the date.

3. *Pharmuthi, day* 7, *corn, tep sacks* $2\frac{1}{2}$ .... 50.
4. *Pharmuthi, day* 17, *corn, tep sacks* $2\frac{1}{2}$ .... 50.
5. *Pharmuthi, day* 27, *corn, tep sacks* $2\frac{1}{2}$ .... 50.
6. *Pachons, day* 7, *corn, tep sacks* $2\frac{1}{2}$ .... 50.

7. *Pachons, day 17, corn, tep sacks* 2½ .... 50.

8. *Pachons, day 27, corn, tep sacks* 2½ .... 50.

9. *Payni, day 7, corn, tep sacks* 2½ .... 50.

10. *Payni, day 17, corn, tep sacks* 2½ .... 50, *together* 56   1170.

11. *Payni, day 27, corn, tep sacks* 2½ .... 50.

12. *Epiphi,*   *corn, tep sacks* 2½ .... 50.

13. *Epiphi,*   *corn, tep sacks* 2½ .... 51¼ (?).

For the last number 51¼ the cipher is not easily to be seen.

The adding sum of 56 + 1 (?) does not quite agree with the sacks Pl. XIX and XX, 10 × 2½ = 25 + ¾ + 13 × 2½ = 32½. Total 58¼. Also the red sum of loaves 1170 is too small. On Pl. XIX, 10 × 54¾ = 546⅔ + 16¼ + 13 × 50 = 650 are 1212 11⁄12, nearly 43 more than is stated.

All particulars are explained above.

We had lastly to speak of a sheet of the same papyrus 1886 = 203. This is dated the 3rd year, the 19 Athyr of Ramenmat (Seti I), it is very defective, so we cite only the beginning.

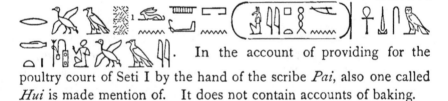

In the account of providing for the poultry court of Seti I by the hand of the scribe *Pai*, also one called *Hui* is made mention of.   It does not contain accounts of baking.

---

[1] Restored by Spiegelberg to ⟨hieroglyphs⟩. Spiegelberg gives this page on Tafel I of his work, the explanation Text, p. 33 f.

A SHORT VOCABULARY OF THE WORDS, PERSONS AND LOCALITIES CONTAINED IN THE ABOVE TREATED PART OF THE ROLLIN PAPYRI.

àutu, "one," XII, 6, 10; XIII, 1; XVI, 3; XVII, 3; "for the king or king's household."

, "a kind of wood," I, 4; III, 2, 3, 5.

àt, tä, ha, XIV, 7; XVII, 9; XIX, 2; "corn in general, not a special kind."

āa pati, "Pharaoh," XIV, 4.

āutu, XIV, 4, "register."

āp, "head, account," V, 1; XII, 2; XVII, 4.

āp, or *tep,* "a sack, kind of measure for grain and flour," VI, 2, 14, 15; VII; XII, 3, 7, 11; XIV, 7; XVII, 9; XIX, 2; XX, 2.

āri, X, 11; XVIII, 10, for the usual   *ārqu,* "the last of the month."

āqu, "aliment, bread," XIII, 2; XIV, 5; XVII, 5, 8.

ākeku, "loaf of bread" of *ca.* $13\frac{1}{2}$ ten = *ca.* $\frac{5}{4}$ kilog., XII, 3, 4, 7, 11, 12.

iu or *nau,* produce V–IX, XII, translated "gives or brought" (*rendement*).

uā neb, VIII, 2; XII, 3, *passim,* "every one."

uí a, rest V 5,   *uta en han,* rest of work, V, 8; VI, 2–6; VII, 2; XII, 4, 9, 13.

boti, "spelt or durra," XIV, 4; XVIII, 1; XIX, 1.

261

⟨glyph⟩ *pēfsu'*, proportion, *em pefsu'* 15 pro sack XVII, 7, "oven" (furnace), XII, 3 ff., ⟨glyph⟩ $\frac{1}{10}$, "loss of oven," *i.e.*, in baking.

⟨glyph⟩ VII, 19; VIII, 2; XII, 14 weight, in coming from the oven.

⟨glyph⟩ *māka*, "flame," p. 95.

⟨glyph⟩ *nut'*, "flour," V, 1, mostly with ⟨glyph⟩ *sek*, "ground flour," V, 5, 6, 10, if the last is not a measure; VI, 5, 6; VII, 2 ff; XII, 1; XVIII, 1, 2.

⟨glyph⟩ *hesāu en māt*, XVII, 4; "the verificators, or the inspectors of the plain."[1]

⟨glyph⟩ XVII, 7, *hestu*, "controlled."[2]

⟨glyph⟩ *hait*, "bakehouse," XIII, 2; XIV, 5; XVII, 5, 6.

⟨glyph⟩ *hanu'*, V, 1; XII, 2, "the works," especially "the *receipts*."

⟨glyph⟩ *haru*, "road," with ⟨glyph⟩ *amenti*, "the western road," XIII, 1.[3]

⟨glyph⟩ *hotep*, "bread, loaves," XX, 1; V, 18.

⟨glyph⟩ *hetera'*, "the tribute, tax," XVII, 4, "taxes, determination."

⟨glyph⟩ *chai*, "consumed," XIII, 8, 13.

⟨glyph⟩ *chennu*, ⟨glyph⟩ *chenti*, "the baker," VI, 1; XVIII, 1, 2; XIX, 1.

⟨glyph⟩ *chennu*, "the hareem, the royal court," XII, 3–5, 7–9, 11–13. XIII, 3.

---

[1] Spiegelberg better ⟨glyph⟩ *Nehesiu* (Negroes), von Mawet.

[2] Spiegelberg, *Neger*, "negroes."

[3] Spiegelberg, better ⟨glyph⟩ *rut*, "district."

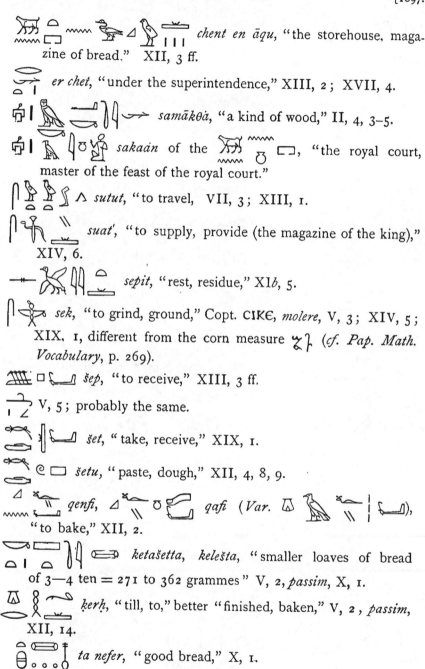

chent en āqu, "the storehouse, magazine of bread." XII, 3 ff.

er chet, "under the superintendence," XIII, 2; XVII, 4.

samākθa, "a kind of wood," II, 4, 3–5.

sakaan of the ⌇⌇⌇, "the royal court, master of the feast of the royal court."

sutut, "to travel, VII, 3; XIII, 1.

suat', "to supply, provide (the magazine of the king)," XIV, 6.

sepit, "rest, residue," XI*b*, 5.

sek, "to grind, ground," Copt. ϭΙΚΕ, *molere,* V, 3; XIV, 5; XIX, 1, different from the corn measure ⌇⌇ (*cf. Pap. Math. Vocabulary,* p. 269).

šep, "to receive," XIII, 3 ff.

V, 5; probably the same.

šet, "take, receive," XIX, 1.

šetu, "paste, dough," XII, 4, 8, 9.

qenfi, *qafi* (*Var.* ⌇⌇⌇), "to bake," XII, 2.

ketašetta, kelešta, "smaller loaves of bread of 3—4 ten = 271 to 362 grammes" V, 2, *passim,* X, 1.

ḳerḥ, "till, to," better "finished, baken," V, 2, *passim,* XII, 14.

ta nefer, "good bread," X, 1.

ten, a weight of 90, 46, grammes, *passim,* XII, 14.[1]

---

[1] Spiegelberg reads ⌇⌇⌇ *teben.*

tálala, "oven, furnace," p. 95.

θes, "a loaf," XII, 9.

ṭet, "hand," *em ṭet-f*, "through his hand," X, 2 ; XIII, 5, 13.

t'a, "received," VIII, 2, *passim*.

LOCALITIES.

"the granary" (of the Pharaoh), XIV, 4.

Pa-ra-nefer-cheper-ka,[1] XII, 1 ; XIV, 3, with

Pa Hathor II, 3.[2]

II, 3.

pa uť'a en chennu, "the magazine of the court," X, 1 ff. ; XIII, 2, 3, 4, 12.

uť'a en pir-āā, "the magazine of the Pharaoh," XIV, 6.

men-nefer, *passim*, Memphis, XII, 6, 10; XIV, 4, 6; XIX, 1.

PERSONS.

King.

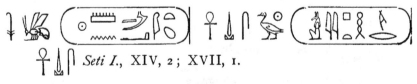

Seti I., XIV, 2 ; XVII, 1.

---

[1] With Spiegelberg we read [cartouche] Ra-āa-cheper-ka Tutmes I.

[2] Doubtful, after Spiegelberg, Tafel XV.

Bakers.

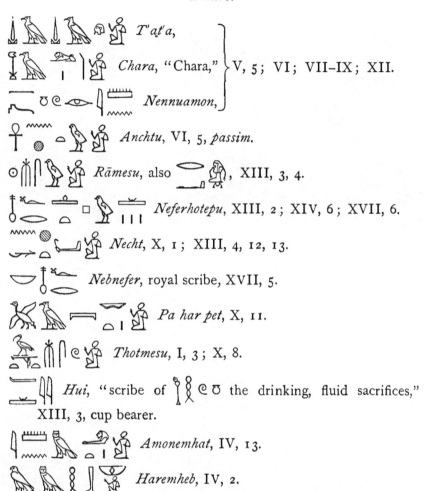

T'aṭ'a,

Chara, "Chara," } V, 5; VI; VII–IX; XII.

Nennuamon,

Anchtu, VI, 5, *passim.*

Rāmesu, also ⌒☖, XIII, 3, 4.

Neferhotepu, XIII, 2; XIV, 6; XVII, 6.

Necht, X, 1; XIII, 4, 12, 13.

Nebnefer, royal scribe, XVII, 5.

Pa har pet, X, 11.

Thotmesu, I, 3; X, 8.

Hui, "scribe of ⚱☖ the drinking, fluid sacrifices," XIII, 3, cup bearer.

Amonemhat, IV, 13.

Haremheb, IV, 2.

Society of Biblical Archæology.

COUNCIL, 1897.

President.

Sir P. le Page Renouf, Knt.

Vice-Presidents.

The Most Rev. His Grace The Lord Archbishop of York.
The Most Noble the Marquess of Bute, K.T., &c., &c.
The Right Hon. Lord Amherst of Hackney.
The Right Hon. Lord Halsbury.
The Right Hon. W. E. Gladstone, M.P., D.C.L., &c.
Arthur Cates.
F. D. Mocatta, F.S.A., &c.
Walter Morrison, M.P.
Sir Charles Nicholson, Bart., D.C.L., M.D., &c.
Alexander Peckover, LL.D., F.S.A.
Rev. George Rawlinson, D.D., Canon of Canterbury.

Council.

Rev. Charles James Ball, M.A.
Rev. Prof. T. K. Cheyne, D.D.
Thomas Christy, F.L.S.
Dr. J. Hall Gladstone, F.R.S.
Charles Harrison, F.S.A.
Gray Hill.
Prof. T. Hayter Lewis, F.S.A.
Rev. Albert Lòwy, LL.D., &c.

Rev. James Marshall, M.A.
Claude G. Montefiore.
Walter L. Nash, F.S.A.
Prof. E. Naville.
J. Pollard.
Edward B. Tylor, LL.D., F.R.S., &c.
E. Towry Whyte, M.A., F.S.A.

Honorary Treasurer—Bernard T. Bosanquet.

Secretary—W. Harry Rylands, F.S.A.

Honorary Secretary for Foreign Correspondence—Rev. R. Gwynne, B.A.

Honorary Librarian—William Simpson, F.R.G.S.

Harrison and Sons, printers in ordinary to her majesty, St. Martin's Lane.

PROCEEDINGS

OF

THE SOCIETY

OF

BIBLICAL ARCHÆOLOGY.

————— ❦ —————

VOL. XIX. TWENTY-SEVENTH SESSION.

Seventh Meeting, November 2nd, 1897.

————— ❦ —————

CONTENTS.

————— ❦ —————

PUBLISHED AT

THE OFFICES OF THE SOCIETY,

37, GREAT RUSSELL STREET, BLOOMSBURY, W.C.

————

1897.

[No. CXLVIII]

SOCIETY OF BIBLICAL ARCHÆOLOGY,

37, GREAT RUSSELL STREET, BLOOMSBURY, W.C.

TRANSACTIONS.

		To Members.		To Non-Members. s. d.				To Members.		To Non-Members. s. d.
Vol.	I, Part 1	... 10	6	... 12 6	Vol. VI, Part 1	... 10	6	... 12 6
,,	I, ,, 2	... 10	6	... 12 6	,, VI, ,, 2	... 10	6	... 12 6
,,	II, ,, 1	... 8	0	... 10 6	,, VII, ,, 1	... 7	6	... 10 6
,,	II, ,, 2	... 8	0	... 10 6	,, VII, ,, 2	... 10	6	... 12 6
,,	III, ,, 1	... 8	0	... 10 6	,, VII, ,, 3	... 10	6	... 12 6
,,	III, ,, 2	... 8	0	... 10 6	,, VIII, ,, 1	... 10	6	... 12 6
,,	IV, ,, 1	... 10	6	... 12 6	,, VIII, ,, 2	... 10	6	... 12 6
,,	IV, ,, 2	... 10	6	... 12 6	,, VIII, ,, 3	... 10	6	... 12 6
,,	V, ,, 1	... 12	6	... 15 0	,, IX, ,, 1	... 10	6	... 12 6
,,	V, ,, 2	... 10	6	... 12 6	,, IX, ,, 2	... 10	6	... 12 6

PROCEEDINGS.

Vol.				To Members.			To Non-Members.
Vol.	I,	Session	1878–79	... 2 0	...	...	2 6
,,	II,	,,	1879–80	... 2 0	...	...	2 6
,,	III,	,,	1880–81	... 4 0	...	...	5 0
,,	IV,	,,	1881–82	... 4 0	...	...	5 0
,,	V,	,,	1882–83	... 4 0	...	...	5 0
,,	VI,	,,	1883–84	... 5 0	...	...	6 0
,,	VII,	,,	1884–85	... 5 0	...	...	6 0
,,	VIII,	,,	1885–86	... 5 0	...	...	6 0
,,	IX,	,,	1886–87	... 2 0 per Part	...	2 6
,,	IX,	Part 7,	1886–87	... 8 0 ,, ,,	...	10 6
,,	X,	Parts 1 to 7,	1887–88	... 2 0 ,, ,,	...	2 6
,,	X,	Part 8,	1887–88	... 7 6 ,, ,,	...	10 6
,,	XI,	Parts 1 to 7,	1888–89	... 2 0 ,, ,,	...	2 6
,,	XI,	Part 8,	1888–89	... 7 6 ,, ,,	...	10 6
,,	XII,	Parts 1 to 7,	1889–90	... 2 0 ,, ,,	...	2 6
,,	XII,	Part 8,	1889–90	... 5 0 ,, ,,	...	6 0
,,	XIII,	Parts 1 to 7,	1890–91	... 2 0 ,, ,,	...	2 6
,,	XIII,	Part 8,	1890-91	... 5 0 ,, ,,	...	6 0
,,	XIV,	Parts 1 to 7,	1891-92	... 2 0 ,, ,,	...	2 6
,,	XIV,	Part 8,	1891–92	... 5 0 ,, ,,	...	6 0
,,	XV,	Parts 1 to 7,	1892–93	... 2 0 ,, ,,	...	2 6
,,	XV,	Part 8,	1892–93	... 5 0 ,, ,,	...	6 0
,,	XVI,	Parts 1 to 10,	1893–94	... 2 0 ,, ,,	...	2 6
,,	XVII,	Parts 1 to 8	1895	... 2 0 ,, ,,	...	2 6
,,	XVIII,	Parts 1 to 8	1896	... 2 0 ,, ,,	...	2 6
,,	XIX,	In progress	1897	... 2 0 (in progress)	2 6

A few complete sets of the Transactions and Proceedings still remain for sale, which may be obtained on application to the Secretary, W. H. RYLANDS, F.S.A., 37, Great Russell Street, Bloomsbury, W.C.

NOTICE.

It has been impossible to make ready in time for ıe present Part of the *Proceedings :—*

The Portrait of the late President, SIR P. LE PAGE RENOUF.

A list of his published Works.

The Plates illustrating PROF. SAYCE's Assyriological Notes.

They will be issued in a future Part.

W. H. RYLANDS.

W. H. Rylands.

LINTEL OF DOORWAY DISCOVERED BY GEORGE SMITH IN THE SOUTH-
EAST COURT OF THE PALACE OF SENNACHERIB, AT KOUYUNJIK.

PROCEEDINGS

OF

THE SOCIETY

OF

BIBLICAL ARCHÆOLOGY.

TWENTY-SEVENTH SESSION, 1897.

Seventh Meeting, 2nd November, 1897.

WALTER MORRISON, M.P., PRESIDENT,

IN THE CHAIR.

The Chairman referred with deep regret to the severe loss the Society had suffered by the death of its distinguished President, SIR P. LE PAGE RENOUF, whose wide acquirements, profound and varied knowledge, and gentleness made it difficult for anyone to follow him. One of the earliest members, Sir Peter had been a constant contributor to the publications from their commencement, and had ever shown the greatest interest and exerted his best efforts for its welfare.

The SECRETARY announced that in accordance with the Bye Laws the Council had proceeded to the election of a President, and that the unanimous vote was in favour of Walter Morrison, Esq., M.P., one of the Vice-Presidents, who was accordingly elected.

The PRESIDENT, having thanked the Society for the kind reception he had met with, expressed the hope that the Society would see fit to elect some well known scholar to occupy the distinguished position of President of the Society.

The following Resolution was proposed, seconded, and carried unanimously, and the Secretary was requested to convey to Lady Renouf and her family this expression of the feelings of the Society :—

"The Council and Members of the Society assembled beg to offer to Lady Renouf and her family their sincere sympathy, and at the same time wish to express the respect and honour they always entertained for their lamented President, Sir P. le Page Renouf, and their great sorrow on hearing the sad news of his death. They feel that their loss, in common with the world of science, cannot be over estimated ; but they will always remember how much the Society has been indebted to him not only for his many gifts to them from his store of learning, his unfailing courtesy towards all who had the privilege of working with him, and for his continuous efforts on behalf of the Society to secure its welfare. Particularly, they will remember his gift of that monumental work, the result of so many years of study, his translation of the 'Book of the Dead.'"

The ordinary business of the Meeting was then proceeded with.

The following Presents were announced, and thanks ordered to be returned to the Donors :—

From the Author :—Prof. C. P. Tiele. The Elements of Religion. Part I, Morphological. Vol. I. 8vo. London. 1897.

'From the Egyptian Exploration Fund :—ΛΟΓΙΑ ΙΗCΟΥ, Sayings of Our Lord. Discovered and edited by Bernard P. Grenfell, M.A., and Arthur S. Hunt. 8vo. London. 1897.

From the Author :—Rev. P. A. C. de Cara, S.J. ; Gli Hethei-
Pelasgi, in Italia. ˙Introduction only. Four Parts. 8vo.
1896 and 1897.

From the Publishers :—Messrs. Houlston and Sons. The Place
of the Crucifixion ; the Walls of Jerusalem, with Plans. 8vo.
1897. London.

From the Author :—Michel M. Alouf. Histoire de Baalbek, par
un de ses Habitants. 8vo. Beyrouth. 1896.

From the Author :—I Cataloghi E. l'Istituto Internazionale di
Bibliografia Osservazioni di D. Chilovi. 4to. Firenze. 1897.

From the Author :—Dr. A. Wiedemann. Notice of Books :
     G. Maspero. Histoire ancienne des Peuples de l'Orient
     classique.

     Ägyptische Urkunden aus den Königlichen Museen zu Berlin.
     Herausgegeben von der Generalverwaltung. Koptische
     und arabische Urkunden. Erstes Band. Erstes Heft.
     Berlin. 1895.

From the Author :—Eberhard Nestle. Zur Umschreïbung des
Hebräischen. 8vo. 1897.

From the Author.—J. J. Griuyer. Bible Chronology, from the
Exodus of the Children of Israel until the fourth year of
Solomon. 8vo. 1897.

From the Author : Rev. Père Lagrange. La Mosaique Géographique de Mâdaba. 8vo. Paris. 1897.
     (Extract, *Revue Biblique.*)

From the Author :—Rev. Père Lagrange. Notre Exploration de
Pétra. 8vo. 1897.

     Monsieur le Marquis de Vogüé. Inscription Nabatéenne de
     Pétra. 8vo. Paris. 1897.
     (Extract, *Revue Biblique.*)

From the Author :—Robert Brown, Jun., F.S.A. The Origin of
the Ancient Northern Constellation Figures. 8vo.
     (*Journ. R.A.S.*, April, 1897).

From the Author :—Dr. J. Hall Gladstone, F.R.S. On the
Transition from the use of Copper to that of Bronze. 8vo.
     (*Journ. Anthrop. Inst.*, May, 1897.)

From the Author:—Prof. Dr. A. Wiedemann. Die neusten Entdeckungen in Ägypten und die älteste Geschichte des Landes.
(*Die Umschau*, Nos. 32 und 33, 1st Jahrg.)

From the Author:—Prof. E. Amélineau. Les Nouvelles Fouilles d'Abydos. 8vo. Angers. 1896.

From the Author:—Prof. E. Amélineau. Les Nouvelles Fouilles d'Abydos, 1896-1897. 8vo. Paris. 1897.

From the Author:—Prof. Sachau. Glossen zu den historischen Inschriften Assyrischer Könige. 8vo. 1897.

From Rev. R. Gwynne:—(Sec. for For. Corr.). Kalender für den Orientalisten-Congress, 1897–98. Den Mitgliedern des XI Internationalen Orientalisten-Congresses sowie Gönnern und Freunden gewidmet von der Officin W. Drugulin in Leipzig.

The following Candidates were nominated for election at the next Meeting on December 7th :—

Dr. Ph. Friedrich Wilhelm Freiher von Bissing, in den Zelten 21, Berlin.

Major-General Francis Eddowes Hastings, 29, Lansdowne Road, Bedford.

Tertius Joynson, Beaumaris.

Dr. Paul Ruben, 2, Warrington Crescent, W.

The Secretary read a Biographical Record of the late President, Sir P. le Page Renouf.

The thanks of the Society were returned to the Secretary for having prepared this record.

BIOGRAPHICAL RECORD OF THE LATE
Sir Peter le PAGE RENOUF.

By the Secretary.

Sir Peter le Page Renouf was the son of the late Joseph Renouf of Guernsey, by his wife Mary, the daughter of the late John le Page of the same place; the name Renouf, of Scandinavian origin, is stated to be composed of $R\grave{e}$ or $R\grave{e}n$ (gods) and ulf (wolf), meaning "wolf of the gods." The early ancestors went to Normandy, where a certain Renouf, Comte de Bayeux, having fought against William the Conqueror, was banished to Guernsey, long holding there the "fief le Comte."

The descent of Sir Peter Renouf's mother is traced back to a certain knight who, having been a page or esquire of Duguesclin, the Constable of France (died 1380), assumed the name of Le Page.

Thus descended from one of the oldest families in the island, he was born in Guernsey, the 23rd of August, 1822. He received his early education in Elizabeth College, and was intended for the Church. Having won a scholarship at Pembroke College, he left Guernsey and went to Oxford, where in the early days of high Tractarian theology, he became the friend of the Rev. John Henry, afterwards Cardinal, Newman; whose friendship and high appreciation of the scholarship and talents of Mr. Renouf only ended with his life.

Mr. Renouf, I have understood, was the author of some of the celebrated Tracts for the Times,* and after the condemnation of

---

* Renouf's first writings were theological and anonymous, the earliest being published in 1841. Shortly after the appearance of Tract XC he published a pamphlet containing a series of evidences from old Anglican authorities, upon a number of points of faith and practice, then in question. This was at first attributed to Newman, but a popular preacher at Carfax (the Rev. Simcox Brecknell) published an elaborate essay proving to his own satisfaction that the real author was Isaac Williams, then candidate for the Professorship of Poetry !

the movement by the heads of the University in 1841, it is perhaps not surprising, with the scrupulous ideas of rectitude which guided him through life, that Renouf, in advance of his friend, and becoming conscious of his true theological position, gave up his career at Oxford, and at Easter, 1842, was received into the Roman Catholic Church at St. Mary's College, Oscott. Here it was that, at the age of nineteen, he commenced the study of Oriental languages together with theology and philosophy, a study which he unremittingly pursued, and which became the guiding passion of his life.

In 1846, his health requiring a change of climate, he undertook the tuition of the present Marquis de Vaulchier, enjoying at the same time, for his own favourite studies, the use of the fine public library at Besançon, then under the care of the learned Dr. Weiss, as well as of the Archiepiscopal library and that of the Theological Seminary. During this lengthened visit abroad, lasting from 1846 to 1855, which included not only France but Switzerland and other countries, Renouf became acquainted with many of the most distinguished scholars of the time, the acquaintance often resulting in a life-long friendship. This friendship included, besides that of the de Vaulchier family, that of Montalambert and M. de Cirecourt, who wished to secure Renouf for the diplomatic service. Throwing aside these chances of a distinguished career, on the foundation, in 1855, by Cardinal Newman, at Dublin, of the Catholic University of Ireland, he complied with the request of his old friend to take part in the new institution. His first work was a series of historical lectures on French literature and the History of Philosophy, but after a short time Renouf was appointed to the Chair of Ancient History, to which was afterwards added the Professorship of Eastern Languages.

His first printed contributions to knowledge, which attracted great attention, appeared in the *Atlantis*, the literary and scientific organ of the university. When Dr. Newman retired from the editorship of this journal, Renouf undertook the literary part, the late Dr. W. K. Sullivan, Professor of Chemistry, who afterwards became President of the Queen's College at Cork, continuing the scientific part. The most important non-Egyptological article written by Renouf is entitled, " A few words on the Arabic Version of the Gospels," a refutation of the theory put forth by Dr. Juynbull of Holland, and repeated by several scholars in England, that the

Arabic version is made not from the Greek but from the Latin Vulgate. At the same time Renouf was taking part in the publication of the *Home and Foreign Review*, for which he wrote several articles, and all the notices of oriental works. In the years 1846 and 1847 he contributed articles to the *Dublin Review*.

The position of Professor was held from 1855 to 1864, during which time he had private classes, in which the members of the university might study Hebrew, Arabic, and Sanskrit. Though the labours of the position were comparatively light, it urged Renouf forward, in order more thoroughly to equip himself for the position he had undertaken, to a further and more extended examination of the materials existing for a study of ancient history from the documents themselves.

He found it necessary personally to examine the exact sense of the Egyptian inscriptions bearing upon history. Observing how few men of learning there were at that time who devoted themselves to the study of the language and literature of ancient Egypt, Renouf, who was admirably fitted for the work from his extensive knowledge of many languages, determined to make himself fully acquainted with all that could tend towards elucidating the history and language of that country. Familiar with the works of all the pioneers in the study of hieroglyphics, he devoted himself with his usual zeal and persistence to the careful examination of all that had been published on the subject, and his efforts were so successful that he soon took a position as one of the first and at the same time one of the most conscientious and reliable Egyptologists of the time; a position which he never lost, but increased year by year, as by unremitting labour he made himself more and more acquainted with the genius of the language.

In 1857, through his marriage with Ludowika, the eldest child of Christian Brentano la Roche, of Frankfort, Renouf formed an alliance and became intimately connected with a family unrivalled in Germany for the literary genius of so many of its members. He was by his marriage the nephew of Bettina v. Arnim, and Savigny, the celebrated jurist and Privy Minister of State.

At this time the works available giving a series of hieroglyphic texts were limited in number, and there were few if any monuments at Dublin. Having obtained the facsimile of the Turin papyrus, published by Lepsius, an idea Renouf had formed at an earlier period took more definite shape, and he decided to undertake the collation of texts, in order to obtain materials for a complete and consecutive translation of the Book of the Dead.

In 1863 appeared, though the essay had then been some time in type, Renouf's masterly article entitled, " Sir G. C. Lewis on the Decipherment and Interpretation of Dead Languages," in which he most exhaustively answered the attack made on Champollion and other decipherers of ancient inscriptions.*

In 1864 he left the Catholic University, retaining the honorary title of Professor of Oriental Languages, and was appointed one of Her Majesty's Chief Inspectors of Schools, a position held by him for nearly twenty years, in which he earned the confidence, admiration, and respect of all those with whom he became associated. Although this work was both exacting and onerous, much time being spent in travelling over the large district under his inspection, Renouf never lost sight of his favourite study; every spare moment was devoted to Egyptology, but more especially to collating and annotating the various texts of the Book of the Dead.

In 1864 he published a letter addressed to Dr. Newman, " by a Catholic Layman," advocating the foundation at Oxford of a College for Catholics. At this time also he found time to contribute a number of articles and short notices to the *Academy* *The North British Review*, and the *Chronicle*.

" The Condemnation of Pope Honorius," an essay which he published in 1868, excited the fury of some ultramontane journals, and on being denounced at Rome, was placed on the Index. The ecclesiastical censure was treated with respectful silence, but the criticisms of opponents was replied to in a second essay published in 1869, " The case of Pope Honorius Reconsidered." It is necessary to say that in attacking the " Personal Infallibility " of the Pope, in the sense in which that doctrine was taught by the *Dublin Review* of that period, no contradiction was offered to the Vatican Decree, which had not yet appeared, and is now generally understood in another sense.

At this time Renouf was appointed Assistant to the Royal Commission on Education in Ireland, and reported on the schools in four of the southern counties.

In 1875 he paid a lengthened visit to Egypt, accompanied by

---

* *Atlantis*, Vol. IV, 1863.

Mrs. Renouf, where he met Mariette and Dümichen, and made a careful examination of many of the monuments. With the original inscriptions before him, many words and characters uncertain in the published copies were examined and new groups identified. The study of Hieroglyphics had become a passion, and he had realized the absorbing interest which Egyptological study inspires in all who indulge in it. Such was the influence the ancient monuments had upon him, that he would often stand almost in a trance centreing his whole mind on some word or little group of characters, oblivious to all else but securing a rational interpretation.

In the year 1879 he was chosen by the Hibbert Trustees to deliver the second series of lectures on Ancient Religions; he naturally took for his subject the Religion of Ancient Egypt. These lectures were printed in the year 1880, passing through several editions, and afterwards translated into several European languages. Like everything else that he undertook, though dealing with a most complicated and difficult subject, they are marked as being the work of a true and conscientious scholar.

At the time of the death of our lamented President, Dr. Birch, which occurred on the 27th of December, 1885, Renouf still held his position as one of H.M. Inspectors of Schools. Though then about the age ordinarily allowed by the Civil Service Minutes, he was selected to succeed Dr. Birch as Keeper of the Egyptian and Assyrian Antiquities in the British Museum, his reputation and learning being so universally acknowledged, that it was felt he was the only person in this country sufficiently learned to fill the post. In March, 1886, then in his 65th year, Renouf was transferred from the Education Department, and entered on his duties in the Museum, having, from love of his favourite studies, surrendered, at pecuniary loss to himself, his position as one of the Inspectors of Schools. At the end of the year 1891, not having completed his seventieth year, he was requested to retire under the ordinary Treasury Minutes as to age, having filled the office of Keeper for less than five years.

While performing the duties of Keeper, in the year 1890 the Trustees of the British Museum issued, under his editorship, "The Coffin of Amamu," a posthumous work of Dr. Birch, and also a full-sized facsimile of the celebrated and beautiful "Papyrus of Ani," principally remarkable for the size and beauty of the coloured vignettes, of which there are a great number. To this work

Renouf added descriptions of the pictures, a help to knowledge here first attempted, as well as an elaborate introduction.

It is perhaps difficult to understand how it was that the scholarship displayed by Renouf so long escaped formal recognition. It came at last, however, when in the year 1896 Her Majesty the Queen, during the present Government, was graciously pleased to confer on him the distinction of Knight Bachelor, an honour well and hardly earned, but which, alas! he has not long lived to enjoy.

In the following year, while spending his holiday in his native place, Guernsey, he over-taxed his strength; returning to London, he was almost continually confined to the house until this summer, when he spent some weeks by the sea. He again returned to London, the change having been of but little benefit. He died on the 14th of October last, at his residence in Roland Gardens, and was buried on Friday the 22nd following, in the crypt of St. Joseph's Church, Guernsey.

The above is a scant record of the more important events in the life-history of Sir Peter Renouf. Though in many ways remarkable, it is really the uneventful career of a scholar, the life of one careless of personal advantage, whose every thought was given to the advancement of knowledge.

I have purposely omitted all mention of his connexion with our Society, in order to place those incidents by themselves. Renouf joined the Society at its commencement, and his name will be found in the earliest list of members, published in 1872, he being then a member of the Council. On the 3rd of June, 1873, he read his first paper, entitled "Note on Egyptian Prepositions," which was printed in the second volume of the *Transactions*. From that date he was a regular contributor to our publications down to the time of his death. When, in the very early years of the Society, the Archaic Classes, as they were called, were commenced, Mr. Renouf, together with Dr. Birch and M. Naville, gave several series of lectures on the language and literature of Egypt. At that time these classes offered the only opportunity in this country for acquiring a knowledge of the subject, and to them must be accorded the credit of fostering and keeping alive the study of the Egyptian language. These lectures resulted in the publication in 1875 of an Elementary Grammar of the Ancient Egyptian Language, printed with the hieroglyphic character, by Mr. Renouf. It was, I believe, the first separate work of the kind printed in the English language. The lectures were continued for some years, and again so late as 1894 Renouf continued the series through many months. They were so successful and so widely appreciated that another series was contemplated, but ill-health prevented the performance of his wishes.

When we met on the 12th of January, 1886, the late Sir Charles Newton occupied the chair. In referring to the recent loss the Society had suffered by the death of its first President, Dr. Birch, he said, " he hoped a worthy successor might be found who, with the memory of Dr. Birch's noble example, would carry forward the work upon which the Society had entered under his guidance since its foundation."

On January the 11th, 1887, Renouf was elected President. How worthily he adhered to the traditions of the Society, and with what kindly consideration and geniality he presided over our meetings is known to those who attended them, as also how modestly he displayed his varied learning in commenting on the many different subjects submitted to the Society. Never absent from his post until illness overtook him, it was much to his sorrow that the doctors forbade him to take his accustomed place among us. Few beyond the members of the Council are perhaps aware of the great amount of time, patience, care and trouble Sir Peter willingly gave to the Society, and how he endeared himself to all. Like his predecessor in the chair, his heart was truly in the work.

The many valuable papers and notes contributed to our publications by Sir Peter Renouf during a period of twenty-four years, were one and all eclipsed by his translation, with commentary and notes, of the Book of the Dead. Several times I had asked him about the possibility of such an undertaking, and during the year 1891 he, at last, after over forty years conscientious study and collation of texts, felt that he was in a position to give to the world a satisfactory and consecutive translation of this book, which always excites so much interest.

It must be remembered that, although translations of a single papyrus, like those of Dr. Birch and M. Pierret, as also of separate chapters, had been printed, no one except Sir P. Renouf has attempted the laborious task of collecting together and reducing to order the scattered and often corrupt portions of the whole work in such a manner as would enable him to make an intelligible translation.

This, the result of the unremitting labour of a lifetime, he freely gave to our Society; and it must ever remain one of the most scholarly and valuable contributions that has ever appeared in the pages of our publications.

From the time of his early college days, when Sir Peter first began to study oriental languages, year by year he had continued to make himself master of any language which might be useful to him in his intended work. Having acquired a knowledge of most of the ancient and modern Semitic, Indo-European, Berber and Finnish languages, within the last few years he became a student of Chinese, for its important contributions to comparative philology. Indeed, there are few, if any, languages with which he was not acquainted. Such was the unique linguistic knowledge which he brought to bear on the Book of the Dead.

The difficulties of the work are well known to those who have paid any attention to the subject; these difficulties were shortly explained in a note by Mr. Renouf himself.* Soon after the appearance of this note the publication of the translation was commenced, and Chapter I was printed in March, 1892.† Part by part this labour of love was continued throughout his illness, down to the very last, at a time when Sir Peter was unable to rise from his bed. He never neglected his favourite study; the latest Part of the *Proceedings*, issued only a few days ago, contains the last Chapters‡ which he considered to be ready for publication.

Sir Peter Renouf literally died in harness, hoping always to see his work finished, and it seems sad indeed that he was not spared to see the completion of a work to which he had given so much mental energy throughout so many long years. But a short time would have enabled him to translate the few chapters that remain unfinished; the book, however, though he himself was not permitted to finish it, must last for ever as a monument of erudition and true scholarship.

Sir Peter ever worked hard for this Society; he loved it, and the best products of his genius were given to it. His character was fitly described in one of the obituary notices which has already appeared:—"His personal character was one of rare simplicity

---

* See *Proceedings*, Soc. Bibl. Arch., Vol. XIV, Part 2, 1st December, 1891.
† *Proceedings*, Soc. Bibl. Arch., Vol. IV, Part 5, 1st March, 1892.
‡ Chapters CXXXVI-CXXXVIII.

and charm.   He was a scholar of the old type, as keen in learned controversy as he was heedless of personal advantage.   His death leaves a gap in the world of learning that will not be easily filled up."   To this I would add, that, like all true scholars, he was ever ready to give to others freely from the stores of his knowledge. No amount of labour and trouble was too much for him in helping a student.   His quiet, modest manner has perhaps led some of those who did not know him intimately, not to appreciate fully the extent of his learning ; to myself, after an association and literary friendship extending over twenty years, his wide and varied knowledge was absolutely overwhelming, and this was joined with one of the gentlest and most kindly natures I ever knew.

ASSYRIOLOGICAL NOTES. No. 3.

BY PROFESSOR A. H. SAYCE.

(I.) An Archaic Babylonian seal-cylinder was shown to me in Cairo, on which are the figures of a priest and the owner of the seal, a space being left for the figure of the deity which has never been filled in. The figures are accompanied by an inscription, in the third line of which the name of the god has been left blank, as well as the word "servant" which should have preceded it. The inscription is as follows (the Assyrian forms of the characters being substituted for the Babylonian forms of the original):

1. 𒀀 𒆠 𒅔 𒈾 𒅋   1. A-ki-in-na-il
2. 𒀀𒁺 𒂍 𒉺 𒌷 𒈬 𒍮   2. arad E-par-ri-mu-tsa
3.   𒅋   3. [arad] il

"Akinna-il the servant of Eparri-mutsa." In the first line the second character is *ki*, not *di*. The name in the second line may be Epar-rimuza for Epar-rimuśa. Both names, however, are difficult to explain.

(II.) A deed of sale (Rm. 2. 19) published by Dr. Peiser, *Sammlung von assyrischen und babylonischen Texten*, IV, pp. 105–107, is dated in the eponymy of Bel-danan (B.C. 734), *ina sanê pu-ri-su*. This Dr. Peiser translates, "in his second period of office," and points out that on the Black Obelisk, ll. 174, 175, we must read: *sanute* SU *pû*[*ri*] [*sa*] *Assur Rammâni akruru* (Layard: *Inscriptions in the Cuneiform Character*, p. 97). Here the translation will be: "for the second time the Pur-festival of Assur and Rimmon I celebrated." The meaning of *akruru* was fixed by Rawlinson many years ago. *Pûru* must signify originally, "lot," or "share," or "allotment," hence "an allotted time" or "term of office," and also a festival at an "allotted" or "fixed time." It would seem from the passage on the Black Obelisk that the festival in question took place at intervals of 30 years. At any rate the Assyrian *pûru* must be the Pûr of the book of Esther, from which the feast of Purim derived its name (Esth. ix. 26). Pûr, it is stated, signified "a lot" (Esth. ix. 24). The feast of Purim was kept by the Jews in the month Adar; in the Assyrian calendar, on the other hand, the preceding month Sebat was sacred to Rimmon, while the intercalary Adar was consecrated to Assur. The Pur-festival mentioned on the Black Obelisk was kept by Shalmaneser II in B.C. 827; if it was regularly kept from that time onwards at intervals of 30 years, one of the celebrations would have fallen in B.C. 467, two years before the death of Xerxes.

(III.) In another text published by Dr. Peiser (*Ib.*, p. 12), which is dated in the reign of Zabum, a monarch of the First Dynasty of Babylon, one of the witnesses is called A-kha-ma-nu. This is the Ahiman of Numb. xiii. 22, Josh. xv. 14. Another witness to the same deed is Pu-la-si-i, which reminds us of the Egyptian Pulasta, the Assyrian Palastu and Pilistu, "Philistia."

(IV.) Among the witnesses to an Assyrian deed of sale of a slave (W.A.I., III. 46, No. 1) are *Suqâ* "the Sukian," *Kuśâ* "the Kusian" (from Kappadokia), Arba-ilâ, "the Arbelite," and Ammâ, the *aba* or "secretary (?) of the Aramæans." Ammâ is literally "the Ammian," and he must have belonged to those " Beni-'Ammô " of whom we hear in Numb. xxii. 5, where it is said that Balaam came from Pethor "which is upon the river (Euphrates), the land of the children of 'Ammô." The country is called Ammiya, Ammi and Amma, in the Tel el-Amarna tablets.

(V.) I have made a fresh collation of the letter from, or to, the king of Arzawa found at Tel el-Amarna (Winckler and Abel, No. 10), which is now in the Gizeh Museum, and have been able to make one or two corrections in the published copies. I have also succeeded in identifying the character 𒍞 which occurs in it. This is the early Babylonian 𒆿, the Assyrian 𒉿 *kit*. As for the name of the country to which the letter is addressed (or from which it was sent), it must have been Arzawa not Arzapi, since 𒉿 elsewhere in the letter has the value of *wa*. Here is my corrected transliteration of the text, with such attempts at translation as our present materials allow to be made :—

1. [um ?]-ma ⌐ Ni-mu-ut-ri-ya   · SAR RAB   SAR MAT
    From (?)   *Nimutriya   the great king, the king of the land*

    Mi-iz-za-ri
    of Egypt;

2. [nu ?]-ud ⟨ Tar-khu-un-da-ra-us   SAR MAT   Ar-za-wa KI-BI-MA
   to (?)   Tarkhundaraus king of the land of Arzawa say :

3. kit-ti-mi   DAMQU-in   BIT-ZUN-mi DAM-MES-mi TUR-MES-mi
   to myself (is) prosperity ; (to) my houses, my wives,   my sons,

4. AMIL-MES GAL-GAL-as   ZAB-MES-mi   D.P. KUR-RA-ZUN-mi
   the officers   of   my soldiers,   my horses,

5. bi-ib-bi-id-mi MAT-MAT-ZUN-mi gan-an-da khu-u-ma-an DAMQU-in
   my chariots,   my provinces   for ever   may there be prosperity!

---

6. ⌐ du-uk-mas kit-ta khu-u-ma-an DAMQU-in   GIS-MES-tu
   In return to thee may there be prosperity! (To) thy trees,

7. BIT-ZUN-ti DAM-MES-ti TUR-MES-ti AMIL-MES GAL-GAL-as
   thy houses, thy wives, thy sons,   the officers

8.   ZAB-MES-ti D.P. KUR-RA-ZUN-ti bi-ib-bi-id-ti, GIS-MES-tu
   of thy soldiers,   thy horses,   thy chariots, thy trees,

9. MAT-ZUN-ti khu-u-ma-an DAMQU-in
   thy provinces may there be prosperity!

---

10. ⌐ ka-a-la-at-ta-mi ⌐ e-nu-un ⟨ Ir-sa-ap-pa
    O my brother!   now   Irsappa

11. AMIL kha-lu-ga-tal-la-an mi-in a-u-ma-ni   TUR-SAL-ti
    messenger   mine I have sent, thy daughter,

12.   AN-UT-mi   [space]   ku-in   DAM-an-ni u-wa-da-an-zi
    O my Sun-god,   for the sake of a wife   he asks

13. nu-us-si li-il khu-ud i-ni   AN   SAK-DU si
    . . .   . *the god head   her (?)*

14. ka-a-la-ta up-pa-akh-khu-un ⟨ śu-kha   la-li-ya   GUSQIN
    O brother,   a gift   one brick (?) have I sent of gold

    DAMQU-an-ta
    as thy present.

---

15. ⌐   a-ni ya-at-ta-la-mu ku-un-da-as kha-at-ra-mu (?)
    . . . . . *my*   . . .   .

282

16. ub-bi   wa-ra-ad-mu [space] ne-it-ta   up-pa-akh-khi   EGIR-an-da
    . . . . . . *my*   *to thee* (?) *a present*   *afterwards*

17. Pal-ta   AMIL   kha-lu-ga-tal-la-at-ti-in   am-me-el-la
    Palta   *thy messenger*   . . . .

18. AMIL   kha-lu-ga-tal-la-an   EGIR   khat   khat-ra-a   khu-u-da-a-AK
    the messenger   *after* . . . .   *may he make* (?)

19. na-i-na-ad   u-wa-an-du
    . . .   .

---

20. ➤ nu-ut-ta   u-wa-an-zi   u (?)-da-an-zi   ku-sa-ta   TUR-
    To thee   *I send*   *an embassy   for the sake of thee* [*and*]

    SAL-ti
    thy daughter ;

21. AMIL   kha-lu-ga-tal-mi-is   AMIL   kha-lu-ga-tal-la ta
    my messenger   [*to*] *thy messenger*

22. ku-is   tu   cl-lu (?)-qar (?) [space] na-as   ag-ga-as
    for   *thee* (?) . . .   .

23. NU-mu   AN-tu   SAL (?)-su-us   ga-as-ga-as   MAT-ya-as
    O my prince (?) *thy god* *women* (?)   *great* (?)   *countries*

    ub-bi is ta us as-su-un
    . . . .

24. zi-in-nu-uk   khu-u-ma-an-da
    . . . .   *may it be.*

---

25. nu   Kha-at-te   sa-as-sa   MAT   E-i-ga-id
    To (?)   *the Hittites   from* (?)   *the land   of Eigaid*

26. nu-ut-ta   GIS KAL-LA   bi-ib-bi   es-li   up-pa-khu-un   la-li
    to thee   usu *wood*   *for a chariot* . . .   *as a gift*   *I sent.*

27. ki-is-sa-ri-is-si ⌐ Ir-sa-ap-pa   AMIL   kha-lu-[ga-tal-la]
    By the hand of   *Irsappa*   *the messenger*

8. ⌐-EN   śu-kha   la-li-ya   GUSQIN   KI-LAL-BI   tu . . .
   one   *brick* (?) *I sent*   *of gold*   *weighing*   . . . .

9. XX ma-na   GUSQIN   III kit   ⊢⌐   III kit   zab-kar- . .
   20 *manehs* *of gold,* 3 kit *of* . . . , 3 kit   *of* . . .

30. III kit   khu-uz-zi   VIII kit   ku-si-it-ti-in
     3 kit   *of . . . ,*   8 kit   *of . . .*

31. C kit   AN-NA   tab al-ga-an   C kit   kha-ab-ri (?) . .
     100 kit   *of lead*   . . . . . ,   100 kit   . . . .

32. C kit   sir-ri-li-ya-as-sa . . .
     100 kit   . . . .

33. IV ABAN   KU-KU-PU   GAL   NI   DUG-GA   VI ABAN   KU-KU-PU   . . .
     4 *jars*   *great of good oil,*   6 *jars*

34. SA NI DUG-GA   III GIS-GU-ZA   SA GIS   pa-na . . .
     of good oil,   3 *seats*   *of . . . wood,*

35. X GIS-GU-ZA   SA   GIS KAL   is-li   bi-ib-bi . . .
     10 *seats*   *of*   usu-*wood*   . .   *for a chariot . . .*

36. X AKH-KHU-UZ   II   GIS-KAL   la-li
     10 *handles*   2 *pieces*   *of* usu-*wood*   *I sent.*

L. 1. The first character is lost, but the traces of it which remain resemble *um*.

L. 2. What is left of the first character is 🖙 . The conjectural translation I have given is that proposed by Prof. Bezold; but since the name of Tarkhundaraus is in the nominative it cannot be right. Moreover it is not probable that the Egyptian king would write in the language of Arzawa, or would call his own county "Mizzari," instead of Mizri. The more likely translation of the lines would accordingly be: "Thus, O Nimutriya, Tarkhundaraus says to thee." *Nutta* seems to mean "to thee" in lines 20, 26.

L. 8. -*As* appears to denote the plural of nouns; *cf.* W. and A. 238. 16, *Khattanas* SAR-*us*, "the king of the Hittites." See also MAT-*yas*, line 23.

L. 10. *La* here has a different form from the *la* of the next line, and might be decomposed into *as-ma*. But in KAL-LA, line 26, we find precisely the same form of character with the value of *la*.

L. 15. *Aniyattala* seems to be compounded with the same word as that which is found in *Khalugatalla*. Perhaps *aniyattala-mu* will signify "my letters."

L. 18. We find EGIR *khat khat-ra-a* and EGIR *khat kha-at-ra-i* in W. and A. 238. 10, 13, which show that ⧾ must here have the value of *khat*.

L. 22. *Aggas*, with the plural termination *as* may be the *aqqâti* or *aggati*, of unknown signification, which occurs in the Babylonian letters of the king of Mitanni (*Winckler and Abel*, No. 22, *Rev.* 30). *Nas aggas* may therefore be " these *aggâti*."

L. 25. The fourth character is *te* not *du* as given by Winckler. With *Khatte*, " the Hittites," compare W. and A. 238. 16, *Khattanas* SAR-*us*, " the king of the Hittites" (or perhaps " of the Khattinâ "). *Nu* may possibly be the ideograph of " prince," the translation being " O prince of the Hittites!" The " land of Eigaid," as I noticed in the *Proceedings* of this Society (June, 1889), must be " the land of Igadâi," mentioned in the Egyptian Travels of a Mohar in connection with " the land of the Hittites."

L. 29. The *kit* must be the Egyptian $\left\{ \begin{smallmatrix} \frown \\ \end{smallmatrix} \right.$ *ket* ($\frac{1}{10}$ of the *ten*).

L. 30. *Kusittin* will be the " *kusiti* garments" mentioned in a letter of the king of Alasia (*Tell el-Amarna Tablets in the British Museum*, 6. 23).*

For an analysis of the grammatical forms see my article in the *Academy*, Aug. 20, 1892, p. 155.

(VI). In Bu. 91–5–9, 296 (*Cuneiform Texts in the British Museum*, II), there are several names belonging to the populations north of Assyria. We have among them Urdiya (or Urkhiya) the son of Iddib-sar (or Idkhib-sar)—which, however, may be Babylonian,—Irisenni the son of Iddibus (or Idkhibus), Akhsir-Tesup the son of I[ri]senni, Ukuya the son of Giskhâ, Kussu the son of Khuluqqa, Durar-Tesup the son of Gil-Tesup, and Akhsir-Babu the *khazannu*, or " governor," the son of Nubanani. Urdiya reminds us of Urdhu, or Ararat, called Urdhes in Vannic (SAYCE, LXXXII. 6), and Iddib-sar of Hittite names like Khata-sar, Khilip-sar, Pi-siris, etc. Khuluqqa seems to be the Assyrian Khilakku and Khiluku " Cilicia," while the god Tesup was the Mitannian Air-god, whose name is found in those of Comagenian kings like Kali-Tesup, and who was worshipped in Armenia under the form of Teisbas. *Gil* in Gil-Tesup must be the Mitannian Giliyas and Gilu-Khipa, and Àkhsir and Irisenni are Mannian. Akhsêri was the king of the Mannâ in the time of Assur-bani-pal, and his grandson was Erisinni. *Eri* enters into the formation of many-Vannic names as well as of *erê-las*, " a king." †

---

* In later Babylonian *Kusitum* denoted an outer garment worn by women.

† See the inscription from Melasgert, published by Dr. Scheil in the *Recueil de Travaux, etc.*, XVIII, p. 75.

As for Babu, a country of Babas is mentioned in the Vannic texts, and its god was worshipped in the neighbourhood of Van (SAYCE, V. 20), while Ukuya resembles the ethnic name Ukkâ. The contract in which these names occur carries them back to the age of the First dynasty of Babylon, and their forms tend to show that similar dialects were spoken at the time from the land of the Minni in the East to Cilicia in the West. In the *Proceedings* of this Society for Feb., 1897 (p. 80), Prof. Hommel has quoted the interesting Hittite name Akhlib-sar from a seal-cylinder in the Berlin Museum. As he points out, this is clearly the same name as the Khilip-sar of the Egyptian texts. Instead of connecting Khilip, however, with Girpa-ruda and Gerba-tusa, as he does, I would see in the word the name of Aleppo, and regard the proper name as belonging to the same class as Khata-sar and Kaui-sar, where the first element must be the Quê or Qaui of the Assyrian monuments. The spelling of Iddih-sar, with the sign for *sarru*, "king," indicates that the vowel of the last syllable is *a*, and perhaps throws light on the meaning of the word.*

Khiliba is the name of a precious stone in the Tel el-Amarna tablets (*Winckler and Abel*, 25. 45, etc.), and was included among the objects sent from Mitanni. I have always believed that it derived its name from the town of Aleppo, like the wood (?) or weights (?) of Carchemish (*Karkamisû*) mentioned in Bu. 88–5–12, 163. 11, and 88–5–12, 19. 8.†

(VII.) I give here a copy of one of my Gyül Tepé texts (S. 1). The following is a transliteration and translation of it :—

1. IV   ma-na   kaśpi   tsa-ru-ba
    Four   manehs   of silver,   refined,

2. a-na   AN   Tar-ku-zar (?)-ba-am
    to   Tarku-zar (?)bu

---

* It is noticeable that Tiglath-pileser I says of the Comagenian king, that he was called "saru-pi," where *pi* is the suffixed article of Mitannian. It would appear, therefore, that in Comagenian *saru* must have signified "king." The word was probably borrowed from Babylonia.

† Since the above was written I have seen Mr. Pinches' article in the *Journ. R.A.S.*, July, 1897, pp. 589–613, in which he gives a translation of the inscription, and draws attention to the linguistic character of the proper names. To those I have given he adds Tekhib-tilla (or Tedib-tilla), Ta-isenni, Sella and Wantia.

3. AN III-ti-da (?)   TUR   Khi-tı-ili
   Salas-ti-da (?)   the son   of Khiti-ili (has lent),

4. is-du   kha-mu-us-tim
   after   the week

5. sa   A-sur-i-me-di
   of   Asur-imedi

6. û   A-sur-rabu   a-na
   and   Asur-rabu :   after

7. IV   sa-na-at
   4   *years*

8. VIII   ma-na   kaśpi
   8   *manehs   of silver*

9. i-sa-gal
   he must pay.

10. Ka-ar-ma-du
    Karmadu (is)

11. li-mu-um
    the eponym,

12. Sa-ga-ti-qad-du-a
    Sagati-qaddua

13. il-ki-śu   ⌐   kaśpa   a-na
    has taken it   viz.   the silver :   for

14. ka-ru-ki-su   kal-la   u-me
    his . . .   all   the time

15. ma-la   AN Tarku-zar (?)-ba
    the whole   Tarku-zar(?)ba

16. i-ga-su-du   û   AN III ti-da (?)
    shall possess,   and   Salas-tida (?)

17. ma-la-su   ma-rab
    the whole of it   entirely

18. i-pa-du-su   -   ma   il-ki
    shall deliver it up,   and   there shall take

19.   a-bit   AN III-ti-da (?)   ru-ku-um
the guaranty   of Salas-tida (?)   who is absent

20. E-ra-tim
Eratim.

21.   Pan   La-li-im
Witnessed by   Lalim

22. pan   Ki-na-nim
and   Kinanim.

I have already given a translation of this tablet in the *Records of the Past*, New Series, VI. p. 131. Its chief interest lies in the fact that the name of Tarku is preceded by the determinative of divinity, showing that I was right many years ago in concluding that Tarku was a god, and in the further fact that mention is made of a god or goddess "Three." The Babylonians knew of a goddess Salas, the mother of the Fire-god (see Tallqvist: *Die assyrische Beschwörungsserie Maqlû* p. 49); though whether her name was connected with *salsu* "three" is questionable. In the Hittite inscriptions there is also a "country III."

L. 1. *Tsaruba* is the Heb. צרף.

L. 3. If Khiti-ili is the right transliteration, the name will be the same as that of Ilu-khite king of Suprê or Subari mentioned by Assur-nazir-pal (W.A.I. I. 20. II. 12.). Compare also Khite-ruadas king of Malatiyeh mentioned in the Vannic inscriptions, with the latter part of whose name that of Garpa-ruda of Gurgum is identical.

L. 4. The mysterious *khamustim*, "a fifth," means, I believe, "a week" in these Cappadocian tablets. The early Latins had a week of nine days (*nundinæ*) the memory of which was preserved among the country people, and the Greeks a week of ten days. The three-fold division of the month of thirty days seems to have been derived from Babylonia, and just as the *kasbu* or "double hour" came to be divided in half, so the long week of ten days might have been similarly halved in Asia Minor. In later Babylonian *khummusu* seems to have signified "a piece of 5 shekels"; see Peiser: *Keilinschriftliche Bibliothek*, IV. p. 183.

L. 16. *Igasudu* represents the Assyrian *ikassadu*.

L. 19. *Abit* is the Assyrian *abûtu*.

L. 20. In GOLÉNISCHEFF, III. 16. Ena-Asur is the son of Erati.

L. 22. Kinanim may be "the merchant."

(VIII.) I add a copy of one of the texts brought by Prof. W. M. Ramsay from Kaisarîyeh of which I have given an imperfect transcription in the *Proceedings* of this Society Nov., 1883. The following is a transliteration and translation of it.

1.   XIII   NER (?)   siqli   kaśpi   a-su-me-ga
      Thirteen and a ner (?) *shekels of silver, thy share* (?)

2. a-na-ku ⧣ kha-bu-ul-ma
    I   have mortgaged, and

3. û Zu-ta-akh-zi-iz   di-ni
    also   Zu-takhziz   judgment

4. i-ti-ma   tsir (?) ga-ga-ad
    has given (?), *and upon   the head*

5. Iz-me-tas   ir-ku-um-ma
    of Izmetas (?) *has declared (saying) :*

6. a-na   sa-la-du-ar
    ' *That they be not returned*

7. e-ti-ru-ma   xv   siqli   kaśpi
    I have paid the 15 *shekels of silver ;*

8. as - ku - ul   a-kha-a-ta   kaśpi
   I have weighed the rest   of the silver,

9. xv   siqli   a-na Sa-ki-[zu]
    15 *shekels, for   Sakizu*

10.   mar   a-khi   su-ku-ul
   the son of my brother, the payment

11. xx ma-na-um   ma-ni   duppi
     of 20 *manehs,   even the manehs of the tablet,*

12. ga-du-um   sa   i-na
     along with what (is) on

13. pi-ikh-su   a-ta-di-na   ma-ni
     its . . . I have given.'   The manehs

14.   i-li-ga-ga
     he has taken for thee,

15. um-ma   A-sur-i-ti-ma
    saying: 'Asur-itima (?)

16. a-na Ma-nu-ki-A-sur
    to   Manu-ki-Asur

17.   DU-DU-ZI   A-sur-ki-na-ra-am
    the grandson (?) *of Asur-ki-naram*

18.   û   AN UD-tab-ba-nahid ki-bi-ma
    and Samas-tabba-nahid has said ;

19. a-na Ma-nu-ki-A-sur   ki-bi-ma
    to   Manu-ki-Asur he has said :

20. XXXIII ma-na-um   i-li-ga
    ' *33   manehs   he has taken,*

21.   ni-ti-ma   a-na-ku . . . ga
    we have known (?), *and   I   thy . . ,*

22. a-na   bit   A-bu-sa-lim
    into the house of Absalom

23.   mar A-sur-e-mu-ki
    the son of Asur-emuki

24. a - ru - ub - ma SAK - a - ta
    have entered,   and the   capital (?)

25. Sa-ki-zu a-na   SAK
    Sakizu for   capital (?),

26. . . I BAR   ma-na-TA   kaśpi
    . . I$\frac{1}{2}$ *manehs   of silver.*

27. a-kha-a-ta   kaśpi   û . . .
    The rest   of the silver   and . . . [*belongs to*

28. Sa-ki-zu   mar   a-khi-MES
    Sakizu   the son of the brothers.

29.   a-sar   sa-khu-śu   ni-
    The place   of his sakhut   we

30. li-h
    have ascended.'

I have already given a translation of this text in the *Records of the Past*, New Series VI, p. 130.

L. 1. In GOLÉNISCHEFF XV. 15, we have *saiel asume rasaum*, which seems to mean "demanding a share of the property." But the word *asume* is obscure. It can hardly be like the Heb. אשם "a sin-offering." The first two words may mean "13 *ner* of shekels."

L. 4. *Iti* may be the Assyrian *idi* "he knows;" see *niti* in l. 21, Here, however, the phrase appears to be *dini iddi*, "has laid down judgment."

L. 5. *Irkumma* from the Assyrian *ragâmu*.

L. 7. *Etiru* is the Ass. *edhiru*.

L. 13. *Pikh* may be the *pukhi* of the Assyrian texts. Perhaps it means "enclosure," from *pikhu* "to close up."

L. 15. Perhaps we should translate: "Asur has known." See note on l. 4.

L. 24. *Arub* seems to be a mistake for *erub*.

L. 26. Or "at the rate of . . 1½ shekels."

(IX.) In GOLÉNISCHEFF XIII. 8, *ki-ra-tim* signifies "gardens" or "plantations," the Assyrian *kiru ; e-zi-e* in the same tablet, l. 14, is "trees," Assyrian *etsi*.

In GOLÉNISCHEFF XX. 8, mention is made of "3 shekels of stamped silver" (*kaśpu ku-nu-ki-ni*). *Kunukini* is derived from *kunuku* "a seal," and must indicate that a seal or stamp was put upon the pieces of silver. The fact is interesting in its bearing on the history of money.

(X.) Some years ago I pointed out that the situation of Qatna, from which two of the Tel el-Amarna letters were sent (*The Tell el-Amarna tablets in the British Museum*, Nos. 36, 37), is fixed by the Annals of Assur-nazir-pal; but if I may judge from recently published remarks on the matter, both my own words, and those of the Assyrian king, have been overlooked. Assur-nazir-pal (W.A.I. I. 23. III. 5–8) states that after leaving Sadikanni, now Arbân, on the Khabûr, he marched to Qatni, then to Dur-Qadlimê and Bit-Khalupê, the modern Helebi (Khalbu, No. 246, in the list of Thothmes III), and then to Sirqi or Circesium at the junction of the Khabûr and Euphrates. The site of Qatni between Arbân and Helebi is therefore clearly determined. In W.A.I. II. 60. 3c. Qatnu is said to be the god of the city of Qatan, where the spelling shows that the second radical is *t* and not *dh* (ט). With the name we may compare the Qadnu of Seti I (No. 9) called Qadnaf by

Amenôthes III (Lepsius, *Denkmäler* III. 88).   It may be added that in a fragmentary letter from Qatna, found at Tel el-Amarna, and now in Berlin (No. 233, line 15), we have the name of [Gar-] ga-mi-is or Carchemish.

(XI.) Mr. Pinches tells me that he has found the name of the Babylonian king which has been variously read Ammi-satana and Ammi-ditana written with ◁ instead of ⟨⟨⟩⟩ in the first syllable of the second element in the compound.   We must therefore read Ammi-dhitana.   The final -*na* I should explain as the suffixed pronoun of the first person plural, as in Samsu-ilu-na or the name of the Hamathite king Irkhu-(i)lê-na, and the name may perhaps signify "Ammi is our leader."   In any case, Ammi is parallel to Samsu, the sun-god, in Samsu-iluna, and Irkhu, the moon-god, in Irkhu-lêna, and like them must be the name of a deity.

(XII.) Among the names found in Babylonian tablets of the age of Khammurabi is one which is read Be-ta-ni.   I should rather read Beta-ili, and compare it with the Biblical Bethuel, and the Beti-ilu of the Tel el-Amarna tablets (*Winckler*, 51. 20, 125. 3. 28).

NOTES.

By F. LL. Griffith.

———◆———

Scarabs belonging to Mr. John Ward.

In looking over the fine collection of scarabs belonging to Mr. John Ward, F.S.A., of Belfast, I note the following as some of the more remarkable from an historical point of view.

1. 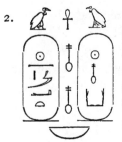, see below, note on the Khyan group of kings.

2. In *A.Z.*, XXXIII, 143, Erman published a scarab in the Berlin collection with the cartouche $M\underline{3}\,^{c}t.n.R^{c}$ (Maat-en-ra) written as here, but associated with ⬭. I have never had any faith in the king "Nefer-Ra," who is incessantly appearing on scarabs: this name is probably a mere blunder, and the present scarab seems to show what the origin of it was. It must be of the XIIIth dynasty, and I agree with Prof. Erman that the other cartouche is probably of King Khenzer. There are several scarabs with the name of Nefer-ka-ra that appear to be of about that age.

3. This is "the King's eldest son Nehesi," who erected an obelisk to Set at Tanis. In Miss Brocklehurst's collection was a scarab of the King Nehesi whose name was found by M. Naville on the base of a statue at Tell Mokdâm. It has since been exchanged with Prof. Petrie.

4. Purchased at Ombos. It has been suggested that this scarab gives the name of the god Sutekh with that of King Apepa, but it will be seen that we have here only an abbreviation of

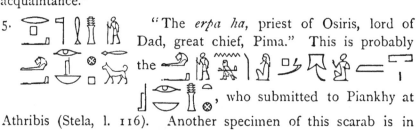

, as in other scarabs (Petrie, *Hist. Sc.*, 382; *cf.* 383, of the same man). Apepa, the name of the Hyksos Apophis, occurs as that of private persons not uncommonly in or about the XIIIth dynasty (see Lieblein). The Apepa of this scarab is a "royal acquaintance."

5. "The *erpa ha*, priest of Osiris, lord of Dad, great chief, Pima." This is probably the , who submitted to Piankhy at Athribis (Stela, l. 116). Another specimen of this scarab is in the Edwards Collection at University College.

6. "King of Upper and Lower Egypt, Taharqa: Son of the Sun, Piankhy." This is the finest glazed pottery scarab that I have seen. It is considerably above the ordinary size, and the back is modelled in the style of the Middle Kingdom, so that it is also a remarkable instance of the revival of an old style. Piankhy must be Piankhy II, who, according to the genealogical table given by Erman, *A.Z.*, XXXV, p. 29, was father of Taharqa. He takes the second place on the scarab.

THE KHYAN GROUP OF KINGS.

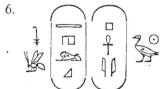

This scarab is not uncommon in collections (see Petrie, *Hist. Scar.*, Nos. 69-86; Petrie, *Hist.* I, p. 103; Catalogue of Hilton Price Collection, No. 169, etc., etc.), but is usually read by collectors Pepa, or Pepy, and both in his scarab book and in his *History* Prof. Petrie has identified the name with that of Pepy II. In all the original instances I have seen, and they number a dozen or more, the reading is either clearly or preferentially ; scarcely , much less , which is the invariable spelling of the name of Pepy. It is evident that the king's name on these scarabs is Shesha; possibly another king of the same group was called *Ppi* (Pepa not Pepy), many of the scarabs seeming to favour that reading as they appear in the publications.

These scarabs are of special importance ; as Prof. Petrie has shown (*Hist.*, I, p. 119), they belong to a remarkable group inscribed with royal names and very distinct in style, the signs being engraved either between vertical lines or within scroll-work open at the top. The name of Pepy, if authentic, would have dated the group, and Prof. Petrie, who has been the first to raise the question in any form, has arranged them at the end of the VIth dynasty and the beginning of the VIIth.   There is room for them both in the great gap between the Old Kingdom and the Middle Kingdom, and in that between the Middle Kingdom and the New; and it is to the later of these two periods that Khyan, the most prominent name among them, has usually been attributed (NAVILLE, *Bubastis*, p. 23, *et seq.*).

As we can see from the *Historical Scarabs* and the illustrations in Petrie's *History*, vol. I, this group of obscure but scarab-loving kings includes [hieroglyphs] and [hieroglyphs] (the [hieroglyph] strangely rendered like [hieroglyph], as always in early scarab work), which cartouches are known by other monuments to have belonged to one king, *Ḥyꜣn*, Khyan.   The rest are more obscure ; their prenomens—arranged from common to rare—are : [hieroglyphs] ; [hieroglyphs] ; [hieroglyphs] ; [hieroglyphs] ; the nomens in similar order are [hieroglyphs] *Šši* (Shesha) ; [hieroglyphs] *Yꜥpḳḥr*, Yapeqher, or as Petrie's newly-acquired specimen reads [hieroglyphs] *Yꜥḳbḥr*, Yaqebher, connecting the name with that of Jacob, as he suggests ; [hieroglyphs] *Nby* (?), Neby ; [hieroglyphs] *ꜥꜣ*, Aa (a doubtful reading).

There is also included a king [hieroglyphs] *Wꜣḏḏ*, Uazed, of whom several scarabs are known : apparently he had no prenomen. It is tempting to pair the four prenomens with the four nomens, but for this there is as yet no sort of proof. The name Uazed, *Wꜣḏḏ*, is most nearly approached by [hieroglyphs] *Wꜣḏḏ*, Uazez (LIEBLEIN, and *Rec. de Trav.*, XII, 11), which seems to me to date from the end of the XIIth or the beginning of the XIIIth dynasty.

Shesha, *Šši*, occurs as a private name on stelae of the VIth dynasty, LIEBLEIN, 43, 1408, and in XIIth—XIIIth dynasty, *Suppl.* 515.

 seems to be for 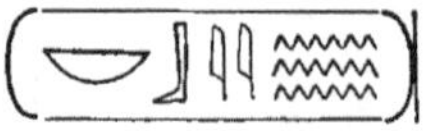 ("Swimmer"?), and as Petrie has pointed out in his *History*, I, p. 113, this name occurs under the form 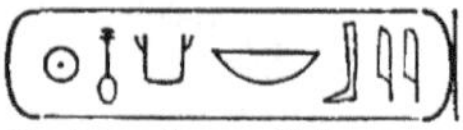, as that of the 43rd king on the tablet of Abydos: Merenra II, of the VIth dynasty, being No. 39, and Neb-kher-ra Mentu-hetep of the XIth being No. 57.  (without the determinative ) curiously enough is a regular name in the New Kingdom.

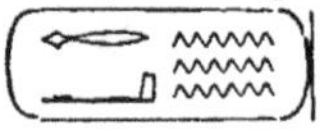? Aa? In the XIXth dynasty we have  as a private name, LIEBLEIN, 639.

The list of Eratosthenes is at present so hopelessly enigmatical, that it is useless to compare Μευρης with *M*ꜣᶜ.*ib.r*ᶜ.

So far the evidence of names is in favour of placing this group of scarabs in the gap between the VIth—XIth dynasties, rather than in that between the XIIIth—XVIIth.

The group may be labelled by the most conspicuous name occurring in it, and called the Khyan group. Monuments of Khyan have been found at Gebelên in Upper Egypt, and at Bubastis in Lower Egypt. His scarabs, too, often come from Thebes and Abydos, and in other cases appear to have been found in Lower Egypt. It is a curious fact that the monuments of this king are associated with those of Apepy both at Gebelên and at Bubastis, and this gives some faint support to the theory that Khyan may belong to the Hyksos period. Also BORCHARDT, *A.Z.*, XXXIII, 142, thinks that the cartouche of Khyan on the statue has been added over an erasure, and that the statue being of the XIIth dynasty style, Khyan must be placed later. The name of Khyan is found on cylinders similar in general style to those of the XIIth dynasty and of Sebekhetep I. Such cylinders are unknown for the XIth dynasty, and are quite different from those of the Old Kingdom. The type of the scarabs seems to be almost as distinct from those known to be Hyksos and XIIIth dynasty, as from XIIth dynasty and earlier types.

Two things, however, still remain to be mentioned: 1st the peculiar title , borne by Khyan upon some of his scarabs and cylinders, and 2nd the strange [hieroglyphs], "beloved of his *ka*," on his statue. [hieroglyphs] is to all appearance a royal title like [hieroglyphs]. It is, I believe, to be read *ḥḳ ḫꜣsḫt* (heqa khaskhet), and as *ḫ* generally changed to ϣ in Coptic, the derivative from the title might very well be something like Ὑκσως. But I do not wish to press this. A good instance of *ḫꜣsḫt* for [hieroglyphs] in certain cases, can be detected in MAR. *Mast.*, p. 188, *mr wd-md nb n stn [didi n]rw Ḥr m* [hieroglyphs], (mer ud med neb en seten dada neru Her em, etc.) where the Aswân tombs have [hieroglyphs]

[hieroglyphs]. The singular of the word seems to be [hieroglyphs]; *cf.* statue A 93 in the Louvre, and examples quoted by Brugsch. If so, the plural form is very abnormal for Egyptian, resembling the broken plurals of the Semitic tongues. In *B.H.I.*, Pl. XXVIII, the petty chief Absha is [hieroglyphs] *ḥḳꜣ ḫꜣst* (?), (heqa khast), "ruler of *a* foreign country," and in *Sanehat*, l. 176, we have the phrase [hieroglyphs], "(His Majesty sent unto me presents as he would unto) the ruler of any foreign country." [hieroglyph] is applied to places not to peoples.

Khyan's title is naturally higher than that of Absha, and means ruler of foreign countries or of deserts, etc. The presence of his name on the lion from Baghdad (read with some uncertainty, owing to the bad engraving), suggested to Prof. Petrie that Khyan may have been the ruler of a great empire. Perhaps he will someday appear as an invader, or otherwise, in the annals of Babylonia. The foreign aspect of the names is sufficiently obvious. And secondly, it is curious that there is only one dedication known in connexion with the whole group of Khyan kings, namely, the abnormal dedication by Khyan himself to his own *ka*, instead of to a divinity.

For my my own part I should prefer an early Hyksos date, if the Manethonean lists in Josephus gave any support to it. And who were the Xoites of the XIVth dynasty? Can they have received this appellation rightly, or by false analogy, from the title [hieroglyphs]? For Khasa, Khasu, *ḫꜣsw* (?), seems to have been the name of Xois, and ⟨glyph⟩, "bull of Khast (?)," was probably its nome sign, while the whole territory of the VIth and VIIth nomes favoured such names. At present, *pace* historians, we have no real information whatever about the XIVth dynasty.

THE ISRAEL STELA.

Dr. Spiegelberg has edited this stela in the *Zeitschrift* with a fulness of knowledge and insight worthy of all praise. He has cleared away many difficulties, and in other cases has opened the way for his successors. The following remarks have occurred to me on reading his edition of the text.

l. 5. ⟨hieroglyphs⟩ ⟨hieroglyphs⟩. For the meaning of *n ḥr-w* (en heru), cf. *Piankhy*, l. 6. "The governors sent to His·Majesty daily, saying, 'Art thou silent to the extent of forgetting the Thebaid and the nomes of the Residence? Tafnekht ⟨hieroglyphs⟩ is *pressing forward* with conquest, and finds none to stay his arm,'" etc. So also *ibid.*, l. 95, at the storming of Memphis. "His Majesty commanded his soldiers (saying,) 'Forward! ⟨hieroglyphs⟩), scale the walls, enter the houses on the river bank!'" Hence, inserting ¦ after *šmw*, I translate this passage nearly as in my rough translation given early last year in the *Contemporary Review : nꜣysn šmw-n-ḥrw* [naysen shemu en heru] must mean "their marchers forward," and the next phrase may mean, "and those who leave the rear behind," the two phrases and following context together being equivalent to, "their boldest soldiers, their feet stayed not, but they ran away," etc. The sense, however, is not very clear.

l. 24. In the pleasing description of the safety of Egypt from the predatory tribes we have the following sentence, "The cattle of the field are let go *to wander loose* ⟨hieroglyphs⟩), *no herdsmen cross the river flood.*" Ordinarily cattle are tethered and watched, and if their pasture should lie across the river, they are conveyed back to the home side on the approach of night. Anyone who has spent a few nights on the western edge of the Delta, knows that the villagers have generally managed to put a canal between themselves and the desert as a protection against cattle-stealers, and that it is exceedingly difficult to persuade one's guards to stop the night on the desert side.

In the illustrative passage quoted by Spiegelberg we have another excellent piece of local colour: "Egypt and the lands are in peace under his rule, the land is like a . . . . . (?), without wrong-doing, so that a woman can go whither she will, *her clothes on her head* $\left(\text{[hieroglyphs]}\right)$, *and her step wide* $\left(\text{[hieroglyphs]}\right)$ to the place she desires." The Egyptian fellâh women, when crossing a piece of desert in twos and threes, or wandering with their female companions in the reedy marshes of the Delta, often gather their clothes up in a bundle *on their heads* to give *free movement* to their limbs. And here I may mention that as a simple waist-cloth was worn by the women in professional dancing and in some domestic avocations (B.H I., Pl. XXIX, grinding corn and spinning thread), the agility thereby gained apparently gave rise to a homely proverb, met with in the Pyramid texts, W. 479 = N. 748 "thou departest from the earth more swiftly (or springing higher) than a girded woman [hieroglyphs]."

Additional Notes to "Egyptian Literature."

In an encyclopaedic publication entitled *"The World's Best Literature"* (New York, Hill and Co., edited by C. Dudley Warner), there is about to appear an article on "Egyptian Literature" containing a number of long translations of inscriptions and papyri made by myself. Here and there in these translations are difficulties which could not well be explained in the footnotes, or which suggest still further comment, and three such additional notes and comments are here submitted to the Society.

Sanehat, l. 268. I have probably made a mistake in speaking of the *menat* bead-strings as "tinkling." More probably they were waved, so as to display their colour and brightness in the hands or round the neck, as part of the accessories of dancing. There is no word corresponding to "tinkle" in the original.

Una, l. 29. Read [hieroglyphs], as shown by a squeeze at Berlin, collated by Crum, and kindly communicated to me. The △ I take to be [hieroglyph], but this may be wrong. The horns of the animal should be waved.

Ibid. l. 30. [hieroglyphs] . The first part reads *phwï ww* (pehui uu), and is identical with [hieroglyphs] in *Piankhy*, l. 3. It is perhaps best to understand it as denoting the coast of the Mediterranean.

Negative Confession, CXXV, 18. " I have not trapped birds, the bones of the gods " (var., " birds of the bones of the gods," " divine birds," etc.). In spite of its strangeness, this is the rendering to which the different texts seem to point, and I have since found a passage in the Pyramid texts, Unas, l. 209, which seems to support and explain it, [hieroglyphs] " thy bones are the divine female hawks which are in heaven." The bones are those of the deceased Unas as Osiris; so it appears that the birds spoken of in the Book of the Dead are those of certain kinds, the sacred hawks at any rate, which were believed to supply the bones, *i.e.*, framework, on which the gods and the ethereal portions of deceased men could fly from earth to heaven; there would be no difficulty in illustrating this view further from the Pyramid texts, but I do not see the way clear at present to prove its correctness absolutely.

HÆMATITE CYLINDER FROM CAPPADOCIA.

By Prof. A. H. Sayce.

The seal-cylinder, of which an impression is here given, was purchased by me at Smyrna in 1879.   It is of hæmatite and

had been brought from Cappadocia along with a gryphon's head in red stone, which is now, I believe, in the Louvre, and which bears upon it, in cuneiform characters, the name of Kuaruman.*   The cylinder is very beautifully engraved, and is in what is termed the " Hittite style."

The two lines of cuneiform characters inscribed upon it are puzzling.   I used to suppose that they were ornamental merely, and had been made by an artist who was as ignorant of the cuneiform syllabary as the Phœnician artists were of the Egyptian hieroglyphs, which they copied for ornamental purposes.   But some of the forged tablets brought from Cappadocia by Mr. Chantre have characters upon them somewhat similar in form, which may have been imitated from genuine inscriptions.   In this case we should have to suppose that the Cappadocians had developed a peculiar cuneiform script of their own.   It is also possible that the engraver has copied his text backwards, the upright wedge being the determinative of an individual.   If so we might read the two lines :—(1) *nun nu* TUR (?) *me khal* (2) *nun* AN SAR *nun nu za*.   But it is more probable that the upright wedge is intended to mark the end of the inscription.

The sun and moon, it will be noticed, are accompanied by the seven stars.   The hare is a common symbol in Hittite art; the object below it seems to be intended for a musical instrument. The cylinder was probably found at the Gyöl Tepé near Kaisariyeh, like the Cappadocian cuneiform tablets and other antiquities which have of late years been offered for sale.

* Published in the *Proceedings* of this Society, Vol. IV, p. 19, and Vol. V, p. 44.

6, GRAY'S INN SQUARE,
6th November, 1897.

DEAR MR. RYLANDS,

I see that in the last Report of the Egypt Exploration Fund, Mr. Crum takes exception to my rendering of the Coptic spell which appeared in the *Proceedings* of May last.   His contention appears to be, that three words in the copy of the text, as it appears in Wessely's *Griechische Zauberpapyri*, from which my translation was confessedly made, have been altered in transcription, and do not correspond with the original.   Or, to mention only one instance, that the word ⲉⲟⲱϣ, which I translate " Ethiopian," is not in the Papyrus at all, its place being taken by some word meaning " on him " (query ⲉⲣⲟϥ?).   This, I understand, he has ascertained by actual inspection of the Papyrus at the *Bibliothèque Nationale*.

If this is the case, Mr. Crum will do me a great service by publishing in the *Proceedings* or elsewhere, his own transcription of the few lines of Coptic which the spell contains.   His reading of the word ⲓⲥⲁⲥⲛⲉ, which I (following therein M. Revillout), took for a divine name, as some word meaning "seven" (query ⲥⲁϣϥ?), if correct, may throw some light on the date when the spell was composed, and the creed of the composer.

Very faithfully yours,

F. LEGGE.

———

The next Meeting of the Society will be held at 37, Great Russell Street, Bloomsbury, W.C., on Tuesday, 7th December, 1897, at 8 p.m., when the following Papers will be read :—

JOS. OFFORD :—Notes on the Congress of Orientalists held at Paris, 1897.

PROF. DR. OPPERT (read by the Rev. C. J. Ball) :—" The Cuneiform Inscriptions and the Book of Kings."

SOCIETY OF BIBLICAL ARCHÆOLOGY PUBLICATIONS.

In 8 Parts. Price 5s. each. The Fourth Part having been issued, the Price is now Raised to £5 for the 8 Parts. Parts cannot be sold separately.

THE EGYPTIAN BOOK OF THE DEAD.
Complete Translation, Commentary, and Notes.

BY THE LATE SIR P. LE PAGE RENOUF, KNT. (*President*);

CONTAINING ALSO

𝔄 𝔖eries of 𝔓lates of the 𝔙ignettes of the different 𝔠hapters.

The Bronze Ornaments of the Palace Gates from Balawat.

[SHALMANESER II, B.C. 859–825.]

Parts I, II, III, and IV have now been issued to Subscribers.

In accordance with the terms of the original prospectus the price for each part is now raised to £1 10s.; to Members of the Society (the original price) £1 1s.

Price 7s. 6d. Only a Limited Number of Copies have been Printed.

THE PALESTINIAN SYRIAC VERSION OF THE HOLY SCRIPTURES.

Four Recently Discovered Portions (together with verses from the Psalms and the Gospel of St. Luke). Edited, in Photographic Facsimile, from a Unique MS. in the British Museum, with a Transcription, Translation, Introduction, Vocabulary, and Notes, by

REV. G. MARGOLIOUTH, M.A.,

Assistant in the Department of Oriental Printed Books and MSS. in the British Museum; formerly Tyrwhitt Hebrew Scholar.

Subscribers' names to be Addressed to the Secretary.

Society of Biblical Archæology.

COUNCIL, 1897.

Harrison and Sons, Printers in Ordinary to Her Majesty, St. Martin's Lane.

PROCEEDINGS

OF

THE SOCIETY

OF

BIBLICAL ARCHÆOLOGY.

VOL. XIX. TWENTY-SEVENTH SESSION.

Eighth Meeting, December 7th, 1897.

CONTENTS.

PUBLISHED AT

"THE OFFICES OF THE SOCIETY,

37, Great Russell Street, Bloomsbury, W.C.

1897.

[No. CXLIX.]

SOCIETY OF BIBLICAL ARCHÆOLOGY,

37, GREAT RUSSELL STREET, BLOOMSBURY, W.C.

TRANSACTIONS.

	To Members.	To Non-Members.		To Members.	To Non-Members.
		s. d.			s. d.
Vol. I, Part 1	10 6	12 6	Vol. VI, Part 1	10 6	12 6
„ I, „ 2	10 6	12 6	„ VI, „ 2	10 6	12 6
„ II, „ 1	8 0	10 6	„ VII, „ 1	7 6	10 6
„ II, „ 2	8 0	10 6	„ VII, „ 2	10 6	12 6
„ III, „ 1	8 0	10 6	„ VII, „ 3	10 6	12 6
„ III, „ 2	8 0	10 6	„ VIII, „ 1	10 6	12 6
„ IV, „ 1	10 6	12 6	„ VIII, „ 2	10 6	12 6
„ IV, „ 2	10 6	12 6	„ VIII, „ 3	10 6	12 6
„ V, „ 1	12 6	15 0	„ IX, „ 1	10 6	12 6
„ V, „ 2	10 6	12 6	„ IX, „ 2	10 6	12 6

PROCEEDINGS.

Vol.				To Members.	To Non-Members.
Vol. I,	Session	1878–79		2 0	2 6
„ II,	„	1879–80		2 0	2 6
„ III,	„	1880–81		4 0	5 0
„ IV,	„	1881–82		4 0	5 0
„ V,	„	1882–83		4 0	5 0
„ VI,	„	1883–84		5 0	6 0
„ VII,	„	1884–85		5 0	6 0
„ VIII,	„	1885–86		5 0	6 0
„ IX,	„	1886–87		2 0 per Part	2 6
„ IX,	Part 7,	1886–87		8 0 „ „	10 6
„ X,	Parts 1 to 7,	1887–88		2 0 „ „	2 6
„ X,	Part 8,	1887–88		7 6 „ „	10 6
„ XI,	Parts 1 to 7,	1888–89		2 0 „ „	2 6
„ XI,	Part 8,	1888–89		7 6 „ „	10 6
„ XII,	Parts 1 to 7,	1889–90		2 0 „ „	2 6
„ XII,	Part 8,	1889–90		5 0 „ „	6 0
„ XIII,	Parts 1 to 7,	1890–91		2 0 „ „	2 6
„ XIII,	Part 8,	1890-91		5 0 „ „	6 0
„ XIV,	Parts 1 to 7,	1891-92		2 0 „ „	2 6
„ XIV,	Part 8,	1891–92		5 0 „ „	6 0
„ XV,	Parts 1 to 7,	1892–93		2 0 „ „	2 6
„ XV,	Part 8,	1892–93		5 0 „ „	6 0
„ XVI,	Parts 1 to 10,	1893–94		2 0 „ „	2 6
„ XVII,	Parts 1 to 8	1895		2 0 „ „	2 6
„ XVIII,	Parts 1 to 8	1896		2 0 „ „	2 6
„ XIX,	Parts 1 to 8	1897		2 0 „ „	2 6
„ XX,	In progress	1898		2 0 „ „	2 6

A few complete sets of the Transactions and Proceedings still remain for sale, which may be obtained on application to the Secretary, W. H. RYLANDS, F.S.A, 37, Great Russell Street, Bloomsbury, W.C.

NOTICE.

Unfortunately it has been found impossible to make ready the plates, etc., named in the November *Proceedings*. Members are therefore requested not to bind this volume until it is complete.

The final proofs of Dr. Oppert's and Mr. Rassam's papers have not arrived in time to be included in this Part of the *Proceedings*, they will however be issued shortly.

W. H. RYLANDS,
Secretary.

PROCEEDINGS

OF

THE SOCIETY

OF

BIBLICAL ARCHÆOLOGY.

TWENTY-SEVENTH SESSION, 1897.

Eighth Meeting, 7th December, 1897.

WALTER MORRISON, M.P., PRESIDENT,

IN THE CHAIR.

The following Presents were announced, and thanks ordered to be returned to the Donors :—

From the Author :—Prof. Ignazio Guidi. Il "Fetha Negast," O. "Legislazione Dei Re," Codice Ecclesiastico E. Civile di Abissinia. 4to. Roma. 1897.

From the Publishers :—David Nutt. Massila-Carthago. Sacrifice Tablets of the Worship of Baal. By Rev. J. M. Macdonald, M.A. 8vo. London. 1897.

From the Editeurs :—M. Bretschneider e. M. Regenberg. Gli Obelischi Egziani. Di Roma Illustraté con Traduzione Dei Testi Geroglifici Da. Orazio Marucchi. 8vo. Roma. 1898.

From the Author :—M. Clermont-Ganneau. Les Tombeaux de David et des Rois de Juda ; et, Le ¡Tunnel-Aqueduc de Silvé. 8vo. Paris. 1897.

From the Author :—Prof. G. Maspero. La Table d'Offrades, des Tombeaux Égyptiens. (Extrait Revue l'Hist. des Relig.) 8vo. Paris. 1897.

From the Author :—Rev. P. A. C. de Cara, S.J. Gli Hethi-Pelasgi in Italia. Gl' Italici Nella Paletnologia Italiana. 8vo. Roma. 1897.

From the Author :—Dr. A. Wiedmann. Menschenvergötterung im alten Ägypten. 8vo. Bonn. 1897.

The following Candidates were nominated for election at the next Meeting to be held on the 11th January, 1898 :—

Admiral Selwyn, 186, Gloucester Terrace, Hyde Park, W.
John Tuckwell, 32, Sarre Road, West Hampstead, N.W.

The following Candidates were elected Members of the Society, having been nominated at the last Meeting, held on the 2nd November, 1897.

Dr. Ph. Friedrich Wilhelm Freiher von Bissing, in den Zelten 21, Berlin.
Major-General Hastings, 29. Lansdowne Road, Bedford.
Tertius Joynson, Beaumaris.
Dr. Paul Ruben, 2, Warrington Crescent, W.

Mr. J. Offord read some Notes on the Congress of Orientalists, held at Paris.

The Rev. C. J. Ball read a Paper by Prof. Dr. Oppert, entitled, "The Cuneiform Inscriptions and the Book of Kings."

Remarks were added by Mr. J. Offord, the Rev. C. J. Ball, Rev. Jas. Marshall, Rev. Dr. Löwy, and the President.

The thanks of the Meeting were returned for these Papers, and to the Rev. C. J. Ball for his trouble.

NOTES ON THE CONGRESS OF ORIENTALISTS, PARIS.

By J. Offord, M.J.S.

Thinking that a short account of some of the proceedings at the recent Congress of Orientalists in Paris by one who enjoyed the privilege of attending there, might be of interest to the members of the *Soc. Bibl. Arch.*, I have put together the following notes :—

Commencing with the Egyptian section, which was very fully attended, and was presided over by M. Naville, two important announcements were made as to forthcoming publications, and in both cases science is to be indebted to the Germans for these works of erudition.

The first of these is a " *Thesaurus verborum aegyptiacorum*," which is as far as possible to contain all the words known both in hiereoglyphic and hieratic texts.   The work is to be so complete and comprehensive that it is not anticipated that the final volume will be issued before 1913.

The second great work is the publication of the journal of Lepsius during his residence in Egypt, together with all the literary matter left in a sufficiently perfect state which he had accumulated at various times with the idea of giving a commentary to his great work the " Denkmäler," and a volume of supplementary plates which were not issued during his lifetime.   These designs, however, are by another member of his expedition, Herr Max Weidenbach.

At the Congress itself, Dr. Pleyte presented a new volume containing many Coptic texts in the museum at Leyden, and the same scholar read a paper upon a demotic papyrus, a palympsest, containing moral precepts.   Photographs where shown of the whole of the document, which is lengthy and very well preserved.

Dr. Krall also read a paper upon a demotic manuscript concerning Bacchoris, but the papyrus itself is of the age of Augustus.

M. Chassinet described the " Ritual of the Vigil of Osiris," and M. Bénédite showed photographs of a collection of Egyptian jewels recently acquired by the Louvre, among which, as pendants to a necklace, were some representations of Egyptian ships.

It was inevitable that the Tel-el-Amarna tablets should come before the section, and the subject was introduced by M. Neteler, who discoursed upon the chronological synchronisms between the tablets and Babylonian and Assyrian records. M. Naville also said a few words in reference to the Stele found by Petrie, which contains a reference to the people of Israel.

In the Assyrian section Dr. Hommel showed some of the plates for his forthcoming work on the pictorial origin of the cuneiform characters, a subject which it is well to remember was first introduced to science in this Society by Dr. Houghton.

Father Scheil announced several new discoveries, notably a tablet presenting a variant version of the Deluge Story. "This tablet contains a similar text to that first published from Nineveh, but is very much older, and Professor Sayce assigns it to the time of Abraham." Also he had found the names of two new kings and a list of geographical names relating to the country of Sirpourla, one of these kings, Tukulti-bil-nisi Père Scheil identifies with Kadasmar-Buryas. It may be mentioned here that upon the official visit to the Louvre, when the monuments were most lucidly explained by M. Heuzey, great interest was deservedly taken in the wonderful cone bearing an historical inscription of Entemena, a preliminary translation of which has been given by M. Thureau Dangin. It is a · regulation of the frontiers of Sirpourla and Gishbau, is in extremely perfect preservation, and of highest historical importance, being of itself, together with various monuments previously known, sufficient to establish a history of the early Telloh kings. There are nearly 220 lines, and it is of great value for filling up lacunæ in the previously published Sirpourla texts. Eannadau, Entemena, a new monarch, Legul-shoug-gour, and a certain Messilem king of Kish appears among its annals. This monument was a private gift to the museum. The Louvre has also some exceedingly large tablets, presented by the Sultan, and, of course, the great inscribed silver vase of Entemena, and a mace head of Messilem's ornamented with eight roaring lions.

In the "Greco-Oriental section" M. J. Reinach again argued that the nude form of goddess of Greece was not derived from Ishtar or any Asiatic prototype, giving as a reason the finding of a nude female figure in a grotto of paleolithic age at Mentone,* whilst

---

* If the forerunners of Greek iconography are to be found so far west and so back, reference might have been made to the very highly realistic female type found at Laugerie Basse (Joly, *Man before Metals*, p. 298), which, as far as I am aware, was not copied by the Aryan Greeks.

in the Assyrian section Father Scheil mentioned a remarkable coincidence between Egyptian and Babylonian thought in a paper upon "Ishtar under the form of a cow," founded upon a representation of Ishtar as a cow suckling a calf.*

The same scholar exhibited proofs of his forthcoming work upon his excavations at Sippara, which city he declines to identify with the Sepharvaim of the Bible.† His researches at Sippara, together with the work of United States' explorers at Niffer, and those of M. de Sarzec at Telloh, will present the most wonderful series of archæological discoveries yet known, forming a fitting termination to these triumphs of the nineteenth century.

Many papers in the Semitic section were offered by Drs. Glaser and Müller upon Arabian inscriptions, the results of whose studies will all ultimately find their way into the "Corpus Inscriptionem Semiticarum." One of these Sabean texts, which Dr. Glaser thought dates from about 500 B.C., is concerned with purifications necessitated by contamination with a corpse, and in cases of certain relations between the sexes; and the expressions used are very similar to some in the Old Testament. Another text of very high antiquity related to the offerings or sacrifices due for sin committed.

In this section great importance was assigned to the fragments of Ecclesiasticus discovered by Mrs. Lewis and Dr. Schechter. M. Halévy started a polemical discussion by showing that the language is somewhat similar to the Mischna, and therefore pre-supposes a much higher antiquity for some of the canonical books, such as the second part of Zechariah, than recent critics had contended.

M. Chabot gave important evidence tending to carry back to a higher date the Arabic version of Tatian's "Diatessaron"; his remarks originated in a letter from M. Cheiko of the University of Beyrout, who has found three pages of an Arabic version, evidently the same as that published by Ciasca, though with some variants.

In this section M. Germer Durand presented the excellent album of photographic plates representing the marvellous Mosaic map of Palestine and the route of the Exodus, discovered by the Dominican Fathers of the St. Stephen Seminary at Jerusalem, at Mâdaba. This map is of the age of Diocletian, and represents the various cities of Palestine and the Delta in a most realistic manner.

---

* Philo of Byblos, professing to quote Sanchoniathon, says Astarte (Ishtar) as a mark of sovereignty placed upon her head a bull's head.

† *Revue Biblique*, vol. iv, 205.

The geographer who directed its execution seems to have been familiar with the "Onomasticon de Locis Hebraicis" of Eusebius, and also with Herodotus.* It is mutilated, but still enough remains to make it an indispensable factor in all future attempts to present

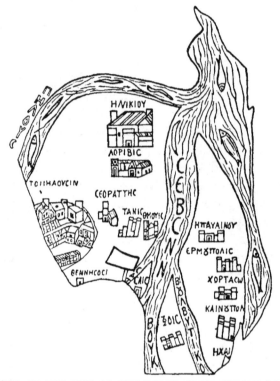

FACSIMILE OF THE MAP OF THE DELTA FROM THE MOSAIC MAP.

a map of ancient Palestine. A curious incident in the map is that Ænon, where John baptised, is shown east of the Jordan, whilst Bethabara is on the west.†

* Herodotus, ii, 17 : "As far as the city of Cercasorus the Nile flows in one stream, but from that point it is divided into three channels ; that running eastward is called the Pelusiac mouth, another bending westward the Canopic mouth; but the direct channel of the Nile is the following : descending, it comes to the point of the Delta, after this it divides the Delta in the middle and discharges itself into the sea, supplying by this channel not by any means the least quantity of water ; this is called the Sebennytic mouth. There are also two other mouths diverging from the Sebennytic and flow into the sea, one the Saïtic, the other the Mendesian mouth. The Bolbitinic and Bucolic mouths are not natural but artificial."

† See Professor W. A. Stevens, in *Journal of Biblical Literature and Exegesis*, 1883, p. 129, and Edersheim, *Jesus the Messiah*, vol. i, p. 657.

Of Egypt only the portion delineating the Delta is legible, and strange to say this gives the site of Chæru,* the city whose true position was first pointed out from a Roman inscription by Mr. Griffith,† in our Society; since my further note on the subject ‡ Père Séjourné has referred to two patristic allusions to this city. One in the Athanasian Chronicle of Verona, which mentions that Athanasius

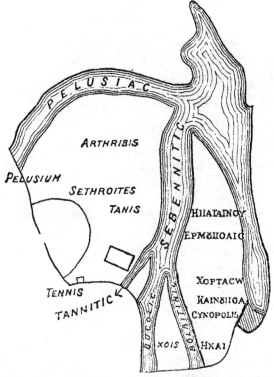

IDENTIFIED NAMES ON THE MOSAIC MAP.

when driven from Alexandria by the Emperor Julian, "commoratus est circa There u;" and in the Life of St. Anthony, where it speaks of Balakios, Duke of Egypt, setting forth from Alexandria with Nestorius, the prefect, to journey to Chæreu, εἰς τὴν πρώτην μονὴν Ἀλεξανδρείας τὴν λεγομενὴν Χαιρέου.

With the kind consent of the Council, a small facsimile of

---

* Marked on the map as HXAI

† See F. Ll. Griffith, *Proc. Soc. Bibl. Arch.*, Vol. XVIII, p. 54.

‡ J. Offord, Vol. XVIII, p. 106, John iii, 26. The disciples of John say to him *at Ænon*, "He that was with thee beyond Jordan," meaning, it would seem, that Ænon was to the west and Bethabara to the east.

the part of the Mosaic map dealing with the Delta, is printed on page 308, so that the three or four Greek names I have been unable to identify may be explained.

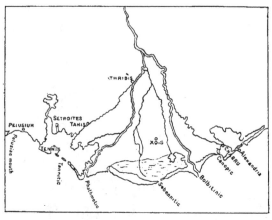

THE DELTA.

There was a paper in the Assyrian section upon a new Vannic inscription from Armavir. Professor Sayce was present, and will doubtless incorporate it in his series of Vannic texts in the *Proceedings of the Asiatic Society.*

I have purposely not alluded at any length to papers which were merely a *résumé* of articles previously published, or of monuments already described in scientific journals, or described in the recently issued report of the *Egypt Exploration Fund.*

Among the ancient manuscripts exhibited was the very old Sanscrit one found by M. Dutreuil du Rhins, who lost his life in the cause of science, and reference was made to other similar manuscripts which Professor Oldenbourg has at St. Petersburg, and there are several fragments in India. Further additions to these relics of still greater importance have been made by the Swedish traveller Sven Hedin, and also by Captain Godfrey at Kathgar, and there can be no doubt but that these discoveries are but the precursors of still better ones.

Among the receptions there was one at the Musée Guimet, which is mentioned because of the fact that its collections have this year been augmented by the successful excavations in the Roman and Byzantine city of Antinoe. The relics from this site are not yet displayed, but they will form the most complete collection of costume and apparel of the early centuries of our era, together with accompanying speciment of jewellery and ornaments of all descriptions.

The prevailing impression of the Congress appeared to be the fact of the immense amount of new material recently placed in the hands of Oriental archæologists.

The number of cuneiform tablets and texts not yet examined, much less deciphered, amounts to many thousands ; whilst hieratic, demotic, and Greek papyri are ever increasing in quantity ; from central Asia and Nepal manuscripts and inscribed monuments are now forthcoming, and there is no reason to doubt that, both in Egypt any Asia, there are far more treasures still buried than have hitherto been rescued.

ASSYRIOLOGICAL NOTES.

By Professor Dr. Fritz Hommel.

§ 31. Of two of the best known Babylonian gods, ⸻𒀭𒉺𒌉 and ⸻𒀭𒅎, the true Babylonian reading is not yet established in a manner which leaves no doubt at all. Only that the readings *Adar* (instead of *Nin-dar* or *Nin-ib*) and *Vul* or *Bin* (instead of *Rammân* or *Bir* or *Dadda* or *Martu*), are false, can be accepted with certainty. I am in a position to give the direct proof for the reading *Rammânu* of ⸻𒀭𒅎. We find sometimes this god written as ⸻𒀭𒅎𒊑, *e.g.*, K. 24, 6, *e-di-im maŝ* ⸻𒀭𒅎 𒊑; W.A.I. IV, 23, Nej., Col. 4, line 21 ⸻𒀭𒅎𒊑 *nugalla - zu - ku*, etc. Meissner, *Beitraege*, No. 4, 6. *Amil* ⸻𒀭𒅎𒊑, No. 21, 25, 26 (the same person), generally transcribed *Amil-mir-ra* (comp. 𒀭𒅎 = *im*, *mir*, and the proper name *Tukulti-me-ir*, king of Khana). But the right reading is ⸻𒀭 *Ram-ma-nu-ri-iḫ-ṣu* (Shurpu, ed. Zimmern, 8, 18), or *Rammânu-ráḫiṣu* (comp. Asurn. 3, 120 *kima* ⸻𒀭𒅎 *ra-ḫi-ṣi*). For 𒊑 = *raḫaṣu*, comp. S[b] 180.

§ 32. The name of the god ⸻𒀭𒉺𒌉 may be read *Nin-dar* or *Nin-ib*. The reading *Nin-dar* would be established by the writing *Nin-* 𒌉 *-ra*, but in the few cases in which we find *Nin-* 𒌉 *-ra*, we are not sure whether *-ra* is put for prolongation, or whether it is the Sumerian postposition. Now in a seal-impression of the time of Samsu-iluna, and published by Mr. Pinches, Collection of Sir Henry Peek, inscribed Babylonian Tablets, p. 61 and 66, we read :—

⸻𒀭𒉺𒌉
𒐈 𒁄 𒄿 𒀀
𒐊 𒀀 𒀀 𒅎 𒀔 𒀭
𒀔 𒌋 (or 𒌋 ?) 𒅅 𒁉

i.e., *Nin-tum* (or *Nin-ib*) *sukal magh gish-kam e-par-par si-di-ne* (or *si-sá-di*) *sig azag šú-ul*, translated by Mr. Pinches "*Nin-ip*, messenger supreme, and hero of E-parparra, director, glorious brightness perfecting" (= who is perfecting gl. brightness). Since Mr. Pinches gives no special note to his reading *Nin-ip*, he seems to hold it as self-evident that ⯈⯈𒀭 *Nin-* 𒌈 is only another manner of writing for the common ⯈⯈𒀭 *Nin-* 𒅁. We would so have a direct proof for the reading *Nin-ib*, for 𒅁 is *ib* and *dar*, whilst 𒌈 is *ib* and *tum*, *ib* being in both cases the identical value. Only if a god *Nin-tum* or *Nin-tum-ma* could exist, the comparison of *Nin-* 𒅁 and *Nin-* 𒌈 would prove nothing, but such a god is not known at all.

A second instance for a male solar deity, ⯈⯈𒀭 *Nin-* 𒌈, I found some weeks ago in a proper name of a contract tablet of the time of Hammu-rabi, viz., Bu. 88–5–12, 210 (publ. by Meissner, *Beiträge*, No. 95). Here we find a certain ⯈⯈𒀭 *Nin-* 𒌈*-a-bi* (comp. the names *Samas-a-bi*, No. 111, and *Marduk-a-bi* No. 100). Meissner reads *Bel-tum* (?)*-a-bi;* but this is impossible ("the goddess Beltis is my father" being nonsense).

On the other side, it is very puzzling to find a second male solar deity named ⯈⯈𒀭 *Nin-* 𒀭𒁯, the consort of the goddess ⯈⯈𒀭 𒌍 (*Ghanna, Gulla*), and therefore most probably *Nirgal*, the old substitute of *Nin-ib* (or *Nin-dar*). Perhaps the original pronunciation of this name was *Nin-dar*, because we meet in the inscriptions of Telloh and in other texts the dialectic variant *Nin-sar* as the name of the wife* of *Nir-gal*, *Nin-gir-gu*, though we find (by the mistake of a later compiler), in the list, W.A.I. V, 43, ⯈⯈𒀭 *Nin-* 𒀭𒁯 *-na*, i.e., *Nin-gunna;* compare too ⯈⯈𒀭 *Nin-dar-a* in the Gudea Inscriptions (*Nin-daya?* or *Nin-sia* for *Nin-saya?*). In the trilingual list of gods, W.A.I. II, 59, we meet ⯈⯈𒀭 *Nin-* 𒀭𒐊 *-a* (*Nin-dan-a*, *Nin-daya?*) as the later pronunciation of ⯈⯈𒀭 *Nin-* 𒅁, comp. my *Sumerische Lesestuke*, p. 35 and 47.

Perhaps Mr. PINCHES is in a position to give us, by a new text, the definitive solution of the original pronunciation of ⯈⯈𒀭 *Nin-*

---

* In the same manner we find ⯈⯈𒀭 *Nin-* 𒀭𒁯 *-an-na* and ⯈⯈𒀭 𒀸 𒀭𒁯 (*eme-sal* for ⯈⯈𒀭 *Nin-* 𒀭𒁯 as mascul., comp. W.A.I. II, 59) employed for the female planetary deity Istar ; see my book, *Semitische Volker und Sprachen*, p. 38 f.

⊨⊣⌐, either as *Nin-ib* (comp. ⊳⊣⌐ *Nin-* ⊵⟨⫮⟩) or as *Nin-dar* (comp.
⊳⊣⌐ *Nin-* ⊱⌐⟨◁⌐ *-a* of the Tellon inscriptions).

§ 33. In Vol. VI of these *Proceedings* Mr. PINCHES gave a
very interesting communication on the Babylonian name of the
falcon, *surdû* (VI, 1884, p. 57–59). In a list, W.A.I. II, 37, 64,
we find *sukhurdû* (*su-khur-du-u* or *su-mur-du-u*) instead of *surdû*
(syn. *kasûsu*), so that we must suppose *sukhurdû* became at first
suvurdû, and finally *surdû*; the original meaning seems to be "the
bird of an unknown region *Sukhurd* or *Suvurd*."

Now we have in the Georgian language *Shazardem* (Svanelic
Shaurden, Mingrelian *shaordeni*), "falcon"; other derivations are,
Persian, *shâhên* (out of *shvarden*, comp. Arm., *mah*, "death," from
marthra, Arm., *shah*=κέρδος, Arm., *Meh* = *Mithra*, Lagarde's law),
"falcon" on the one side and Turkish *chakyr*, Arabic *tzakr* (صَقْر),
middle Latin *sacer*, Slavonic, *sokol*, "falcon," on the other side.
No doubt the original home of this interesting and noble bird was
somewhere in Asia Minor; if I am right, it is the bird either of
Separad* or, if *sukhurdû* is the oldest form, of the Sagartians, a
people southwards from the Caspian sea, the latter being, however,
less probable than the former.

§ 34. In DELITZSCH's *Handwörterbuch* we read, p. 393 :—

> *madâdu*, "to love," S^b 205, RAM (*a-ka*) = *ma-da-du*;
> *namaddu*, "the beloved," Tigl., 4, 35; 7, 56, Assurn.
>   1, 33, and p. 642;
> *shudadu* = *râimu* [*i.e.*, "loving"], W.A.I. V, 28, 20.

Now the sign RAM is, as I have shown in my *Sumerische
Lesestücke*, originally the picture of "measure," ⊵⌐≥ (comp. S^b 196
and 197, *gur*, Heb. כֹּר, and *ninda*, Semitic *namandu*) with inscribed ⊵◁⊨⌐ (*ram, lam*, originally *rag, lag*, comp. ⊵◁⊨⌐ = *lam*
and ⊳⟨⊵◁⌐ = *ag*, from *lag*). So we have S^b 205, not *madâdu*,
"love," which does not exist at all, but *madâdu*, "to measure."
Namaddu (to be read *nawaddu*) and *shîdadu*, however, are to be
derived from *wadâdu*, "to love" (comp. Arabic *wadd*, "love"), and
are borrowed from Arabic in the time of the Arabic dynasty of
Hammurabi; for the possibility of such borrowing at that time, see
the 3rd and 4th chapters of my book, *Ancient Hebrew Tradition*.

---

* Sardes, too, was originally Saparda; but our Separad must have been
situated in Kappadocia or Pontus, and so probably the Biblical Sepharad.

§ 35. The well-known expression *akhulâpi* = *adî matî* (written
a-ḫu-la-pi and *a-ḫu-lab*, Delitzsch's *Handw.*, p. 43) is to be
transcribed *aḫulâwi*, *aḫulaw*, and so the proper noun *A-ḫu-law-ia*,
not only for the sake of אֲחֻלִי, אַחֲלֵי, but because the word *a-ḫu-
la-a*, "beyond" (lit., "on yon side") is identical with it. As the
Arabic ذُو *dhû*, pl. أُلُو *ulû* is both "yon" and "which" (demonst.
and relat.), so the *ulâ* (comp. أُلَاء and أُلَى, *ulâ 'i* and *ulâ*, plural
of ذَا, *dhâ*) in the Babylonian *akhulâwa*, *akhulâi* is both demonstr.
(*aḫulâi*, "beyond") and relative (*aḫulâwi* = *adî matî*, "how long
then, how long still?"). Comp., too, *amêlu ki-i-pi ša a-ḫu-ul-la-'a*,
Strassm., *Neb.*, 109, 22 (Peiser, *K.B.*, IV, p. 188). Even in the
period of Hammurabi we find names like *A-ḫu-la-ab-Samas*
(Meissner, No. 11), which we must speak *Akhulaw-Samas*.

In similar manner, the names *Sin-ṣi-pi-di*, *Samas-ṣi-pi-di-im*
(Meissner, No. 3 and 32, time of *Apil-Sin* and *Sin-muballit*) are
to be read *Sin-ziyâdi* and *Samas-ziyâdim ;* comp. Arab. زِايَاد, *Ziyâd*,
originally *Zi'âd* (زِأد, 𐩭𐩱𐩹) of the Sabaean inscriptions, whilst
زَيْد *Zaid*, is زيد, 𐩭𐩱𐩹. So too, in the names with -*pi-ḳar*,
e.g., *A-bu-pi-ḳar*, *A-bu-um-pi-ḳar* (not *A-bu-um-pi-am*, as Mr. Pinches
has shown some time ago), we have to read -*waḳar* (יקר).

§ 36. The Babylonian *umâmu*, "beast," stands for *ubhâmu*,
buhâmu ; comp. בְּהֵמָה, بَهِيمَة *bahîmat ;* comp. *ubânu*, "finger,"
with إِبْهَام *ibhâm*, Hebrew בֹּהֶן.

§ 37. In Delitzsch's *Handw.*, p. 548, a *pishannu* of a temple
and the work (*dullu*) of a *pishannu* is mentioned. It is the same
word as *epishannu*, p. 119, "workman," and from my friend Prof.
Hilprecht I learn a third variant, viz., *epishnu*, Camb. 61, 4 ;
66, 7 ; 121, 6.

§ 38. Babylonian *ashlaku* (comp. Delitzsch's *H.W.*, p. 145)
seems to me to be compared with Arabic *silk*, plur. *aslâk*, "thread,"
and so to mean the rope maker, cord maker.

The Anniversary Meeting of the Society will be held at 37, Great Russell Street, Bloomsbury, W.C., on Tuesday, 11th January, 1898, at 8 p.m., when the usual business will be transacted.

The Rev. C. J. Ball will read a paper, entitled : "Puzzles in Picture Writing."

THE FOLLOWING BOOKS ARE REQUIRED FOR THE LIBRARY OF THE SOCIETY.

Members having duplicate copies, will confer a favour by presenting them to the Society.

ALKER, E., Die Chronologie der Bücher der Konige und Paralipomenōn im Einklang mit der Chronologie der Aegypter, Assyrer, Babylonier und Meder.

AMÉLINEAU, Histoire du Patriarche Copte Isaac.

——————— Contes de l'Égypte Chrétienne.

——————— La Morale Egyptienne quinze siècles avant notre ère.

AMIAUD, La Légende Syriaque de Saint Alexis, l'homme de Dieu.

——————— A., AND L. MECHINEAU, Tableau Comparé des Écritures Babyloniennes et Assyriennes.

——————— Mittheilungen aus der Sammlung der Papyrus Erzherzog Rainer. 2 parts.

BAETHGEN, Beiträge zur Semitischen Religiongeshichte. Der Gott Israels und die Götter der Heiden.

BLASS, A. F., Eudoxi ars Astronomica qualis in Charta Aegyptiaca superest.

BOTTA, Monuments de Ninive. 5 vols., folio. 1847–1850.

BRUGSCH-BEY, Geographische Inschriften Altaegyptische Denkmaeler. Vols. I—III (Brugsch).

——————— Recueil de Monuments Égyptiens, copiés sur lieux et publiés par H. Brugsch et J. Dümichen. (4 vols., and the text by Dümichen of vols. 3 and 4.)

BUDINGER, M., De Colonarium quarundam Phoeniciarum primordiis cum Hebraeorum exodo conjunctis.

BURCKHARDT, Eastern Travels.

CASSEL, PAULUS, Zophnet Paneach Aegyptische Deutungen.

CHABAS, Mélanges Égyptologiques. Séries I, III. 1862–1873.

DÜMICHEN, Historische Inschriften, &c., 1st series, 1867.

——————— 2nd series, 1869.

——————— Altaegyptische Kalender-Inschriften, 1886.

——————— Tempel-Inschriften, 1862. 2 vols., folio.

EBERS G., Papyrus Ebers.

ERMAN, Papyrus Westcar.

Études Égyptologiques. 13 vols., complete to 1880.

GAYET, E., Stèles de la XII dynastie au Musée du Louvre.

GOLÉNISCHEFF, Die Metternichstele. Folio, 1877.

——————— Vingt-quatre Tablettes Cappadociennes de la Collection de.

GRANT-BEY, Dr., The Ancient Egyptian Religion and the Influence it exerted on the Religions that came in contact with it.

HAUPT, Die Sumerischen Familiengesetze.

HOMMEL, Dr., Geschichte Babyloniens und Assyriens. 1892.

JASTROW, M., A Fragment of the Babylonian "Dibbarra" Epic.

JENSEN, Die Kosmologie der Babylonier.

JEREMIAS, Tyrus bis zur Zeit Nubukadnezar's, Geschichtliche Skizze mit besonderer Berücksichtigung der Keilschriftlichen Quellen.

JOACHIM, H., Papyros Ebers, das Älteste Buch über Heilkunde.

JOHNS HOPKINS UNIVERSITY. Contributions to Assyriology and Comparative Semitic Philology.

KREBS, F., De Chnemothis nomarchi inscriptione Aegyptiaca commentatio.

LEDERER, Die Biblische Zeitrechnung vom Auszuge aus Aegypten bis zum Beginne der Babylonische Gefangenschaft mit Berichtigung der Resultate der Assyriologie und der Aegyptologie.

LEDRAIN, Les Monuments Égyptiens de la Bibliothèque Nationale.

LEFÈBURE, Le Mythe Osirien. 2me partie. "Osiris."

LEGRAIN, G., Le Livre des Transformations. Papyrus démotique du Louvre.

LEHMANN, Samassumukin König von Babylonien 668 vehr, p. xiv, 173. 47 plates.

LEPSIUS, Nubian Grammar, &c., 1880.

MARUCHI, Monumenta Papyracea Aegyptia.

MÜLLER, D. H., Epigraphische Denkmaler aus Arabien.

NOORDTZIG, Israel's verblijf in Egypte bezien int licht der Egyptische outdekkingen.

POGNON, Les Inscriptions Babyloniennes du Wadi Brissa.

RAWLINSON, CANON, 6th Ancient Monarchy.

ROBIOU, Croyances de l'Égypte à l'époque des Pyramides.

——— Recherches sur le Calendrier en Égypte et sur la chronologie des Lagides.

SAINTE MARIE, Mission à Carthage.

SARZEC, Découvertes en Chaldée.

SCHAEFFER, Commentationes de papyro medicinali Lipsiensi.

SCHOUW, Charta papyracea graece scripta Musei Borgiani Velitris.

SCHROEDER, Die Phönizische Sprache.

STRAUSS and TORNEY, Der Altägyptische Götterglaube.

VIREY, P., Quelques Observations sur l'Épisode d'Aristée, à propos d'un Monument Égyptien.

VISSER, I., Hebreeuwsche Archaeologie. Utrecht, 1891.

WALTHER, J., Les Découvertes de Ninive et de Babylone au point de vue biblique. Lausanne, 1890.

WILCKEN, M., Actenstücke aus der Königl. Bank zu Theben.

WILTZKE, Der Biblische Simson der Agyptische Horus-Ra.

WINCKLER, HUGO, Der Thontafelfund von El Amarna. Vols. I and II.

——— Textbuch-Keilinschriftliches zum Alten Testament.

WEISSLEACH, F. H., Die Achaemeniden Inschriften Zweiter Art.

WESSELEY, C., Die Pariser Papyri des Fundes von El Fajum.

Zeitsch. der Deutschen Morgenl. Gesellsch., Vol. XX to Vol. XXXII, 1866 to 1878.

ZIMMERN, H., Die Assyriologie als Hülfswissenschaft für das Studium des Alten Testaments.

SOCIETY OF BIBLICAL ARCHÆOLOGY PUBLICATIONS.

In 8 Parts. Price 5s. each. The Fourth Part having been issued, the Price is now Raised to £5 for the 8 Parts. Parts cannot be sold separately.

THE EGYPTIAN BOOK OF THE DEAD.
Complete Translation, Commentary, and Notes.

BY THE LATE SIR P. LE PAGE RENOUF, KNT. (*President*);

CONTAINING ALSO

𝔄 𝔖𝔢𝔯𝔦𝔢𝔰 𝔬𝔣 𝔓𝔩𝔞𝔱𝔢𝔰 𝔬𝔣 𝔱𝔥𝔢 𝔙𝔦𝔤𝔫𝔢𝔱𝔱𝔢𝔰 𝔬𝔣 𝔱𝔥𝔢 𝔡𝔦𝔣𝔣𝔢𝔯𝔢𝔫𝔱 𝔠𝔥𝔞𝔭𝔱𝔢𝔯𝔰.

The Bronze Ornaments of the Palace Gates from Balawat.

[SHALMANESER II, B.C. 859–825.]

Parts I, II, III, and IV have now been issued to Subscribers.

In accordance with the terms of the original prospectus the price for each part is now raised to £1 10s.; to Members of the Society (the original price) £1 1s.

Price 7s. 6d. Only a Limited Number of Copies have been Printed.

THE PALESTINIAN SYRIAC VERSION OF THE HOLY SCRIPTURES.

Four Recently Discovered Portions (together with verses from the Psalms and the Gospel of St. Luke). Edited, in Photographic Facsimile, from a Unique MS. in the British Museum, with a Transcription, Translation, Introduction, Vocabulary, and Notes, by

REV. G. MARGOLIOUTH, M.A.,

Assistant in the Department of Oriental Printed Books and MSS. in the British Museum; formerly Tyrwhitt Hebrew Scholar.

Subscribers' names to be Addressed to the Secretary.

SOCIETY OF BIBLICAL ARCHÆOLOGY.

COUNCIL, 1897.

President.

WALTER MORRISON, M.P.

Vice-Presidents.

THE MOST REV. HIS GRACE THE LORD ARCHBISHOP OF YORK.
THE MOST NOBLE THE MARQUESS OF BUTE, K.T., &c , &c.
THE RIGHT HON. LORD AMHERST OF HACKNEY.
THE RIGHT HON. LORD HALSBURY.
THE RIGHT HON. W. E. GLADSTONE, M.P., D.C.L, &c.
ARTHUR CATES.
F. D. MOCATTA, F.S.A., &c.
SIR CHARLES NICHOLSON, BART., D.C.L., M.D., &c.
ALEXANDER PECKOVER, LL.D., F.S.A.
REV. GEORGE RAWLINSON, D.D., Canon of Canterbury.

Council.

REV. CHARLES JAMES BALL, M.A.
REV. PROF. T. K. CHEYNE, D.D.
THOMAS CHRISTY, F.L.S.
DR. J. HALL GLADSTONE, F.R.S.
CHARLES HARRISON, F.S.A.
GRAY HILL.
PROF. T. HAYTER LEWIS, F.S.A.

REV. ALBERT LÖWY, LL.D., &c.
REV. JAMES MARSHALL, M.A.
CLAUDE G. MONTEFIORE.
PROF. E. NAVILLE.
J. POLLARD.
EDWARD B. TYLOR, LL.D., F.R.S., &c.

Honorary Treasurer—BERNARD T. BOSANQUET.

Secretary—W. HARRY RYLANDS, F.S.A.

Honorary Secretary for Foreign Correspondence—REV. R. GWYNNE, B.A.

Honorary Librarian—WILLIAM SIMPSON, F.R.G.S.

HARRISON AND SONS, PRINTERS IN ORDINARY TO HER MAJESTY, ST. MARTIN'S LANE.

PROCEEDINGS

OF

THE SOCIETY

OF

BIBLICAL ARCHÆOLOGY.

———— ✳ ————

VOL. XIX. TWENTY–SEVENTH SESSION.

APPENDIX.

———— ✳ ————

CONTENTS.

———— ✳ ————

PUBLISHED AT

THE OFFICES OF THE SOCIETY,

37, GREAT RUSSELL STREET, BLOOMSBURY, W.C.

———

1898.

SOCIETY OF BIBLICAL ARCHÆOLOGY,

37, Great Russell Street, Bloomsbury, W.C.

TRANSACTIONS.

				To Members.		To Non-Members.						To Members.			To Non-Members.
				s.	d.	s.	d.						s.		d.
Vol.	I, Part	1	...	10	6	... 12	6	Vol.	VI, Part	1	..	1	6 ... 12	6
,,	I, ,,	2	...	10	6	... 12	6	,,	VI, ,,	2	...	1 0	... 12	6
,,	II, ,,	1	...	8	0	... 10	6	,,	VII, ,,	1	..	1 9	... 10	6
,,	II, ,,	2	...	8	0	... 10	6	,,	VII, ,,	2	..	1	... 12	6
,,	III, ,,	1	...	8	0	... 10	6	,,	VII, ,,	3	...	1	... 12	6
,,	III, ,,	2	...	8	0	... 10	6	,,	VIII, ,,	1	...	1	... 12	6
,,	IV, ,,	1	...	10	6	... 12	6	,,	VIII, ,,	2	..	1 0	... 12	6
,,	IV, ,,	2	...	10	6	.. 12	6	,,	VIII, ,,	3	...	1 8 0	... 12	6
,,	V, ,,	1	...	12	6	... 15	0	,,	IX, ,,	1	...	1 0 6	... 12	6
,,	V, ,,	2	...	10	6	... 12	6	,,	IX, ,,	2	...	10 6	... 12	6

PROCEEDINGS.

Vol.				To Members.			Non-Members.	
Vol.	I,	Session	1878–79	... 2	0	...	... 2	6
,,	II,	,,	1879–80	... 2	0	...	... 2	6
,,	III,	,,	1880–81	... 4	0	...	... 5	0
,,	IV,	,,	1881–82	... 4	0	...	. 5	0
,,	V,	,,	1882–83	... 4	0	..	... 5	0
,,	VI,	,,	1883–84	... 5	0	...	... 6	0
,,	VII,	,,	1884–85	... 5	0	...	... 6	0
,,	VIII,	,,	1885–86	... 5	0	...	... 6	0
,,	IX,	,,	1886–87	... 2	0 per Part	...	2	6
,,	IX,	Part 7,	1886–87	... 8	0 ,, ,,	...	10	6
,,	X,	Parts 1 to 7,	1887–88	... 2	0 ,, ,,	...	2	6
,,	X,	Part 8,	1887–88	... 7	6 ,, ,,	...	10	6
,,	XI,	Parts 1 to 7,	1888–89	... 2	0 ,, ,,	..	2	6
,,	XI,	Part 8,	1888–89	... 7	6 ,, ,,	...	10	6
,,	XII,	Parts 1 to 7,	1889–90	... 2	0 ,, ,,	...	2	6
,,	XII,	Part 8,	1889–90	... 5	0 ,, ,,	...	6	0
,,	XIII,	Parts 1 to 7,	1890–91	... 2	0 ,, ,,	...	2	6
,,	XIII,	Part 8,	1890–91	... 5	0 ,, ,,	...	6	0
,,	XIV,	Parts 1 to 7,	1891–92	... 2	0 ,, ,,	...	2	6
,,	XIV,	Part 8,	1891–92	... 5	0 ,, ,,	...	6	0
,,	XV,	Parts 1 to 7,	1892–93	... 2	0 ,. ,,	...	2	6
,,	XV,	Part 8,	1892–93	... 5	0 ,, ,,	...	6	0
,,	XVI,	Parts 1 to 10,	1893–94	... 2	0 ,, ,,	...	2	6
,,	XVII,	Parts 1 to 8	1895	... 2	0 ,, ,,	...	2	6
,,	XVIII,	Parts 1 to 8	1896	... 2	0 ,, ,,	...	2	6
,,	XIX,	Parts 1 to 8	1897	... 2	0 ,, ,,	...	2	6
,,	XX,	In progress	1898	... 2	0 ,, ,,	...	2	6

A few complete sets of the Transactions and Proceedings still remain for sale, which may be obtained on application to the Secretary, W. H. Rylands, F.S.A., 37, Great Russell Street, Bloomsbury, W.C.

APPENDIX.

CHRONOLOGICAL LIST OF PUBLICATIONS OF THE LATE SIR P. LE PAGE RENOUF.

[*In the compilation of the following list I have had the kind assistance of Lady Renouf, the Rev. Francis T. Lloyd of Oscott College, Mr. F. Wetherell, formerly editor of the Chronicle and the North British Review, The Very Rev. Canon Moyes (Dublin Review) an[?] others, to whom I would offer my thanks. A copy of the Home a[?] l Foreign Review, with the author's names added by Lord Acton, ᴡ ᴀs very kindly examined by Dr. L. Brentano.—*W. H. RYLANDS.]

1841.

The Doctrine of the Catholic Church in England on the Holy Eucharist, illustrated by extracts from her great Divines. With an Appendix on various other points of Faith and Practice. 64 pp. 8vo. Oxford, Parker. 1841.

1843.

Carlyle's Past and Present. *Dublin Review*, Vol. XV, No. 29, Art. IX. August, 1843.

The Character of the Rev. W. Palmer, M.A., of Worcester College, as a controversialist, particularly in reference to his charge against the Right Rev. Dr. Wiseman, of quoting as genuine works of the Fathers, spurious and heretical productions : considered in a letter to a friend at Oxford, by a late Member of the University. 76 pp. 8vo. London, Dolman. 1843.

1844.

Veneration of Saints in the Early Church. *Dublin Review*, Vol. XVI, No. 32, Art. II. June, 1844

Appendix to Art. II.   *Ib.*, Art. XII.

Scriptural Difficulties of Geology.   *Dublin Review*, Vol. XVI, No. 32, Art. III.   June, 1844.

Papal Supremacy anterior to the division of East and West.   *Dublin Review*, Vol. XVII, No. 34, Art. VII.   Dec., 1844.

Church and Empire in the Thirteenth Century.   *Dublin Review*, Vol. XVII, No. 34, Art. VIII.   1844.

1845.

Difficulties of the Ante-Nicene Fathers.   *Dublin Review*, Vol. XVIII, No. 36, Art. III, 39 pp.   8vo.   June, 1845.

1847.

The Greek and Anglican Communities.   A Letter respectfully addressed to the Rev. T. Allies, Rector of Launton, by P. le Page Renouf, late of Pembroke College, Oxford [dated 9.12.46].   Published by James Tovey.   38 pp.   8vo. London, 1847.

1859.

Seyffarth and Uhleman on Egyptian Hieroglyphs.   *Atlantis*, Vol. II. No. 3, January, pp. 74–98.   8vo.   (Plate.)   Re-issued, 1860.

Hieroglyphic Studies.   No. I.   *Atlantis*, Vol. II, No. 4, July pp. 333–378.   (Plate.)   [See 1862.]

1860.

Traduction d'un chapitre du Rituel Funéraire des Anciens Égyptiens. Lettre adressée à M. le Professeur Merkel (Bibliothécaire Royale à Aschaffenbourg).   Avec 2 planches.   *Aschaffenbourg*, 1860.   pp. 1–16 (lithographed).   8vo.

1861.

Saint Worship and Monotheistic Religion.   *Dublin Review*, Vol. L. No. 100, Art. I.   August, 1861.

1862.

Note on some Negative Particles of the Egyptian Language. 8vo.
London, 1862. Letter to Wycliff Goodwin, Esq. (lithog.).

The Early Epochs of Authentic Chronology. *Home and Foreign
Review.* Vol. I, p. 420. Oct. 1862.

Hieroglyphic Studies. No. II. *Atlantis*, Vol. III, No. 5, pp. 127–
156. (Plates.)

Hieroglyphic Studies. No. III. A Prayer from the Egyptian Ritual.
Translated from the hieroglyphic text by P. Le Page Renouf.
Atlantis, Vol. III, pp. 423–41.

Dr. Seyffarth and the *Atlantis* on Egyptology. *Atlantis*, Vol III.
No. 6, pp. 306–38.

1863.

Sir G. C. Lewis on the Decipherment and Interpretation of Dead
Languages. From the *Atlantis*, Vol. IV, pp. 23–57. 8vo.
London, 1863.

A few words on the supposed Latin origin of the Arabic Version of
the Gospels. Reprinted from the *Atlantis*, Vol. IV, pp. 241–
259. 8vo. London, 1863.

Notice on an Unpublished Translation of the Pentateuch. By
Father Richard Simon. *Atlantis*, Vol. IV, pp. 259–68.

Notices in " Contemporary Literature ":—

The Home and Foreign Review, Vol. II, January 1863.

2. Ueber den aeltesten Zeitraum der indischen Geschichte
mit Ruecksicht auf die Litteratur. Ueber Buddha's
Todesjahr u. einige andere Zeitpunkte in der aelteren
Geschichte Indien's. 2 Abhandlungen v. N. L. Wester-
gaard, ordentl. Prof. der oriental. Sprachen an der Univ.
Kopenhagen. Aus dem Daenischen uebersetzt.

3. Indische Studien : Beitraege fuer die Kunde des indischen
Altherthum's. Im Vereine mit mehreren Gelehrten
herausgegeben v. Dr. Albrecht Weber. 5ter Band,
2tes. u. 3tes Heft.

4. Five Jâtakas: Containing a Fairy Tale, a Comical Story, and Three Fables. In the original Pâli text, accompanied by Translation and Notes. By V. Fausboell.

5. E. de Rougé : Rituel funéraire des anciens Égyptiens. Texte complet en écriture hiératique, publié d'après le Papyrus du Louvre. Liv. 1 et 2.

6. Recueil de Monuments Égyptiens, dessinés sur les lieux et publiés sous les auspices de S. A. le Viceroi d'Égypte, par le Dr. Henri Brugsch. Vol. I.

7. Ed. Roeth : Geschichte unserer abendlaendischen Philosophie. Entwickelungs- geschichte unserer spekulativen sowohl philosophischen als religioesen Ideen v. ihren ersten Anfaengen bis auf die Gegenwart. 2 Bde.

8. V. der mannigfachen Bedeutung des Seienden nach Aristoteles v. Franz Brentano.

15. Constitutiones Apostolorum. P. A. de Lagarde edidit.

16. Theophili Episcopi Antiocheni ad Autolycum libri tres. Ad optimos libros Mss. recensuit etc. Joan. Carol. Theol. Otto. Accedunt Theophili qui feruntur Commentarii in 4 Evangelia, nunc primum castigiatores.

18. Mani, seine Lehre und seine Schriften. Herausgegeben v. G. Fluegel.

19. Macoudi: les Prairies d'Or. Texte et traduction par C. Barbier de Meynard et Pavet de Courteille. Tome I.

20. A Grammar of the Arabic Language. Translated from the German of Caspari, and edited, with numerous additions and corrections, by W. Wright. Vol. II.

21. Temudschin der Unerschuetterliche. Nebst einer geographisch- ethnographischen Einleitung und den erforderlichen besondern Anmerkungen und Beilagen. Von Prof. Dr. F. v. Erdmann.

31. Anecdota Adriani Sexti, Pont. Max. quae partim ex codice ipsius autographo, partim ex apographis edidit, etc. E. H. J. Reusens.

Home and Foreign Review, April, 1863.

4. Rudimenta Linguae Hebraicae. Dr. C. H. Vosen. Editio altera.

5. Elements of Comparative Philology.   By R. G. Latham.

6. Essai sur le Veda, ou études sur les Religions, la Littérature, et la Condition sociale de l'Inde, depuis les temps primitifs jusqu'aux temps Brahmaniques; ouvrage pouvant servir d'introduction à l'étude des Littératures occidentales.   Par Emile Burnouf.

7. Expédition scientifique en Mésopotamie, exécutée par ordre de Gouvernement de 1851 à 1854, par MM. Fulgence Fresnel, Felix Thomas, et Jules Oppert; publiée sous les auspices de S.E.M. le Ministre d'État, par Jules Oppert.   Tome I, Relation du Voyage et Résultats de l'Expédition.

8. Recueil de Monuments Égyptiens ; par le Dr. Henri Brugsch.   2ième partie.   Planches LI–CVII.

12. Geschichte der Entwickelung der grieschischen Philosophie, und ihrer Nackwirkungen im roemischen Reiche.   Von C. A. Brandis.   Erste groessere haelfte.

13. Grundriss der Geschichte der Philosophie der vorchristlichen Zeit.   Von Dr. F. Ueberweg.

14. VII. Buecher zur Geschichte des Platonismus.   H. v. Stein.

18. Eusebii Pamphili Episcopi Caesariensis Onomasticon Urbium et Locorum sacrae Scripturae.   Graece cum Latina Hieronymi interpretatione ediderunt F. Larson et G. Parthey.   Accedit Tabula Geographica.

19. Dogmengeschichte der vornicaenischen Zeit.   Von Dr. Jos. Schwane.

21. Geschichte des Abbasiden Chalifats in Egypten.   Von Dr. G. Weil.

22. Notices et Extraits des Manuscrits de la Bibliothèque Impériale et autres Bibliothèques.   Tome 19, première partie.

23. Ibn-el-Athiri Chronicon quod perfectissimum inscribitur, Vol. octavum, annos H. 295–269 continens ; ad codices Parisinos et Upsalienses edidit C. J. Tornberg. Publico sumptu.

Volume III, *July*, 1863.

1. An Introduction to the Old Testament ; critical, historical, and theological, containing a Discussion of the most important Questions belonging to the several books.   By S. Davidson, D.D., of the University of Halle, and LL.D.

2. The History of the Jews from the earliest period down to modern times.   By H. H. Milman, D.D., Dean of St. Paul's.   3 vols.   (Third edition.)

3. The Pentateuch and Book of Joshua critically examined. By the Rev. J. W. Colenso, D.D., Bishop of Natal. Part 3.

4. Notes by the Bishop of Natal on an examination of Part 1 of his work on the Pentateuch by the Rev. Dr. M'Caul, Professor of Hebrew, and Testament Exegesis, King's College, London.

6. Novum Testamentum Graece.   Ad fides Codicis Vaticani recensuit Ph. Buttmann.

7. Novum Testamentum Sinaiticum sive N. T., cum Epistula Barnabae et Fragmentis Pastoris, ex codice Sinaitico, auspiciis Alexandrii II omnium Russiarum Imperatoris ex tenebris protracto descripsit Aenotheus Fridericus Constantinus Tischendorf.

8. Kirchengeschichte des 19ten Jahrhundert's.   V. Dr. F. C. Baur.   Herausgegeben v. E. Zeller.

9. The Tuebingen School and its antecedents.   R. W. Mackay.

10. Histoire générale et Système comparé des Langues Semitiques.   E. Renan.   Première Partie : " Histoire générale des Langues Semitiques."   3me édit.

11. Croyances et Légendes de l'Antiquité.   Essais de Critique appliquée à quelques points d'Histoire et de Mythologie. Par L. F. A. Maury.

13. Essays and Lectures chiefly on the Religion of the Hindus. By the late H. H. Wilson.   Collected and edited by Dr. R Rost.   In 2 vols.   Vol. II.

14. Original Sanskrit Texts on the Origin and History of the People of India, their Religion and Institutions. Collected, translated into English, and illustrated by Remarks by J. Muir. Part IV.

15. La Médecine chez les Chinois. P. Dabry.

17. Recherches sur le nom égyptien de Thébes, avec quelques Observations sur l'Alphabet sémitico-égyptien et sur les singularités orthographiques. Par F. Chabas.

18. A compendious Grammar of the Egyptian Language as contained in the Coptic, Sahidic, and Bashmuric Dialects; together with Alphabets and Numerals in the Hieroglyphic and Enchorial Characters. Rev. H. Tattam.

19. Lexicon Linguae Aethiopicae. C. F. A. Dillmann.

20. An Arabic-English Lexicon. By E. W. Lane. Book I. Part 1.

21. The Gulistan of Shaikh S'adī of Sh'iraz. New edit., with a Vocabulary. By F. Johnson.

22. Anecdota Syriaca. J. P. N. Land.

Vol. III, *October*, 1863.

2. Anmerkungen zur Griechischen Uebersetzung der Proverbien. P. de Lagarde.

3. The Holy Gospels translated from the original Greek. With notes and critical appendix. By G. W. Brameld.

4. Les Évangiles. Par G. d'Eichthal. Première partie. "Examen critique et comparatif des Trois premiers Évangiles." Tomes I et II.

5. Histoire du Canon des Écritures Saintes dans l'Église Chrétienne. Par E. Reuss.

6. Vie de Jésus. Par E. Renan.

8. Die Weissagungen des Alten Testaments in den Schriften des F. Josephus und das angebl. Zeugniss von Christo. Dr. E Gerlach.

13. Wissenschaftliche Richtungen auf dem Gebiet des Katholicismus in neuester u. in gegenwaertiger Zeit. Dr. A. Schmid.

16. Das Orakel u. die Oase des Ammon.   Von. G. Parthey.

17. Ἀριστοτέλους περὶ ζῴων ἱστορίας βιβλία θ', ἐφ᾽ οἷς καὶ δέκατον τὸ νόθον. Ἐπιμελείᾳ καὶ ἐιορθώσει Ν. Σ. Πικκόλου, Ἰατροῦ. (Paris: Firmin Didot frères).

52. L'Archipel des Iles Normandes, Jersey, Guernsey, Auregny, Sark, et dépendances.   Institutions communales, judiciaires, féodales de ces iles: avec une carte pour servir à la partie géographique et hydrographique.   Par Théodore Le Cerf.

1864.

University Education for English Catholics.   A Letter addressed to the Very Rev. J. Newman, D.D., by a Catholic Layman. pp. 49.   London, Burns and Lambert.

Orientalism and Early Christianity.   *Home and Foreign Review*, Vol. III, p. 118.

Notices in "Contemporary Literature":—

Home and For. Review.   Vol. IV, January.   pp. 248–271.

1. Das Alter des Menschengeschlechts, die Entstehung der Arten, und die Stellung des Menschen in der Natur. von M. J. Schleiden.

2. Ueber das Gesetzbuch des Manu, von. Dr. Fr. Johaentgen.

3. The Bhamini Vilasa of Pandita Jagannath.   Edited by Pandit Yadu Nath Tarkaratna.

4. Avesta: die heiligen Schriften der Parsen, von Dr. Friedrich Spiegel.

5. Zoroastrische Studien, von Fr. Windischmann.

6. Das Ursprünglische Zendalphabet, von Richard Lepsius.

7. The Pharaoh of the Exodus, by D. W. Nash.

8. Die Grabstele des Priesters Ptah'emwa, von Dr. S. Reinisch.

9. On Two Egyptian Tablets of the Ptolemaïc Period, by Samuel Birch, Esq., LL.D., F.S.A. (*Archæologia*, Vol. XXXIX).

10. Ausfühliches Lehrbuch der hebräischen Sprache des Alten Bundes, von Heinrich Ewald.

11. Das Buch Judith als geschichtliche Urkunde vertheidigt und erklärt, von O. Wolff.

12. Die deuterocanonischen Stücke des Buches Esther von D. T. Langen.

13. Das vierte Ezrabuch, nach seinem Zeitalter, seinen Arabischen Uebersetzungen und einer neuen Wiederherstellung, von H. Ewald.

14. Einleitung in das Neue Testament von Fr. Bleek.

15. Patrum Apostolicorum Opera, ... Versione Latina passim correcta, prolegominis, indicibus instruxit Albertus Rud. Max. Dressel. Editio Altera.

Review of Dr. Smith's Dictionary of the Bible. *Home and For. Review*, Vol. IV, pp. 623–666.

Notices in "Contemporary Literature":—

Home aud For. Review, Vol. IV, pp. 700–703, 705–707.

1. Ueber die Quellen zum Leben des Confucius, namentlich seiner sog. Hausgespräche (Kia-iü). von Dr. John Heinr. Plath.

2. Yu Kiao Li. Les Deux Cousines, Roman Chinois, ... par Stanislas Julien.

3. Indische Sprueche: Sanskrit und Deutsch, von Otto Böhtlingk.

4. Dei Tentativi fatti per spiegare le antiche Lingue Italiche e specialmente l'Etrusca. Pietro Risi.

7. Biblical Essays, by Rev. John Kenrick, M.A., F.S.A.

8. La Chaldée chrétienne . . . par Adolphe d'Avril [probably].

1865.

Miscellaneous Notes on Egyptian Philology. A Letter to S. Birch, Esq. (Additional Remarks). 8vo. London, 1865. (*Lithographed*).

1866.

Miscellanea.   No. I.   *Zeitschrift für Aegyptische Sprache*, pp.
58–60.   1866.   [See also 1867, 1868, 1872, 1877.]
> (Variants found in monuments of Saitic origin, and
> corrections to Miscellaneous Notes.)

1867.

Miscellanea.   No. II.   *Zeitschrift für Aegyptische Sprache.*   32, 41,
52. pp.   No. III.   60, 65, 96. pp.   [See also 1866, 1868,
1872, 1877.]   (Values of various hieroglyphic signs.)

Articles.   An Hieroglyphic Dictionary and Egyptian Grammar [in
Bunsen's *Egypt's Place in Universal History*].   *The Chronicle*,
Aug. 24th, pp. 513–15, continued.

Egyptian Grammar, Notice of Egypt's Place, etc., and De Rougé's
Chrestomathie Égyptienne, Sep. 7th, pp. 562–65.

Coptic Versions of the Bible.   (Lagarde, Der Pentateuch Koptisch.)
The Chronicle, Dec. 14th, fol., pp. 897–98.

Notice of Westropp's Handbook of Archæology.   *The Chronicle*,
p. 114.   fol.   London.   April 27th, 1867.

Notice of Hyak Nin-Is'shiu, p. 163.   *The Chronicle.*   May 11th,
1867.

Notice of Miss Freer's the Regency of Anne of Austria, Regent of
France, mother of Louis XIV.   *The Chronicle*, p. 259.
June 8th.

Notice, C. Piazzi Smyth's Life and Works at the Great Pyramid.
The Chronicle, p. 330, June 29th, 1867.

Notice of Brugsch, Hieroglyphich-Demotisches Wörterburch, I, II,
III, IV, V.   *The Chronicle*, pp. 667–68.   Oct. 5th.

Notice.   A. H. Layard's Nineveh and its Remains, and Nineveh and
Babylon.   *The Chronicle*, p. 832.   Dec. 7th.

Notice.   Chronique de Abou-Djafar Mohammed-Ben-Djarir-Ben
Yezid Tabari.   *The Chronicle*, p. 905.   Dec. 14th.

Notice.   F. G. Eichoff, Grammaire Générale Indo-Européenne.
The Chronicle, p. 929.   Dec. 21st.

Notice.   Hébreu Primitif, par Ad. Lethierry-Barrois.   *The Chronicle*,
p. 953.   Dec. 28th.

1868.

The Condemnation of Pope Honorius, by P. le Page Renouf,
Ὀνωρίῳ αἱρετικῷ ἀνάθεμα.   Longmans, Green, and Co., 46 pp.

8vo. London, 1868. It was translated into Dutch, with an Introduction, by J. A. van Beek. 8vo. Dordrecht, 1869.

> (See Bottalla (P.), Pope Honorius before the Tribunal of Reason and History. 8vo. 1868. (A reply to Renouf's " The Condemnation of Pope Honorius.") (See Beek (J. A. van), Beschouwingen over de Pauselijke Onfeilbaarheid, etc. (A reply to Renouf's " The Condemnation of Pope Honorius." 8vo. 1869).

Astronomical Observations in the fifteenth century before Christ (Calendar at Biban-el-Moluk). *The Chronicle*, pp. 81–84. Folio. January 25, 1868.

Notice. Ludwig Schulze; Vom Menschensohn und vom Logos. *The Chronicle*, pp. 113, 114. February 1.

Notice. W. Wattenbach, Anleitung zur griechischen Palaeographie. *The Chronicle*, p. 163. February 15.

Miscellanea, Part III, continued :—

> *Zeitschrift für Aegyptische Sprache*, p. 7. 1868. (See also 1866, 1867, 1871, 1872, 1877.)

—————— Part IV, pp. 45–48.

1869.

The Case of Pope Honorius reconsidered, with reference to recent apologies. Nihil est pium nisi quod idem verum est. By P. Le Page Renouf. pp. 100. 8vo. London, Longmans, 1869.

Notices in " Contemporary Literature ":—

North British Review. No. 101. October.

Chrestomathie Égyptienne. De Rougé.

Traduction comparée des Hymnes au Soleil, etc. Lefébure. Hymne au Nil, publié et traduit par Maspero.

St. Paul, par Ernest Renan.

1870.

Notices in " Contemporary Literature ":—

North British Review. No. 102. January.

Resultate der 1868 nach Aegypten entsendeten Archäologish-photographischen Expedition. Dümichen.

Paulus der Apostel der Heiden : Krenkel [most probable].

Dir Gliederung des Buches Isaias als Grundlage seiner Erklärung, etc. Neteler.

The Homilies of Aphraates, the Persian Sage.   Wright.

Synesius von Cyrene.   Volkmann.

Maçoudi : Les Prairies d'Or.   Barbier de Meynard.

Histoire de Calife le Pecheur, etc.   Clermont-Ganneau.

Geschichte der Sprachwissenschaft und orientalischen Philologie in Deutschland. Benfey. No. 103. April.

Le Calendrier des Jours fastes et néfastes de l'année Égyptienne. Chabas.   .

Eine vor 3000 Jahren abgefasste Getreiderechnung.   Dümichen.

Buddhaghosha's Parables.   Rogers.

Geschichte des Volkes Israel, etc.   Hitzig.

Canones S. Hippolyti, etc.   Haneberg.

Chronologie der römischen Bischöfe, etc.   Lipsius.

Beiträge zur Geschichte der Chemie.   Kopp. [Probable.]

Le Diwân de Nâbiga Dhobyânî.   Derenbourg. [Most probable.] *North British Review*, No. 103. April.

The Writings of Methodius, etc.   Ante-Nicene Library. *North British Review*, No. 104. July.

Liber Diurnus, etc. De Rozière. [Probable]. *North British Review*, No. 105. October.

1871.

On several Hieroglyphic Words.   Letter addressed to M. Chabas. *Zeitschrift für Aegyptische Sprache.* pp. 129–37. 1871.

Notice in " Contemporary Literature ":—
    The Decree of Canopus, Sharpe. *North British Review*, No. 106. January.

1872.

On the sign 𓄿, and the words in which it occurs. *Zeitschrift für Aegyptische Sprache*, pp. 91–96. 1872.

Assimilation of Letter. *Zeitschrift für Aegyptische Sprache*, p. 25. [Referring to Letter addressed to M. Chabas. *Ib.*, 1871.]

On the Metal ⚴, *Zeitschrift für Aegyptische Sprache*, pp. 119
23. 1873.

Note on the Medical Papyrus of Berlin. P. le Page Renouf.
Zeitschrift für Aegyptische Sprache, p. 123. 1873.

Note on Egyptian Prepositions. P. Le Page Renouf. *Trans. Soc.
Bibl. Arch.*, Vol. II, part 2, pp. 301–20. 8vo. London,
1873.

Notes to a paper called the Serpent Myths of Ancient Egypt, by W.
R. Cooper. *Transactions of the Victoria Institute*, Vol. VI,
pt. 24. With illustrations. (Privately printed), pp. 86. 8vo.
London, 1873.

1874.

Notes on Egyptian Prepositions. P. Le Page Renouf. Reprinted
from the *Trans. Soc. Bibl. Arch.*, Vol. II, pp. 301–320.
8vo. London, 1873.

The Royal Tombs of Bībān-el-Molūk and "enigmatical" writing.
P. Le Page Renouf. *Zeitschrift für Aegyptische Sprache*, pp.
101–105. 1874.

Tale of the Two Brothers (Translation). P. Le Page Renouf.
Records of the Past, Vol. II, pp. 131–52. 1874.

Calendar of Astronomical Observations found in Royal Tombs of
the XXth dynasty. P. Le Page Renouf. (Woodcuts.)
Reprinted from the *Trans. Soc. Bibl. Arch.*, Vol. III,
pp. 400–21. 1874.

List of further Egyptian Texts for further Translation (tentative list only). *Records of the Past*, Vol. II, pp. 170–73. 1874. (Repeated, Vol. IV, 1875, pp. 154–57, and other volumes.)

Notes on the Medical Papyrus of Berlin. *Zeitschrift für Aegyptische Sprache*, p. 123.

1875.

Tale of Setnau. (Ancient Egyptian). Translation. P. Le Page Renouf. *Records of the Past*, Vol. IV, pp. 129–48.

An Elementary Grammar of the Ancient Egyptian Language, in the Hieroglyphic Type. P. Le Page Renouf. 4to. pp. iv, 66. London, 1875. (Archaic Classics, Bagster.)

Second edition, 1890 ; Third edition, 1893.

An Elementary Manual of the Egyptian Language ; with an Interlineary Reading Book in the Hieroglyphic Character. In two Parts. Part I, Grammar. Part II, Reading Book. (with Exercise Sheets.) 4to. London, Bagster, 1875. [The Second Part was never published.]

Review of Records of the Past. Vol. II, Egyptian Texts. *Academy*, No. 140. January, 1875.

Correspondence of our oldest MS., and who mutilated it. *Academy*, No. 142. January 23rd. [Reply of T. ffoulkes, see No. 143.]

Second Article on our oldest MS. [Reply to T. ffoulkes.] [Reply of T. ffoulkes.] *Academy*, No. 144. February.

1876.

Inscription of Aahmes, son of Abana. P. Le Page Renouf. *Records of the Past*, Vol. VI, pp. 5–10. 1876.

Abstract of Criminal Proceedings in a Case of Conspiracy in the time of Rameses III. Translated. *Records of the Past*, Vol. VIII, pp. 53–65. 1876.

1877.

The Negative Particle . Letter addressed to M. Naville. P. Le Page Renouf. *Zeitschrift für Aegyptische Sprache*, pp. 91–97. 1877.

Reply to M. Golenischeff, ⎡𓄿⎤, ⎡𓄿⎤ never a conjunction, but always preposition, like 𓅓𓄿 \\, 𓅓𓄿 |. P. Le Page Renouf. *Zeitschrift für Aegyptische Sprache*, pp. 106-11. 1877.

Miscellanea. No. VI. *Zeitschrift für Aegyptische Sprache.* pp. 97–106. [See also 1866, 1867, 1868, 1871, 1872.]

The Royal Tombs of Biban el Mohul, and Enigmatical Writing. *Zeitschrift für Aegyptische Sprache*, p. 101.

Review of the Doctrine of Addas the Apostle, by Dr. Phillips, President of Queen's College, Cambridge. *Academy*, No. 244, January 6th, p. 13.

Review. Der Bau des Tempels Salomos nach der Koptischen Bibelversion von Brugsch-Bey. Leipzig, 1876. *Academy*, No. 250. February 17th.

1878.

Lists of Further Texts, Assyrian and Egyptian. Selected by the late George Smith and P. le Page Renouf. *Records of the Past*, Vol. X, p. 165, 1878.

The Pastophorus of the Vatican. P. Le Page Renouf. *Records of the Past*, Vol. X, pp. 45–54. 1878.

Review. Die Aethiopishe Uebersetzung des Physologus verdeutscht mit historischer Einleitung. Hommel. *Academy*, No. 313. April 27th.

Review. Koptische Untersuchungen von Karl Abel, Berlin. *Academy*, No. 225. July 27th.

> *See* Abel (Carl). Zur ägyptischen Kritik. A reply to a criticism by P. Le Page Renouf upon the "Koptische Untersuchungen" of C. Abel, pp. 16. 8vo. Berlin, 1878.

1879.

On the True Sense of an important Egyptian word (𓂓 *ka*). Reprinted from the *Trans. Soc. Bibl. Arch.*, Vol. VI, pt. 2, pp. 494–508. 1879. Cf. *Proc.*, Vol. I, pp. 26, 27. 1878.

Note. The Belief in the Soul in Ancient Egypt. Maspero. *Academy*, No. 369. May 31st.

1880.

Lectures on the Origin and Growth of Religion, as illustrated by the Religion of Ancient Egypt. P. le Page Renouf. Delivered in May and June, 1879 (Hibbert Lectures, 1879), pp. x, 259. 8vo. London, 1880.

Second edition, pp. xxvi, 259. 8vo. London, 1884.

Letter. Nuk Pu Nuk. The Use of Obelisks as Lightning Conductors. *Academy*, No. 425. June 20th.

1881.

The Meaning of the Word Hotep. P. le Page Renouf. *Proc. Soc. Bibl. Arch.*, Vol. III, pp. 117–21.

Inscription of Queen Hatasu, on the base of the Great Obelisk of Karnak. *Records of the Past*, Vol. XII, pp. 127–36.

1882.

On the Value of the Hieroglyphic Sign ⟨glyph⟩, etc. P. le Page Renouf. *Proc. Soc. Bibl. Arch.*, Vol. V, 1882, pp. 13–18.

Note on some Negative Particles of the Egyptian Language. P. Le Page Renouf. Lithographed. 8vo. pp. 8. London, 1882.

Brugsch's Interpretation of Pihahiroth. (Ex. xvi, 2.) P. Le Page Renouf. *Proc. Soc. Bibl. Arch.*, Vol. V, No. 33, pp. 13–18.

Vorlesungen über Ursprung und Entwickelung der Religion der alten Aegypter. (Autorisirte Uebersetzung.) P. Le Page Renouf. 8vo. pp. vii–248. Leipzig (Hinrichs), 1882.

Wrong Values commonly assigned to Hieroglyphic Groups. *Proc. Soc. Bibl. Arch.*, Vol. IV, pp. 60–68. 1882.

Note on the 125th Chapter of the Book of the Dead. *Proc. Soc. Bibl. Arch.*, Vol. V, p. 6. 1882.

An Egyptian Preposition. *Proc. Soc. Bibl. Arch.*, Vol. V, p. 135. 1882.

1884.

Lectures on the Origin and Growth of Religion as illustrated by the Ancient Religion of Egypt . . . . Second Edition. P. le Page Renouf. pp. xxvi–259. 8vo. London (Williams and Norgate), 1884.

The Egyptian Prepositions ⟨glyph⟩ and ⟨glyph⟩ ⟨glyph⟩ ⟨glyph⟩. P. le Page Renouf. *Proc. Soc. Bibl. Arch.*, Vol. VI, pp. 93–95. 1884. (*See* 1890.)

The Bow in the Egyptian Sky. P. le Page Renouf. *Proc. Soc. Bibl Arch.*, Vol. VI, pp. 131, 132. 1884.

Egyptian Mythology, particularly with reference to Mist and Cloud. P. le Page Renouf. *Proc. Soc. Bibl. Arch.*, Vol. IV, pp. 75–76, 1882. *Trans. Soc. Bibl. Arch.*, Vol. VIII, pp. 198–29. [1882] 1884.

The Negative Particle ⟨glyph⟩. *Proc. Soc. Bibl. Arch.*, Vol. VI, pp. 95–101. 1884.

The Egyptian God ⟨glyph⟩ ⟨glyph⟩. P. le Page Renouf. *Proc. Soc. Bibl. Arch.*, Vol. VI, pp. 187–89. 1884.

The Horse in the Book of the Dead. P. le Page Renouf. *Proc. Soc. Bibl. Arch.*, Vol. VII, pp. 41, 42. 1884.

Is the Hebrew word Cherub of Egyptian origin? P. le Page Renouf. *Proc. Soc. Bibl. Arch.*, Vol. VI, pp. 189–93. 1884.

The Egyptian word for Battle, ⟨glyph⟩. P. le Page Renouf. *Proc. Soc. Bibl. Arch.*, Vol. VI, pp. 229–31. 1884. (See 1885, 1887, 1891.)

1885.

The Eclipse in Egyptian Texts . . . *Proc. Soc. Bibl. Arch.*, Vol. VII, pp. 163–70, etc. 8vo. London, 1885.

The Title of the Book of the Dead. P. le Page Renouf. *Proc. Soc. Bibl. Arch.*, Vol. VII, pp. 210–13. 1885.

Seb, the Great Cackler. P. le Page Renouf. *Proc. Soc. Bibl. Arch.*, Vol. VII, pp. 152–54. 1885.

The Egyptian Silurus Fish and its Functions in Hieroglyphics. The true phonetic value of the sign ⟨glyph⟩, ideograph of Strife and War, and its homophones. P. le Page Renouf. *Proc. Soc. Bibl. Arch.*, Vol. VII, pp. 100–108. 1885. (See 1884, 1887, 1891.)

1886.

Some Religious Texts of the Early Egyptian Period preserved in hieratic papyri in the British Museum. P. le Page Renouf. *Proc. Soc. Bibl. Arch.*, Vol. VII, p. 6. 1884.

The Myth of Osiris Unnefer. P. le Page Renouf. *Proc. Soc. Bibl. Arch.*, Vol. VIII, pp. 111–116.; *Trans. Soc. Bibl. Arch.*, Vol. IX, pp. 281–84. London [1886]. 1893.

The Name (1) of the Ithyphallic Horus ⟨glyph⟩, and (2) of the Heliopolitan Nome ⟨glyph⟩. P. le Page Renouf. *Proc. Soc. Bibl. Arch.*, Vol. VIII, pp. 246–53.

The Name of the Blind Horus. P. le Page Renouf. *Proc. Soc. Bibl. Arch.*, Vol. VIII, pp. 155–57. 1886.

The Name of the Winged Solar Disk on Egyptian Monuments. P. le Page Renouf. *Proc. Soc. Bibl. Arch.*, Vol. VIII, pp. 143, 144.

Egyptian Texts of the Earliest Period from the coffin of Amamu in the British Museum, with a translation by the late S. Birch; a prefatory note by P. le Page Renouf, and coloured illustrations [by F. Compton Price]. pp. 14. Folio. London, 1886.
[Published by order of the Trustees of the British Museum.]

Assyrian Antiquities. Guide to the Nimroud Central Saloon of the British Museum, by P. le Page Renouf. pp. x, 128. 8vo. London, 1886.
[Published by order of the Trustees of the British Museum.]

The Egyptian god ⟨glyph⟩ Àpuat. P. le Page Renouf. *Proc. Soc. Bibl. Arch.*, Vol. VIII, pp. 157–58. 1886.

Remarks on the Two Bilingual Inscriptions, Phœnician and Cypriote, with translation of Cypriote text. P. le Page Renouf. *Proc. Soc. Bibl. Arch.*, Vol. IX, pp. 49–51. 1886.

1887.

Mueller (Max), of Nuremberg. The supposed Name of Judah in the list of Shoshenq, etc. Remarks by P. le Page Renouf. 8vo. 1887. *Proc. Soc. Bibl. Arch.*, Vol. X, pp. 83–86.

132 ; Vol. XI, p. 76, 1889.   London, 1887–89.

The Name of the God Seb . . .   P. le Page Renouf.   *Proc. Soc. Bibl. Arch.*   Vol. IX, pp. 83–97.   8vo.   London, 1887. (See 1893.)

Appendix on the Transcription of Egyptian Words.   P. le Page Renouf.   *Proc. Soc. Bibl. Arch.,* Vol. IX, pp. 95–97. 1887.

Note on the Silurus fish ⟨hieroglyphs⟩, *āba,* and the hieroglyphic sign of battle ⟨hieroglyph⟩.   P. le Page Renouf.   *Proc. Soc. Bibl. Arch.,* Vol. IX, pp. 313–17.   8vo.   London, 1887. (See 1884, 1885, and 1891.)

Note on the Inscription of Amenophis III.   *Proc. Soc. Bibl. Arch.,* Vol. IX, p. 206.   1887.

Conscience in Egyptian Texts [Funereal Scarabæi].   *Proc. Soc. Bibl. Arch.,* Vol. IX, pp. 207–10.   1887.

1888.

Is אַבְרֵךְ (Gen. xli, 43) Egyptian?   The thematic vowel in Egyptian. P. le Page Renouf.   *Proc. Soc. Bibl. Arch.,* Vol. XI, pp. 5–10, 1888.   8vo.   London.

Two Vignettes from the Book of the Dead.   P. le Page Renouf. *Proc. Soc. Bibl. Arch.,* Vol. XI, pp. 26–28.   8vo.   London, 1888.

Pronominal Forms in Egyptian.   Three Letters, controverting the views of A. H. Sayce, in his Presidential Address to the Philological Society, 1888.   P. le Page Renouf.   *Proc. Soc. Bibl. Arch.,* Vol. X, pp. 247–64, 1888; Vol. XI, pp. 18–21, 1888; Vol. XI, pp. 82–83, 1889.   8vo.   London, 1888–89.

Note on the values of the Sign ⟨hieroglyph⟩.   P. le Page Renouf.   *Proc. Soc. Bibl. Arch.,* Vol. X, pp. 571–78, etc., p. 8.   8vo.   London, 1888.   (See 1884, 1890.)

The Ḳenbetu and the Semitic South.   P. le Page Renouf.   *Proc. Soc. Bibl. Arch.,* Vol. X, pp. 373–76.   8vo.   London, 1888.

1889.

Inscription at Kūm-el-aḥmar. *Proc. Soc. Bibl. Arch.*, Vol. X, pp. 73–78. Note, *ib.*, 132. Errata, *ib.*, XI, 76. 1889.

A Coptic Transcription of an Arabic Text. P. le Page Renouf. *Proc. Soc. Bibl. Arch.*, Vol. XI, pp. 155–58. 8vo. London, 1889.

Egyptian Phonology. P. le Page Renouf. *Proc. Soc. Bibl. Arch.*, Vol. XI, pp. 107–15. 8vo. London, 1889.

Parallels in Folk-Lore. P. le Page Renouf. *Proc. Soc. Bibl. Arch.*, Vol. XI, pp. 177–89. 8vo. London, 1889.

Pronominal Forms in Egyptian. *Proc. Soc. Bibl. Arch.*, Vol. XI, pp. 82–83. 1889.

Remarks on Jacob-el and Joseph-el. *Proc. Soc. Bibl. Arch.*, Vol XI, pp. 283–85. 1889.

1890.

The Priestly Character of the earliest Egyptian Civilization. P. le Page Renouf. *Proc. Soc. Bibl. Arch.*, Vol. XII, pp. 355–62. 1890.

Seb or Qeb : Sechet and Sechemet. P. le Page Renouf. *Proc. Soc. Bibl. Arch.*, Vol. XII, pp. 363–67. 1890.

The Sun Stroke in Egyptian. P. le Page Renouf. *Proc. Soc. Bibl. Arch.*, Vol. XII, pp. 460–61, 1890. 8vo. London.

The Name of Isis and Osiris. P. le Page Renouf. *Proc. Soc. Bibl. Arch.*, Vol. XII, pp. 343–46. 1890.

Neith of Sais. P. le Page Renouf. *Proc. Soc. Bibl. Arch.*, Vol. XII, pp. 347–52. 1890. 8vo. London.

The Book of the Dead. Facsimile of the Papyrus of Ani in the British Museum (in 37 plates). With an Introduction by P. le Page Renouf. pp. 19. Folio. London, 1890.
[Published by order of the Trustees of the British Museum.]

Nile Mythology. P. le Page Renouf. *Proc. Soc. Bibl. Arch.*, Vol. XIII, pp. 4–11. 1890.

Note on the phonetic values of the Sign ☺. P. le Page Renouf. *Proc. Soc. Bibl. Arch.*, Vol. XIII, pp. 119–20. 1890. Remarks, *ib.*, pp. 281–82. 1891. (See 1884, 1888.)

Egyptian Grammar. 1st ed., 1875. 2nd. ed., 1890. 3rd ed. 1893.

Note on the signs ⟨signs⟩, etc. P. le Page Renouf. *Proc. Soc. Bibl. Arch.*, Vol. XIII, p. 316. 1891. (See 1885, 1887.)

The Tablet of the Seven Years' Famine. P. le Page Renouf. *Proc. Soc. Bibl. Arch.*, Vol. XIII, pp. 443–44. 1891.

Who were the Libyans? P. le Page Renouf. *Proc. Soc. Bibl. Arch.*, Vol. XIII, pp. 599–603. 1891.

The Horus Standard and the Seat of Horus ⟨signs⟩ plague or fog. ⟨signs⟩ not the king of Upper Egypt, and not to be read *bit* or *bat*. P. le Page Renouf. *Proc. Soc. Bibl. Arch.*, Vol. XIV, pp. 17–25. 1891. (See 1892.)

The Book of the Dead. Introductory. *Proc. Soc. Bibl. Arch.*, Vol. XIV, pp. 37–38. 1891.

A Difficult Passage in the Pyramid Text of King Teta. P. le Page Renouf. *Proc. Soc. Bibl. Arch.*, Vol. XIV, pp. 108–11.

An Ambassador Royal of Rameses the Great. P. le Page Renouf. *Proc. Soc. Bibl. Arch.*, Vol. XIV, pp. 163–65. 1892.

The Book of the Dead. Chapter I. *Proc. Soc. Bibl. Arch.*, Vol. XIV, pp. 213–22. 1892.

The Regnal Years of the Egyptian Kings. The Egyptian Year. P. le Page Renouf. *Proc. Soc. Bibl. Arch.*, Vol. XIV, pp. 264–65. 1892.

The Book of the Dead. Chapters II to XIV. *Proc. Soc. Bibl. Arch.*, Vol. XIV, pp. 270–79. 1892.

The Egyptian Book of the Dead. Meanings of certain primitive words. P. le Page Renouf. *Proc. Soc. Bibl. Arch.*, Vol. XIV, pp. 349–51. 1892.

The Book of the Dead. Chapters XV and XVI. *Proc. Soc. Bibl. Arch.*, Vol. XIV, pp. 352–63. 1892.

The Book of the Dead. Chapter XVII. *Proc. Soc. Bibl. Arch.*, Vol. XIV, pp. 377–95. 1892.

A Second Note on the Royal Title . P. le Page Renouf.
Proc. Soc. Bibl. Arch., Vol. XIV, pp. 396–402. 1892. (See
1891.)

The Book of the Dead. Chapters XVIII to XX. *Proc. Soc. Bibl.
Arch.*, Vol. XV, pp. 4–12. 1892.

The Pharaoh of the Exodus. P. le Page Renouf. *Proc. Soc. Bibl.
Arch.*, Vol. XV, pp. 60–62. 1892.

The Book of the Dead. Chapters XXI to XXV. *Proc. Soc. Bibl.
Arch.*, Vol. XV, pp. 63–69. 1892.

The Book of the Dead. Chapters XXVI to XXXB. *Proc. Soc.
Bibl. Arch.*, Vol. XV, pp. 98–107. 1893.

The Book of the Dead. Chapters XXXI to XXXVII. *Proc. Soc.
Bibl. Arch.*, Vol. XV, pp. 155–63. 1893.

The Book of the Dead. Chapters XXXVIII to XLI. *Proc. Soc.
Bibl. Arch.*, Vol. XV, pp. 219–28. 1893.

The Book of the Dead. Chapters XLII to LVI. *Proc. Soc. Bibl.
Arch.*, Vol. XV, pp. 276–90. 1893.

The Book of the Dead. Chapter LVII to LXIIIB. *Proc. Soc. Bibl.
Arch.*, Vol. XV, pp. 377–84. 1893.

The Gods Akar and Seb. P. le Page Renouf. *Proc. Soc. Bibl.
Arch.*, Vol. XV, pp. 385–86. 1893. (See 1887.)

The Name of Pharaoh. P. le Page Renouf. *Proc. Soc. Bibl. Arch.*,
Vol. XV, pp. 421–22. 1893.

The Book of the Dead. Chapter LXIV. *Proc. Soc. Bibl. Arch.*,
Vol. XVI, pp. 3–12. 1893.

The Book of the Dead. Chapters LXV to LXX. *Proc. Soc. Bibl.
Arch.*, Vol. XVI, pp. 27–32. 1893.

The royal titles . P. le Page Renouf. *Proc. Soc. Bibl. Arch.*,
Vol. XVI, p. 53. 1893.

An Elementary Grammar of the Ancient Egyptian Language in the
Hieroglyphic Type. P. le Page Renouf. Third Edition,
pp. viii, 78. 8vo. London, 1896. First Edition, 1875.
Second Edition, 1890.

1894.

The Book of the Dead. Chapters LXXI to LXXVI. *Proc. Soc. Bibl. Arch.*, Vol. XVI, pp. 64–72. 1894.

The Book of the Dead. Chapters LXXVII to LXXVIII. *Proc. Soc. Bibl. Arch.*, Vol. XVI, pp. 100–103. 1894.

Where was Tarshish? I. P. le Page Renouf. *Proc. Soc. Bibl. Arch.*, Vol. XVI, pp. 104–108. 1894.

Where was Tarshish? II. P. le Page Renouf. *Proc. Soc. Bibl. Arch.*, Vol. XVI, pp. 138–41. 1894.

Where was Tarshish? III. P. le Page Renouf. *Proc. Soc. Bibl. Arch.*, Vol. XVI, p. 307. 1894.

The Book of the Dead. Chapters LXXVIII to LXXXII. *Proc. Soc. Bibl. Arch.*, Vol. XVI, pp. 123–30. 1894.

The Book of the Dead. Chapters LXXXIII to XCI. *Proc. Soc. Bibl., Arch.*, Vol. XVI, pp. 179–87. 1894.

Greek and other Legends of the Deluge. P. le Page Renouf. *Proc. Soc. Bibl. Arch.*, Vol. XVI, pp. 177–78. 1894.

The Book of the Dead. Chapters XCII to XCVIII. *Proc. Soc. Bibl. Arch.*, Vol. XVI, pp. 218–24. 1894.

The Book of the Dead. Chapters XCIX to CVII. *Proc. Soc. Bibl. Arch.*, Vol. XVI, pp. 263–73. 1894.

The Book of the Dead. Chapters CVIII to CIX. *Proc. Soc. Bibl. Arch.*, Vol. XVI, pp. 293–98. 1894.

1895.

The Book of the Dead. (Note to Chapter CIX.) Chapters CXI. to CXVI. *Proc. Soc. Bibl. Arch.*, Vol. XVII, pp. 6–15, 1895.

The Bow in the Egyptian Sky, II. P. le Page Renouf. *Proc. Soc. Bibl. Arch.*, Vol. XVII, pp. 37, 38. 1895.

The Book of the Dead. Chapter CX. *Proc. Soc. Bibl. Arch.*, Vol. XVII, pp. 51–56. 1895.

The Book of the Dead. Notes, Chapter CX. *Proc. Soc. Bibl. Arch.*, Vol. XVII, pp. 97–102. 1895.

The Book of the Dead.   Chapters CXVII to CXXIII.   *Proc. Soc. Bibl. Arch.*, Vol. XVII, pp. 123–29.   1895.

The Book of the Dead.   Chapters CXXIV.   *Proc. Soc. Bibl. Arch.*, Vol. XVII, pp. 192–94.   1895.

Note on Length and Breadth in Egyptian.   *Proc. Soc. Bibl. Arch.*, Vol. XVII, p. 191.   1895.

The Book of the Dead.   Chapter CXXV.   Parts I and II.   *Proc. Soc. Bibl. Arch.*, Vol. XVII, pp. 216–19.   1895.

1895.

Remarks on the Translation of the Papyrus of Ani.   *Academy*, No. 1200.   May 4th.

Fragments of Sahidic Version of the Bible.   P. le Page Renouf.   *Proc. Soc. Bibl. Arch.*, Vol. XVII, pp. 251–53.   1895.

The Book of the Dead.   Chapter CXXV, Part III.   *Proc. Soc. Bibl. Arch.*, Vol. XVII, pp. 273–77.

1896.

The Book of the Dead.   Chapter CXXV, Part IV.   *Proc. Soc. Bibl. Arch.*, Vol. XVIII, pp. 7–16.   1896.

The Book of the Dead.   Notes to Chapter CXXV, continued.   *Proc. Soc. Bibl. Arch.*, Vol. XVIII, pp. 47–53.   1896.

The Book of the Dead.   Notes to Chapter CXXV, continued.   *Proc. Soc. Bibl. Arch.*, Vol. XVIII, pp. 81–85.   1896.

The God [hieroglyphs].   *Proc. Soc. Bibl. Arch.*, Vol. XVIII, pp. 111–12.   1896.

The Book of the Dead.   Notes to Chapter CXXV, continued.   Vol. XVIII, pp. 113–17.   1896.

The Book of the Dead.   Chapters CXXVI, CXXVII.   *Proc. Soc. Bibl. Arch.*, Vol. XVIII, pp. 149–55.   1896.

The Book of the Dead.   Notes to Chapter CXXVIII.   *Proc. Soc. Bibl. Arch.*, Vol XVIII, pp. 165–69.   1896.

1897.

The Book of the Dead. Chapters CXXIX to CXXX. *Proc. Soc. Bibl. Arch.*, Vol. XIX, pp. 65–67. 1867.

The Book of the Dead. Chapters CXXX to CXXXII. *Proc. Soc. Bibl. Arch.*, Vol. XIX, pp. 107–12. 1897.

Lay of the Threshers. *Proc. Soc. Bibl. Arch.*, Vol. XIX, pp. 121–22. 1897.

The Book of the Dead. Chapters CXXXIII to CXXXV. *Proc. Soc. Bibl. Arch.*, Vol. XIX, pp. 125–31. 1897.

Hypocephalus from Luxor. *Proc. Soc. Bibl. Arch.*, Vol. XIX, pp. 144–46. 1897.

The Book of the Dead. Chapters CXXXVIA and CXXXVIB. *Proc. Soc. Bibl. Arch.*, Vol. XIX, pp. 160–64. 1897.

Young and Champollion. *Proc. Soc. Bibl. Arch.*, Vol. XIX, pp. 188–209. 1897.

The Book of the Dead. Chapters CXXXVIIA to CXXXIXB. *Proc. Soc. Bibl. Arch.*, Vol. XIX, pp. 225–28. 1897.

Biographical Record of the late Sir P. le Page Renouf, by W. H. Rylands (*Secretary*). *Proc. Soc. Bibl. Arch.*, Vol. XIX, pp. 271–79. 1897.

List of Writings of the late Sir P. le Page Renouf. Collected by W. H. Rylands. *Proc. Soc. Bibl. Arch.*, Vol. XIX, Supplement, p. 25. 1898.

SOCIETY OF BIBLICAL ARCHÆOLOGY PUBLICATIONS.

In 8 Parts. Price 5s. each. The Fourth Part having been issued, the Price is now Raised to £5 for the 8 Parts. Parts cannot be sold separately.

THE EGYPTIAN BOOK OF THE DEAD.

Complete Translation, Commentary, and Notes.

BY THE LATE SIR P. LE PAGE RENOUF, KNT. (*President*);

CONTAINING ALSO

𝔄 𝔖eries of ℜlates of the 𝔙ignettes of the different 𝔠hapters.

The Bronze Ornaments of the Palace Gates from Balawat.

[SHALMANESER II, B.C. 859–825.]

To be completed in Five Parts.

Parts I, II, III, and IV have now been issued to Subscribers.

In accordance with the terms of the original prospectus the price for each part is now raised to £1 10s. ; to Members of the Society (the original price) £1 1s.

Price 7s. 6d. Only a Limited Number of Copies have been Printed.

THE PALESTINIAN SYRIAC VERSION · OF THE HOLY SCRIPTURES.

Four Recently Discovered Portions (together with verses from the Psalms and the Gospel of St. Luke). Edited, in Photographic Facsimile, from a Unique MS. in the British Museum, with a Transcription, Translation, Introduction, Vocabulary, and Notes, by

REV. G. MARGOLIOUTH, M.A.,

Assistant in the Department of Oriental Printed Books and MSS. in the British Museum; formerly Tyrwhitt Hebrew Scholar.

Subscribers' names to be Addressed to the Secretary.

Society of Biblical Archæology.

COUNCIL, 1898.

President.

Prof. A. H. Sayce, LL.D., &c., &c.

Vice-Presidents.

The Most Rev. His Grace The Lord archbishop of York.
The Most Noble the Marquess of Bute, K.T., &c., &c.
The Right Hon. Lord Amherst of Hackney.
The Right Hon. Lord Halsbury.
Arthur Cates.
F. D. Mocatta, F.S.A., &c.
Walter Morrison, M.P.
Sir Charles Nicholson, Bart., D.C.L., M.D., &c.
Alexander Peckover, F.S.A.
Rev. George Rawlinson, D.D., Canon of Canterbury.

Council.

Rev. Charles James Ball, M.A.	Rev. Albert Löwy, LL.D., &c.
Rev. Prof. T. K. Cheyne, D.D.	Rev. James Marshall, M.A.
Thomas Christy, F.L.S.	Claude G. Montefiore.
Dr. J. Hall Gladstone, F.R.S.	Prof. E. Naville.
F. Ll. Griffith, F.S.A.	J. Pollard.
Gray Hill.	Edward B. Tylor, LL.D., F.R.S.,
Prof. T. Hayter Lewis, F.S.A.	&c.

Honorary Treasurer—Bernard T. Bosanquet.

Secretary—W. Harry Rylands, F.S.A.

Honorary Secretary for Foreign Correspondence—Rev. R. Gwynne, B.A.

Honorary Librarian—William Simpson, F.R.G.S.

HARRISON AND SONS, PRINTERS IN ORDINARY TO HER MAJESTY, ST. MARTIN'S LANE.

CPSIA information can be obtained
at www.ICGtesting.com
Printed in the USA
BVHW08*1300021018
529052BV00009B/731/P

9 780484 595568